# Media Innovation and Entrepreneu

# MEDIA INNOVATION AND ENTREPRENEURSHIP

Edited by Michelle Ferrier & Elizabeth Mays

Chapters by Jake Batsell, CJ Cornell, Geoffrey Graybeal, Mike Green, Mark Poepsel, Jessica Pucci, Ingrid Sturgis, Betty Tsakarestou, Foreword by Jan Schaffer, Sidebars from Lori Benjamin, Dana Coester, Chris Dell, John Dille, Dalton Dellsperger, Amy Eisman, Francine Hardaway, Coury Turczyn, Georgann Yara, Interviews with Ebony Reed, Daniel Zayas, and Research from Cheryl Cuillier

## Rebus Community

This book was created with support from the Rebus Community for Open Textbook Creation,  where we are building new collaborative models for creating & sustaining open textbooks. Would you like to collaborate on an open textbook? Join the Rebus Community at forum.rebus.community.

Are you a faculty member or administrator with questions about this book, or about open textbooks generally? Please get in touch with us at contact@rebus.community.

# CONTENTS

## Marketing Your Venture to Audiences

## Entrepreneurship Abroad: Cultural and International Perspectives and Challenges

## Instructor Resources

# FOREWORD
*Jan Schaffer*

## The Case for Learning about Media Entrepreneurship: An Important Gateway to Your Future

If you are enrolled in a journalism or communications program, you should shudder if your school never teaches you how to post stories to a content management system.

You should flinch if you hear the word "convergence"[1] dominating course offerings but never hear about design thinking or audience-engagement strategies.

And while you should pursue grammar literacy, be wary if you are not learning how to parse the language and patterns of disruptive innovation, particularly the media disruption happening in front of you daily.

As U.S. journalism and mass communications programs revamp to prepare you to succeed in today's rapidly evolving media landscape, there is—bar none—no better place to embrace and refine nearly every skill you will need to know than learning about media entrepreneurship and innovation.

In the course of envisioning, prototyping and launching, you will integrate multimedia production, social media distribution, design thinking,[2] data collection and analysis, and audience engagement strategies.

As added benefits, you will develop business skills, begin to understand how to develop a product, how to discover customers, and how to manage all these activities so that you can deliver a new entrepreneurial startup. Or you may go the intrapreneurial route and spearhead a new venture inside your existing media organization.

## The Time Is Now

Face it: You will be stepping into a world where media entrepreneurship is at an all-time high.

Hundreds of downsized journalists are watering community media deserts by launching hyperlocal news startups. Scores of statewide nonprofit news ventures are bringing back accountability journalism to state capitals. Startup founders are embracing single-topic niche sites, doing deep dives into climate change, health care, arts and culture, public education, and more. And, of course, venture capitalists have turned the likes of *Vice*, *Vox* and *BuzzFeed* into $1 billion-plus unicorns,[3] so confident are they of a return on their investment.

Of course, all of these initiatives not only need your journalistic skills, they also need outreach, social media sharing, ad sales, contact databases, event planning, membership drives, grant proposals, and the creation of regular quarterly or annual reports to let supporters know what they have accomplished. That's where innovations in public relations skills are critical.

How can there be so many new media ventures starting up at the same time legacy news organizations wring their hands, erect paywalls, and cut their way to attempted profitability?

Clearly, something more than new business models is at play here. It's important for you to learn about this.

It's clear that media entrepreneurs are articulating some new value propositions for their audiences. Nowadays, entirely new breeds of journalism are emerging from the imaginations of news entrepreneurs: mission-driven journalism, restorative narratives,[4] soft-advocacy journalism,[5] solutions journalism[6] and activist journalism. Moreover, new media ventures are reaching out and engaging audiences in fresh, new ways, often building robust civic communications ecosystems.

In learning about media innovation, you will be part of the creative process and a contributor to these new trends.

So why should you learn about media entrepreneurship, intrapreneurship, and innovation?

## Skills With a Purpose

Let's count the ways:

### Advancing Digital Smarts

To create a media startup, be it a website, an app, a tool or something else, students have to know how to create a minimum viable product, update it, monitor metrics, and employ various social distribution platforms to attract users. Instead of learning these skills as end goals in themselves, you will integrate them in the context of turning your ideas into a venture imbued with your passions.

### Identifying Opportunities

Entrepreneurs meet success when they have identified a need in the marketplace, a job to be done—one that no one else is doing. Or one they think they can do better. Craigslist identified a job to be done in classified advertising; Facebook in social sharing; Google for search; YouTube for video; Sirius for satellite radio. Again and again, mainstream media comes up missing in action in recognizing these possibilities. Media entrepreneurs, however, are identifying gaps or problems and using design thinking to craft solutions. If you want to be a media player, this is where a lot of the action is.

## Engaging Audiences

It's not enough to build a startup. An entrepreneur must find ways to engage a target audience to become successful. Whether that's social media, crowdsourcing, commenting, news games, virtual reality, drones, or augmented reality, you will learn that media has to be more than a commodity these days. Media ventures have to be participatory experiences to find a following.

As news entrepreneurs quickly learn, engaging audiences is more involved that counting web page views or social media shares. The depth of engagement is what will convert readers into donors, advertisers, content contributors, or volunteers, as we found in J-Lab's 2012 report,[7] "Engaging Audiences, Measuring Interaction, Engagement and Conversions."

Engagement might entail hiring a graphic artist to do a before-and-after visualization[8] of a streetscape to invite a community to consider redevelopment options, as *UrbanMilwaukee.com* did in 2009. It might involve launching niche newsletters[9] on numerous topics as *The New York Times* has done. Another option is webcasting[10] civic meetings as *Nowcastsa.com* does in San Antonio.

## Developing Data Skills

To be sure, students need to learn how to collect, analyze, and visualize data to do enterprise reporting. A media entrepreneurship student, however, will also learn about the need to gather data to report on the outcomes of any grants or donations or to measure impact of stories. And you will see that you must build contact databases to even begin to send out a newsletter, produce events, or launch a crowdfunding campaign.

## Building Revenues

Courses in the business of media have long been overlooked in many communications programs. A grounding in media entrepreneurship will challenge you to figure out how to build a business with multiple revenue streams to help sustain and grow activities. And it can teach you that there are other creative opportunities in the media world than simply enjoying the act of writing.

## Pitching Ideas

Good ideas go nowhere if you can't convince others of the merits. Pitching is a skill that can attract advisors or investors to a startup. But the same skill can attract an editor's support for a story idea or an intrapreneurial initiative that begs to be launched inside a media organization. Media entrepreneurship courses will require you to distill your ideas into a cogent framework that identifies needs, opportunities, and challenges.

## Different Definitions

Be sure you understand what your school means by media entrepreneurship before you enroll. A spring 2016 survey[11] of educators teaching media entrepreneurship courses revealed striking disparities in how professors defined the field. I conducted the survey for CUNY's Tow-Knight Center for Entrepreneurial Journalism. Some respondents saw media entrepreneurship as starting a project that can be monetized. Others saw it as using multimedia tools to tell stories. Still others defined it as building a freelance business. Go for the programs that prepare you to envision and establish a new idea.

There's some other good news about media entrepreneurship and innovation programs. They can help reassure your parents that you will have excellent job prospects in the future.

Media entrepreneurship programs can play a key role in preparing you for many different futures. They can be the fulcrum for the ultimate Gateway Degree,[12] one that can get you a job just about anywhere, not just at a news outlet or a public relations firm. Integrating research, writing, digital, and business skills, as media entrepreneurship programs do, opens the doors to careers in startups, nonprofits, the diplomatic corps, commercial enterprises, the political arena, and tech giants, in addition to law and medical school.

That's because participating in such a Gateway program means you've learned how to generate a specific outcome.

It also means you've opened the door to many new definitions of success that you can achieve as a graduate.

*Jan Schaffer is executive director of J-Lab: The Institute for Interactive Journalism,[13] a journalism incubator where she has vetted thousands of proposals and funded 220 media startups and innovation projects around the U.S. She teaches media entrepreneurship at American University and social journalism at the CUNY Graduate School of Journalism. She has been on the SXSW Accelerator Advisory Board since 2012. Reach her on Twitter at @janjlab.*

## Leave feedback on this chapter.

## *Notes*

1. Terry Flew, "Media Convergence," *Brittanica*, https://www.britannica.com/topic/media-convergence.

2. "Design Thinking," *IDEO U*, https://www.ideou.com/pages/design-thinking.

3. "Unicorn (finance)," *Wikipedia*, https://en.wikipedia.org/wiki/Unicorn_(finance).

4. Mallary Jean Tenore, "Defining Restorative Narrative, a Strength-based Storytelling Genre," *IVOH*, May 20, 2016, http://ivoh.org/restorativenarrative/.

5. Jan Schaffer, "A New Kind of Activist Journalism: When Finding Solutions are Part of Journalists' Jobs, Too," *NiemanLab*, June 4, 2013, http://www.niemanlab.org/2013/06/a-new-kind-of-activist-journalism-when-finding-solutions-are-part-of-journalists-job-too/.

6. *Solutions Journalism Network*, http://solutionsjournalism.org/.

7. Jan Schaffer and Erin Polgreen, "Engaging Audiences, Measuring Interactions, Engagement and Conversions," *J-Lab*, August, 2015, http://www.j-lab.org/wp-content/uploads/2015/08/engaging-audiences-EngagementReport_web.pdf.

8. Jan Schaffer, "A New Kind of Activist Journalism: When Finding Solutions are Part of Journalists' Job, Too," *J-Lab*, June 4, 2013, http://www.j-lab.org/2013/06/04/a-new-kind-of-activist-journalism-when-finding-solutions-are-part-of-journalists-job-too/.

9. Email Subscriptions, *The New York Times*.

10. *Nowcast San Antonio*, http://nowcastsa.com/.

11. Jan Schaffer, "Teaching Media Entrepreneurship. What Does That Mean?" *Medium*, June 28, 2016, https://medium.com/teaching-media-entrepreneurship/teaching-media-entrepreneurship-what-does-that-mean-36f9c24647d4.

12. Jan Schaffer, "Reimagining Journalism School as a 'Gateway Degree' to Anything," *MediaShift*, November 19, 2014, http://mediashift.org/2014/11/reimagining-journalism-school-as-a-gateway-degree-to-anything/.

13. J-Lab, http://www.j-lab.org/.

# PREFACE FROM THE EDITORS

*Michelle Ferrier and Elizabeth Mays*

Web phenomenons such as Google and Facebook were started by student entrepreneurs. Google began in March 1996 as a research project by Larry Page and Sergey Brin, both Ph.D. students at Stanford University. No one could have ever guessed that the algorithm-powered Google search engine, invented for a university library, would become the world's most powerful search engine. Facebook was created in February 2004 by Mark Zuckerberg, a psychology major at Harvard University, who simply wanted to create a way for upperclassmen to check out incoming classmates on the Web. Now this once-modest social network made $9.1 billion dollars in the second quarter of 2017 in advertising revenue alone.[1]

In 2000, Michelle Ferrier taught her first multimedia journalism course at a small, liberal arts college. The course required students to create an online business, then use their multimedia skill sets to develop a prototype and win their first customer. Students developed solo business ideas like a regional bride guide, a boy scout online education site for earning merit badges, or a takeout taxi service. Students learned HTML, web marketing, and usability testing skills. They figured out how to generate revenue with their businesses. And they learned to think like an innovator, solving problems and creating solutions that worked for their customers.

As the Internet disrupted the business of journalism, an entrepreneurial mindset emerged as the must-have job skill for recent journalism graduates to help reshape the journalism and mass communication industries. In response, forward-thinking journalism and mass communications programs sought to cultivate this entrepreneurial mindset by making entrepreneurship a staple of their curricula. Today, many faculty in media, communication and journalism programs have been tasked with teaching entrepreneurial journalism, media innovation labs, business of journalism, or media entrepreneurship.[2] In some degree programs, this manifests as a full class. In others, it surfaces as a module or modules within existing course topics–reporting, media management, audience engagement, student media, and others. Educators have also created graduate programs, competitions, and other structures to advance media entrepreneurship within the curriculum.

In her foreword, Jan Schaffer mentions a spring 2016 survey[1] that revealed educators teaching media entrepreneurship courses defined media entrepreneurship quite differently. "Some respondents saw media entrepreneurship as starting a project that can be monetized. Others saw it as using multimedia tools to tell stories. Still others defined it as building a freelance business," Schaffer writes.

But as educators who've been tasked with teaching entrepreneurship, we wanted a textbook that explained entrepreneurship in the context of the disruptions and opportunities in media and journalism. There was no one seminal text that covers the key concepts of media innovation and entrepreneurship that media, communication, or journalism students need, especially as the development of content and technology businesses is very different than traditional brick-and-mortar entrepreneurship.

When we embarked on this project, it was our aim to build the resource we ourselves needed, and make it freely available for use to others teaching media innovation and entrepreneurial journalism courses across the globe. While the original text was built with the needs of such courses front of mind, we have intentionally made the book modular, and open, so that parts of it can serve related courses, and be built upon.

The Rebus Community, a Canada-based publishing company, allowed us to experiment with an open textbook format, meaning the textbook would be created collaboratively and live as a dynamic document for others to share, remix, and reuse. Published under the Creative Commons CC BY[3] license, this text will be remixable, expandable, and easily updated, with attribution to original authors and contributors.

The first version–itself a "minimal viable product or MVP,"–was available to instructors for beta testing in their classrooms in Fall 2017. Students and educators were (and will continue to be) able to send feedback to the authors and editors. This input was incorporated into the "official" Version 1.0 release of the book in December 2017.

For now, Version 1.0 is envisioned to include a dozen chapters. The text is structured to move students from ideation to securing funding. The work can be used as a whole or in standalone modules. Version 2.0 (spring 2018) will build on this and add a chapter on Project Management and Team Leadership, as well as new sidebars. It will also incorporate feedback that didn't make the deadline to get Version 1.0 into print-on-demand in time for spring. (These changes will be added into the online version sooner, as they come in.) With Version 3.0, we will include instructor resources such as activities, ancillary materials, case studies, and more.

We'd like to thank our collaborators from across the globe, to the educators, students, and entrepreneurs who engaged with us on Facebook groups, in private conversations, or on our webinars. This textbook is much richer because of the diversity of ideas and experiences you contributed.

And because we believe in eating our own medicine, we will continue to listen to you, adapt, and add to this textbook, ever ensuring that we are meeting your needs as media innovators and entrepreneurs.

*Dr. Michelle Ferrier, associate professor, E.W. Scripps School of Journalism, Ohio University*

*Elizabeth Mays, adjunct faculty, ASU; operations manager, Rebus Community*

————————

## What is CC BY?

For educators and for students, the CC BY license has many benefits we think you'll appreciate, a few of which we'll highlight here:

- It observes the 5Rs.[4] You won't have any license limitations or restrictions in allowing students to do what you want them to do with the text. They can read it, they can download it, you can have your bookstore print it, all without fear of legal repercussions. It's also not gated behind an email opt-in or an expensive access code that students need to purchase. And it won't suddenly become unavailable based on the publisher's whims.
- No barriers to access. The textbook will be freely available in the numerous formats students ask for–publicly on the web, downloadable as an ebook, printable as a PDF. And we'll be taking care to make the textbook accessible, not only for those with disabilities, but also taking into account the multiple modalities (mobile, offline, etc.) through which students desire to study.
- It won't make your students #textbookbroke. It will be available free (though we will also make a print version available at a price not much above cost for those who prefer not to print at home).
- You can adapt this resource. You can continue to build upon this collaboratively created work as an instructor (in fact, it's our goal that you will want to do so!). You can use just the chapters you like, and add more of your own (send them back to the repository we will create so others can also utilize these additions). You can produce your own version tailored to the modules and progression of your own class. You can translate it into your language. You can pull just the resources you need. You can even do an open pedagogy project with your class to expand it.
- This book is a two-way, iterative product. Meaning you can interact with it in never-imagined-before ways. Found a typo? Please let us know. Found something confusing or feel something has gone out of date or could be improved? We the authors and editors want to hear from you. And we'll push out updates to the book as it evolves.

A final note: This book is produced with the support of the Rebus Community,[5] whose mission is to build a new, collaborative process for open textbook publishing. Rebus Community is funded by the William + Flora Hewlett Foundation, and the folks there are building a cadre of resources and technology to help connect global collaborators wanting to do similar open textbook projects. If you share that desire, you can connect with them in the Rebus Community Forum.[6]

## *Notes*

1. Marty Swant, "Facebook Raked in $9.16 Billion in Ad Revenue in the Second Quarter of 2017," *Adweek*, July 26, 2017, http://www.adweek.com/digital/facebook-raked-in-9-16-billion-in-ad-revenue-in-the-second-quarter-of-2017/.

2. James Breiner, "How J-schools Are Helping Students Develop Entrepreneurial Journalism Skills," *Poynter.org*, May 17, 2013, https://www.poynter.org/2013/how-j-schools-are-helping-students-develop-entrepreneurial-journalism-skills/213701/.

3. "Licensing," *Rebus Community*, https://about.rebus.community/licensing/.

4. "Defining the Open in Open Content and Open Educational Resources," *Opencontent.org*, http://opencontent.org/definition/.

5. *The Rebus Community*, https://about.rebus.community/.

6. *Rebus Community Forum*, https://forum.rebus.community/.

# DEVELOPING THE ENTREPRENEURIAL MINDSET

by Mike Green

## Summary

The U.S. media industry has been experiencing major disruption. Learn how the media landscape is evolving and why an entrepreneurial mindset and intrapreneurial skills are in demand.

---

### Learning Objectives

- Learn how the evolution of the U.S. economy has impacted the journalism industry.
- Understand what is meant by the "innovation economy" and how media are affected by it.
- Differentiate between "intrapreneurs" and "entrepreneurs" and discover which you might be.
- Grasp the entrepreneurial ecosystem and why journalists need to understand it.
- Learn about some of the personal attributes—such as resilience—that are essential to innovation.

---

## Inside this Chapter

- Developing the Entrepreneurial Mindset
- From the Field: Taking Risks and Building Resilience on the Path to Innovation, by Dana Coester
- From the Field: Q&A With a Young Innovator, by Dana Coester
- What's an Intrapreneur? And How Do I Become One? Interview with Ebony Reed

*Mike Green is a New York Times Leadership Academy Fellow and award-winning journalist with 20 years' experience. He is co-founder of ScaleUp Partners, a national consultancy specializing in economic inclusion and competitiveness strategies, plans, and policy. Reach him on Twitter at @amikegreen2.*

# DEVELOPING THE ENTREPRENEURIAL MINDSET

*Mike Green*

The twenty-first century ushered in an era of rapidly evolving new technologies and disruptions of consumer behavior across all industries. New entrepreneurial opportunities were born amid the chaos of industry responses. Barriers to entry were lowered or obliterated. New, fast, and nimble competitors entered the markets. And a new economic paradigm was introduced to media companies that would leave many print news organizations struggling.

---

**View data and charts**[1] from Pew Research Center's Newspapers Fact Sheet, part of its State of the News Media report. The Media Deserts Project[2] also has maps showing the decline of local newspapers in various regions.

---

On the employee level, industry disruptions have changed what a career means. Since 2004, the industry has contracted 37 percent, from more than 65,000 reporters and editors employed in 2004 to just 41,400 in 2015 (the last year of available data collected by Pew Research and published June 1, 2017).[3] Behind those data is deeper insight; Pew Research will need to gather information for the next publishing cycle because the News Media Alliance (NMA), formerly Newspaper Association of America (NAA), can no longer supply it.[4] Accurate industry research is another victim of the industry-wide upheaval.

No one can expect to get hired anywhere in the country and work for the same company for most of their careers until retirement. That's a twentieth-century concept rendered obsolete in the first decade of the twenty-first. For media, this is especially true.

## Dog Eat Dog

Buying and selling of media companies is consolidating the landscape. The plummeting value of major media properties, like the 140-year-old *Washington Post* (founded in 1877) that sold for $250 million[5] in 2013, can result in a sale for less than digital newcomers like *Huffington Post*. *Huffington Post* was born in 2005 and sold for $315 million[6] to AOL in 2011.

While the Graham family nurtured a multigenerational national media operation for about 68 years that was built on a foundation of award-winning journalism, Arianna Huffington started a blog and generated more market value from it in six years than the Graham family could manage from the *Washington Post* in decades. In case you're inclined to think AOL overpaid for *Huffington Post*, last year the telecom company Verizon bought AOL and all of its media properties for $4.4 billion. By contrast, The New York Times Company was worth $1.8 billion[7] on the market at the time AOL was purchased. Meanwhile, startup media company *Vox*, at fourteen years old, was valued at $1 billion in late 2016.[8] Today, AT&T hovers over Time Warner (which owns CNN) waiting for the government to approve its $85 billion offer.[9]

The media industry has changed, and journalism is changing too. Gone are the days of college grads cutting teeth at the local level and honing their reporting chops before embarking on a series of tours, from low-wage local jobs to regional, and up the career ladder to higher pay with national news chains. Gone too, is the wall of demarcation that divided the production of editorial news content from the business of operating a media company.

Local media used to be the trusted place where consumers learned about their schools, city council, sports teams, and happenings in their community. But the consolidation of media across the nation has reached the local level. And corporate ownership of local media has ramifications for journalists. Sinclair Broadcast Group is on the verge of purchasing[10] the Tribune Media Company this year. This purchase is sending tremors across the media landscape due to its size and scope.

Before the Sinclair deal can be confirmed, allegations[11] of political bias by the company have been raised. These include requiring stations to carry "must run" segments produced by the corporation and mandatory insertions of political commentary into local news broadcasts. The ability of corporations to purchase media in local markets in bundles is having an impact on the integrity of the journalism profession. The evolution of the industry, as it is being disrupted by new media and new players, introduces uncertainty in the media market and changes the dynamic of the career trajectory for journalists entering the profession.

## Death of Past; Birth of Future

*Newspaper Death Watch*[12] keeps tabs on the decline of the news industry, noting that 15 major city dailies have shuttered since *NDW* started tracking in 2007. The loss of 15 major daily newspapers in the past 10 years doesn't inspire confidence in the future of the media industry. Lying in the grave alongside those relics are also notions that journalists are dispassionate objective observers, set apart from the communities they serve. Gone too is the standard of objective robotic reporting. The way journalism will be conducted in the future will look different than it did during the past century.

**It's important to note: journalism is not dead.**

The craft and industry are evolving. And technology is playing a key role in that evolution. Both the media industry and its truth-seeking, storytelling, content-producing members will continue to play a vital role in society. However, the double-digit profits that made the former newspaper landscape an influential and prosperous "Fourth Estate" have evaporated along with the attention span of audiences. The sudden disappearance of financial scaffolding provided by the advertising industry, which enabled the profession of journalism to grow, has caused the collapse of media companies and the loss of thousands of journalism jobs.

Today, even under the recent renewed interest in journalism that national newspapers are seeing due to the public's concerns with "fake news," the media industry is racing to keep up with technologies and new consumer behavior that have transformed a centuries-old U.S. industry in a decade. And the most unnerving revelation of all is that this new era of tech-innovation driving the evolution of media is in its infancy.

## Economic Evolution

Journalists who wish to survive in this new era must think beyond the boundaries of an employee performing tasks for an employer. The industry is filled with underpaid and overworked professionals who do their best work because of their love for journalism and service to the public. Ironically, it is this passion and love for the work that fits in the next phase of journalism in the twenty-first century.

Today, journalists must consider themselves as more than masters of their craft, whether they are writers and editors, photographers and videographers, television producers or newsroom managers. Every journalist who intends to make media and/or journalism a career must consider their role as either an _intrapreneur_ or _entrepreneur_.

These terms are so important that we'll define them here.

> An entrepreneur is someone with a market-driven pursuit of a conceptual idea, who seeks a viable business model that succeeds in a target market.

> An intrapreneur is an employee who innovates and thinks entrepreneurially to develop new lines of business, programs or products within an existing organization or corporation.

It is important to understand how and why the era of entrepreneurship arrived and will remain. The national economy has transformed itself three times over the past 100 years. America was once a profitable agrarian economy and land ownership was the key to prosperity in the nineteenth century. With overseas wars in the twentieth century came the need for mass production and an evolution of America into a manufacturing economy. Ownership of a factory and the means to production was a pathway to wealth. Manufacturing included the production and dissemination of information as news. And journalists were needed to gather, edit, and produce the content.

With the introduction of venture capital investing as an industry in the late 1960s, the buying and selling of businesses became a profession by the late 1990s. Another evolution of the U.S. economy occurred. America had given birth to a creative, knowledge-based, tech-driven innovation economy.

By the turn of the twenty-first century, this "new economy" (as it was initially called; today it is known as the "innovation economy") began to reward disruptive ideas in the marketplace, and the marketplace is global. With the advent of the Internet and collaborative technologies that continue to emerge from global connectivity, the age of information exploded.

Investors began to view the growth of teams of entrepreneurs starting their own companies as high-risk, high-reward opportunities for investing capital. This kind of direct investment into a young company is rewarded in an exchange for a portion of ownership. When the company grows and attracts buyers, the investors will get their share of the purchase depending on the percentage of shares they own in the company. This direct investing into startup companies, typically by angel investors[13] (individuals and/or groups who invest their personal funds), accounted for more than $21 billion in 2016, according to the Center for Venture Research.[14]

One of the major impacts upon the media industry since the turn of the century was the number of digital media startups,[15] fueled by money from investors and venture capitalists. Niche markets were targeted by new digital platforms such as *Techcrunch*, *Venturebeat*, *Mashable*, *ReadWriteWeb*, and others leveraging the power of journalism to cover new areas of the economy. In addition, journalists, laid off from their legacy media jobs, started hyperlocal online news sites, small geographic regions where they focused the news on a zip code, neighborhood, or city/town. These hyperlocals were bootstrapped startups, for the most part, that relied on self-funding, or friends and family to start. *CJR* maintains a database[16] of such sites. With the growth of mobile usage, mobile applications and other new technologies in the hands of consumers, the need for content has exploded[17] over the past few years. Adding to that explosion are new technologies such as virtual reality (immersive) and augmented reality (blended real and imagined). Learn the difference.[18] These new platforms require the skill of storytellers to produce content that engages consumers.

The hope of getting money from investors is one of the drivers that's motivating creative storytelling solutions. But entrepreneurship isn't only about chasing those dollars, but rather pursuing the journey of giving the industry a solution based upon an innovation. However, without startup funding, ideas can die in the minds of innovators. The age of startup companies was fueled by laptops, tablets, smartphones, and software apps that keep making it easier for anyone with a connection to the Internet to develop a website to get their idea into the marketplace quickly.

Media was one of the first industries to feel the disruption of fast-paced, tech-driven production, and dissemination of information in the hands of millions of people. The ability of almost anyone with a computer, software, and the Internet to produce the written and spoken word, photos and video, and upload it to the world to consume became a challenge to the media industry. Industry executives learned that anyone with a blog, a comment, or a tweet on the Internet could compete with the journalism profession for attention of the masses. Yet, that was the reality. A YouTube star[19] could be born in the bedroom of any home. And media would have yet another player in the market competing for attention in a 24-hour daily cycle.

That initial recoiling by media was a mistake. It opened the door to early adopters of new publishing platforms, and the race was on to grab market share in the digital space. While media companies challenged the quality and accuracy of content being produced in America's basements, bedrooms, and garages nationwide, entrepreneurial ventures developed as digital media platforms for this content. Since the turn of the century, hundreds of media platforms have entered the market to compete with the "legacy" media. Ironically, social media platforms like Google and Facebook understood the power of online engagement with audiences long before legacy media began to switch their business model from print distribution of news products to invest in development of digital platforms that encourage audience participation versus passive consumption.

## Entrepreneur or Intrapreneur?

Journalists eventually began to understand the power they had to establish a brand, develop a platform, and connect with an audience. And, as the media industry contracted, journalists turned to entrepreneurship, as self-employed freelancers and CEOs of new media ventures.

Former *CBS News* anchor Dan Rather now produces content for his News & Guts[20] platform. Former CNN news anchor Soledad O'Brien produced the series Black in America, which aired on CNN. When she was fired in 2013, she took the series with her. O'Brien had established a brand of matter-of-fact journalism during her career at MSNBC, CNN, Al Jazeera America, and HBO. After CNN, she transitioned from journalist to founder and CEO of Starfish Media,[21] where she retains ownership of her brand and continues to produce content for broadcast media, like HBO and her own platform, *MatterofFact.tv*.[22]

Of course, not everyone is able to be the CEO of their own company. But in this era of innovation, there are no guarantees of a twenty- or thirty-year career with one employer or even in one industry. Even those who fear entrepreneurship must learn to think like an entrepreneur while serving as an employee. An employee with an entrepreneurial mindset is known as an <u>intrapreneur</u>. And these are the most valued and coveted kinds of employees. Let's take a look at the definition of an entrepreneur and examine why employees prefer intrapreneurs.

> "Entrepreneurship is the pursuit of opportunity beyond resources currently controlled," said Johnathan Holifield, former NFL player, attorney and author of the critically acclaimed book, The Future Economy and Inclusive Competitiveness.[23]
> "That's how Harvard professor Howard Stevenson describes it, which underscores my own passion for it. Entrepreneurship is about the relentless pursuit of opportunity

that results in business formation, educational attainment and everything else worth having."[24]

Simply put, entrepreneurs are innovators. They are creative problem-solvers, critical thinkers, collaborators, and calculated risk-takers. They are sacrificial, tenacious, motivated, and driven toward measurable outcomes. They are team players and team leaders. Entrepreneurs pursue their goals with passion and determination to succeed, despite obstacles.

---

*An entrepreneur is someone with a market-driven pursuit of a conceptual idea, who seeks a viable business model that succeeds in a target market.*

---

*Social* entrepreneurs are a unique type in that they seek to introduce solutions into the marketplace that produce both profit and measurable social impact.

The entrepreneur is engaged in a process of creating, innovating, monitoring, measuring, tweaking, pivoting[25] (shifting strategy when necessary) … and all the while searching for a formula that delivers market adoption with a desired return on investment.

Contrary to the experimental world of the entrepreneur, a business owner is managing the operations of a proven business model. One example is becoming a business owner through purchase of a franchise operation and getting the training to run it based on an established model for that business. While this approach still contains a certain amount of risk, the experience of the franchise corporation helps reduce the risk of the investment made by the franchisee owner to offer a more solid foundation from which to launch. Learn more[26] about the difference between an entrepreneur and business owner.

Of course, entrepreneurs don't necessarily make good business owners and managers. Given their penchant and passion for creativity and constant search for a business model that works, too often startup CEOs who are stuck in the mindset of the entrepreneur find themselves tweaking a business that doesn't need it. This is a problem venture capital investors find in some startups that have successfully penetrated a market and competed for a share of it.

Investors who write multimillion dollar checks to provide the company enough cash for it to grow will often ask the startup CEO to step aside and assume a different role in their own company. This is due to the need for the CEO to manage the process of scaling up the company based on the successful business model. The former CEO, who still yearns to innovate, can do so within the company without detracting from the core business model. Thus, he or she is now in the position of being an employee with an entrepreneurial mindset. This kind of employee, the intrapreneur, is valuable to any company that seeks to remain innovative and keep pace with what is happening in the industry.

In the near future, all journalists will decide whether they are intrapreneurs or entrepreneurs.

And yes, you can be both. At different times in a journalist's career, both will be valued traits that generate opportunities in-house and in the marketplace.

Given the nature of a changing landscape, journalists who leverage their entrepreneurial mindset to identify problems and offer solutions will make themselves invaluable to the media company. At the same time, every media company will be impacted by the market and need to make decisions that can result in layoffs. Journalists who prepare for such an inevitability will have generated opportunities outside of their employer's shop.

## Innovation: Sustainable & Disruptive

Inside media companies, the quest to keep up with the changing nature of the industry is a constant challenge. New technologies and innovations (new tweaks on existing products and services) are changing consumer behavior, which affects how media reach their audiences. Journalists are asked to do more to ensure their content is produced in multiple formats for multiple platforms and screens. Virtual Reality (VR) is a new technology, complete with hardware for immersive engagement of media content. Alternately, Augmented Reality (AR) is less invasive by incorporating something new into existing technology used by consumers. An example would be the game Pokemon Go.[27] Using a smartphone, anyone who knows how to use the camera and the phone's GPS can instantly play the game, which inserts an imaginary character into real-world scenes, as viewed through the camera. Thus, Pokemon Go's augmented reality is an innovation of existing technology, rather than a new technology altogether.

Today's media consumers are primarily digital and view media across a variety of screens, ranging from television to laptops and tablets, to smartphones (the preferred screen of younger audiences).[28] The Internet is a visual medium, which means audiences prefer video and photos to long-form prose on their screens. Consider what it's like to read a lot of text on the television. That's a recipe for losing an audience. The same can be true for smaller screens. That said, there are ways of presenting articles to audiences in readable format via any screen. But each year, media must consider how the behavior of their audiences changes and adapts. This is known as sustainable innovation.

An example of sustainable innovation is CNN's *Great Big Story* startup, which began inside of CNN. Bloomberg's June 20, 2017 article,[29] "CNN to Invest $40M in its Video Startup *Great Big Story*," illuminates the point.

CNN's investment in *Great Big Story* is one example of a fast-moving convergence in television, where traditional channels are pouring money into online startups to make shows for a younger, cord-cutting generation of millennials and Gen Z. Recent research from the Pew Research Center indicates that in the 18-29 age category, mobile usage is 100 percent in 2017, with 92 percent having access to a smartphone. NBCUniversal, for instance, has invested $400 million in *BuzzFeed* and $200 million in *Vox Media*. Recently, Time Warner said it would invest $100 million in making shows and buying ads on Snapchat.[30]

It may seem odd that CNN would invest in a media venture separate from itself. But consider the benefits. CNN's investment is growing its younger audiences[31] (25-35-year-olds) and opening a new market, like NBCUniversal's investments in *BuzzFeed* and *Vox Media*. The risk taken is by the startup entity. The capacity for the startup to respond to market demands and experiment with new ideas far exceeds a large corporation's capacity. Remember that corporations operate on proven business models while entrepreneurial ventures are in search of a business model that delivers the desired return on investment. *Great Big Story* already has found an approach in the market and is delivering a return on investment to CNN in a period of time. As the startup grows, it will become yet another valuable asset of CNN, its investor. If *Great Big Story* is sold via a liquidity event[32] (i.e. merger and acquisition or initial public offering), CNN will benefit.

Throughout the life cycle of the startup, from development to market impact to sale, CNN will benefit. As the challenge to generate profits in the media industry grows difficult, and with more non-journalism players jumping into the media industry (technology companies, telecom and cable operators, app developers) and competing for market share, more pressure is placed upon media companies to pay attention and continue to be creative in how they gather, produce, and deliver content to their audiences, as well as how they engage their audiences in participatory journalism. The ability to sustain a competitive level in the media marketplace depends directly upon the priority placed on creativity that can lead to marketable products, services, and increased audience engagement.

Journalists should always be on the lookout for innovation in the market. Not just the journalism/media market, but the advertising/marketing industry as well. When these markets are hit by a disruption that impacts existing business models, changes will occur as companies adjust to the disruption. That adjustment can take many forms, but one is layoffs. The advertising industry is a volatile landscape that is evolving today. As technologies enable major advertisers to dispense with third-party ad agencies and go direct to the consumer of their products and services, media companies suffer a loss of revenue. And since most media operate on an advertising business model, the loss of that revenue means cuts in expenses. That domino hits the newsroom.

But disruptions in the media and marketing industries are also doors of opportunity waiting to be opened. Consider the fact that with more screens (and here comes the growth of virtual reality and augmented reality) there is a need for more content. With more cable channels, there is more need for broadcast material. With more corporate brands seeking to tell their story to consumers in a way that holds some integrity, they need the skills of professional journalists. Storytelling is the most valued commodity across all platforms of distribution. Stories inform. Stories influence. Stories have impact. Stories move people to feel and act on their feelings. The media and marketing industries, regardless of how they evolve, and how quickly they evolve, will always need storytellers.

Journalism is changing. But that's not a bad thing. Remnants of the familiar remain. But the landscape is evolving. And while no one has a clear vision on where this industry is headed, the doors of creative opportunity are expanding. And that empowers both entrepreneurs and intrapreneurs to contribute their innovative ideas to help steer the industry into the future.

## Resources

- What's an Intrapreneur? And How Do I Become One?[33]
- Quiz: Are You an Intrapreneur or an Entrepreneur? [34]
- What's an Intrapreneur, and How to Be One[35]

**Mike Green** *is a New York Times Leadership Academy Fellow and award-winning journalist with 20 years' experience. He is co-founder of ScaleUp Partners, a national consultancy specializing in economic inclusion and competitiveness strategies, plans, and policy. Reach him on Twitter at @amikegreen2..*

## Leave feedback on this chapter.

# Notes

1. "Newspapers Fact Sheet," *Pew Research Center,* http://www.journalism.org/fact-sheet/newspapers/.

2. *The Media Deserts Project,* https://mediadeserts.wordpress.com/.

3. "Newspapers Fact Sheet," *Pew Research Center,* http://www.journalism.org/fact-sheet/newspapers/.

4. "Newspapers Fact Sheet," *Pew Research Center,* http://www.journalism.org/fact-sheet/newspapers/.

5. Eugene Kim, "Amazon CEO Jeff Bezos Signed the $250 Million Washington Post Deal With no Due Diligence," *Business Insider,* March 24, 2016, http://www.businessinsider.com/amazon-ceo-jeff-bezos-bought-washington-post-with-no-due-diligence-2016-3.

6. "AOL Agrees To Acquire The Huffington Post," *Huffington Post,* May 25, 2011, http://www.huffingtonpost.com/2011/02/07/aol-huffington-post_n_819375.html.

7. Benjamin Mullin, "With New Investment, BuzzFeed Would be Worth Almost as Much as The New York Times," *Poynter,* October 21, 2016, http://www.poynter.org/2016/with-new-investment-buzzfeed-would-be-worth-almost-as-much-as-the-new-york-times/435647/.

8. Benjamin Mullin, "With New Investment, BuzzFeed Would be Worth Almost as Much as The New York Times," *Poynter,* October 21, 2016, http://www.poynter.org/2016/with-new-investment-buzzfeed-would-be-worth-almost-as-much-as-the-new-york-times/435647/.

9. Cecilia Kang, "AT&T's Words on Time Warner Deal Say 'Underdog.' Its Actions Speak Otherwise," *The New York Times,* April 23, 2017,  https://www.nytimes.com/2017/04/23/technology/att-time-warner-merger-cable-regulation.html.

10. Jeff Guo, "The Imminent Conservative Takeover of Local TV News, Explained," *Vox,* May 15, 2017, https://www.vox.com/2017/5/15/15598270/sinclair-broadcast-imminent-conservative-takeover-of-local-tv-news-explained.

11. Jeff Guo, "The Imminent Conservative Takeover of Local TV News, Explained," *Vox,* May 15, 2017, https://www.vox.com/2017/5/15/15598270/sinclair-broadcast-imminent-conservative-takeover-of-local-tv-news-explained.

12. *Newspaper Death Watch,* http://newspaperdeathwatch.com/.

13. "The Notable Angel Investors in Media Technology," *MediaTech,* https://mediatech.ventures/mediatech-angel-investors.

14. *Center for Venture Research,* http://paulcollege.unh.edu/research/center-venture-research.

15. *Crunchbase,* https://www.crunchbase.com/

16. "The News Frontier Database," *CJR,* http://archives.cjr.org/the_news_frontier_database/.

17. "Research," *Content Marketing Institute,* http://contentmarketinginstitute.com/research/.

18. "What Is the Difference Between AR and VR? A Lesson in Altered Realities," *Cramer*, http://cramer.com/story/the-difference-between-ar-and-vr/.

19. Nathan McAlone, "These Are the 18 Most Popular YouTube Stars in the World — and Some Are Making Millions," *Business Insider*, March 7, 2017, http://www.businessinsider.com/most-popular-youtuber-stars-salaries-2017.

20. *News and Guts*, https://www.newsandgutsmedia.com/.

21. *Starfish Media Group*, http://www.starfishmediagroup.com/.

22. *Matter of Fact with Soledad O'Brien*, http://matteroffact.tv/.

23. *Johnathan M. Holifield*, http://johnathanholifield.tech/.

24. Source: personal interview with Johnathan M. Holifield

25. Avishai Abrahami, "3 Rules for Making a Successful Pivot," *Entrepreneur*, July 3, 2014, https://www.entrepreneur.com/article/235168.

26. Shobhit Seth, "Entrepreneur vs. Small Business Owner, Defined," *Investopedia*, http://www.investopedia.com/articles/investing/092514/entrepreneur-vs-small-business-owner-defined.asp.

27. "How Does Pokémon Go Actually Work?" *DigitalFoundry YouTube Channel*, July 13, 2016, https://www.youtube.com/watch?v=tV9Jc3KFmPA.

28. "Mobile Fact Sheet," *Pew Research Center*, http://www.pewInternet.org/fact-sheet/mobile/.

29. Gerry Smith, "CNN to Invest $40 Million in Its Video Startup Great Big Story," *Bloomberg*, June 20, 2017, https://www.bloomberg.com/news/articles/2017-06-20/cnn-to-invest-40-million-in-its-video-startup-great-big-story.

30. Fitz Tepper, "Time Warner Will Spend 100M on Snapchat Original Shows and Ads," June 19, 2017, https://techcrunch.com/2017/06/19/time-warner-will-spend-100m-on-snapchat-original-shows-and-ads/.

31. Sarah Kessler, "CNN Launches Great Big Story," *Fast Company*, https://www.fastcompany.com/3051812/cnn-launches-great-big-story-its-answer-to-vice-and-buzzfeed.

32. "Liquidity Event," *Investopedia*, http://www.investopedia.com/terms/l/liquidity_event.asp?lgl=rira-baseline-vertical.

33. "What's an Intrapreneur? And How Do I Become One?" *Media Innovation & Entrepreneurship*, https://press.rebus.community/media-innovation-and-entrepreneurship/chapter/whats-an-intrapreneur-and-how-do-i-become-one/.

34. "Quiz: Are You an Intrapreneur or an Entrepreneur," *Virgin*, https://www.virgin.com/entrepreneur/quiz-are-you-intrapreneur-or-entrepreneur.

35. Elizabeth Mays, "What's an Intrapreneur, and How to Be One," *Medium*, https://medium.com/@theeditress/whats-an-intrapreneur-and-how-to-be-one-eba2af04269d.

# TAKING RISKS AND BUILDING RESILIENCE ON THE PATH TO INNOVATION

*Dana Coester*

## Finding Joy in Taking Risks

### "We don't know what will happen, but let's try this!"

Resiliency—the ability to weather change and bounce back from failure—is an essential mindset for entrepreneurs. In innumerable blog posts and articles, industry leaders describe resilience as a cornerstone to innovation, frequently citing Thomas Edison's famous quote: "I have not failed. I have just found ten thousand ways that won't work."

Resilience is more than a buzzword; it's a survival skill. And it's a skill that you will need to develop to become successful at navigating today's dynamic business environment. With predictions suggesting that today's worker may hold more than twelve jobs in their lifetime, you will need to build your capacity for resilience for the future. Sometimes you are forced to be resilient when dealing with an uncertain or difficult situation, such as losing your job or having to relocate. But while life experiences lay the groundwork, here are a few additional perspectives you can explore to build on your core of resiliency.

### "The future is on top of us."

One of the first steps in building resiliency is to fully appreciate the magnitude and pace of change that technology drives across almost all fields. This insight will even give you an edge over entrenched leaders, who continue to underestimate the pace of change[1] in their industries. Read carefully and internalize this bold statement about exponential change from Ray Kurzweil's now cult-classic 2001 essay, Law of Accelerating Returns:[2]

*"Human culture will change in the next 100 years as much as it has changed in the past 25,000 years."*

According to Kurzweil, the default setting within organizations for anticipating change is based on an intuitive linear view of progress—the idea that change happens at a steady and predictable pace with just a few dramatic turns. This false perception results in consistently underestimating change, which can happen at a far more accelerated rate. In fact, Kurzweil described the far-reaching implications of what the "acceleration of acceleration" would mean for industries grappling with technology-driven change, anticipating the profound disruption to come in the years since 2001.

The gist is that all exponential change is flat for a very long period of time—but exponential change always reaches a point where the graph becomes vertical.

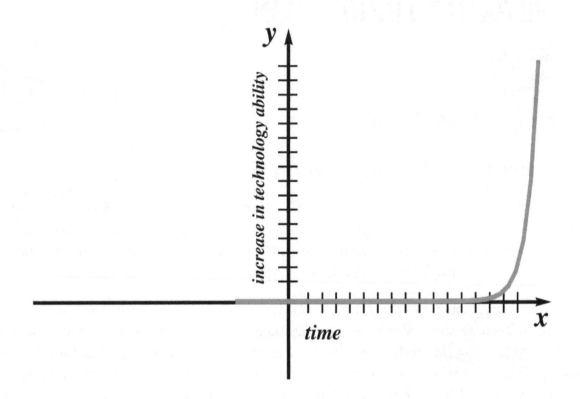

*We are at the point where the curve goes vertical.*

You may ask, why does 100 years from now matter if you're just looking to start your own business a few years from now? If you were on this curve back in 1980, and you were making plans for your future, you can see that the location of the future was exactly where you'd expect it—far off on a gentle and still relatively flat slope.

But if you're at the point where the graph becomes vertical, you need to ask yourself, "Where does the future lie now?"

A young media college student in an entrepreneurship class recently answered that question, by saying: "The future is on top of us."

## "We don't know what will happen."

John Keefe, a "bot developer" and product manager at innovative startup publication Quartz,[3] teaches classes in innovation and evangelizes "DIY hackery" as part of the maker community. The maker movement represents a thriving community of hobbyists and entrepreneurs alike who conduct home-grown, DIY experiments in technology and product development as well as other creative problem solving that helps drive innovation across industries.

Keefe says experimenting take takes trial and error, and that innovation by nature is a risky prospect. He challenged himself to risk failure repeatedly in his public experiment "Make Every Week,"[4] where he built a new DIY "thing" (almost) every week for a year.

"Being creative might lead to failure," Keefe says, "but it could lead to something awesome."

In Keefe's case, it led to breakthroughs in groundbreaking sensor journalism,[5] new job opportunities and a book,[6] but it was also a valuable exercise in acclimating himself to taking risks. Not unlike embarking on an exercise regime, acclimating yourself to potential failure through repeated exposure to trial and error on a small scale helps build resilience.

For Keefe, these serial experiments included working with students on a beta sensor-reporting project as part of an experimental journalism class he taught at West Virginia University. Each week he said to students:

*"We don't know what will happen...but let's try this."*

As simple as that statement seems, it bears breaking down and repeating, because it captures attributes of innovation you can start to emulate now. When you say out loud to your classmates or teammates, "We don't know what will happen, but let's try it," you are helping to build a culture of resiliency and a safe space to experiment in that moment. Here's how:

"We don't know what will happen…" expresses:

- a matter-of-fact expectation that uncertainty is a given
- a transparent acknowledgement of vulnerability without anxiety or shame
- that you're willing to risk asking questions that don't have answers

"But let's try it…" expresses:

- an eagerness to conduct hands-on experimentation
- a commitment to being collaborative and inclusive
- joyful curiosity

Confronting the reality of accelerating change empowers you to prepare for a different kind of future than the one your predecessors faced. Building resiliency gives you a remarkable edge for both anticipating, and navigating, the many changes to come.

*Dana Coester is an associate professor at West Virginia University Reed College of Media, where she is creative director for the College's Media Innovation Center and leads the Center's Knight-funded Innovators-in-Residence program. She is also the creative director and executive editor for the digital media startup 100 Days in Appalachia.[7] Reach her on Twitter at @poetabook.*

## Leave feedback on this sidebar.

## Notes

1. Steven Kotler, "The Acceleration of Acceleration: How The Future Is Arriving Far Faster Than Expected," *Forbes,* February 6, 2015,  https://www.forbes.com/sites/stevenkotler/2015/02/06/the-acceleration-of-acceleration-how-the-future-is-arriving-far-faster-than-expected/#13f677ce3b18.

2. Ray Kurzweil, "The Law of Accelerating Returns," *Kurzweil Accelerating Intelligence,* March 7, 2001, http://www.kurzweilai.net/the-law-of-accelerating-returns.

3. Quartz, https://qz.com/.

4. "Make Every Week: Lunch Bot," *Johnkeefe.net,* http://johnkeefe.net/make-every-week-lunch-bot.

5. Matt Waite, "How Sensor Journalism Can Help Us Create Data & Improve Our Storytelling," *Poynter,* April 17, 2013, https://www.poynter.org/2013/how-sensor-journalism-can-help-us-create-data-improve-our-storytelling/210558/.

6. "Make Every Week Begets a Book," *Johnkeefe.net,* http://johnkeefe.net/make-every-week-lunch-bot.

7. 100 Days in Appalachia, http://www.100daysinappalachia.com/.

# FROM THE FIELD: Q&A WITH A YOUNG INNOVATOR

*Dana Coester*

## From the Field

"Fail fast." "Fail often." "Reward failure." It's easy to evangelize a fast-fail philosophy in spirit, but it may be especially difficult in the classroom—after all, an F in college is not exactly a badge of honor. Add to this millennials' oft-cited propensity for perfection, desire to please and conform, and you don't exactly have a recipe for high-risk innovation. Although some studies have painted a portrait of this generation as risk averse,[1] many young entrepreneurs are pushing back at that assessment.

Meet Jillian Clemente, a member of the Young Innovators program[2] at West Virginia University pursuing a dual major in Journalism and Wildlife and Fisheries Resource Management. She is also a two-time veteran of the Media College's Innovators-in-Residence Experimental Storytelling program, where she worked closely with John Keefe and inventors at MIT Public Lab in her environmental sensor work, helping to pioneer new projects and classes in the College's "Maker Lab." She is also a member of Launch Lab, which is the University's business incubator for student entrepreneurs. As a young entrepreneur juggling multiple passions, she shares firsthand what it's like to jump into the deep end and offers some advice to fellow students.

**What's your advice for fellow students on cultivating resiliency and taking risks in their entrepreneurship journey?**

**Ask for help!**

I've needed teachers and leaders to help me up quite a bit, and I've learned that it's okay to ask for help, whether you're starting from scratch, or starting over again. It can be scary to do something new from scratch and maybe come out with no tangible new "thing," but I can promise you the process is worth it.

As a sophomore Jillian Clemente took the lead in her sensor journalism project. Now she leads workshops for community media and citizen scientists in how to build and use water sensors and other DIY electronics. Photo by David Smith.

**Acknowledge the fear. Now throw it away.**

Fear is dumb. Innovate because you want to, not for anything else. Don't do it to impress people and don't take more than you can handle. If you're doing the work for the right reasons, you'll be pleased with the process and the project as a whole. There's never a reason to worry that "nothing will come out of it." Something positive always comes out of it.

**You are going to fail, but you're not a failure.**

First, know your worth as a person—you yourself are a unique innovation. Now give it your all. The end result may not be a "success" as in "hey, this thing works," but it will be successful in giving you problem-solving skills and insight into your resilience as a human being. Try listing out your new skills after a project or experiment (regardless of its "success" or "failure") for your resume, and you'll be pleasantly shocked.

**Accomplishments can be tiny—hey, look, you MADE something!**

Remember when you gave your parents a drawing and they got so excited about how amazing it was, even if it wasn't perfect? Get that way about your own accomplishments, no matter how small. It's an achievement to make one component of a final piece. Yes, there are always more miles to travel, but you did something. You made it to a goal and, in a field of so many unknowns (um, innovation), it's the showing up, the tiny steps, the trial and error that makes way for expertise and breakthroughs.

**Groups are good.**

Don't shut people out—listen to all. Pride is an idea killer. Plus, if an idea doesn't work, you'll still have some backups to test out, too. Also, acknowledge the introverts and extroverts. Some people may need longer breaks alone to perform best.

**Have fun.**

You're choosing to spend your time doing these things. Choose joy. Enjoy the process. Enjoy the failures. Enjoy collaboration and the betterment of yourself and, possibly, the world.

*Dana Coester* *is an associate professor at West Virginia University Reed College of Media, where she is creative director for the College's Media Innovation Center and leads the Center's Knight-funded Innovators-in-Residence program. She is also the creative director and executive editor for the digital media startup 100 Days in Appalachia.[3] Reach her on Twitter at @poetabook.*

## Leave feedback on this sidebar.

## Notes

1. Ruth Simon and Caelainn Barr, "Endangered Species: Young U.S. Entrepreneurs," *Wall Street Journal*, January 2, 2015, https://www.wsj.com/articles/endangered-species-young-u-s-entrepreneurs-1420246116.

2. *WVU Young Innovators Program*, http://younginnovators.wvu.edu/.

3. 100 Days in Appalachia, http://www.100daysinappalachia.com/.

# WHAT'S AN INTRAPRENEUR? AND HOW DO I BECOME ONE?

*Interview with Ebony Reed*

*In this interview, Elizabeth Mays interviews intrapreneur Ebony Reed for a class on Business & Future of Journalism.* **Ebony Reed** *is director of innovation and the RJI Futures Lab at the Reynolds Journalism Institute and an associate professor at University of Missouri-Columbia. Previously she was director of business development for U.S. (local) markets at the Associated Press. Reach her on Twitter at @EbonyReed.*

## Q: Can you give our readers some ideas of the types of projects or initiatives or interesting things that you've done as an intrapreneur in newsrooms?

**ER:** Sure. About three years ago I was working as a regional sales manager for the Associated Press, and we started to place more emphasis in the local markets on selling to nontraditional news customers, which were startups and also companies that aren't even in the news business. That included some companies that were doing things with artificial intelligence and needed news to put the metadata that's on it, maybe companies that wanted to use news for competitive intelligence, just a variety of use cases. And so my job at that time was to drive that new business and to look for those new markets and to grow that revenue, which grew about a million dollars year over year in that time that I was in that role. I worked with 24 sales representatives across the U.S. that were working in their local markets driving the initiatives that I was identifying.

## Q: How did you get tapped as an entrepreneur to begin with? You have a series of intrapreneurial roles on your career path, but you didn't walk into a newsroom as an intrapreneur, did you?

**ER:** Right. Part of it was luck. Part of it was fate. I was working for the Associated Press as a deputy bureau chief. That's how I was recruited into the AP in June 2010 from the *Detroit News*.

I was 90 days into my job and the AP went through a re-organization and said, "Hello all of you bureau chiefs. We're now changing your jobs, and you now have a complete focus on revenue and we're removing you from being involved with the news report and the news operation.

You'll come into headquarters in October. You'll get trained from the Harvard Business School, and that'll be your new job."

So I was asked at that time whether or not I wanted to continue down that path, or whether I wanted them to find me [another] place. I just sort of embraced the opportunity that had been placed in front of me and I just said, "You know what? I've got a master's in media management, I have a father that was a longtime advertising executive on the buy side, I've got an uncle that is a VP of operations for one of the largest urban radio station chains in the U.S.," and I just said, "I'm just going to go with this and see what happens." And so to my surprise, I actually was pretty good at sales and then that opened the door to people listening to me about new products and services.

The other thing that I did was that I wasn't quiet about my ideas. The AP had a business plan competition. I had an idea for a mobile political product. At the time it was something that AP wasn't doing and I put forth my idea and I was one of the top 12 global finalists in that competition. So that really got the attention of senior management within the organization to want to hear my ideas and listen to them, even though the AP didn't make the product.

## Q: From your perspective, what does it mean to be an intrapreneur in a newsroom environment?

**ER:** To me it means that you have new ideas about new ways to do things. It may be that you have new ideas about creating an experience for your digital clients or your digital users, or it may be that you have a new idea tied to a new product and service, and that you can say, "This is how this ties into our core mission. And it's new and it's different, and this is why we should do it." I think being able to understand the revenue piece too is really key, because at the end of the day, all of these media companies really need to be able to make revenue.

## Q: How would you encourage young people who have great ideas and are afraid they won't be listened to by others within the organization?

**ER:** So I hate to link everything back to revenue, but that's so much of the big piece. So right now, I'm doing advertising sales as a manager at the *Boston Business Journal*, which is part of American City Business Journals, and I would say while I'm not on the product team there, if I have an idea about something that's new that we need to do in this market, I can move that idea forward by linking it to how much revenue potential I see. I know that my boss and her bosses want that from me, expect that from me, would be open to that. So what I would say is to anyone that's considering a proposal for something that's new, I would just say how solid is your business case? What is the value proposition? Why should this media company do what you're proposing? Are you saving them time, are you saving them money, are you saving them both? There has to be an element to it that has a benefit that's tied to financials and it's not just cool and fun.

One of the questions I would have, and that I think students should ask, is who else in the organization is doing this and why do we think that this will work inside of this organization? Because really what you're doing is you're almost building a business, building a product, building something that doesn't exist anywhere else inside the organization and if you don't have the support from the top down, you're just kind of spinning your wheels.

### Q: Why do you enjoy this kind of a role? That sounds like hard work and a lot of numbers. What are the best and worst parts of being an intrapreneur in the newsroom today?

**ER:** So my work on the advertising side … technically I'm not in the newsroom, although I work for a news company. I would say that the best part is recognizing that the work that I'm doing to make things fiscally strong and financially strong is ensuring that great journalism gets to continue happening at the organization where I am and for the industry.

I would say one of the hardest parts of this type of work is when you're a reporter, when you're an editor, everyone wants to talk to you. Everybody wants to tell their story. Everybody has something they want to say, but when you're on the revenue side, it is hard. It is tough. We get a lot of no's. I tell my team, "We need three times as much revenue in our pipeline to be able to hit our revenue goals." What that means is, is if we're doing outreach to 100 prospects, in the back of my mind I only think 25 to 30 of them are going to be warm towards us. That means we have a lot of people telling us no. That's just a part of the job, but at the same time, when you come from a side of the house where everybody is warm and engaging and wants to talk and then you come over to this side, it's a totally different experience. Totally.

### Q: Do you think hearing the word "no" is really unique to that advertising side or do you think that's also part of just being in journalism? Shouldn't my students be prepared to have some sort of a thick skin?

**ER:** They will definitely hear "no" in other parts of their work, even if they're not working full-time on the revenue side. What I would say to that is when people say no, what I say to my team is then your next question is why. If they said no, ask why. Is it because the idea isn't realistic? Is it because the resources are not there? Is it because they don't think the revenue would be there, and if so, why?

Then when it's even not clear after that, ask for an example. It's another way of really getting down to the nitty gritty of what the issue and how you can make your proposal better so that maybe it could become a business plan that could be utilized.

### Q: What traits do you think would make someone a good fit for newsroom or news organization intrapreneurship, media intrapreneurship? Or what traits would make

them someone who's a better fit not to do that and just to be a newsroom employee and what traits would make them better to be an entrepreneur than an intrapreneur?

**ER:** Let me separate the two terms first. So, entrepreneur means of course, you're starting your own company, you're solely responsible, you're going to employ yourself and other people, and it's all on you. Intrapreneurial is you're inside of a big organization. So to some extent you like working inside of a big company. Maybe you like the resources that it provides. Maybe you like having the amount of colleagues you can bounce ideas off of. Maybe you like having the credibility of the name of where you work, but you're inside of a big organization. So to me, one of the first big differences is that the intrapreneur is very comfortable and okay with moving through that maze of that larger organization. The entrepreneur might like a much more flat organization to work within and might not want to deal with the level of bureaucracy to get decisions made.

When you're intrapreneur, you've got to not only put forth new and creative ideas, but you've got to also really, really understand the organization you are maneuvering within politically. You've got to understand it from a fiscal perspective. You've got to understand how it fits into the greater context of the industry as a whole, which an entrepreneur has to understand too.

## Q: Do you have any rules that have held true about pitching your ideas throughout organizations or are your pitches very specific to each organization?

**ER:** I think it really depends on the organization, and I think it depends on the organization's mission. I think it depends on who the players are within the organization. I think it depends on timetables, how long you would take to get something crafted that's new. So I don't have any set ground rules. What I would say is that I have never put forth an idea inside of an organization where someone did not ask me what is the timetable to get this off the ground, what are the resources that you need, and what is the revenue potential? That's something that's been part of every conversation.

*This interview has been edited for length.*

## Leave feedback on this sidebar.

# LOOKING AHEAD

## Looking Ahead

You've read why entrepreneurship (and intrapreneurship) are important in Developing the Entrepreneurial Mindset, the Foreword and Preface. In order to better understand the entrepreneurial process, it's time to come up with an entrepreneurial idea. Read on to learn about methods for Ideation.

# IDEATION

by Michelle Ferrier

## Summary

How do you come up with good ideas for a potentially viable product that will meet a real need and find a market? What makes a business idea worth pursuing?

**Learning Objectives**

- Define innovation and entrepreneurship and how it has generated innovations in new, digital-only media entities, distribution, content, engagement, and other technologies.
- Define ideation.
- Examine creative processes for exploring possibilities.
- Learn about human-centered design (HCD) and its use in problem solving, ideation, and design.
- Acquire techniques for ideating within HCD.
- Understand intellectual property and whether your idea can be protected.
- Encourage students to look outside their own domain for ideas.

# Inside this Chapter

- Ideation

*Michelle Ferrier is an associate professor in the E.W. Scripps School of Journalism at Ohio University. She is the founder of Troll-Busters.com, an online pest control service for women journalists. Reach her on Twitter at @mediaghosts.*

# IDEATION

*Michelle Ferrier*

"Creativity, as has been said, consists largely of rearranging what we know in order to find out what we do not know. Hence, to think creatively, we must be able to look afresh at what we normally take for granted."
— George Kneller, author of *The Art and Science of Creativity*

**How do you know if your good idea is the next big thing?** Whether you are an intrapreneur, working within an existing business, or an entrepreneur looking to create a business startup, or a student creating an idea for a class project, this question is the one that should drive you to find answers. Unfortunately, it is not a question that can be answered on its own. It takes answering a bunch of other questions of your potential customers, of your own motivations, and of your idea as well. Two key qualities required to begin this journey include curiosity and creativity. As a communicator or a student at a mass communication program, you should already possess an innate curiosity about people, storytelling, and problem solving. Creativity is a skill that can be cultivated as an individual or as part of group or team exercises, to develop unusual connections, breakthroughs in processes, or insights that lead to product development. Often, the journey to a good idea begins with asking "What if?"

Ideation is the process of coming up with an idea. It is using creativity and questions like "What if?" to imagine ways something can be done differently. The ideation stage is critical to ensure that you are generating good ideas from the start. It involves seeing problems and opportunities, brainstorming around the problems you identify, and doing research to test your assumptions about the market, your customers, and your idea. Refining that initial idea involves assessing the market, looking at trends, and asking questions (and more questions)—and learning from potential customers, investors, and research whether your idea is a good one. The design process consists of a series of steps to test assumptions and ideas. Ideation falls within a larger design process that begins with understanding who you are serving; empathizing, understanding and defining the needs of that target audience; then ideating around what is needed (Figure 1):

In the Stanford School Design Thinking Process, there six stages to design[1]:

- Empathizing
- Defining
- Ideating

- Prototyping
- Testing
- Sharing

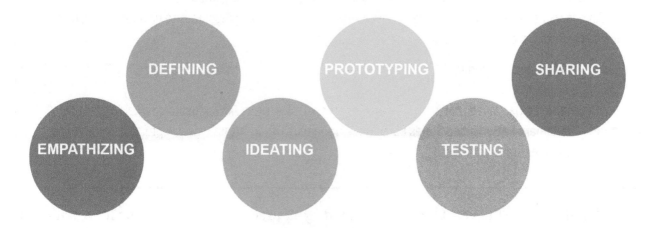

Figure 1. Represents six areas of design as defined by the Stanford School of Design Thinking Process.

According to 2012 research by Harvard Business School instructor Shikhar Ghosh, 75% of venture-backed startups fail.[2] Ideas are like opinions—everyone has one. If the founders of those failed companies could have answered that question as to whether *their idea* was the next big thing…well everyone wants that guarantee. But entrepreneurship is risky. Startups are risky. You and your team are using your time and your intellectual property (ideas) to create something new. Generating a great idea from the start is part of a larger set of success factors such as the expertise of the founders, the competitive landscape, speed to market, and other factors.

These other success factors include:

- The composition of the team itself;
- The execution of the concept. Is the team adaptable, effective and efficient?
- The structure or business model shows a clear revenue path and immediate revenue stream;
- The structure of funding; and
- The timing of the idea and its entry into the marketplace.

What ultimately matters most is not the idea, but the ability of the team to work together, execute and test an idea, and get their idea out into the marketplace. So the ideation stage is about minimizing the risk of failure by coming up with ideas that the world needs or wants. Successful startups begin with a quality idea, one that is novel, encapsulates a "truth," and will have good barriers to competitors.

Students will often come to me and say, "I've got this great idea, but I'm afraid to share it because someone might steal it." I often coach students that their fear is preventing them from finding other teammates, coaches, potential investors, and mentors. Timing and execution are king; ideas, well, everyone has one. So if you're hoarding your ideas, you are limiting one of your key assets, which is timing.

---

Is an idea something that can be protected? Ideas themselves cannot be copyrighted, but original expressions of ideas in a tangible medium can earn legal protection. Review the following resources to understand what can and can't be protected under U.S. copyright, patent or trademark law.

- **FAQs About Copyright,** United States Copyright Office, https://www.copyright.gov/help/faq/index.html[3]
- **Patent FAQs,** United States Patent and Trademark Office, https://www.uspto.gov/help/patent-help[4]
- **Trademark FAQs,** United States Patent and Trademark Office, https://www.uspto.gov/learning-and-resources/trademark-faqs[5]

---

But what if you don't have a great idea? How do you practice stretching your imagination to be more creative? And what is creativity anyway? A recent article in the alumni magazine for the University of Central Florida[6] spoke to the entrepreneurial culture that has been a part of the DNA of the institution since its founding as a technical school in 1963. Administrators and faculty from all types of disciplines were asked to weigh in. Michael Pape, Dr. Phillips Entrepreneur in Residence, says creativity is the hunt for an answer to a secret:

> "Creativity is a process of bringing something new into existence that challenges prevailing assumptions. It's fundamental to human existence. To challenge prevailing assumptions, you need to discover secrets." Pape says "to observe, embrace chaos, and try to frame it into form, you might uncover those secrets in the process."

Rick Hall, production director for the Florida Interactive Entertainment Academy, says that creativity is a teachable skill.

> "Creativity is really just your ability to associate two disparate ideas in a way that others haven't thought of before. You've got to proceduralize creativity. And never let a good mistake go to waste."

I once interviewed a student at the University of Pittsburgh who got involved in entrepreneurship because he thought himself to be someone who was creative.

> "I always wanted to pursue new ideas," he said. "It just seemed like the current system is kind of rigid in the sense that the older you get, the more you have to start pruning away some of your ideas and get a more precise focus. And for me, I kind of like things open-ended, and I like to really explore all these ideas that I feel is like part of one big puzzle. And when you put that together, that's how you get the best products because it draws from a number of inspirations."

## Scanning the Environment

Pape says the creative process begins with observation. As a curious journalist, I am always on the lookout for problems, opportunities and new ideas, observing what is happening around me, listening to what my neighbors are talking about, and what people are struggling with in their everyday lives. And as Hall suggests, we can "proceduralize creativity" by increasing the juxtapositions, the opportunities for the collisions of disparate ideas that might spark the next idea.

As an avid reader and a bit of a science geek, I am always scanning publications inside and outside my field that feature innovations in science, medicine, technology, and journalism such as *Wired, FastCompany,* and *Scientific American.* First, I'm learning about innovations and how others leveraged their ideas into businesses. Second, I'm learning how founders adapt their ideas as they learn. Third, I begin to see the world through others stories, experiences, and disciplines that help me to "look afresh" at the world as George Knelle suggests.

Scanning the environment like this is what led me to create Troll-Busters.com in 2015 as I observed what was occurring in social media spaces online and the challenges of women journalists and journalists of color in maintaining a voice online in the midst of targeted online harassment. While the idea began because of my own personal experience and the current news of Gamergate attacks,[7] I quickly validated that this was a common experience among journalists and media organizations. The idea for TrollBusters was validated initially by the response from female journalists themselves at a hackathon. However, we quickly began diving into global scholarly research that further pointed to the scope and scale of the problem we were addressing.

Through deep interviews with women journalists, we discovered a reluctance to report abuses and a lack of knowledge about what to do next after an attack. The interviewees also talked about the lack of support from peers and management. We started by developing awareness campaigns and online courses that made visible what was happening all over the world and helped women journalists take control of their own protection and speak up about the online harassment they are experiencing.

Look to the work of futurists and others who attempt to predict the future of technology, education, manufacturing, and other fields. Amy Webb,[8] founder of the Future Today Institute, examines trends in technology, media, and communications. In her new book, *The Signals are Talking,*[9] she says there are "signals" that everyone can watch for, beyond what is covered in the technology press. She says "It's not like there's a singular source where you would go to find the unusual suspects at the fringe. Instead, it's a series of guiding questions she uses in her explorations:

- Who do I know of that's been working directly and indirectly in this space?
- Who's funding this work?

- Who's encouraging experimentation?
- Who might be directly impacted if this technology succeeds one way or the other?
- Who could be incentivized to work against any change?
- Who might see this technology as just the starting-off point for something else?"

Then the curious, like Amy, get going. They start asking questions. And reading. And listening.

The New Media Consortium started asking these questions of its employees, who were trying to keep up with the changing technology landscape. They realized that many policy makers, industry leaders, innovators, educators, and others struggled to keep up with technology trends. They started the NMC Horizon Project[10] to chart emerging technologies and their implications for teaching, learning, and creative inquiry. Accenture, a strategy and consulting company, creates a technology trends report. Its 2017 Technology Vision[11] report details disruptive technology trends and deep industry knowledge. CBInsights tracks trends across multiple industry sectors including automotive, financial tech, the Internet of Things, artificial intelligence, AR/VR, and other technology areas.

In the media field, I've mentioned publications like *Wired* and *FastCompany* that provide a deep dive into media and technology innovations. The Pew Research Center[12] offers deep research into social, religious, technology, and media trends and usage. Other media-focused publications include *MediaShift, TechCrunch, Mediagazer,* and *VentureBeat.*

*CrunchBase* is a database of startups, product development timelines, funding rounds, and other information. Add in subscriptions to online newsletters for the startup and entrepreneurship world like *Entrepreneur* and *Fast Company, Inc.* and others to keep an eye out on emerging, competing ideas in the market. Find these types of sources and scour them to cultivate new ways of seeing the world, the first step to creating innovative ideas.

## Thinking Creatively With Human-Centered Design

LUMA Institute defines human-centered design: "Human-Centered Design (HCD) is the discipline of developing solutions in the service of people."[13] Human-centered design (HCD) is being adopted now by more organizations, strategists, and development practitioners and has been taught in places like Stanford's D-School (Design School). HCD views people as the core focus of design and development. According to LUMA Institute,[14] which works with organizations seeking to innovate:

> "Every story of a good innovation — whether it's a new product, a new service, a new business model or a new form of governance — begins and ends with people. It starts with careful observation of human needs, and concludes with solutions that meet or exceed expectations."

When I teach innovation, I separate the Human-Centered Design process into three phases:

1. **Inspiration Phase:** Learn directly from the people you're designing for as you immerse yourself in their lives and come to deeply understand their needs.
2. **Ideation Phase:** Make sense of what you learned, identify opportunities for design, and prototype possible solutions.
3. **Implementation Phase:** Bring your solution to life and eventually to market. And you'll know that your solution will be a success because you've kept the very people you're looking to serve at the heart of the process.

Individuals, teams, and other groups use brainstorming and ideation to come up with better ideas — ideas that speed processes, ideas that create new products, ideas that create innovations, and ideas that solve problems. But usually that activity happens in a vacuum —a team sits around a whiteboard coming up with ideas. With human-centered design, inspiration comes through exploration of actual people, their problems, and their needs. So ideation is like an incubator for experimentation. The better you become at asking questions of potential customer and getting them answered quickly, the better you can be at shaping your idea into something that meets a need.

Ideation also involves knowing your outcome/deliverable. If you are creating ideas for a student competition, you'll want to know the rules and what the judges will be evaluating. Some competitions give you the problem you are attempting to solve. Your measure of success will be in how closely your idea aligns with the competition goals. I've often judged student competitions where there are different rubrics. The simplest I've used asks founders to ask themselves three questions:

1. **Feasibility:** Can we do this?
2. **Viability:** Should we do this?
3. **Desirability:** Do they want this?

The most valuable design sits at the intersection of these three questions and will help guide you in positioning your ideas to meet market needs.

The rubric I developed for an international innovators cup competition provides a good template to use to determine if your idea is innovative:

- Presentation was compelling, easy to understand, and described the problem and a "fresh"? solution.
- Meets the threshold for innovation. Judges should be guided by the reality that truly transformational innovation is rare. Incremental innovation is more the norm but is equally valuable in our competition so long as it provides an inspired solution to the challenge that has been posed.
- Takes full advantage of new media tools, platforms, technologies, and applications in use today. These might include things like interactive design, gaming, geolocation-based tools, informational graphics, and all aspects of social media, etc.

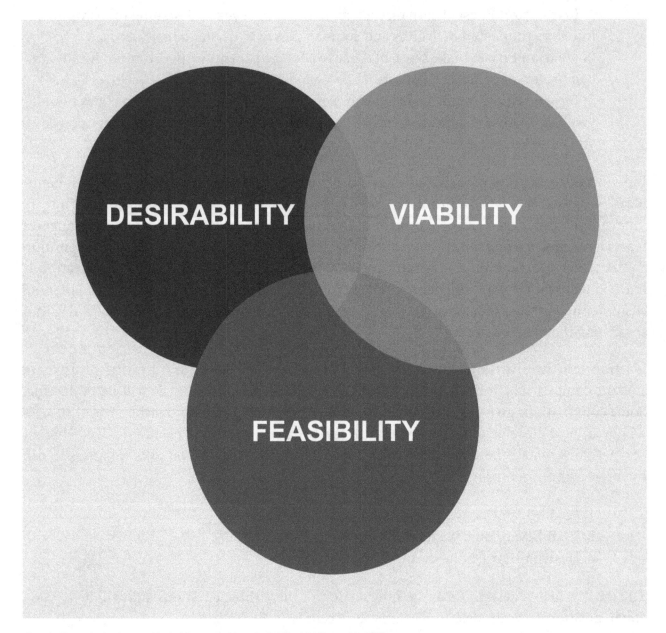

Figure 2. Three criteria often used for judging competitions: Desirability, Viability, and Feasibility.

- Addresses the problem within its context. It should demonstrate that it is offering an idea or approach that is supported by facts and/or research and demonstrates an understanding of today's media and communication landscape, including familiarity with any similar products, apps, or services.
- Understands possible roadblocks, competition, and need for a sustainable advantage. The solution shows an understanding of the roadblocks that need to be overcome, the competition, and how the solution can be sustainable.
- Provides a solution that clearly describes its main features and benefits and presents a valid value proposition with the key activities clearly outlined.

I also added this "diversity enhancement" component to the competition questions to ensure student teams thought about and integrated the needs of underserved and underrepresented users/customers/audiences in their solutions.

- Solution embraces diverse viewpoints, populations, or audiences. The solution realistically includes the potential to expand media diversity, including serving underserved populations:

Later in the chapter, we'll look at specific team exercises to get your group thinking expansively, increasing the juxtaposition of disparate ideas, and generating ideas that we can test. But first let's examine the media landscape and see if we can find interesting juxtapositions and questions that can help us find novel ideas.

## The Media Innovation Landscape

Media innovation and entrepreneurship brings together journalism, technology, and business to create new projects inside and outside of traditional media organizations. For the media industry, there are significant opportunities in the disruption to business models and technological changes. This seismic shift in the monolithic news and information business has created a landscape that has allowed new forms of journalism and technology to emerge, driven by innovation, creativity, and entrepreneurship. The report "The Big Thaw: Charting a New Future for Journalism" by Tony Deifell of Q Media Labs[15] details the new competitive landscape for today's media enterprises (Figure 3).

As Deifell's report describes, this disruption can be seen as opportunity. Each of the four areas: new competitive landscape, new sources of value, new distinctive competencies, and new business models presents challenges, questions, and spaces providing fertile ground for new ideas. His four questions challenge us to continue to look to the media industry and communication professions for opportunities by asking ourselves:

1. How are media organizations structured to capture value?
2. What needs can be met, problems solved, or desires fulfilled?
3. How is the landscape changing?
4. What new capabilities are needed to succeed?

For example, look under "New Competitive Landscape." The media industry has had to respond to new devices and convergences. Existing companies have had to innovate and design products to maximize the mobile experience for users of their content and products. Think about news apps such as BBCNews[16] for traditional news entities that expanded their existing brand into a new device. We can also point to startups like FlipBoard,[17] a tool designed solely to solve the problem of making reading content easier on a mobile device. Mike McCue, the founder of FlipBoard, says he never intended to start another company after he sold his prior company TellMe to Microsoft. His new company started by asking

Vol. 2 | New & Emerging Realities

Four strategic questions frame the new challenges and opportunities for media organizations (outlined in the diagram below).

## Vol. 2: **New & Emerging Realities**

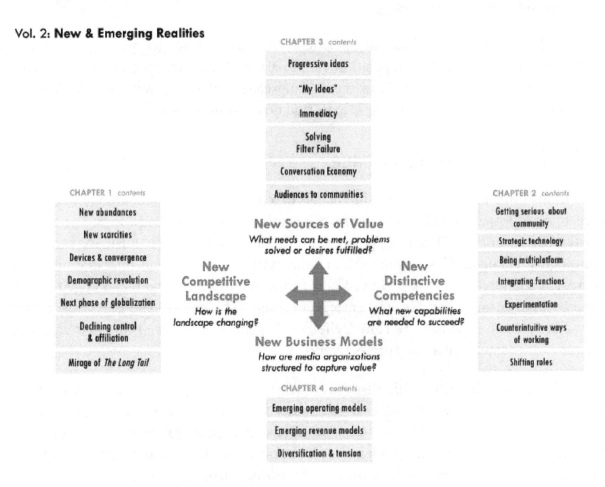

Figure 3. New and emerging realities from the Knight Commission reports. From "The Big Thaw: Charting a New Future for Journalism" by Tony Deifell. This image is Copyright The Media Consortium. All Rights Reserved. Used with permission.

the question "What if?" that started him thinking about redesigning the web interface from scratch.

The mashup of disciplines and technology yields new forms of media entrepreneurship. The chart from *The Big Thaw: Report on New Competitive Landscape*, p.11 (Figure 4) shows the new media paradigm that is driving these changes.

It was at the intersection of three disciplines — business, nutrition, and journalism — that I developed the idea for LocallyGrownNews.com, which won a News Media Women's Entrepreneur grant of $20,000 from the McCormick Foundation in 2009. The idea — Women's Community News Franchise — provided the infrastructure—technical, education, writing, publishing, software, and advertising support — to develop online community news

| OLD PARADIGM | | NEW PARADIGM | |
|---|---|---|---|
| **Mainstream Media** | **Independent Journalism** | **All Media** (mainstream & independent converging) | |
| | | *Current* ➡ | *Emerging?* |
| **Industry competition** | Stable | | Unstable & rapid | |
| | Competing against existing commercial players. | Competing against mainstream elites (corporate & government) | Competition from all directions. "No more mainstream." ➡ | Fighting against populist hegemony & group-think. |
| **Distribution limits** | **Scarcity of information** organized around physical distribution limitations.<br><br>Scarcity of independent voices. | | **Scarcity of Attention** caused by abundance of info & "filter failures." ➡ | **Scarcity of reputation & authenticity** (real-name identity).<br><br>Increasing control of Internet pipeline vs. "Net Neutrality." |
| **Platforms & devices** | **Distinct platforms** for different media (print, radio, TV, film). Limited media devices. | | **Convergence** of multiple platforms. **Device proliferation.** ➡ | **Multisensory convergence** & mass mobile-media. |
| **Demographics** (in U.S.) | **Majority + Minorities** | | **Majority minorities.** Millennial generation: "net native" & different attitudes. | |
| **Geography** | **National, regional & local.** High geographical constraints on production. | | **Increasingly global & hyper local.** Low geographical constraints on production. | |
| | | | Rise in non-western values. ➡ | Decline of local reporting. Nation-state censorship. |
| **Institutional control** | **Greater institutional control,** affiliation & trust. | | **People acting free of institutions.** People less tied to publications. | |
| **Consumer habits** | **Power Law:** more locked in. | | **Power Law:** many fast changing dynamics. | |

Figure 4. From "The Big Thaw: Charting a New Future for Journalism" by Tony Deifell of Q Media Labs. This image is copyright The Media Consortium. All Rights Reserved. Used with permission.

and information franchises. Citizen journalists and community members can focus on what they are most passionate about — building their community conversation through good local information and networking.

The business structure for LocallyGrownNews.com came from the franchise business model of providing services and growing a prototype model. The content topic came from the local food movement that was gaining favor nationwide. Geography and journalism became my way to solve the problem of access to fresh, local food. How could I help people live a local food lifestyle through LocallyGrownNews.com? By providing a website with information about local producers, farmers markets, and timely alerts of seasonal goods, I was able to solve the problem of getting good information about the local produce market to my audiences. I'd found a niche at the intersection of the growing local food movement, distributed networks of content creators, services, and a need for good information.[18]

## Defining the Problem Space

Before you design a solution, you need to know what problem you are trying to solve. I often have students who want to create startup ideas that solve a personal problem. One of my students wanted a better way to share music. Another wanted to create a way to earn Boy Scout merit badges online. However, each of these students needs to define the problem space to determine whether their solutions—online education and peer-to-peer recommendations—were really a problem for other people. In other words, is this problem a pain point for just you or are there others? Is there a real problem with a large enough market that needs a solution? To define the problem space, we need to start with a more expansive view of what we are dealing with to determine what might be the best solution.

Remember the three questions we asked earlier in the chapter?

> 1. **Feasibility:** Can we do this?
> 2. **Viability:** Should we do this?
> 3. **Desirability:** Do they want this?

At this point in the process, we are trying to answer the desirability question...Do they want this? So we have to define who is the "they" in this question, and then brainstorm to discover the "this" or solution in the question we want to test. We can use human-centered design to experiment and match our solutions to customer needs at the sweet spot in the center of feasibility, viability, and desirability.[19]

## Working the Problem Space

So let's say you are trying to develop concierge college admissions services, that's the business you want to create. But what is the problem you are trying to solve? Often, students jump to a solution before diving deeply into understanding the problem space. Who is experiencing pain? Is it painful enough that people are seeking solutions and willing to shell out money?

Stanford University's D-School has developed exercises for brainstorming and developing ideas. LUMA Institute and IDEO.org are two additional companies that help organizations think more expansively and deliver ideas that meet human needs.

# Stakeholder Mapping

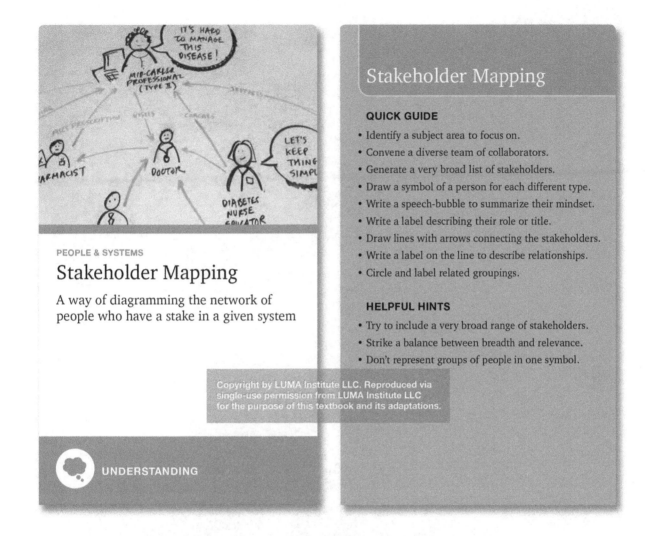

Figure 5. Stakeholder Mapping Card. Source: Innovating for People: Human-Centered Design Planning Cards. Copyright by LUMA Institute LLC. Reproduced via single-use permission from LUMA Institute LLC for the purpose of this chapter and its adaptations. www.luma-institute.com

To visualize who is impacted by the problem you are trying to solve, you can use a stakeholder map to get a sense of the problem space, the actors in it, and who your solutions might address.

For example, students in a social media class were attempting to create tools and strategies to reach out to potential undergraduate students for college admissions. Of course, they started with the pain points and perspective of high school students having recently been in the search for colleges themselves. However, by identifying other stakeholders that play a role in the admissions process, the students were able to identify other pain points and possible solutions that addressed parents, admission counselors, and other stakeholders in the map (Figure 6).

To begin, you need stickies and limited drawing ability. Also a large blank canvas of paper.

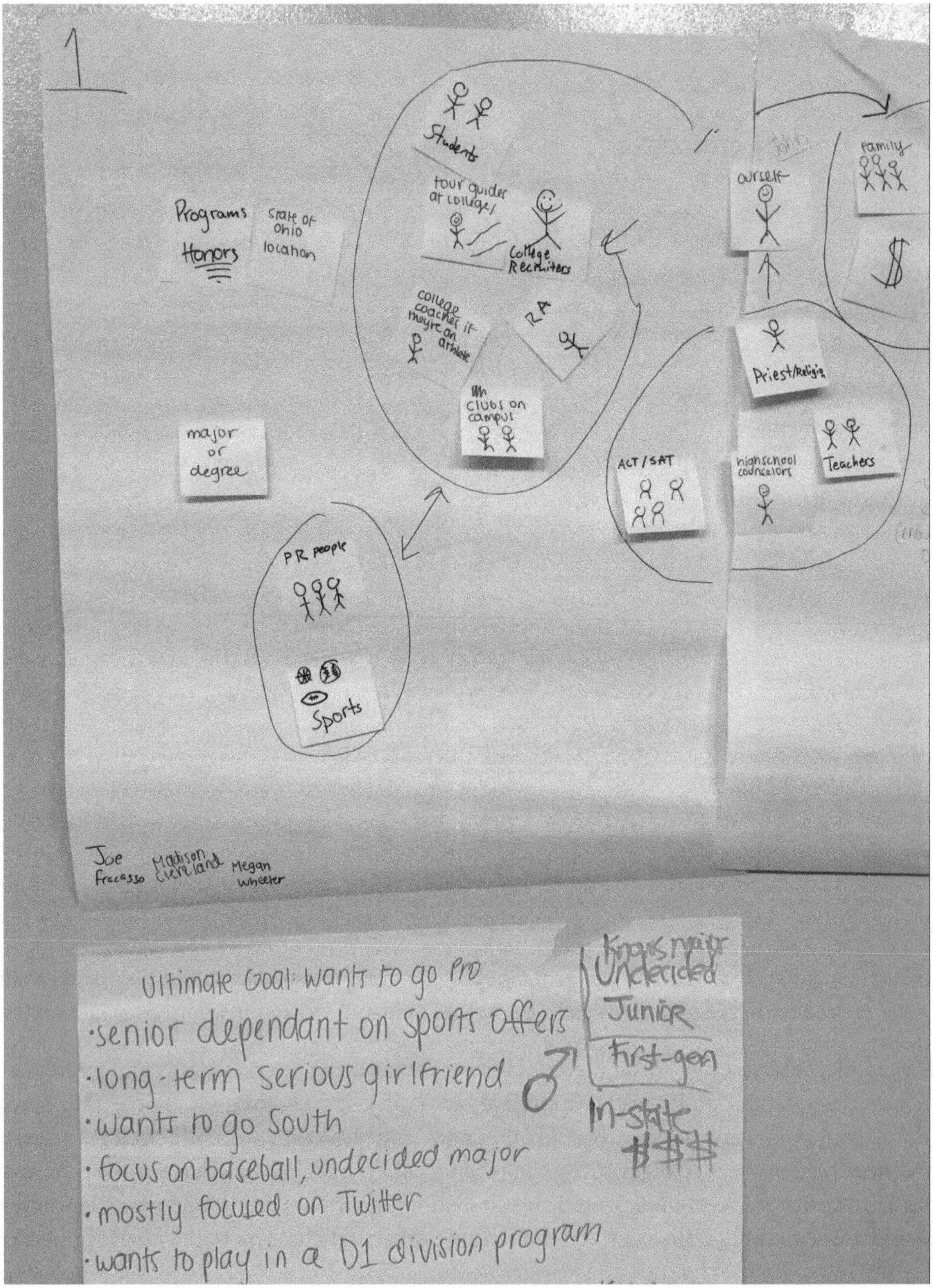

Figure 6. A partial image of a stakeholder map representing the problem space of college admissions and enrollment.

- Create small teams of two to six people. Each person in the team gets sticky notes and a marker.
- Independently, team members are invited to brainstorm potential stakeholders in the problem space. In our example above, we went beyond the college organization to look at the role of parents, high school counselors, government agencies, and others play in the college decision process. Individual work should be given about one minute.
- Collectively, the team goes through its stakeholders, identifying commonalities and defining the roles more clearly by adding a visual element or a speech bubble to suggest what the person may be saying or thinking. These stakeholder stickies are put up on the blank canvas by consensus of the group.
- Organize the stakeholders by grouping entities that are linked by geography or processes. Use lines to draw relationships between stakeholders. For example, a line between parents and the financial aid office of a college might be drawn with dollar signs on it.
- Discuss in the group where there are breakdowns, pain points, and other places where innovation might help to solve the problem. These discussions can then be used to refine who the customer might be for your efforts — students, parents, college administrators, etc. — and who will pay for your solution.
- Select the stakeholders that you will continue to ideate around as potential customers.

## Statement Starters

One exercise, found at LUMA Institute,[20] is designed to ask "What if?" types of questions: open-ended questions that become the jumping point for brainstorming. Sample statement starters include: What if_____? or How might we_____? These statement starters are then attached to the problems you've identified in your stakeholder mapping exercise. Brainstorming then happens around the problem you've identified.

IDEO has a design kit[21] with many examples.

## Other Tools You Can Use

- IDEO's Design Kit resource[22] will help you work with students in brainstorming exercises like the Mash Up which encourages students to think outside of the box to create brilliant proposals and solutions.
- Check out this collection of Human-Centered Design methods[23] you can use to guide students in the ideation phase.
- LUMA offers an online platform[24] to help people implement Human-Centered Design using LUMA's "flexible, repeatable and easy-to-learn" system of Human-Centered Design.
- Exploring your hunch[25] is a huge part of Human-Centered Design. Here is a useful

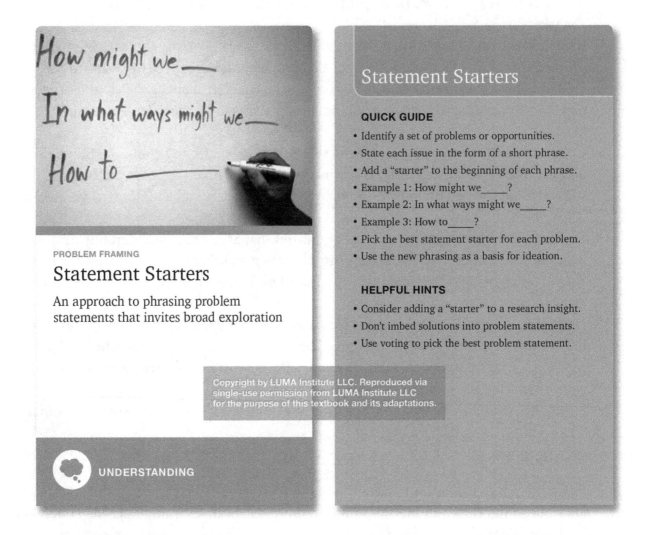

Figure 7. Source: Innovating for People: Human-Centered Design Planning Cards. Copyright by LUMA Institute LLC. Reproduced via single-use permission from LUMA Institute LLC for the purpose of this chapter and its adaptations. www.luma-institute.com

tool to get those ideas and creative juices flowing by exploring and testing your hunch.

- The card game Aha![26] created by the City University of New York allows students to juxtapose an emerging technology with an audience or need.
- Help students to prioritize, communicate, and strategize using this synthesis tool and team activity.[27]
- Try these pointers to structure and organize brainstorming sessions[28] to ensure they are truly engaging, meaningful, and successful.

## Validated Learning

Eric Ries of The Lean Startup advocates "failing fast." What he's suggesting is that teams quickly move through the ideation stage to customer discovery and testing phases, tossing out assumptions and ideas that fail to meet customer needs.

IDEAS → BUILD (CODE) → MEASURE (DATA) →LEARN

You and your team will engage in a process of validated learning...confirming your assumptions through user testing, research, interviews, or ethnography. You may also build test sites or "smoke tests"—fake websites that walk users through the solution to see if they will pull out their wallet and buy (but don't use your real domain name for these tests). You may pivot or change ideas after getting feedback or may find yourself back at the empathy stage, gathering more information about the problem space before creating new solutions. The idea is to stay lean and iterate quickly through ideas: build, measure, and learn.

With validated learning, you can test your value hypothesis — the value proposition that you are offering to your customers — or your growth hypothesis, how you intend to scale your company by testing new markets, or types of users. A hypothesis template looks like this:

We believe that _____ will cause [the users] to [do this action/behavior] because of [value proposition].

An example might be:

We believe that an augmented reality shopping app will cause brick-and-mortar shoppers to walk into stores more frequently because of the urgency and proximity of the deals and discounted offers.

Hypotheses are tested using the traditional research methodologies and a prototype or minimum viable product (MVP) of your idea. A prototype is a reduced version of your actual product or service, featuring just key features or functions. Version One of your product has every feature and function that users might need. A prototype can be developed in a few hours or days, while your first full version make take months.

Your team will define the hypothesis, determine how you will test the hypothesis, and assess what you learned from the results. Developers use A/B testing to try two different solutions and see which one gets the best response. This testing might be two different designs of a home page, testing color schemes or even two different solutions.

Before you spend valuable time and money rolling out a product that no one needs, a prototype and idea testing can help refine your ideas and discard or enhance your product or service features.

## SWOT Analysis

Once you have identified the problem your group intends to solve, you must ask if another product already addresses it. If so, how? Conduct a SWOT (Strengths, Weaknesses, Opportunities, and Threats) analysis from the point of view of the competition. (Download a free worksheet.[29]) Do this for each close competitor, large or small, until you clearly identify your niche and are able to refine your target market.

# Resources for Students and Faculty

## READINGS

Links to articles that describe brainstorming, ideation, and design thinking.

- The Creativity Imperative in the Innovation and Entrepreneurship Curriculum: A Dilemma in the Scholarship of Teaching[30]
- Fostering Creativity – a Holistic Framework for Teaching Creativity[31]
- A Taxonomy of Innovation[32]
- The 7 All-Time Greatest Ideation Techniques[33]
- A Guide to Journalism and Design[34]
- Introduction to the Essential Ideation Techniques which are the Heart of Design Thinking[35]
- 10 Longtime Brainstorming Techniques that Still Work[36]
- 6 Types of Brainstorms that Help Create Awesome Ideas[37]
- Ideation – Learn More About Your Innate Talents from Gallup's Clifton StrengthsFinder![38]

## OPPORTUNITIES

### Media Ideation Fellowship

Voqal.org offers a Media Ideation Fellowship for social entrepreneurs.[39] The technology accelerator is interested in founders who will "transform progressive politics or remedy a social inequity."

### National Grants and Competitions for Media Ventures

You'll read more about other sources of nontraditional funding and resources in the Startup Funding chapter of this open textbook. Here is one crowdsourced list[40] of such opportunities.

**Michelle Ferrier** *is an associate professor in the E.W. Scripps School of Journalism at Ohio University. She is the founder of Troll-Busters.com, an online pest control service for women journalists. Reach her on Twitter at @mediaghosts.*

## Leave feedback on this chapter.

# *Notes*

1. "Stanford School Design Thinking Process," https://goo.gl/jua3VS

2. Faisal Hoque, "Why Most Venture-Backed Companies Fail," *Fast Company*, December 10, 2012, https://www.fastcompany.com/3003827/why-most-venture-backed-companies-fail.

3. FAQs About Copyright, *United States Copyright Office*, https://www.copyright.gov/help/faq/index.html.

4. Patent FAQs, *United States Patent and Trademark Office*, https://www.uspto.gov/help/patent-help.

5. Trademark FAQs, *United States Patent and Trademark Office*, https://www.uspto.gov/learning-and-resources/trademark-faqs.

6. Eric Michael, "What is Creativity?" https://www.ucf.edu/pegasus/what-is-creativity.

7. Jay Hathaway, "What is Gamergate, and Why? An Explainer for Non-Geeks," *Gawker*, October 10, 2014, http://gawker.com/what-is-gamergate-and-why-an-explainer-for-non-geeks-1642909080.

8. *Amy Webb*, http://amywebb.io/.

9. Amy Webb, *The Signals Are Talking*. (New York: Public Affairs, 2016).

10. *NMC Horizon Project*, https://www.nmc.org/nmc-horizon.

11. "Top 5 Technology Trends 2017," *Accenture*, https://www.accenture.com/us-en/insight-disruptive-technology-trends-2017.

12. *Pew Research Center*, http://www.pewresearch.org/.

13. *Innovating for People Handbook of Human-Centered Design Methods* (Pittsburgh: LUMA Institute, 2012), https://www.amazon.com/Innovating-People-Handbook-Human-Centered-Methods/dp/0985750901.

14. *LUMA Institute*, http://www.luma-institute.com/.

15. Tony Deifell, "The Big Thaw: Charting a New Future for Journalism," *The Media Consortium*, http://www.thebigthaw.com/.

16. "BBC News on Your Mobile," *BBC News*, June 29, 2015, http://www.bbc.com/news/10628994.

17. Erick Schonfeld, "(Founder Stories) How Mike McCue Came Up With Flipboard: 'What If We Accidentally Deleted The Web.' *TechCrunch*, June 12, 2011, https://techcrunch.com/2011/06/12/founder-stories-mike-mccue-flipboard.

18. I developed the site over three years, building advertising revenue during that time. However, LocallyGrownNews.com was only sustainable as a side hustle, and a job opportunity in another state forced me to shutter the site.

19. "The Value of Balancing Desirability, Feasibility, and Viability," *Crowd Favorite*, https://crowdfavorite.com/the-value-of-balancing-desirability-feasibility-and-viability/.

20. "Innovating for People: Human-Centered Design Planning Cards," *LUMA Institute*, https://goo.gl/efaZc8.

21. "Field Guide to Human-Centered Design," *IDEO.org*, http://d1r3w4d5z5a88i.cloudfront.net/assets/guide/Field%20Guide%20to%20Human-Centered%20Design_IDEOorg_English-ee47a1ed4b91f3252115b83152828d7e.pdf.

22. "Ideation Method Mashup," *IDEO.org*, http://www.ideou.com/pages/ideation-method-mash-up.

23. "Human-Centered Design," *IDEO.org*, http://www.designkit.org/human-centered-design.

24. "LUMA Workplace," YouTube, https://www.youtube.com/watch?v=qDyElJ0xe2o.

25. "Explore Your Hunch," *IDEO.org*, http://www.designkit.org/methods/32.

26. *Aha!*, http://towknight.org/aha/

27. "Top 5," *IDEO.org*, http://www.designkit.org/methods/15.

28. "Brainstorm Rules," *IDEO.org*, http://www.designkit.org/methods/28

29. "SWOT Analyis," *MindTools*, https://www.mindtools.com/pages/article/newTMC_05.htm.

30. Peter Schmidt and Sarah Kim, "The Creativity Imperative in the Innovation and Entrepreneurship Curriculum: A Dilemma in the Scholarship of Teaching" *Advances in Business-Related Scientific Research Conference 2014*, https://goo.gl/rdsSdR.

31. Holger Berg, Vesa Taatila, and Christine Volkmann, "Fostering Creativity – a Holistic Framework for Teaching Creativity," *Development and Learning in Organizations: An International Journal*, http://www.emeraldinsight.com/doi/full/10.1108/14777281211272242.

32. "A Taxonomy of Innovation," *Harvard Business Review*, https://hbr.org/2014/01/a-taxonomy-of-innovation.

33. "The 7 All-Time Greatest Ideation Techniques," *Innovation Management*, http://www.innovationmanagement.se/2013/05/30/the-7-all-time-greatest-ideation-techniques/.

34. "A Guide to Journalism and Design," *Tow Center for Digital Journalism*, http://towcenter.org/a-guide-to-journalism-and-design/.

35. Rikke Dam and Teo Siang, "Introduction to the Essential Ideation Techniques Which are the Heart of Design Thinking," *Interaction Design*, https://www.interaction-design.org/literature/article/introduction-to-the-essential-ideation-techniques-which-are-the-heart-of-design-thinking.

36. John Boitnott, "10 Longtime Brainstorming Techniques that Still Work," *Inc.com*, http://www.inc.com/john-boitnott/10-longtime-brainstorming-techniques-that-still-work.html.

37. "6 Types of Brainstorms that Help Create Awesome Ideas," *Pace*, http://www.paceco.com/insights/strategy/brainstorm-techniques/.

38. "Ideation - Learn More About Your Innate Talents from Gallup's Clifton StrengthsFinder!" *Gallup Strengths Center on YouTube*, https://www.youtube.com/watch?v=55ZC1u42Xww.

39. "Media Ideation Fellowship," *Voqal.org,* http://voqal.org/initiatives/voqal-fund/media-ideation-fellowship/.

40. https://goo.gl/981PxS

# LOOKING AHEAD

| Looking Ahead |
| --- |
| You've come up with an entrepreneurial idea. Now, how do you identify and find customers for it? The next chapter, Customer Discovery, will help. |

# CUSTOMER DISCOVERY

by Ingrid Sturgis

## Summary

This chapter focuses on a fundamental dilemma for entrepreneurs: How to identify your customer or market, or in this case, your readers, viewers or listeners. To develop a successful media company, entrepreneurs must know who the audience is and how to reach it. Making the exercise a bit more tricky today is that the customer for news and information is very different than in the past. Influenced by an ever-evolving media ecosystem, today's audience or customers are not just in a single place. They hang out on social media, use smartphones or gaming devices, or even watch streamed programming on television, sometimes all at once. Understanding the new media ecosystem will help entrepreneurs to understand who they are trying to reach, the scope of their business venture, and how to best allocate financial and human resources.

### Learning Objectives

- Understand the new media ecosystem and how disruption and convergence has reshaped the media marketplace.
- Conduct effective audience research to define your customer and understand the differences between segments of the audience.
- Develop a systematic approach to identify and understand the needs of your customer.
- Identify and refine a target audience for a media product.
- Develop skills to discover market demographics and build your customer's psychographic profile.

## Inside this Chapter

- Customer Discovery for Content and Tech Startups

*Ingrid Sturgis is an associate professor in the Cathy Hughes School of Communications at Howard University. She was a reporter and editor for* The Philadelphia Inquirer, *the* Times-Herald Record, *and* The Poughkeepsie Journal *as well as founding managing editor for magazine startups BET* Weekend *and* Savoy. *She has worked online as a senior programming manager for AOL's Black Voices, and as editor-in-chief for Essence.com. Sturgis is the author of the anthology* Are Traditional Media Dead: Can Journalism Survive in the Digital World, *and co-editor of* Social Media: Pedagogy and Practice. *Reach her on Twitter at @isturgis.*

# CUSTOMER DISCOVERY FOR CONTENT AND TECH STARTUPS

*Ingrid Sturgis*

## What Is a Media Ecosystem?

Derived from the physical science term ecosystem, which describes the interdependence of organisms and their physical environment, a media ecosystem is the system of interdependency among media-related entities such as newspapers, magazines, radio, television, as well as the Internet, and user-generated content, including blogs, audio and video platforms, social networks, and communications devices such as tablets and smartphones.

To define the new media ecosystem, you have to go back in time to understand what the media business was like before the Internet (Figure 1). Back then, the high costs of traditional publishing— paper, printing presses, newsroom personnel, unions, equipment, and distribution—ensured a high barrier to entry for would-be newspaper publishers. Scarce resources allowed publishers to control all levels of the news production process, including distribution and sales. They also created an environment that helped advertising agencies grow. Advertising became one of the primary revenue streams for publishers to offset the expensive production process. Reporters and editors were the gatekeepers who determined what stories and information would be covered and disseminated. Customers were observers. They consumed what they were given. Their input with the publishing process was typically as part of a community board, if a news organization had one, or as writers of letters to the editor to complain or praise the coverage of a news story. In the days of mass media, news and information content was designed to be delivered to the largest audiences, whose attention and engagement fueled the ecosystem.

In the mid-1990s, the Internet began to upend the newspaper business. The digital, interactive technology spurred the convergence, or merging, of mass media including print, television, radio, the Internet, and telecommunications into a digital format. Barriers like million-dollar printing presses had kept competitors out of the marketplace for content and audiences. With digital products, the barriers to entry into the marketplace fell. Today, anyone can be a publisher, or as professor Jay Rosen[1] of New York University put it, "the people formerly known as the audience now have some control of the message and access to dissemination." Everyone is contributing to this larger media ecosystem. The advantages for mass media

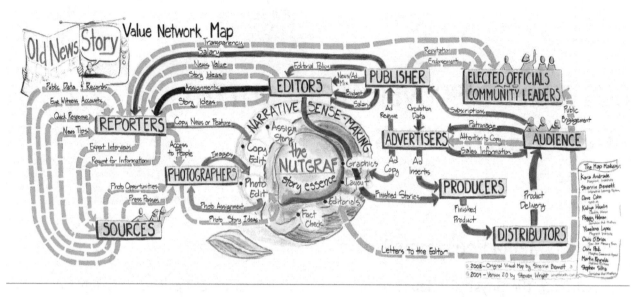

Figure 1. Old News Story Value Network Map image courtesy of Journalism That Matters, Seattle, Washington. www.journalismthatmatters.org.

publishers have shrunk dramatically, creating a fundamental shift in the balance of power between traditional media and its customers. Traditional media is no longer the gatekeeper of news as new voices and niche content continue to grow online (Figure 2). Social media platforms and online tools have allowed customers to talk back, talk to each other, as well as create, share, and alter information outside traditional media organizations (Figure 3).

The social media space has spawned much of the disruption of the distribution model of publishing. Peer-to-peer technologies have dislodged industry "middle men" and challenged many media industries including music, software, and other fields like travel. Innovations in digital technologies disrupted media spaces, connecting consumers to each other in spaces like eBay and etsy.com or in streaming music spaces like Pandora or in the recommendations and review sections of websites like Amazon and in forums like Reddit.

The 2017 Conversation Prism Version 5.0 (Figure 4), is an ever-changing attempt to visualize these social networks and spaces emerging on the web. The graphic, originally created in 2008,[2] maps the evolving "conversation space" that includes such digital behemoths as Facebook and Twitter, but also new spaces and innovations in areas such as the quantified self where we digitally capture human body functions through wearables or virtually compete in a run with friends. The Conversation Prism Knowledge Wiki[3] created by Dr. Michelle Ferrier and her undergraduate students at Ohio University provides a deeper look at each of those tools and platforms in the prism and includes a general overview of the tool/platform, the history of the space, the technological events that caused the tool to emerge, as well as current and future challenges. Each area of the prism is explored more fully, including a pro-con analysis of the top tools in each area and their functions, along with user personas of those using the tool and target audiences.

In the past decade, the digital revolution has transformed the media, disrupting traditional

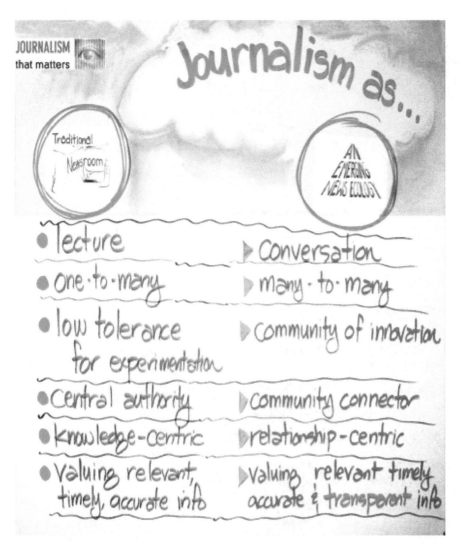

Figure 2. Journalism as... This diagram shows the shift in the newspaper industry pre and post the introduction of the Internet and social media tools. The left takes a traditional look at the distribution and values; the right examines how roles and values shift in the digital age. Image courtesy of Journalism That Matters, Seattle, Washington; www.journalismthatmatters.org.

methods of reporting, distribution, and news presentation. The development of high-speed Internet-connected tablets, smartphones, touch-screen displays, large screens, and small monitors provides content creators with an evolving array of platforms on which to imagine, redesign, and create innovative multimedia news products. Worldwide adoption of social media—Facebook, Twitter, Google, YouTube, Snapchat, WhatsApp, and others—has changed the flow of information and redefined the media ecosystem. The shift is more than just losing market share to the latest fad in widgets; it has expanded the media ecosystem.

Today, like a thriving wildlife habitat, there is a dynamic news ecosystem made up of many people, organizations, Internet Service Providers, and media companies working to meet the news and information needs of communities. For example, Jeff Jarvis,[4] director of the Tow-Knight Center at the City University of New York Graduate School of Journalism, resides in New Jersey, where he says the media ecosystem, "has a growing and disorganized

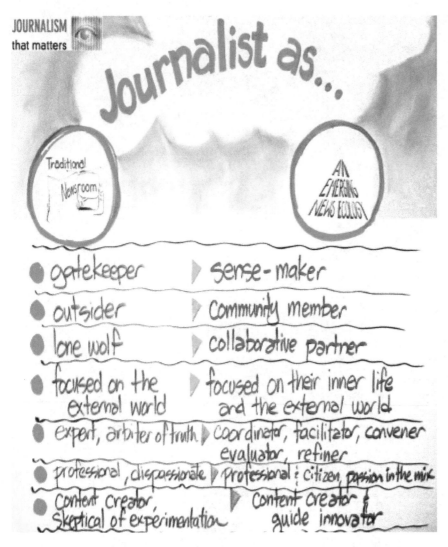

Figure 3. Journalist as... This diagram looks at the shift in the perspective and positioning of the journalist vis à vis the audience. Image courtesy of Journalism That Matters, Seattle, Washington; www.journalismthatmatters.org.

hodgepodge of sites, services, communities, and individuals that operate on various platforms with different motives, with more or fewer resources, and with business models from none to not-for-profit to hoping-for-profit to profitable. They all contribute to a larger ecosystem of information in the state and its communities."

In addition, new social media platforms and technologies are continuing to reshape the media landscape. In the content space with the proliferation of niche and individualized content and the technology and new devices and network spaces, new media startups continue to shape a very different digital information culture and marketplace.

Figure 4. Conversation Prism 5.0

# Define the Market

## What to call your customer: Or is it the audience or the public?

A customer is the person who buys what you are selling. The audience are the people who see your work. The audience is generally larger than your customer base and may include some of your customers. Users are the people who engage with your publication through digital media and technology.

How do you go about learning what your empowered customer or audience wants? The first step is called "customer discovery."[5] The objective is to refine the problem you are solving for the customer and to determine which market segment is the target of the solution. The market segmentation graphic shows that your idea may target any of these market segments—demographic, psychographic, behavioral, or geographic—individually or in combination (Figure 5):

## Main Bases of Segmentation

| Geographic | Demographic | Behavioural | Psychographic |
|---|---|---|---|
| e.g. "Customers 10 miles or more outside of a major metropolitan area." | e.g. "College students ages 18-24." | e.g. "Customers wanting a competitive edge on graduate admissions applications." | e.g. "Students who are interested in sustainability and environmental issues." |
| Location Region City/Town/State | Age Gender Occupation Socio-economic Group | Benefits sought Loyalty status Ready to buy Early adopters | Lifestyle Attitude Education Level Class Personality |

Figure 5. Main Bases of Segmentation

For example, Blavity[6] founders Morgan DeBaun and Aaron Samuels knew they wanted to create a community for black millennials and multicultural influencers. They identified both a demographic and a psychographic market segment underserved by other media companies. The two founders developed some basic assumptions about their customer and identified the problem they needed to solve for the customer. They were then able to turn those assumptions into hypotheses that they could test.

They were able to tap into several prevailing assumptions and trends:

- African-Americans millennials were valued as trendsetters and influencers in popular culture as well as "early adapters" of new technology—early adopters who remix and adapt current technologies.

- African-Americans were frustrated by a low level of inclusion of Blacks in television programs, advertising and point-of-purchase communication; and,
- African-American-oriented news media were losing circulation and struggling to find advertising revenue.

As a result of its sharp content focus on surfacing the voice of this underserved community and the use of digital technologies to develop its content platform, Blavity has grown to become one of the fastest-growing digital media outlets on the web, reaching nearly 7 million users a month[7] since its launch in 2014. DeBaun and Samuels say their focus on user-generated content, video, and a custom-designed backend, offers a space for black millennials to own their story and share their perspective.

These founders are practicing what entrepreneur and author Johnathan M. Holifield calls "inclusive competitiveness," which he defines as "a framework that allows businesses to capitalize on the potential of underserved audiences to help fuel the next generation economic vitality in a way that is more inclusive and durable."[8]

Inclusive competitiveness, Holifield says in his 2017 groundbreaking book, seeks to tap the talents of diverse, disconnected workers, including blacks, Latinos, women, and residents of low-income communities, to participate in the global innovation economy.

## Conducting Market Research

Audience analysis is a key component of customer discovery. Good product or service solutions come from a human-centered approach to design. Likewise, the business model will evolve as you explore your customers' needs. Identifying your initial target market will help you more clearly define the scope of your project and plan for the first several years of operations. It also will help you figure out how to allocate your scarce resources—time and money. For an entrepreneur to be successful, they must have a firm perspective of the people they are trying to serve, including their needs, habits, aspirations, and environment.

To engage in audience analysis is easier today with all the demographic resources available online. There are a number of market research reports to help entrepreneurs refine segmentation, consumer preferences, as well as compile demographic profiles that can help them discover motivations and buying patterns.

Websites such as Forrester,[9] eMarketer,[10] Pew Research Center, Nielsen, and American Press Institute offer demographic data that can be used to get a better sense of the digital skills, income, lifestyle, and news and entertainment habits of your target market. The data provided by these organizations—some of which is released for free—can be used to fill in demographic and psychographic information about your potential users.

For example, entrepreneurs can start with gathering demographic information, such as age, ethnic background, income, gender, and more from the U.S. Census Bureau,[11] which offers a birds-eye view of demographic trends in everything from the economy to entrepreneurship to workforce and population shifts. Similarly, the Bureau of Economic Analysis (BEA)[12] focuses on the economy by providing relevant data on issues such as economic growth, regional economic development, inter-industry relationships, and the United States' position in the world economy.

For media research, Pew Research Center[13] is a think tank and an excellent repository of trends and data on news and information, audience engagement, social media, and emerging news providers. The American Press Institute[14] has developed a tool called Metrics for News, content analysis software that helps publishers better measure audience engagement. Local Independent Online News (LION) Publishers[15] offers workshops to help small publishers to develop skills to build their audiences. Kantar Media[16] offers international consumer insights for advertisers, agencies, and media owners to reach key consumer audiences. In addition to its focus on online and offline consumer behavior, attitudes, and media consumption, Kantar specializes in sports, healthcare markets, and new technology. Finally, Nielsen[17] offers information on consumer trends and habits worldwide.

## Creating User Personas

Now that you have discovered the demographics of your audience, you have a good idea as to whether your customers are using the devices you are designing for, whether they use other media, and where they are located. But this data is for your whole target audience. How can you focus on the needs and design for your "ideal user"? User personas are tools that entrepreneurs can use to drill down into the ideal audience member and add psychographic information such as behaviors and lifestyle information. According to HubSpot, a company that provides social media marketing, content management, web analytics, and search engine optimization services, demographics explain who your customer is while psychographics explain why they buy.[18]

Usability.gov, a leading resource for guidelines and best practices in user experience online, says the purpose of personas is to "create reliable and realistic representations of your key audience segments for reference."[19] When used as part of a strategy called user-centered design or human-centered design, personas can help to tell the story of your customers' needs. They also help to define your brand and your mission, as well as how to market your site. Often, a user persona will include demographic data like "50-year old, African-American female, married, earns $75K a year," as well as specifics like "picks children up from school at 3 p.m. and drives to after-school activities three times a week." Some teams give their user personas names and even draw or find an image that represents their ideal customer. The goal is to know how your ideal user goes about his or her life and how your product or service will intersect with their lifestyle.

Entrepreneurs must learn to dig deeply into their customers' media consumption habits. Consider:

- **Information needs.** What information or activities will serve the user's needs? Will they need to perform online transactions to purchase products, such as event tickets?
- **Research modes.** Where does your targeted user search for information? How do they prefer to access information?
- **Expertise.** Is your targeted user knowledgeable about the information you provide? Or do they need explainer videos with background information, like those provided by Vox?[20]
- **Technology.** How will users access your information? Will they use mobile devices or laptops? Will they be comfortable with the latest technology trends or will they need help navigating to new technology on your site?

How do you develop psychographic information for user personas? Many large corporations use observation. This can take the form of field trips or site visits to meet their customers where they are likely to be. For example, cosmetic companies will visit college campuses during homecoming to meet students they view as their target market. *Essence* magazine holds a music festival in New Orleans every year with empowerment and editorial meet-and-greet sessions to develop a deeper understanding of readers' needs. Local newspapers often attend community events like weekly farmers markets to meet their customers. Others conduct focus groups where potential customers discuss their interests, activities, and opinions.

But it does not have to be that organized. As media entrepreneurs, you can use your journalism training to meet and interview potential customers everywhere from the grocery store line to the car wash to the street fair to collect information to create user personas. Interview them about their reading and shopping habits. Do they read magazines or read stories via smartphones using Snapchat? Do they access the web via tablet or laptop? Do they send email or text messages? Do they binge-watch on Netflix or seek out must-see TV? Ask about their values, personal goals, opinions, hobbies, interests, shopping habits, entertainment interests, and lifestyle. Use their answers to develop a solid understanding of your audience.

## User Persona Tools

Once you have identified where you want to conduct your psychographic research, consider the information you need to build your profiles. There are a number of resources to help develop psychographic user personas. *Smashing Magazine*[21] offers a closer look at personas.

Behance,[22] a creative talent website, has a helpful tool to help entrepreneurs envision features and services that would benefit specific users. Marketing company XPLANE has created the Empathy Map, a tool that can help to create a user focused profile. XPLANE's worksheet focuses on getting at what's most important for your customers—defining their goals and aspirations as well as their preoccupations. It also asks about their environment and influences as well as their behavior toward others. The Empathy Map worksheet[23] focuses on six questions that media entrepreneurs can use to develop strong psychographic profiles.

1. What does your customer think and feel?
2. What does your customer hear?
3. What does your ideal customer see?
4. What does your ideal customer say and do?
5. What are her pains, fears, frustrations, obstacles?
6. What are her gains, wants, needs, measures of success?

Two important elements that should not be overlooked in developing these personas are culture and language. The U.S. Census Bureau forecasts major demographic shifts that can significantly impact businesses serving consumers. According to Johnathan M. Holifield,[24] diversity remains a strong economic driver and entrepreneurs must adopt a strategy that embraces diversity through inclusive competitiveness.

In addition, media entrepreneurs must also make sure to take into consideration their target customers' media habits. For example, when talking with a young man working as a cashier at Target, a media entrepreneur was able to learn that he was a student at a local college. He said he thought print publications were growing extinct and digital was the way to go. He got his news and information from ESPN and GQ channels using the Snapchat app on his smartphone. If you are targeting a customer like him, choosing the right platforms to reach him is important.

Here is a very basic user persona based upon what we know about the ideal customer for a women's magazine (Figure 6):

## DENISHA

- from Atlanta
- graduate of a historically black university or college (HBCU)
- Happily single, but wants to marry one day and have kids
- Account exec who wants to own her own company to take her supervisor's job
- Has 401K, some stock, and owns a condominium
- Owns laptop, smartphone; uses social media
- Travels, works out, has active social life
- Goes to site for networking, fitness, finances, and fun; eats well and doesn't want health problems of her parents and elders

*Denisha, 29*
*Account Executive*

Figure 6. Psychographic profile of a young online magazine reader.

Here is what a set of user personas might look like for a general interest newsmagazine (Figure 7):

**Figure 7**

| Mindy, 40 | Brett, 36 | Soraya, 35 | Malcom, 25 | Denisha, 29 |
|---|---|---|---|---|
| Experienced communications professional, specializing in crisis management, media relations, writing, editing, message development, and online marketing. | Associate Producer for Hearst Television, Washington, D.C. bureau. | Life coach. | First-year graduate student at University of Maryland, pursuing a Master's degree in Speech Language Pathology. | Account exec who wants to own her own company to take her supervisor's job. |
| Also specializes in artist development, and as a crowdfunding specialist to help launch careers for young creatives. | Digitally literate. Works on the cutting edge of journalism. Specializes in using social media to advance storytelling. Travels a great deal for work. | Went size 18 to a size six in seven months. Wants to be an inspiration to anyone who has been struggling with their weight. Recently compiled recipes for a cookbook to help people overcome eating disorders. | Wants to use degree to help improve lives of those with speech disorders related to autism. Works as graduate teaching assistant and part-time job as research assistant for speech pathologist. | HBCU graduate. Has 401K, some stock and condo. Laptop, smart phone, social media. |
| From Harlem, New York. | Originally from England. Trains for body-building competition. Loves to read magazines for relaxation. Engaged to get married in a year. | Originally from Cleveland. Now vegetarian and self-taught home cook. Church-goer who uses positive affirmations to help maintain her weight loss. Works out daily. | From Charleston, South Carolina. Runs marathons. | From Atlanta. Travels, works out, has active social life. Happily single, but wants to marry one day and have kids. Goes to site for networking, fitness, finances and fun; eats well and doesn't want health problems of her parents and elders. |

# Check Website Analytics

Once your site is up and running, you can examine the data from the content to get a good idea what has moved people to click, call, or buy. Basic tools like Google Analytics[25] can give a snapshot of the user, as will Facebook or Twitter[26] analytic tools. Other more commercial marketing analytics include HubSpot,[27] Alexa, Chartbeat and Viafoura.

The *Wall Street Journal* online media kit[28] uses information gathered from the commercial analytics tool comScore Media Metrix. In this sample from the first quarter of 2017,[29] WSJ.com gathered information from users who visited the site on its digital platforms in the past 30 days with a household income of $100,000 or higher. According to the media kit, WSJ.com reaches top management and has a reach of 42 million digital readers per month, all seeking news and information critical to their businesses and personal lives. Their users are made up of more men than women with an average age of 43. The users have an average household income of $242,000 and an average net worth of $1.5 million. Most have graduated from college and slightly less than half are considered millionaires.

# Do a Competitive Analysis

A competitive analysis allows you to unearth your direct and indirect competitors. You may think you're competing with a known competitor (let's say another media outlet in your same niche) but on the Internet, everyone has the potential to be your competitor for audience. This is especially true when we think about "search," meaning when potential users are looking for a product like yours. Where do they end up?

If you have a Google Adwords account, you can use Google's Keyword Planner[30] tool without placing an ad. You can also get data from Google Trends,[31] though if your product is in a less mainstream niche, it may not be helpful.

With paid software, such as SEMRush[32] and SpyFu,[33] you can see what your potential audience (and your competitors' existing audience) is searching for that is resulting in traffic to their site.

For instance, on SpyFu, you can type in the URL of a competitor's website and the software shows you its organic competitors on the Internet.

Let's say you were the editor of Entrepreneur magazine. You could type in https://www.entrepreneur.com and find out that your competitors not only include Inc Magazine but also bplans.com. You could see which keywords are especially valuable (attracting lots of traffic). And you can see where your keywords intersect, and where you're doing better and worse than competitors at capturing an audience interested in topics relevant to your media business and outlet. You can sort and use this information to determine where it might make sense for you to add content to serve the needs of your niche (as demonstrated by search) and compete better in search.

These tools are also useful if you do paid advertising to attract people to your site. They let you see whether competitors are placing PPC (pay-per-click) ads, and in some cases, the best-performing PPC ads themselves.

All of this competitive intelligence can help you make decisions about your editorial narrative and content direction, as well as your ad strategy and marketing in general. We'll talk more about Marketing in the Marketing & Analytics chapter.[34]

## Conduct a User Survey

You can gather information to validate your assumptions by conducting a survey. It is another useful source of information on potential customers' habits, needs, and consumption patterns. Surveys can be designed and distributed online, or conducted by telephone or in person. Research gleaned from surveys allows you to see similarities among target users. For example, a survey may reveal that many of your users take yoga classes. Your research may show that millennials indicated an interest in trap yoga, that seniors seek chair yoga, or that men are trying bro yoga. A survey can help identify your audience's needs. You can then use the survey information to fine-tune your unique value proposition and distinguish your product from your competition. For example, *The Texas Tribune* describes itself as the "only member-supported, digital-first, nonpartisan media organization that informs Texans—and engages with them—about public policy, politics, government and statewide issues."[35] According to a report by Southern Methodist University journalism Professor Jake Batsell for the John S. and James L. Knight Foundation, "Earning Their Keep: Revenue Strategies From the Texas Tribune and Other Nonprofit News Startups,"[36] *The Texas Tribune* conducted an audience identification survey in 2012 that revealed that most of their readers were college graduates who voted in the last election and that half had household incomes of more than $100,000. This research helped the Tribune raise $300,000 from one sponsor to reach its affluent, intellectual audience. Instead of seeing itself as a competitor to other local news organizations, the Tribune calls itself a supplemental news source for Texas. Where other news organizations have cut back on statehouse coverage, *The Texas Tribune* covers it and supplies it to newspapers around the state. The Tribune's unique value proposition is that it is filling a need that was going unmet for its audience (readers) and it has made customers of competitors by providing in-depth political coverage.

Now that you have acquired your audience, what can you do to keep them and make them pay for your products and services?[37]

## 1. Create opportunities for in-person engagement.

Face-to-face events help to develop audience loyalty, according to Batsell.[38]

Some examples include *The Texas Tribune* Festival, which engages Tribune readers as well as sponsors and advertisers. The events can include readings with local and well-known authors, meet-the-staff sessions, coffee shop or interest group meetups, summer festivals, or discounted group outings. The idea is to deliver unique experiences, Batsell says, that are worth the time. The payoffs can be building trust with your audience as well as increased online engagement and corporate support.[39]

## 2. Crowdsource the news.

Use your users as a news resource. User Generated Content is any type of content — text, YouTube videos, audio, testimonials, tweets, Facebook posts, etc. that has been created by unpaid contributors, which publishers may distribute on their sites and use to promote their brands.

For example, Off The Bus 2012[40] was an Open Reporting initiative of *Huffington Post* and News Assignment to cover the 2012 election. It encouraged readers to attend political events, record them, and submit them to the online publication. Twelve thousand people signed up. Public participation gave readers an inside view of the projects that the site was reporting on, spurred reader trust, and improved communication with its audience. Using readers in this way can help build trust and develop a stronger story because the user may have some access or knowledge that the news organization does not. However, be careful of online commenting. Some news organizations have had to find improved ways to manage the troubling comments that arise from some stories.

## 3. Serve a niche.

Social media technology allows news organizations to serve a narrow, but passionate niche. Called passionate verticals, this niche can be defined by geography or interests. One example is SCOTUSblog, a law blog that focuses on the Supreme Court of the United States (abbreviated as SCOTUS) by tracking live cases as well as maintaining an archive of cases argued before the court. Written by lawyers, law professors, and law students, the site leadership also live-blogs court decisions and hosts symposiums with influential experts on important court cases.

## 4. Develop alternative story forms.

Advances in technology have made it easier and more affordable to give your targeted audience new interactive experiences that can spur engagement and keep them on-site longer. Use of gaming techniques and data-driven graphics and immersive video projects can give users an opportunity to explore a subject deeply or to provide entertainment. For example, the *New York Times* garnered praise for "Snow Fall,"[41] an interactive, seamless multimedia blending of video, photos, and graphics in a series about an avalanche. Similarly, *Wired* magazine's "Cutthroat Capitalism" game[42] brought home the geopolitical social and economic issues that drove desperate Somali fishermen to hijack and capture ships for ransom. Both interactive projects entertained and informed readers as well as provided professional buzz for the work of the news organizations.

## 5. Develop paying customers for your product.

There was a time when newspapers relied on advertising for most of their revenue. A trope was that readers would not pay for content, and many news organizations opted to make their content free to everyone online. As their online audiences grew, many media entrepreneurs were hesitant to ask them to pay. That mindset has thankfully passed. Now sites like the *New York Times, Wall Street Journal* and *Washington Post* feature "metered" pay walls that give users a glimpse of their news product and entice them to pay after a certain number of views. Other media entrepreneurs have used crowdfunding to raise money for their sites and others offer modest subscription rates, which indicate readers are willing to pay for news. But users paying for news may not be enough to fund a project. Media entrepreneurs have to develop a variety of products for their audience. They can include events; special news products, such as special commemorative issues; access to specialized data; access to technology tools; and company promotional and branding souvenirs.[43]

Once you learn how to identify and understand your customer, you will gain an invaluable skill that will serve you greatly as an entrepreneur as well as in other endeavors. Overall, be willing to adapt and change as your market evolves and grows.

| Exercise |
| --- |

**TRY IT: STAKEHOLDER MAPPING**

Visualize the ecosystem of your service or product to learn how different stakeholders influence your customer's experience.

Stakeholder mapping in four steps:

1. Define your stakeholders.
2. Analyze stakeholders by impact and influence.
3. Plan stakeholder communications and reporting.
4. Engage with your stakeholders.

Use these steps along with the stakeholder maps and templates to manage your stakeholders effectively and turn them into project champions!

Source: Stakeholder Mapping https://www.stakeholdermap.com/[44]

---

### Exercise

**TRY IT: BRAINSTORM STAKEHOLDERS / SOLUTIONS**

- Topics for discussion: Any other burning questions/challenges to address?
- Identify people for groups.
- Identify stakeholders on sticky notes.
- Convene in breakout rooms and pick top six stakeholders.
- Create a column for each stakeholder.
- Ideate with one idea per sticky.
- Reconvene in a large room with your stakeholder/solutions list.

Source: http://media-entrepreneurship-course-development.wikispaces.com[45]

For more stakeholder mapping exercises, see the chapter on Ideation.[46]

---

# RESOURCES:

## Readings

- The GV Library website has a guide to design research.[47]
- Michael Mergolis's article, "Seven Tips for Lean Market Research,"[48] answers many questions students may have about customer discovery, market, and customer behavior.
- Learn more[49] about the value of the customer-focused experience and the innovation process.
- This resource on customer discovery[50] is based on the first of four steps of Steven G. Blank's Customer Development Model from his book, *The Four Steps to the Epiphany*.[51]

Beyond demographics, the use of psychographics helps designers and marketers better understand audience perceptions and behavior.

- How to Use Psychographics in Your Marketing: A Beginner's Guide[52]
- Psychographics Are Just as Important for Marketers as Demographics[53]

- Why the Lean Start-Up Changes Everything[54]
- Using the Crowd as an Innovation Partner[55]

## Video

- Building Product, Talking to Users, and Growing (Adora Cheung)[56]
- Paying for news: Why People Subscribe and What it Says About the Future of Journalism[57]
- How to Create and Execute a Niche Content Strategy[58]
- Engaged Journalism: Lessons From Professor Jake Batsell[59]
- Clark Atlanta University Leveraging Concept of Inclusive Competitiveness[60]
- Entrepreneurship & Small Business: Target Market[61]

*Ingrid Sturgis* *is an associate professor in the Cathy Hughes School of Communications at Howard University. She was a reporter and editor for* The Philadelphia Inquirer, *the* Times-Herald Record, *and* The Poughkeepsie Journal *as well as founding managing editor for magazine startups* BET Weekend *and* Savoy. *She has worked online as a senior programming manager for AOL's Black Voices, and as editor-in-chief for Essence.com. Sturgis is the author of the anthology* Are Traditional Media Dead: Can Journalism Survive in the Digital World, *and co-editor of* Social Media: Pedagogy and Practice. *Reach her on Twitter at @isturgis.*

## Leave feedback on this chapter.

## *Notes*

1. Jay Rosen, "Bio," *Pressthink,* http://pressthink.org/bio.

2. Michelle Ferrier, "The Social Web: A Map for Visual Learners," *Poynter.org,* August 21, 2008, https://www.poynter.org/2008/the-social-web-a-map-for-visual-learners/91038.

3. Michelle Ferrier, "Conversation Prism Knowledge Wiki," http://socialmediaplatforms.wikispaces.com/.

4. Jeff Jarvis, "Ecosystems and Networks: What Now for News?— Part III," *Medium,* February 10, 2014, https://medium.com/whither-news/ecosystems-and-networks-1d76e62d1ee2.

5. "Create a Succinct Value Proposition: 'Customer Discovery' and the Customer Development Model," *Marsdd.com,* December 16, 2011, https://www.marsdd.com/mars-library/developing-your-value-proposition-an-overview-of-customer-discovery/.

6. *Blavity,* www.Blavity.com.

7. "About," *Blavity.com,* https://blavity.com/about.

8. Johnathan M. Holifield, *The Future Economy and Inclusive Competitiveness: How Demographic Trends and Innovation Can Create Economic Prosperity for All Americans.* (New York: Palgrave Macmillan, 2017), 27.

9. *Forrester,* https://www.forrester.com/search?N=10001&range=504005&sort=3&searchRefinement=report.

10. *eMarketer,* https://www.emarketer.com.

11. *United States Census Bureau,* https://factfinder.census.gov/faces/nav/jsf/pages/index.xhtml.

12. *Bureau of Economic Analysis,* https://www.bea.gov/regional/.

13. *Pew Research Center,* http://www.pewresearch.org.

14. American Press Institute, https://www.americanpressinstitute.org/.

15. *Local Independent Online News Publishers,* https://www.lionpublishers.com.

16. *Kantar Media,* http://www.kantarmedia.com/us.

17. *Nielsen,* http://www.nielsen.com/us/en/insights/news.html?sortbyScore=false&tag=Related:multicultural.

18. Alisa Meredith, "How to Use Psychographics in Your Marketing: A Beginner's Guide," *HubSpot.com,* https://blog.hubspot.com/insiders/marketing-psychographics.

19. Dan Brown, "Personas," *Usability.gov,* https://www.usability.gov/how-to-and-tools/methods/personas.html.

20. Vox, "Explainers," *Vox,* https://www.vox.com/explainers.

21. Shlomo, Goltz, "A Closer Look At Personas: What They Are And How They Work," *Smashing*

*Magazine*, August 6, 2014, https://www.smashingmagazine.com/2014/08/a-closer-look-at-personas-part-1.

22. Crystal Ruth Bell, "User Personas," *Behance*, July 6, 2014, https://www.behance.net/gallery/18164949/User-Personas.

23. "DNA of Change," *HubSpot*, http://cdn2.hubspot.net/hub/375601/file-1450136163-pdf/worksheet_03_visual_alignment.pdf?t=1500065553883.

24. Johnathan M. Holifield, *The Future Economy and Inclusive Competitiveness: How Demographic Trends and Innovation Can Create Economic Prosperity for All Americans.* (New York: Palgrave Macmillan, 2017).

25. *Google Analytics,* https://analytics.google.com.

26. *Twitter Analytics,* https://analytics.twitter.com.

27. *HubSpot Marketing Analytics,* https://www.hubspot.com/products/marketing/analytics.

28. *Wall Street Journal Media Kit,* http://www.wsjmediakit.com.

29. *comScore Media Metrrix,* http://www.comscore.com/Products/Audience-Analytics/Media-Metrix.

30. "Keyword Planner," *Google Adwords,* https://adwords.google.com/home/tools/keyword-planner/.

31. *Google Trends,* https://newslab.withgoogle.com/trends.

32. *SEMRush,* https://www.semrush.com/.

33. *SpyFu,* https://www.spyfu.com/.

34. Jessica Pucci and Elizabeth Mays, "Marketing & Analytics," *Media Innovation & Entrepreneurship,* https://press.rebus.community/media-innovation-and-entrepreneurship/part/marketing-your-venture-to-audiences/.

35. "About Us," *The Texas Tribune,* https://www.texastribune.org/about/.

36. Jake Batsell, "Earning Their Keep: Revenue Strategies From the Texas Tribune and Other Nonprofit News Startups," *Knight Foundation,* April 2015, https://s3.amazonaws.com/kf-site-legacy-media/feature_assets/www/nonprofitnews-2015/pdfs/KF-NonprofitNews2015-Tribune.pdf.

37. Anna Jasinski, "Ways to Engage With Digitally Empowered News Audiences," *Media Blog PR Newswire,* May 19, 2016, https://mediablog.prnewswire.com/2016/05/19/5-ways-to-engage-with-digitally-empowered-news-audiences.

38. Jake Batsell, "Earning Their Keep: Revenue Strategies From The Texas Tribune and Other Nonprofit News Startups," *Knight Foundation,* April 2015, https://s3.amazonaws.com/kf-site-legacy-media/feature_assets/www/nonprofitnews-2015/pdfs/KF-NonprofitNews2015-Tribune.pdf.

39. Anna Jasinski, "5 Ways to Engage With Digitally Empowered News Audiences," *Media Blog, PR Newswire,* May 19, 2016, https://mediablog.prnewswire.com/2016/05/19/5-ways-to-engage-with-digitally-empowered-news-audiences/.

40. Amanda Michel, "Get off the Bus: The Future of Pro-am Journalism," *CJR*, March/April 2009, http://archives.cjr.org/feature/get_off_the_bus.php.

41. John Branch, "Snow Fall: The Avalanche at Tunnel Creek," *The New York Times*, December 20, 2012, http://www.nytimes.com/projects/2012/snow-fall/#/?part=tunnel-creek.

42. "Game Design: Smallbore Webworks, Visual Design: Dennis Crothers 'Cutthroat Capitalism: The Game,'" *Wired*, July, 20, 2009, https://www.wired.com/2009/07/cutthroat-capitalism-the-game.

43. Mike, Green, "Inclusive Competitiveness Glossary of Terms," *Slideshare*, September 23, 2013, https://www.slideshare.net/amikegreen2/inclusive-competitiveness-glossary-of-term.

44. "Stakeholder Analysis, Project Management, Templates and Advice," *Stakeholdermap.com*, https://www.stakeholdermap.com.

45. Michelle Ferrier, "Media Entrepreneurship Course and Ecosystem Resources," *Media Entrepreneurship Course Development Wikispaces*, 2012, http://media-entrepreneurship-course-development.wikispaces.com.

46. Michelle Ferrier, "Ideation," *Media Innovation & Entrepreneurship*, August 2017, https://press.rebus.community/media-innovation-and-entrepreneurship/chapter/ideation-2/.

47. John Zeratsky, "GV Guide to Research," *GV Library*, July 17, 2012, https://library.gv.com/gv-guide-to-research-847cfb08fcef#.2sgz1dpd7.

48. Michael Margolis, "Seven Steps for Lean Market Research,"*GV Library*, November, 13, 2012, https://library.gv.com/seven-tips-for-lean-market-research-76934c58abfe.

49. Peter Lavers, "Forging the Link Between Customer Experience and Innovation," *IBM*, December 28, 2016, https://www.ibm.com/think/marketing/forging-the-link-between-customer-experience-and-innovation-2.

50. "Create a Succinct Value Proposition: 'Customer Discovery' and the Customer Development Model." *Mars*, December 16, 2011, https://www.marsdd.com/mars-library/developing-your-value-proposition-an-overview-of-customer-discovery.

51. Steven G. Blank, *The Four Steps to the Epiphany*. (Pescadero, CA: K&S Ranch, 2013).

52. Alisa Meredith, "How to Use Psychographics in Your Marketing: A Beginner's Guide," *HubSpot*, "December 20, 2012, https://blog.hubspot.com/insiders/marketing-psychographics.

53. Alexandra Samuel, "Psychographics Are Just as Important for Marketers as Demographics," *Harvard Business Review*, March 11, 2016, https://hbr.org/2016/03/psychographics-are-just-as-important-for-marketers-as-demographics.

54. Steve Blank, "Why the Lean Start-Up Changes Everything," *Harvard Business Review*, May 2013, https://hbr.org/2013/05/why-the-lean-start-up-changes-everything.

55. Kevin J. Boudreau and Karim R. Lakhani, "Using the Crowd as an Innovation Partner," *Harvard Business Review*, April 2013, https://hbr.org/2013/04/using-the-crowd-as-an-innovation-partner.

56. Sam Altman, "Building Product, Talking to Users, and Growing (Adora Cheung)," *Startup Class*, October 2, 2014, http://startupclass.samaltman.com/courses/lec04/.

57. American Press Insittute, "Paying for News: Why People Subscribe and What it Says About the

Future of Journalism," *American Press Institute,* May 2, 2017. https://www.americanpressinstitute.org/publications/reports/survey-research/paying-for-news.

58. Millie Tran, "How to Create and Execute a Niche Content Strategy," *American Press Institute,* May 7, 2015, https://www.americanpressinstitute.org/publications/reports/strategy-studies/create-niche-strategy.

59. Jeff Andrews, "Engaged Journalism: Lessons From Professor Jake Batsell," *Parse.ly,* April 20, 2015, https://blog.parse.ly/post/1804/engaged-journalism-lessons-from-professor-jake-batsell/.

60. Maria Saporta, "Clark Atlanta University Leveraging Concept of Inclusive Competitiveness," *Saporta Report,* April 25, 2016, http://saportareport.com/clark-atlanta-university-leveraging-concept-inclusive-competitiveness.

61. "Entrepreneurship & Small Business: Target Market," http://libguides.colorado.edu. http://libguides.colorado.edu/Entrepreneurship/ConsumerTargetMarket.

# LOOKING AHEAD

## Looking Ahead

You have an idea of what problem you're solving and for whom. Now, whether you're a nonprofit, for-profit or freelance professional, it's time to think about your business model. What will you charge people for in order to make your business sustainable? Business Models for Content & Technology Ventures, Nonprofit Models and Freelancing & Consulting as Business Models will give you some ideas.

# BUSINESS MODELS FOR CONTENT & TECHNOLOGY VENTURES

by Geoffrey Graybeal

## Summary

This chapter will provide an overview of business models, revenue models, and business plans, and how they are developed, including the use of the business model canvas and other ideation tools. The chapter will discuss traditional media business models, some common forms of business models for content and technology plays, and some of the various legal and regulatory issues facing media startups and entrepreneurs. This chapter primarily focuses on for-profit businesses. The following chapter explores nonprofit business models more in-depth.

---

### Learning Objectives

- Analyze the media environment to identify opportunities for media entrepreneurship.
- Propose innovative solutions that capitalize on those opportunities.
- Be able to identify and explain a business model.
- Be able to identify and explain a revenue model.
- Identify types of business models for content and technology plays.
- Be able to identify and explain a business plan.

---

## Inside this Chapter

- Business Models for Content & Technology Ventures
- From the Field: Refining Our Business Plan Was the Key to Attracting Our First Investor, by Dalton Dellsperger
- Writing a Business Plan & Budget, by John Dille

*Geoffrey Graybeal is a clinical assistant professor in the Entrepreneurship and Innovation Institute at Georgia State University. Previously he was an assistant professor at Texas Tech University. He is a media management scholar and entrepreneur who uses economic and management theory to explore issues of media sustainability. Graybeal teaches courses on media entrepreneurship, media management, media economics, and innovation. Reach him on Twitter at @graybs13.*

# BUSINESS MODELS FOR CONTENT AND TECHNOLOGY PLAYS

*Geoffrey Graybeal*

## Dive In

A business model helps to clarify a company's main purpose, such as who they're serving, how they help, and how the company can sustain its operations. A business model is distinctly different from an organization's strategy, which typically addresses product, pricing, and marketing decisions. A formal business plan, however, may include some of these elements as part of the company's long-term goals and objectives.

## Defining Key Terms

| Business Model | Business Plan | Revenue Model |
| --- | --- | --- |
| **Business Model** | **Business Plan** | **Revenue Model** |
| A business model provides a rationale for how a business creates, delivers and captures value, and examines how the business operates, its underlying foundations, and the exchange activities and financial flows upon which it can be successful. | A business plan is a formal document that typically describes the business and industry, market strategies, sales potential, and competitive analysis as well as the company's long-term goals and objectives. | A revenue model outlines the ways in which your company will make money (e.g. revenue streams). |

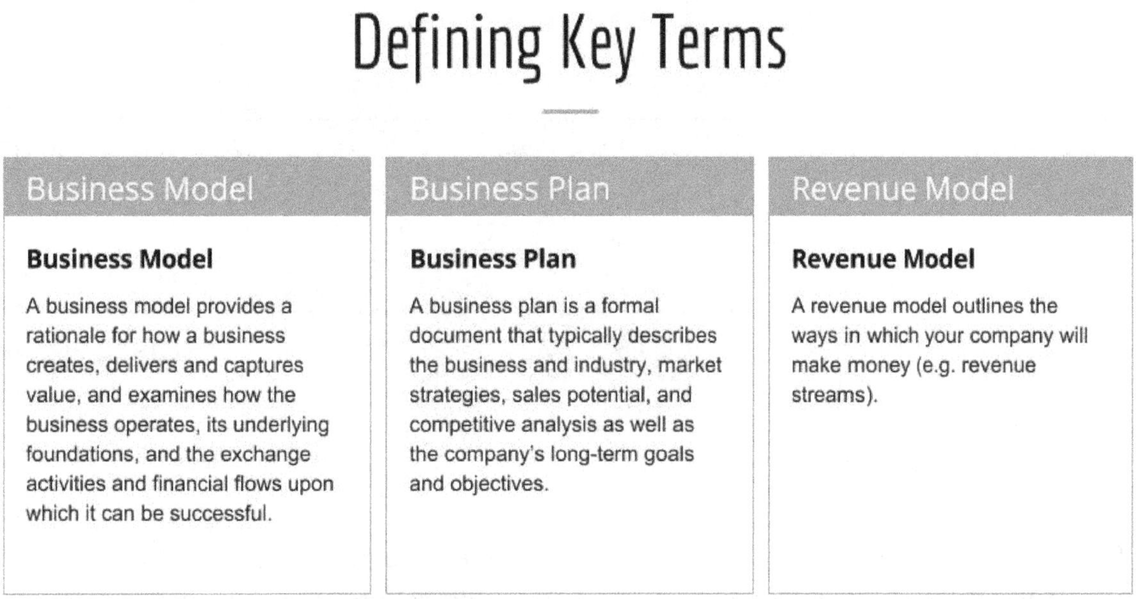

Figure 1. Chart produced under CC BY license.

Each business model is unique to a company. There is not an industry-wide business model per se although companies may coalesce around a dominant company's successful business model and seek to emulate it.

Business models provide a rationale for how a business creates, delivers, and captures value,[1] and examine how the business operates, its underlying foundations, and the exchange activities and financial flows upon which it can be successful.[2]

A business model canvas is a tool to map out and plan the different components to a business model. The components vary based on the canvas tool you use, with the most widely used one developed by Osterwalder and Pigneur in the book Business Model Generation, or available online through a series of customizable tools and canvases available for a fee on strategyzer.com.

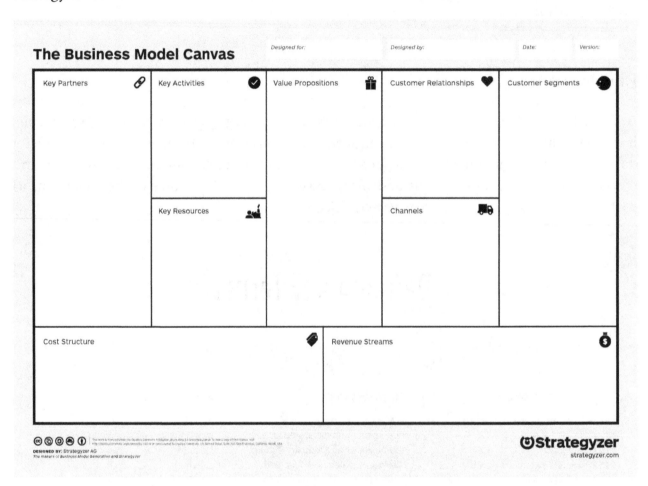

Figure 2. This image is licensed CC BY-SA 3.0. The Business Model Canvas is included here with permission from Strategyzer. Download the canvas at https://strategyzer.com/canvas/business-model-canvas.

The Osterwalder and Pigneur canvas blocks[3] include revenue stream, customer segments, value proposition, cost structures, channels, key activities, key partners, key resources, and customer relationships.

Early on, your greatest focus should be on the right side of the canvas because:

- These are in many ways the most critical aspects of starting a new venture (customer segments, value proposition, channels, and revenue streams).
- The most fluid (revenue streams, channels, and value propositions will likely differ for

the differing customer segments and as you iterate and pivot throughout the customer discovery process could likely change).

- It follows a logical temporal order (there's no need to focus on the costs of building a company if you won't have customers).

In a follow up to Business Model Generation, the Strategyzer team created a second canvas, the Value Proposition Canvas. Value Proposition Canvas[4] is a new tool that pulls out the customer segment and value proposition blocks of the business model canvas and encourages more in-depth exploration of those blocks to achieve "fit" between the two. The Value Proposition Canvas tool looks at customer pains, gains and jobs-to-be-done on the customer side and painkillers, gain creators, and products and services on the value proposition side.

A revenue model focuses on an organization's revenue streams, e.g., how a company will make money, whereas a business model also concerns itself with other issues such as who the product is serving, how it is distributed and promoted, and key partnerships used in implementing it. In short, a revenue model is just one component of a business model. As a typical business model has multiple elements (nine in the case of the Osterwalder and Pigneur model), a revenue model is primarily focused on how a company will make money.

For traditional legacy media outlets, such as a newspaper, revenue streams typically encompassed advertising and consumer payment either through subscription or alternate payment methods like single-sale purchases.

Hayes and Graybeal (2012) provide an overview of categorizations of online business models from the late 1990s to late 2000s from scholars and industry practitioners, including many online content plays. Revenue models were the most common components found in all forms of business model classifications. Value streams and logistical streams were also equally important in e-commerce models.[5]

Think of a business model canvas as an ideation tool to help brainstorm and flesh out your startup concept. The business model is a more adaptable, flexible tool that can be used to formulate the ideas that would later be fleshed out in a more formal business plan.

A business plan is a formal document, presented to prospective investors, that typically includes elements such as an executive summary, business description, marketing strategy, and competitive analysis. A business plan may also include a business model canvas as supplemental material in an appendix.

You should usually develop a business model before a business plan. But before you get to a business model, first and foremost, you need an idea. There are numerous resources for brainstorming activities and entrepreneurial processes to help develop an idea and flesh it out to be "market-ready." (see previous chapter on Ideation[6]) Original ideas are sometimes hard to come by.

Early research into competitors helps as a starting point. Who else has had this idea? Has this idea been tried before and failed? That's not necessarily a dealbreaker. As renowned media economist Robert Picard notes, just because an idea failed at one point in time, under a certain set of circumstances, that doesn't mean a failed idea can't be revisited.[7]

Another entrepreneurial startup truism is that no matter how great your idea may be, if no one will use your product, then you're dead on arrival. So startup ideas need customers to become a business. Thus, the various entrepreneurial processes, whether that is business model canvas tools, lean startup principles and methodologies, or other approaches, focus a great deal on the customer.

The Osterwalder and Pigneur book describes a process of creating a customer empathy map to distill down your ideal target customer. Bring to life an individual, and delve into his or her fears, dreams, aspirations, and what she or he does in the everyday life. After identifying your target customer, you can begin to segment your audience. But start with an individual customer, idealized or actualized, and distill deeply into that customer profile.[8]

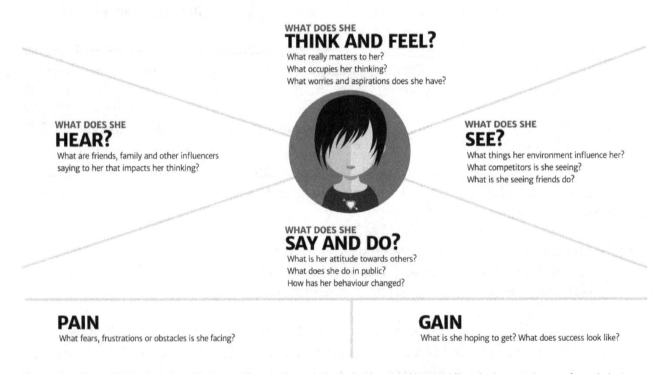

Figure 3. Empathy map by Paul Boag, Copyright Boagworld, used with permission. https://boagworld.com/usability/adapting-empathy-maps-for-ux-design/

The Customer Empathy Map is an idealized portrayal of your fictionalized target customer, the most promising candidate from your customer segments. Give him or her a name and demographic characteristics, such as income, marital status, and so forth, before delving into the pains, gains, thoughts, feelings and surroundings of this individual you bring to fruition.

This is an approach that has long been used in media and communication fields such as advertising and strategic communication. Advertisers and marketers often create customer personas–fictional, generalized representations of ideal or existing customers–as part of campaign plans, pitches, strategy, and creative concept delivery.

When you peel away the language used to describe business models, the early startup planning stages come down to asking a series of questions. Another popular framework used in entrepreneurial circles when it comes to formulating a business model for a startup concept is that of <u>desirability-feasibility-viability</u>.

This forces the entrepreneur to address broad questions about the startup concept.

**Desirability:** How desirable is the product? Who will use it and why?

**Feasibility:** How feasible is this idea? What are the costs to make it? How practical is the concept?

**Viability:** Will this idea remain viable? How will it make money? How will it be sustained over time?

These questions then begin to connect together to form a narrative about where the startup concept came from, who it serves, why it's needed, how it will make money, and how it will be sustained in the future.

Strategyzer also has a great "Ad-lib" template[9] that will help you figure out a few potential value propositions. They also offer other resources[10] you can access after signing up for a free account.

## Business Models

Although there is not a single definition to the term business model and usage varies widely, in standard business usage a "business model" can denote how costs will be covered as well as how a business creates and delivers value for itself and its customers, including the ways in which products are made and distributed. Academic strategists tend to use the term business model to describe the configuration of resources in response to a particular strategic orientation.[11][12][13]

Most people are familiar with Business to Consumer models (also referred to as BTC or B2C). In a Business-to-Consumer model, the business primarily provides services to consumers. Many of the common media content plays are considered B2C. Newspapers, television shows, films, and video games are primarily B2C companies. Many apps that individual users download and then consume content from are B2C. Because media companies are typically providing content that is of value to consumers, they look like a B2C, however, they use the attention of those consumers to sell advertising space to businesses, effectively operating as a B2B. Business to business to consumer (or B2B2C or BtoBtoC) is another prominent e-commerce model, that combines Business to Business and Business to Consumer in a complete product or service transaction.

Nascent startup Shine, which officially launched its inspirational text message service in Spring 2016, is an example of following a classic Business-to-Consumer model. (Full disclosure: I taught one of the founders.) Through automated texts, Shine delivers daily self-help, encouragement and advice to its subscribers via either SMS or Facebook Messenger. Anyone can use the free service, but it is primarily aimed at millennials and about 70 percent of users are female.

On the Brooklyn-based company's one-year anniversary in April 2017, the Shine team announced that it had obtained half a million users. Co-founders Marah Lidey and Naomi Hirabayashi raised $2.5 million to further develop Shine in a funding round led by Betaworks and Eniac Ventures, and including Female Founders Fund, Felix Capital, Comcast Venture, BBG Ventures, *The New York Times*, and Ed Zimmerman.

They want to expand the service to be included on other platforms like Line and WeChat.

The problem Shine tackles is that "self-help is broken" and its value proposition addresses in part what is known as "the confidence gap," often cited as a barrier that holds women back when it comes to advancing in their careers, raising money, investing, and planning retirement.

Shine has four pillars it is built to address: mental health, confidence, daily happiness, and productivity.

In 2015, Hirayabashi and Lidey began to focus on turning their idea into a reality. The two met at and worked together at DoSomething.org, a youth-oriented global nonprofit organization. They conducted a closed test with 70 individuals before publicly releasing Shine in beta in October 2015. They formally left DoSomething.Org in April 2016 and Shine was born.

While the messaging service is free, the company has experimented with adding revenue streams through additional consumer services. Shinevisor provides advice and guidance from real people who are certified life, career, and school coaches. That service currently runs $15.99 per week billed on a 12-week basis. Shinevisor is an early effort of Shine to add additional services that bring in revenue, as multiple revenue streams are most often needed for a company to succeed.

While Shine, apps and a majority of content plays are primarily B2C, the other predominant business model is that of a Business to Business, also commonly referred to as B2B or BTB. Whereas Shine is a business whose product serves customers, in a Business to Business model, a company primarily serves other businesses, not individual consumers.

MailChimp, an Atlanta-based company, began as a B2B in 2001. More than 15 million people and businesses around the world use MailChimp. MailChimp enables many B2B marketing transactions. A leading marketing automation platform, MailChimp sends more than a billion emails a day. MailChimp's primary customers were businesses that used the platform to send marketing emails, automated messages, and targeted campaigns to its individual users.

Historically, media companies that provide analytic services have sold that data and analysis to other businesses. Bloomberg's financial terminals sold to businesses around the world is a classic example of a B2B service.

Küng, Picard & Towse (2008) also note "elements of different business models can be combined [so] in that sense, every business model of a company is unique."[14] For those reasons, a business model can be a source of competitive advantage, with business model design and product-market strategy serving as complements, not substitutes.[15] Strategy functions like an architect creating a homeowner's design, while the detailed floor plan based on choices in the design process would constitute a business model design.[16]

When you go to get funding for your startup (more on this in a later chapter),[17] having an understanding of your business model will come in handy.

## Regulation

Media are among the handful of industries that face industry-specific policies and regulations that other businesses do not face. The broadcast industry is regulated in the U.S. through the Federal Communication Commission. The print media industry is impacted by certain postal and governmental notice regulations. Banking and pharmaceuticals are other industries that face such industry-specific regulations. Reduced barriers to entry, promotion of trade, promotion of small enterprises, and regulation of consolidation and concentration are among some of the policies and regulations media must face. Media strategy can be influenced by these environmental factors, firm factors, industry factors, and media-specific factors, among others.[18] Some regulation can hinder startups.

That's why policy is one of the domains of enabling an entrepreneurial ecosystem. Government supports can come in the forms of tax breaks and incentives, regulatory frameworks, venture-friendly legislation, institutional investments, financial support, and policy initiatives.[19] Regulation and policy limitations to the strategic choices available to media companies are two examples of media-specific characteristics.

Regulation can help or hinder incumbents or startups based on policies that are set. For example, regulations pertaining to net neutrality have been debated for years, with many startups of the past decade arguing that without net neutrality they would have faced disadvantages instead of the environment that enabled them to grow and prosper. Many technology startups, for example, banded together in July 2017 to form a protest over FCC proposals to eliminate Obama-era net neutrality rules. Y Combinator, a popular technology startup incubator, was among the backers of the protest, along with companies like Kickstarter, Etsy, GitHub, Amazon, and Reddit.

Government policies can also support entrepreneurship. Some U.S. cities have staff dedicated to innovation and entrepreneurship. New York City for example uses revenue from its film and television projects to fund media entrepreneurship efforts like the NYC Media Lab.

New York City's media and tech startup scene, so-called "Silicon Alley," is no longer confined to a small alleyway in NYC's financial district and is more of a concept than a location. Media companies such as Google and IAC/InterActiveCorp make up part of NYC's media ecosystem. In 2012, the Center for Urban Future proclaimed that NYC witnessed over 1,000 media startups including *Tumblr* and *Mashable*.

During this time, NYC was also witnessing the growth of media cooperative working spaces, accelerators and incubators including New York University's (NYU) Polytechnic Institute Tandon Future Labs supported by the New York City Economic Development Corporation. During this time Mayor Bloomberg advanced tax breaks and funding opportunities for media startups in NYC as part of his five-borough economic plan.

The NYCEDC, in a public-private partnership, also helped launch the NYC Media Lab in 2010. The primary goal of NYC Media Lab is to connect the media industry during the dot-com revival in NYC and colleges and universities in the area to advance media entrepreneurship. The consortium, which includes Columbia University, New York University, The New School, the City University of New York (CUNY), the IESE Business School, and the Pratt Institute, work under the NYC Media Lab umbrella to generate media research and development and advance media entrepreneurship. The Combine serves as NYC Media Lab's incubator and its main goal is to position NYC as the media capital of the world by advancing and launching "one-of-a-kind" media and communication technologies. Specifically, the Combine aims at supporting and growing media startups from faculty and students from collaborating universities with a high potential to launch. The Combine is funded by the NYCEDC, the Mayor's Office of Media and Entertainment, and NYC Media Lab's corporate members.

Some current projects include an experiment with metadata extraction from book manuscripts for Audible, a market research project for MBA students in New York City on augmented reality products for Hearst Ventures, an augmented reality fellowship in design and engineering through Bloomberg and Lampix, and a virtual reality fellowship for Viacom NEXT.

Many European countries also provide funding for entrepreneurial initiatives. In 2004, the Flemish government established iMinds, a digital research center and business incubator to focus on information and communication technology. The European Union and other European nations routinely fund innovation and entrepreneurial projects.

# Applicable Techniques

## Content Models

Revenue streams are a common element of most definitions of business models, particularly ones used to address electronic commerce.[20] Many online news business models, historically, have been similar to traditional business models, as subscription, advertising, and transactional are the most common categories of online business models.[21][22]

Advertising and subscription still remain the most dominant forms of revenue streams used in most content business models. Content plays involve the creation and dissemination of content, such as news or entertainment, which users will want to receive.

Here's an example to help you better understand what I mean by a content company. There's an excellent episode in the first season of Startup,[23] the podcast about creating a startup from Gimlet Media in which the founders, Alex Blumberg and Matthew Lieber, debate whether Gimlet is a content company or a technology company. In the episode, Gimlet Media thus far has gone the route of being a content company. The company produces content—in this case compelling podcasts—that are then distributed on other technology platforms, such as through Apple or Spotify. If Gimlet became a technology company, it would launch a proprietary podcast-playing platform. For comparison's sake, Spotify provides a platform for streaming audio but does not produce the content—the music, the songs, the podcasts that play on that platform.

See the additional resources included at the end of this chapter for lists of many revenue streams for many digital media, mobile, and ecommerce companies.

Some of the most common forms of revenue streams used in content companies include:

### Subscription

When the newspaper industry moved into online content delivery, many companies initially gave its content away online for free. Within the past decade or so, most newspaper companies have offered digital-only subscriptions and bundled online delivery along with the traditional print product. Within the United States, the leading paywall system was developed by PressPlus. Paywalls offer users a certain number of free page visits, before being blocked with subscription, the primary means to gain additional access.

Many digital media companies that offer content, particularly those that offer content that compete with traditional companies such as newspapers, magazines, and broadcasters, have implemented a Paywall approach. A paywall can be *hard* where the only way to access the content is to pay for it, usually through a subscription, or *soft*, where the user is given a certain number of free visits or views per month before being asked to subscribe.

Another common subscription model used for content and technology plays is that of a <u>freemium</u> model. Under a freemium model, access to basic content is free, but users can choose to subscribe to premium content for a fee that provides improved access (such as an ad-free experience) or additional services. The online music streaming service Spotify is a classic example of a freemium model, with basic access to ad-supported music online available for free, with monthly premium subscriptions for a fee. Dropbox is another commonly used digital startup that relies on a freemium model. The cloud-based file storage service offers free storage up to a certain amount, and charges a monthly fee beyond that.

<u>Membership</u> is another subscription model. Under a membership model, the content can either be free or paid, but users who purchase a membership receive perks and bonus materials, exclusive access to supplemental materials, and so forth. In many instances, these content companies have been focused on a certain content form (technology, politics, sports) rather than general interest publications. Musician fan clubs and sporting teams are classic examples of non-digital content entities that excel at offering memberships. That same model is applied to media companies, typically ones that diversify their offerings through some of the other miscellaneous revenue streams discussed later (such as events and conferences; archival data, etc.).

Classic subscriptions, of course, are the most prevalent. Netflix is probably the most well-known media content company that offers access to its content through monthly subscription options. As previously mentioned, some media companies offer subscription access based on content delivery mechanism (online, mobile delivery/web, all access).

Increasingly, more and more entertainment content is being sold through subscription packages, with over-the-top services independent of cablevision subscriptions being offered for individual channels (HBO, Showtime, ESPN) or in packaged bundles (Sling, Hulu, Amazon Prime, etc.).

## Advertising

There are various forms of advertising for content and technology companies, with many forms specific to the delivery mechanism and form of the company. Traditional legacy media companies sell local direct advertising (newspapers, broadcasters), classified advertisements, sponsorships (most common in broadcasting) and are part of national advertising networks, among other forms.

Advertising networks are still prevalent for digital media content and technology companies, alongside selling direct advertising on various platforms. Native advertising, the use and sale of microsites dedicated to paid clients, the use of Google AdSense, and the sale of Outbrain-style links to external sites are common on web-based content and technology plays.

Content and technology companies can sell display advertising, search advertising, video ads, text/SMS advertising, mobile and digital forms of advertising, and location-based advertising among other forms, particularly in the mobile space. Content and technology startups can also develop their own proprietary forms of advertising content based on the system. For example, Twitter developed and sold promoted tweets and sponsored ads in its platform. Sponsorships, particularly used in podcasts, are another form of advertising available for content and technology plays.

Mobile advertising ("in-app ads" and "mobile display" ads) and variations of charging for content are the most prominent ways traditional media have sought to monetize content thus far, but there are many other alternative business models under consideration, including free and paid SMS alerts, social media platform distribution, and free applications.

### Transactional/e-Commerce

Content and technology plays often employ various forms of transactional, or e-commerce revenue streams. Some of these allow for an in-between option for users who want access to content, whether that be one-time or more, but don't want a full subscription option. Let's explore some of the most common.

### Micropayments

Micropayments are small payments, typically $5 or less, for an individual piece of content. Every time you buy an individual song from Apple for download, for instance, you've made a micropayment. The iPod popularized the consumption of individual forms of music, chiefly song downloads, disaggregating individual song purchases from complete albums.

Virtual currencies can be a form of micropayment, typically employed within videogames or on online platforms, such as Facebook or Twitch, where users are making individual small purchases for virtual items, such as increased game playing ability, items used within game, or donations to other users.

Newspapers, magazines, and other forms of micropayments for news and digital delivery of content were tried unsuccessfully in the late 1990s and early 2000s, with companies like Flooz, Beenz, CyberCash, Bitpass, Peppercoin and DigiCash just a few examples of failed micropayment companies from its first era.

From about 2010 or so onward, additional efforts at micropayments have had varying success, usually within various regions. *Blendle*, a Dutch-based online news startup, has probably had the most success at selling access to individual news articles and magazine content, both in Europe and the United States.

Kachingle, CarrotPay, Knack.it, and Ganxy are a few other companies that offered various forms of micropayment platforms for content companies to utilize in recent years.

My colleague Jameson Hayes and I developed theoretical modified micropayment models for news and media content that introduce the ability for users to microearn for sharing content in addition to having to micropay for it but there are no functioning platforms that fully execute that conceptual vision.[2425] Many tend to agree that micropayments must be used in tandem with other revenue streams and can't alone sustain a media operation.

Failure itself is widely embraced by the entrepreneurial community, as the entrepreneurial process encourages and promotes a series of failures along the way that lessons can be learned from (pivots, etc.) Entrepreneurs have even held annual FailCon conferences in which speakers share entrepreneurial failures and lessons learned in cities around the world.

Failure doesn't mean an idea can't be revisited. Micropayments were tried unsuccessfully in the 1990s, but with the advent of Blockchain and Ethereum digital transactions have found more success in recent years. With the creation of browsers like Brave, some predict micropayments and digital transactions to become more mainstream in the not-too-distant future. Management and economics scholars have predicted that blockchain has the potential to transform intellectual property and content licensing, access to information and digital goods, and increase the value of curation of digital content. They envision artists who license music on Apple or Spotify being able to easily track how many times songs are played by consumers, backers on crowdfunding sites obtaining royalties each time a song is played, digital goods priced and delivered using a blockchain for payment, contract enforcement, and authentication.

Some newspapers abandoned early efforts at digital subscriptions and for the better part of two decades the industry norm was free online content. Now, of course, digital content payments have been adapted by many companies. Blockchain enables an easy ability for micropayments to be implemented in a browser where users could pay a single subscription and navigate between different newspapers.

## Donations

Some media organizations, such as *The Guardian*, allow for direct donations from readers. These outlets may make a direct plea on their homepage, or at the beginning or end of articles. Donations are also much more commonly used in nonprofits as outlined in the next chapter, but soliciting donations from users can also be done by for-profit media ventures.

## Merchandise

Whether you're a nascent startup or a more established company, selling merchandise with your company's brand, name, logo, and slogans can serve as an additional revenue stream in addition to serving marketing purposes. T-shirts, mugs, keychains, and hats are commonly sold merchandise. Google, for example, has a physical store on its main campus that sells all sorts of Google-branded merchandise. Companies can also sell merchandise online.

Some other forms of e-commerce:

## Crowdfunding

Crowdfunding, defined as "an open call, essentially through the Internet, for the provision of financial resources either in form of donation or in exchange for some form of reward and/or voting rights in order to support initiatives for specific purposes." offers a novel way of funding projects.[26]

Crowdfunding involves creators of a project soliciting donations from funders, or backers, of the project, through an online platform that features the project request.

Five basic kinds of crowdfunding models have attained widespread reach: donation-based, pre-purchase based, reward-based, lending-based, and equity-based.[27] In donation-based crowdfunding, the backers support a particular cause with no expectation of any kind of returns.[28] However, in reward-based crowdfunding, the backers are provided with non-monetary benefits in exchange for their support. Kickstarter and Indiegogo are the most well-known and commonly used rewards-based crowdfunding platforms.

A pre-purchase model is similar to rewards. A backer receives the product the entrepreneur is making, such as a music album. Lending-based crowdfunding platforms offer a loan to small-scale lenders with an expectation for a return on capital investment. For instance, Kiva is the most premier lending crowdfunding platform that operates in 66 countries. Equity-based crowdfunding is that in which the backers receive an equity or stake in the profits of the project they have invested in. The Jumpstart Our Business Startups (JOBS) Act of 2012 allowed equity funding in the U.S. for the first time. Title III of this act allows small-sized business owners and entrepreneurs to retail investment that was previously restricted to select accredited investors and potential investors on various Internet-based crowdfunding platforms.

Crowdfunding gained popularity somewhere in the late 2000s. Since then it has shown unprecedented growth and is particularly common among startup entrepreneurs and investors. Circleup, Equity Net, AngelList, and Wefunder are examples of some popular equity-based crowdfunding sites.

## Retail/Marketplace

One revenue stream for media startups could come from a "digital retail mall" or "transactional experiences" like shopping purchases through a digital credit card or online payment system.

## Group Buying

Popularized and most well-known by the startup Groupon, this method provides discounted deals en masse to groups of consumers who scoop up the coupon-like savings that can be purchased and used at a later date.

## Applicable techniques

### Technology Plays

Many of the models previously mentioned for content plays (subscription, advertising, and transactional) are also applicable for technology plays, and we'll discuss some miscellaneous categories beyond the Big Three for both.

One of the considerations for technology plays is the distribution mechanism, whether the product is available online, or mobile, some combination of the two, or neither. If the technology play is an Internet-dependent one, such as an app, then the choices are whether it is accessible through the mobile web (HTML5 is a common tool), or proprietary app stores. If it's an app, then you must decide whether it will be formatted and available in Apple's iOS format or Google and Android capability. Many universities and cities hold appathons or hackathons that bring together interdisciplinary teams to work on the creation of an app and/ or the business plan and pitch for an app concept over a weekend. These are useful and can help flesh out some of the necessary steps and considerations for startup tech plays. Look for such efforts at your university or city. *MediaShift* also sponsors a popular hackathon several times a year that brings together students, faculty, and professionals from universities across the country.

If you are creating an app, decisions include whether the download is free or if you charge a one-time download fee. Then, you can consider some of the above-mentioned revenue streams, such as subscription, and mobile advertising.

Some other revenue models commonly employed in technology plays include:

### Auction

eBay is probably the most well-known auction site, where users can post items for sale and get bids from other users.

### Sharing Economy

Apps and websites that take advantage of the sharing economy have proliferated in recent years. Also referred to as the collaboration economy, this business model is predicated on collaboration, whether that is sharing an apartment or home (as is the case in Airbnb), sharing a ride (Lyft or Uber), or sharing office space (coworking spaces).

Misc. revenue streams for both content and technology plays:

### Events/Conferences

Mainstream media outlets like *The New York Times* excel at organizing live events and conferences as an alternative revenue stream, but startups can also do the same. Media organizations sponsor live events, such as conferences and banquets, and charge a fee to attend.

### Foundation Funding

See resources elsewhere in this textbook for lists of foundation funding sources. Many nascent entrepreneurs and media startups have benefited from foundation funding in the past. The Knight Foundation historically has been a large funder of media entrepreneurial efforts. The Lenfest Institute for Journalism is a new funding source for entrepreneurial journalism efforts. And organizations like the Kauffman Foundation and VentureWell fund entrepreneurial efforts writ large. Grants and competition prizes from foundations focusing on entrepreneurship are worth exploring as a funding source.

### Sell Archival Access

Content companies who have created archives of past content can sell access to the archives to users for a fee.

### Sell Data and/or Analytic Services

Analytics are usually more of a B2B play, where the business sells access to user data and analytics to other companies. In some instances, companies can sell analytic tools and services to users as well.

### Licensing

Commonly used in technology plays, licensing as a revenue stream involves licensing out some form of proprietary technology, such as software or analytics tools, for use by other companies for a fee.

## Conclusion

This chapter has introduced the concepts of business model, revenue model, and business plan. You should have an understanding of what comprises a business model and business plan, some common revenue streams used in traditional media companies, and revenue streams available for content and technology startup plays, along with the role regulations and government can play among startups. You can start to develop the business model for your startup concept by sketching out the basic idea and its target customer, then identifying how it will make money through one or more revenue streams discussed in this chapter.

## TRY IT: NAPKIN SKETCH

Sketch out the start of a startup concept on the back of a napkin.

I would encourage doing this assignment after you've developed a customer empathy map and have a target customer segment in mind for your concept.

Address the following questions in your napkin sketch:

1. What is your idea (concept) and why is it valuable (value proposition)?
2. Who will it serve (target customer)?
3. How will it make money (revenue streams)?

For the first question, you'll want to keep it succinct. The equivalent of a 140-character or less tweet is a good starting point. This forces brevity, as does using an actual napkin for this exercise. There's only so much space on a napkin.

Napkin sketches are a commonly used brainstorming tool. The napkins at Walk-Ons Bistreux and Bar, a sports bar started by Louisiana college basketball players in 2001, include the original napkin sketch for the sports bar concept.

When my Lede, LLC cofounder Jameson Hayes and I first sketched out our idea for a news micropayment business model, we did so on a napkin over beers and fried pickles at the Blind Pig Tavern in Athens, Georgia. While the napkin sketch is somewhat of a cliché, I can attest firsthand that when inspiration hits you have to use whatever you have handy to put it on paper– even if that is in fact an actual napkin.

If your concept is a content play or a technology play, you may want to mention that as well.

The napkin sketch and brainstorming activities, such as the customer empathy map, are good tools to begin the process of formulating a business model for your startup concept. The customer segments and revenue streams are two of the nine blocks for the business model canvas tool anyway.

This chapter has discussed a number of different revenue streams and business models that are ideal for media startup companies. You can pull one or more revenue streams from some of the models mentioned in this chapter for the third question.

Value chiefly what's referred to as the value proposition, is also important to consider. This directly connects to the customer segments. What value will you offer the customer? Essentially this also addresses the "why?" question. Why you? Why would anyone use this product and/or pay for it? What value is offered?

Before fleshing out additional blocks of the business model canvas, it's useful to continue to ask and answer a series of questions.

Chris Guillebeau's book, *The $100 Startup*, provides a nice resource in the form of the one-page business plan. You're encouraged to answer each question on the form with one to two short sentences.

## Suggested Readings

- Guillebeau, Chris. *The $100 Startup: Reinvent the way you make a living, do what you love, and create a new future.* Crown Pub, 2012.
- Osterwalder, Alexander, and Yves Pigneur. *Business Model Generation: a handbook for visionaries, game changers, and challengers.* John Wiley & Sons, 2010.
- Ries, Eric. *The Lean Startup: How today's entrepreneurs use continuous innovation to create radically successful businesses.* Crown Books, 2011.
- Maurya, Ash. *Running Lean: iterate from plan A to a plan that works.* "O'Reilly Media, Inc.," 2012.

## Resources

- Strategyzer video series[29]

- Strategyzer Ad Lib Value Proposition Template[30]

- Hackpad[31]

- The Ultimate Master List of Revenue Models Used by Web and Mobile Companies[32]
- 76 Ways to Make Money in Digital Media[33]

*Geoffrey Graybeal is a clinical assistant professor in the Entrepreneurship and Innovation Institute at Georgia State University. He is a media management scholar and entrepreneur who uses economic and management theory to explore issues of media sustainability. Graybeal teaches courses on media entrepreneurship, media management, media economics, and innovation. Reach him on Twitter at @graybs13.*

## Leave feedback on this chapter.

## *Notes*

1. Osterwalder, Alexander; Pigneur, Yves. *Business Model Generation* (Hoboken, NJ: Wiley, 2013).

2. Picard, Robert. "Changing Business Models of Online Content Services: The Implications for Multimedia and Other Content Producers." *International Journal on Media Management* 2 (2000): 60-68.

3. Osterwalder, Alexander; Pigneur, Yves. "Business Model Canvas," https://en.wikipedia.org/wiki/Business_Model_Canvas#/media/File:Business_Model_Canvas.png.

4. "The Value Proposition Canvas," *Strategyzer*, https://strategyzer.com/canvas/value-proposition-canvas.

5. Hayes, Jameson L and Graybeal, Geoffrey M. "Synergizing Traditional Media and the Social Web for Monetization: A Modified Media Micropayment Model." *Journal of Media Business Studies* 8 (2011): 19-44.

6. Michelle Ferrier, "Ideation," *Media Innovation and Entrepreneurship*, https://press.rebus.community/media-innovation-and-entrepreneurship/chapter/ideation-2/.

7. Picard, "Changing Business Models," 60-68.

8. Osterwalder and Pigneur, "Business Model Generation."

9. "Ad Lib Value Proposition Template," *Strategyzer*, https://assets.strategyzer.com/assets/resources/ad-lib-value-proposition-template.pdf.

10. "Resources," *Strategyzer*, https://strategyzer.com/platform/resources.

11. Johnson, Mark. *Seizing the White Space: Business Model Innovation for Growth and Renewal* (Boston: Harvard Publishing Company, 2010).

12. Küng, Lucy. Strategic Management in the Media: From Theory to Practice. (Los Angeles: Sage, 2008).

13. Picard, "Changing Business Models," 60-68.

14. Küng, Lucy, Picard, Robert and Towse, Ruth. *The Internet and the Mass Media* (Sage: Los Angeles 2008). 153.

15. Zott, Christoph and Amit, Raphael. "The Fit Between Product Market Strategy and Business Model: Implications for Firm Performance." *Strategic Management Journal* 29 (2008): 1-26.

16. Zott, Christoph, Amit, Raphael, and Massa, Lorenzo. "The Business Model: Recent Developments and Future Research." *Journal of Management* 37 (2011): 1019-1042.

17. CJ Cornell, "Startup Funding," *Media Innovation & Entrepreneurship*, https://press.rebus.community/media-innovation-and-entrepreneurship/part/startup-funding/.

18. Picard, Robert. "Environmental and Market Changes Driving Strategic Planning in Media Firms." In R.G. Picard (Ed.). *Strategic Responses to Media Market Changes 2.* (Sweden: Jonkoping International Business School, 2004): 65-82.

19. Isenberg, Daniel. "The Entrepreneurship Ecosystem Strategy as a New Paradigm for Economic Policy: Principles for Cultivating Entrepreneurship." Presentation at the Institute of International and European Affairs (2011).

20. Laudon, Kenneth C. and Traver, Carol Guercio. *E-commerce: Business. Technology. Society* (Upper Saddle River: Prentice Hall, 2008).

21. Graybeal, Geoffrey M. and Hayes, Jameson L. "A Modified News Micropayment Model for Newspapers on the Social Web." *International Journal on Media Management* 13 (2011). 129-148.

22. Mings, Susan B. and White, Peter B. "Profiting From Online News: the Search for Viable Business Models." *In Internet Publishing and Beyond.* Kahin, B. & Varian, H.R. (Eds.) The President and Fellows of Harvard College (2000).

23. *StartUp podcast*, https://gimletmedia.com/startup/.

24. Graybeal and Hayes, "Modified News Micropayment Model"

25. Hayes and Graybeal, "Synergizing Traditional Media"

26. Schwienbacher, Armin and Larralde, Benjamin, Crowdfunding of Small Entrepreneurial Ventures (September 28, 2010). *Handbook of Entrepreneurial Finance*, Oxford University Press.

27. Mitra, Devashis. "The Role of Crowdfunding in Entrepreneurial Finance." *Delhi Business Review* 13, no. 2 (2012): 67.

28. Bradford, C. Steven. "Crowdfunding and the Federal Securities Laws." (2012).

29. Strategyzer video series, *YouTube*, https://www.youtube.com/watch?v=wwShFsSFb-Y.

30. "Ad Lib Value Proposition Template," *Strategyzer*, https://assets.strategyzer.com/assets/resources/ad-lib-value-proposition-template.pdf.

31. "Web And Mobile Revenue Models (final)," *Hackpad*, Accessed July 13, 2017. https://hackpad.com/Web-And-Mobile-Revenue-Models-final-EgXuEtSibE7.

32. Kumar, Abash, "The Ultimate Master List of Revenue Models Used by Web and Mobile Companies," *YourStory.com*, March 20, 2014, Accessed July 13, 2017, https://yourstory.com/2014/03/ultimate-master-list-revenue-models-web-mobile-companies/.

33. Plotz, David, "76 Ways to Make Money in Digital Media," *Slate Magazine*, August 29, 2014, Accessed July 13, 2017, http://www.slate.com/blogs/moneybox/2014/08/29/_76_ways_to_make_money_in_digital_media_a_list_from_slate_s_former_editor.html.

# FROM THE FIELD: REFINING OUR BUSINESS PLAN WAS THE KEY TO ATTRACTING OUR FIRST INVESTOR

*Dalton Dellsperger*

## From the Field

When I first had the idea of what would be our company, TownWave,[1] I never imagined I would have to break it down into such detail that would eventually match up with a traditional business model. We started with a lean startup canvas model, as most startups do, and expanded it from there.

My team's biggest struggle was identifying our value proposition. As a "web-based artist/music discovery platform," we were going into an oversaturated market of social sound platforms that all ideally promised the same thing for their customers. We had to differentiate ourselves in our business model canvas from the start to assure we would not make the same mistakes as our competitors.

At the same time, we had to make sure we were identifying our market properly and knew how we would eventually pitch ourselves to a board of investors. Once we found an interested investor, my partner and I started to create a detailed business plan, filled with information and research from our potential customer market. Some of the information gathered included amount of time people spent searching to discover new music, their preferred platform for music discovery, and the average amount of time listeners spent listening to music each day.

Finding data and information that proved there was a need for our product in the industry was the most important part for our investor. Investors don't care how much a company believes in its projected success, you must provide them with numbers that back up your claim and give the investor confidence they are investing in something special.

We had to conduct our own polls and research studies to prove that there was a massive market of opportunity for our company to thrive in. Our business plan is single-handedly the most important document we have ever worked on. It's roughly 30 pages of one single idea, TownWave, broken down into claims that our product will deliver on its promise, which is all backed by research. We were offered $200,000 for 33% equity in our company from an angel investor and though this was exciting news for us, we eventually turned down the offer and continued with our app's development. We felt giving away such a high percentage of our company that early in our company's development was not right for TownWave's future success. Since then, we have been developing our product into something much greater and have since been offered multiple investments of $100,000 for 10% equity, which valuates our company much higher than the original offer would have. We are now in the process of releasing our finished product into the market and using SAFE agreements to lock down a few investors to help us push our product into the hands of millions of listeners and artists.

*Dalton Dellsperger* graduated from Texas Tech in May 2017. He is now working full time on his entrepreneurial venture, TownWave. Reach him on Twitter at @dalton_townwave.

## Leave feedback on this sidebar.

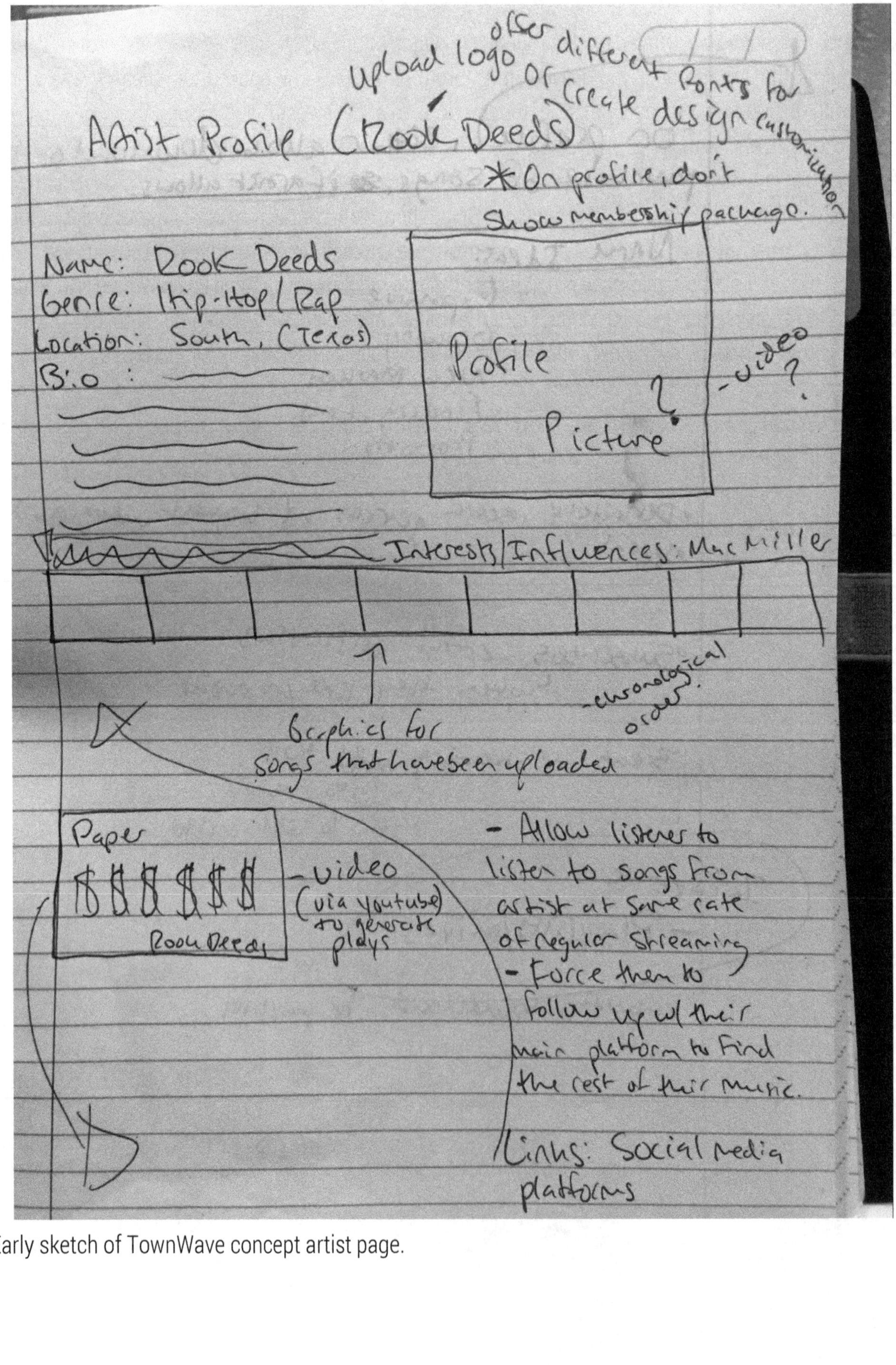


Early sketch of TownWave concept artist page.

## *Notes*

1. *TownWave*, http://townwave.com/.

# FROM THE FIELD: WRITING A BUSINESS PLAN & BUDGET

*John Dille*

## Build a Business Plan & Budget

"A goal without a plan is a wish-"–old management adage

If the value proposition is the compass, the business plan is the roadmap, and the budget and the metrics used are the waypoints that guide the promised goals home.

### What's in a Business Plan?

There is no one specific template every investor expects when they ask for a business plan. But usually, a business plan will include some combination of the following:

- What you want from investors *(aka your "ask")*
- A clear summary of the business, its product and the market you will serve *(key activities, value propositions and customer segments from the Business Model Canvas)*
- Financial information about the business—pricing, revenue, P&L, cash flow, return on investment, and pro forma (three-year) budget *(cost structure and revenue streams from the BMC)*
- Background about your company, its history and legal status, and the team
- A bit on your "secret sauce" that will enable you to be competitive *(key resources, channels, customer relationships, key partnerships from the BMC)*
- The metrics by which you'll measure success
- Whether and why the business is worth doing or investing in financially

Today's media marketplace is an on-demand, platform-specific landscape with a myriad of options available to consumers. Anyone in the media business these days knows the chaos that surrounds it and the search for new and more creative methods to monetize its content. Planners must be responsive to these historically disruptive conditions. Whatever plan you start out with, you'll probably iterate and maybe even pivot to respond to user and customer needs and changes in the marketplace.

That said, having a flexible business plan remains central to the success of any project.

What follows is a look at the essential financial components of a basic business plan.

## Developing a Pro Forma Budget

Assuming we have the other parts of the business plan in place, it is the budget process that can give the business plan the credibility and durability that both operators and investors seek.

The pro forma budget for new content or product is usually on a three-year schedule. From start to some level of market acceptance or rejection, three years provides a reasonable look. It is the last step in making the plan real. It is the quantification of the strategies and tactics included in the plan. Inasmuch it must ask, indeed force, the questions that engage the issues facing the enterprise.

The budget employs metrics that must be selected to accurately evaluate performance as well as offer tools that can guide actions that result in meeting desired goals.

Media lives at the convergence of the organization's ability to create compelling and relevant content and its skill at converting it to money. The organization must do this in a digitally created on-demand landscape and in a marketplace whose players are moving at an uneven pace.

Still, fundamentals remain and the need to retain existing customers, upsell them where possible, and to constantly recruit new ones persists. The repeat customers are critical.

**There are four primary components to a pro forma budget.**

**REVENUE** — For our purposes we should think of revenue, not as one big number, but as the sum of a collection of smaller numbers. Revenue is the result of two numbers, for example, number of units, broadcast spots or ads or whatever times the price per unit sold. That then holds true for every income stream the operation offers the market.

A newspaper historically has had two primary sources of revenue: advertising and circulation sales or subscribers. In the digital space this converts to clicks and paywalls.

The real challenge facing media outlets and their revenue is monetizing smaller audiences in a way that remains of value to the advertiser.

- All sources of revenue

These can be from third parties, such as advertisers, or directly from consumers. Go to the chapters on Business Models and Nonprofit Models for ideas on potential sources of revenue.

- What is the durability of these revenue or income streams?

  How often do buyers buy?

- What are the pricing models?

  What exactly are the buyers buying?

  - Content
  - Access to this content's consumers?
  - What will the profiled buyer pay? More, less or the same as competitors?

  If the marketplace competition is such that it will not support the desired price, is the value proposition still viable? Or can it be adjusted without disrupting the cost model?

  For decades media has priced on a Cost per Thousand readers/viewers/listeners basis. That model is now under attack as being imprecise and inadequate. This too, is under re-evaluation.

The message here is that the budget process must remain nimble enough to accommodate change quickly should the need arise.

**COST STRUCTURE** – All costs associated with the designated project. These include outsourcing costs as well as internal payroll and other costs used to fund the operation.

Fixed and variable costs

- Media has traditionally been a high fixed cost business. This means that regardless of the number or consumers, readers/viewers, the cost to produce the content is essentially the same.
  - Office rent or insurance would be fixed costs.
  - The cost of producing content will vary based on the volume and type of content you produce, and whether you use full-time or freelance employees. However, as a media business, you will always have this overhead.
  - A building contractor, on the other hand, would hire carpenters and buy materials only when he had a building to construct.

Costs will vary depending on strategies chosen in the business planning process

- Some elements of an operation may be higher. For example, an enterprise focused on building a specialized product may have higher service costs than an operation offering a one-size-fits-all product.
- The budget will need to take this into account.

**METRICS** – Metrics used to measure performance are critical. If they are not employed in sync with the business plan they can provide not only incorrect information but misleading data and flawed conclusions.

* Some metrics look back and are used as performance indicators. Income statements produced monthly include the predetermined budget for comparison between what revenues planners thought would come in versus what actually did happen.
* Retrospective information, for instance when comparing a monthly budget to actual costs, answers the question, "how'd we do?"
* Equally important are metrics that predict success. For example, sales managers know that the number of sales calls made by a seller of media on existing or prospects matters. There is a direct correlation here. Sellers who underperform usually aren't making enough calls. This metric can guide an operation. Similarly, if a seller is selling, but his or her orders aren't priced correctly, the total revenue generated will be insufficient.
* With this kind of predictive data, management can direct actions of employees and others to the desired goals.

**PROFIT or MARGIN** — Revenue minus Expenses equals Profit.

* Was it worth it? This is the question asked by all concerned. How did our effort on this project compare to what we could have done?
    * Investors in particular ask this, but operators do as well.
* Breakeven analysis and Return on Investment are two more important data points available from the information created in the pro forma budget process.
    * What do we need to do to break even or not lose money?
    * What is the ROI on this course of action vs. our next best alternative? For instance, would we sell more advertising if we priced it at $2,500 instead of at $5,000?
    * Or, in harsh reality, whether the project should be undertaken at all.

All of this is at the heart of the business plan and is the "reality check" any plan requires.

*John Dille is the president and CEO of Federated Media.*

## Leave feedback on this sidebar.

# NONPROFIT MODEL DEVELOPMENT

by Jake Batsell

## Summary

This chapter will explore revenue strategies that have worked for nonprofit news outlets in the digital age. It begins with an in-depth look at *The Texas Tribune*, which over the past decade has gained a reputation as a national model for nonprofit news. The chapter also explores best practices in revenue strategies as pursued in recent years by the Tribune and many of its peers in nonprofit news.

---

### Learning Objectives

- Understand how nonprofit news organizations are different and similar to for-profit news enterprises.
- Through the lens of a case study on *The Texas Tribune*, familiarize yourself with some common ways nonprofit news venues generate and diversify their revenue streams.
- Learn which of these strategies have led to success and sustainability for other nonprofit news organizations in the United States and abroad.

---

## Inside this Chapter

- Nonprofit Model Development
- From the Field: The Knoxville Experiment, by Coury Turczyn
- Exercise: Being a Media Nonprofit

*Jake Batsell is an associate professor at Southern Methodist University's Division of Journalism in Dallas, where he teaches digital journalism and media entrepreneurship. His book, "Engaged Journalism: Connecting with Digitally Empowered News Audiences" (Columbia University Press, 2015) was one of three national finalists for the Tankard Book Award administered by the Association for Education in Journalism and Mass Communication. Reach him on Twitter at @jbatsell.*

# NONPROFIT MODEL DEVELOPMENT

*Jake Batsell*

An *earlier version of this chapter was published as "Earning Their Keep: Revenue Strategies From The Texas Tribune and Other Nonprofit News Startups,"*[1] *Knight Foundation, April 2015. The author has updated the current version with new information while editing for content and focus. It is republished here with permission and gratitude to the Knight Foundation.*

The rise of digital media in the new millennium has triggered an irreversible plunge in print advertising revenues. Consequently, the newspaper industry is shedding jobs. By mid-2016, the American newspaper workforce alone had lost about 20,000 jobs[2] over the previous 20 years, and most in the industry expect that trend will continue. With ad-supported mass media mired in what seems to be a permanent cycle of disruption, a growing number of journalists have shifted their career path toward nonprofit news, a realm that traditionally has depended on more altruistic forms of funding such as memberships and philanthropic donations.

The *Institute for Nonprofit News,*[3] founded in 2009 by 27 investigative news organizations, had grown to more than 120 members by mid-2017. And in the aftermath of the 2016 U.S. presidential election, the nonprofit news sector—a category that includes public radio and television stations, established investigative newsrooms, and newer startups covering a specialized topic or region—saw an unprecedented surge in donations[4] from readers and foundations hungry for independent watchdog journalism. In March 2017, The Center for Investigative Reporting, the Center for Public Integrity and ProPublica each received $3 million in grants from the Democracy Fund and First Look Media, prompting *Inside Philanthropy* to proclaim in a blog post headline: "It's Official: Donald Trump is the Best Thing That's Ever Happened to Nonprofit Journalism."[5]

Seven-figure grants can pay for plenty of accountability journalism, but news nonprofits can't pin their long-term survival on big checks from foundations. The term "nonprofit" generally means that an organization exists to fulfill some sort of social purpose, not to make money for corporate owners. But the bills still need to be paid. If you talk business strategy with any of the civic-minded entrepreneurs who run news nonprofits, you'll quickly hear a common theme: "nonprofit" is not, by itself, a business model—it's simply a tax status. Yes, once they clear a lengthy review by the Internal Revenue Service,[6] nonprofit news organizations benefit from 501(c)(3) status, which exempts them from certain taxes and enables them to collect charitable donations. Still, tax-exempt status brings no automatic guarantee of financial success. To stay afloat, today's news nonprofits must constantly seek revenue from a diverse array of sources including corporate sponsorships, events, subscriptions, and crowdfunding while also cultivating new members and philanthropic donations.

This chapter will explore revenue strategies that have worked for nonprofit news outlets in the digital age. We'll begin with an in-depth look at *The Texas Tribune*, which over the past decade has gained a reputation as a national model for nonprofit news. Later in the chapter, we'll explore best practices in revenue strategies as pursued in recent years by the Tribune and many of its peers in nonprofit news.[7]

## Earning Their Keep: *The Texas Tribune*

*The Texas Tribune* launched on November 3, 2009, with seventeen employees and the mission "to promote civic engagement and discourse on public policy, politics, government, and other matters of statewide concern." It has since grown to fifty-three employees and now has more full-time statehouse beat reporters than any other U.S. news organization.[8] The Tribune has collected a heap of national and regional awards, including a 2017 Peabody Award[9] shared with fellow nonprofit ProPublica for a collaborative investigation revealing Houston's vulnerability to a Katrina-caliber hurricane. It also has raised more than $40 million through a combination of donations, memberships, corporate sponsorships, events, and other sources of revenue. It all adds up to a diversified business model that funds the work of a growing and respected newsroom.

What lessons can be gleaned from *The Texas Tribune*'s journey? How much of the Tribune's experience is unique, and to what degree can its revenue-generating prowess be replicated by other news outlets? For a year, these questions guided my work as a visiting research fellow[10] funded by the John S. and James L. Knight Foundation.

While based in the Tribune's Austin newsroom from August 2013 to July 2014, I investigated best practices in the business of nonprofit news. I sat in on staff and board meetings, conducted interviews with employees, and also visited some of the Tribune's nonprofit news peers around the country. The fellowship afforded me unusual access to directly observe the Tribune as it evolved beyond its startup roots and adopted business strategies designed to build an enduring organization. Meanwhile, my travels to other news nonprofits enabled me to compare and contrast the Tribune's revenue strategies with those of its peers.

If there are generalizable lessons to be learned from the Tribune's experience, they do not add up to a rigid recipe but rather a handful of strategic concepts that other news startups might consider. This much is clear: Among the past decade's wave of nonprofit news startups, *The Texas Tribune* stands out as the most aggressively entrepreneurial.

The sheer scale of what the Tribune has achieved in Texas may not be replicable to other settings. But other nonprofit news outlets may wish to emulate some of the tactics that have propelled the site's success. Among the most replicable concepts are revenue diversity, entrepreneurial creativity, and a shared sense of editorial and business mission.

## The Birth of *The Texas Tribune*

The story of *The Texas Tribune* began in late 2006, when software investor John Thornton began researching how his Austin-based venture capital firm might profit by acquiring stakes in financially troubled newspapers. As Thornton dug into the news industry's changing economics, he became convinced that public-interest journalism—which had been subsidized for decades by a now-vanishing system of mass media advertising—could not survive as a stand-alone product. His interest in journalism shifted from a potential business opportunity to a philanthropic pursuit.

Observing the diminished presence of mainstream media outlets covering the state Capitol, Thornton donated the first $1 million to start a nonpartisan news source. During the spring of 2009, he formed an official corporation and quickly applied to the IRS for tax-exempt status, which was granted within months and, crucially, enabled the Tribune to raise funds as a public charity. (Other aspiring news nonprofits during this era were not as fortunate when seeking tax-exempt status from the IRS, which was baffled about how to handle these new entities. Some startups who began under these shaky regulatory grounds waited in vain for nonprofit status, ultimately either dying in infancy or partnering with an already established nonprofit organization that could act as a fiscal sponsor.[11] The lesson, once again: nonprofit is a tax status, not a business model.)

To lead the new venture, Thornton enlisted his friend Evan Smith—who, as the longtime editor of *Texas Monthly* magazine, brought deep connections within the state's political, business and media circles. The pair teamed up with another veteran political journalist, Texas Weekly editor Ross Ramsey, and the three co-founders assembled a talented crew of young reporters and developers during the summer of 2009.

The Tribune then embarked on a remarkable fundraising spree to bolster the initial $1 million from Thornton. Boosted by the journalistic credibility of Smith, Ramsey, and a cast of rising stars poached from legacy newsrooms, the fledgling nonprofit landed a flurry of five- and six-figure sums from an array of wealthy donors and foundations (including $250,000 from the Knight Foundation).[12] It also signed up more than 1,400 members who contributed at least $50 each, and around sixty corporate sponsors who pitched in at least $2,500 apiece. By the end of 2009, the Tribune had raised roughly $4 million.

## Proving the Concept During the "Runway" Phase

The initial $4 million fundraising haul provided vital early breathing room for what Thornton called a two-year "runway" phase—a period during which the Tribune would need to prove the value of its journalism while figuring out its long-term business strategy.

Somewhat unexpectedly, the site's early traffic magnet was its series of searchable databases, which allowed readers to easily snoop through government employees' salaries, contributions to political campaigns, and state prison inmates' convictions and sentences. The databases were controversial to some readers, who considered them an invasion of privacy even though they contained public information. But the databases were undeniably popular—at one point during the site's first year, they were drawing three times as many pageviews as traditional news stories. And each curious click created more digital impressions for corporate sponsors' messages.

Offline, the Tribune launched a series of events that expanded the site's visibility. Tanya Erlach, hired from *The New Yorker* to serve as the Tribune's full-time director of events, developed a morning event series featuring on-the-record interviews with high-profile political figures. The events—hosted by Smith, a skilled questioner with his own PBS interview show—drew a strong following among political insiders, attracting crowds of as many as 200 to 300 people to a downtown ballroom directly across from the Tribune's offices. And these events, underwritten by corporate sponsors, were free to attend regardless of whether one was a Tribune member.

From the start, Thornton sought to wean the Tribune from philanthropic support as soon as possible. In an early brochure distributed to potential supporters in 2010, a chart labeled *"The Texas Tribune's* path to self-sufficiency" predicted that within three to four years, the site would no longer require major gifts from donors and foundations. Instead, according to the chart, three equal revenue streams would sustain the Tribune: memberships, specialty publications, and corporate sponsors and events. However, even as the Tribune's journalism gained prominence across the state, it soon became clear that those revenue categories were not developing quickly enough to keep the Tribune afloat.

## Accelerating Business Capacity

During the latter half of 2010, the Tribune made a series of adjustments designed to ratchet up revenue. Thornton agreed to donate another $1 million—but this time, in the form of a matching grant that would kick in whenever the Tribune landed major donations of $5,000 or more. As executive editor Ross Ramsey recalled, "You've got to raise a million to get a million. The most important part was raising the million."

Smith brought in a new director of business development, his former *Texas Monthly* colleague April Hinkle, who as the magazine's publisher had more than two decades of experience selling advertising to the state's corporate crowd. "He said, 'I want your for-profit brain for my nonprofit," Hinkle recalled. One of her first moves was to expand corporate sponsorships beyond the basic $2,500 level offered during the Tribune's launch phase. Originally, Tribune sponsorships offered little more than a tax write-off and a rotating logo box on the site's homepage, but Hinkle began to develop more comprehensive programs that included event sponsorships, more visible logo placements and other customized elements for a higher price.

Hinkle said her singular mission upon joining the nonprofit was "using all Tribune assets I could possibly get my hands on to create custom programs."

Around this same time, the Tribune also sought to boost membership revenue by introducing an "editor's circle" program focused on securing multi-year pledges. The circle program, which requires a three-year commitment of up to $5,000 annually, created a stable pipeline of support. "It was really genius in a box in terms of revenue growth," said Maggie Gilburg, the Tribune's former director of development. And on the news side, the site struck a syndication deal with *The New York Times* to provide eight stories a week for the iconic newspaper's Texas editions.

These were all promising revenue developments, but by the end of 2010 the Tribune remained heavily dependent on philanthropic support. Nearly two-thirds of the Tribune's $2.25 million in overall revenue that year came from individual donors and foundations, according to internal figures.[13] Earned revenue—an industry term referring to self-generated income such as corporate sponsorships and events—remained a much smaller part of the mix.

## Building Entrepreneurial Momentum

Two factors in 2011 helped the Tribune build more entrepreneurial momentum. During the spring, the site for the first time covered a state legislative session, which in Texas convenes only once every two years. Hinkle's revamped sponsorship packages offered businesses and institutions a new, more targeted option to get their messages in front of a politically savvy audience during the urgency of a session. Corporate sponsorships more than doubled from $306,000 in 2010 to $637,000 in 2011, according to internal figures.

Perhaps even more significantly, in September the site hosted its first annual Texas Tribune Festival, a weekend-long bonanza for policy wonks that drew more than 1,300 attendees to the University of Texas campus. The festival—organized by events director Erlach, who previously ran a similar festival for *The New Yorker*—featured big-name keynote interviews and panel discussions, along with networking at cocktail receptions and trendy food trucks. Ticket sales helped cover costs, but festival sponsorships accounted for the biggest windfall. The festival, combined with more than 40 additional events throughout the year, pushed annual event revenues to $702,000, more than tripling the total from the previous year. The festival grew even bigger in 2012, offering forty-five sessions and 150 speakers on topics including health, race, and criminal justice. Attendance climbed to nearly 1,700, and sponsorships for the three-day festival approached $400,000. "It's just a real you-have-to-be-there vibe that we've been able to create," Erlach told me at the time. The growth of the festival pushed total yearly event revenue to almost $900,000.

Also in 2012, the Tribune tallied enough major philanthropic donations to fully redeem Thornton's $1 million matching pledge. But earned revenue was beginning to drive the business model. That year, for the first time, revenue from corporate sponsorships and events (together, roughly $1.9 million) surpassed major donations and grants ($1.8 million). Memberships rose to $510,000, nearly equaling the total raised during the previous two years combined. After adding in syndication, subscriptions, and other revenue sources, the Tribune hauled in more than $4.5 million overall.

The trend continued in 2013, as sponsorships and events each topped $1.1 million. The Tribune Festival, a growing juggernaut, swelled to nearly 2,500 attendees and produced more than $700,000[14] by itself. By the end of its fourth full year, the Tribune raked in a total of $5.1 million from a balanced assortment of revenue streams: 45 percent from sponsorships and events, 34 percent from philanthropic sources, 13 percent from memberships, and 8 percent from syndication, subscriptions, crowdfunding, and other sources.

It was a dramatically different financial formula from its first full year, when foundations and wealthy donors supplied nearly two-thirds of the Tribune's annual revenue. And by the end of 2016, the Tribune's annual revenue had swelled to $6.9 million from roughly the same combination of sources: 45 percent from sponsorships and events, 40 percent from philanthropic donors, 11 percent from memberships, and 4 percent from syndication, subscriptions, and other sources. While philanthropy provided the initial boost and continues to be crucial, the Tribune gradually has figured out ways to earn more of its keep.

## New Challenges—and More Scrutiny

The corporate sponsors[15] fueling the Tribune's transformed business model—companies, lobbying firms, universities, advocacy groups—all have their own agendas at stake in the world of state government. While these sponsorships have accelerated the Tribune's revenue growth, they also have triggered scrutiny from media watchdogs.

In February 2014, Austin-based political author Jim Moore, a former journalist, published a series of blog posts denouncing the Tribune's financial model as fundamentally "corrupted." "What believers hoped was going to be a watchdog has turned into a lapdog by taking big dollars from lobbyists and corporations," Moore argued.[16] Commercial media, of course, have long battled similar perceptions that their news coverage was beholden to advertisers' interests. But as veteran Texas journalist and professor Bill Minutaglio would later observe,[17] Moore's four-part attack—entitled "The Trouble With the Trib"—underscored "how fine a line the brave new world of nonprofit journalism has to tread in the search for viable business models."

The Tribune always has listed all financial contributors on its site, but the criticism from Moore and others accelerated a series of changes[18] that editors had already been considering to improve transparency. Corporate sponsors would now be listed not only by name, but also by the specific amount of their sponsorships—a higher degree of disclosure than practiced by most, if not all, of the Tribune's nonprofit peers. In addition, disclosures would be appended to any story that mentioned people or institutions who had given the Tribune more than $1,000.

Also, event descriptions would include language to reinforce that sponsors "do not have any role in selecting topics, panels or panelists."

A point often overlooked when discussing the ethics of fundraising for nonprofit news is that, collectively, an expanding roster of corporate sponsors dilutes the ability of any single financial backer to wield undue influence. In one instance I watched unfold in the newsroom during the spring of 2014, Ramsey, the site's co-founder and executive editor, agreed to moderate a corporate forum in Dallas in exchange for an honorarium to the Tribune. The week before the event, organizers sent the Tribune a list of 10 pre-scripted questions for panelists. Ramsey objected, making clear that he would moderate only if he had discretion over the questions. "They wanted a paid performance, and we don't do that," Ramsey said. The company found another moderator, and the Tribune lost the honorarium. Both sides moved on. It's just one example, but it highlights how diverse revenue streams and journalistic integrity can help protect a news organization from the whims of any particular financial supporter.

In recent years, Tribune has sought to widen its audience while also doing everything it can to monetize the diehard politicos who already read it every day. The Tribune has developed strategies to extract more revenue from its most loyal followers, raising the subscription price for its insider political newsletter and offering VIP experiences at the Texas Tribune festival. It hired its first chief audience officer[19] and created a sister op-ed site, TribTalk,[20] whose content consists of volunteer submissions and clearly labeled "paid placement" posts authored by corporate sponsors.

The sheer scale of what *The Texas Tribune* has achieved may not be replicable in the world of nonprofit news, at least at the regional and local level. The Tribune has uniquely benefited from a generous founding investor who combines a venture capitalist's business acumen with a personal passion for public-interest journalism; a charismatic CEO with a well-honed public presence; and, of course, the "everything's bigger in Texas" effect. Texas is a vast, pro-business state whose 27 million residents also share a distinct sense of cultural identity. In other areas of the country, even the most dedicated founders of local digital news outlets have ultimately succumbed to "founder fatigue" — in May 2015, after nine years of running the community news site *DavidsonNews.net* in North Carolina, editor David Boraks announced the site's closure in a farewell column: "We're in debt, we're exhausted, and it's time to go."

Still, fellow news nonprofits may wish to emulate some of the tactics that have propelled the Tribune's success. Below, I have outlined key elements of the Tribune's business model that are most likely to be mirrored elsewhere:

- **Persistent focus on revenue diversity.** From the outset, Thornton sought to establish multiple streams of revenue, a strategy he jokingly called "revenue promiscuity"[21] during the Tribune's early days. It's worth noting, though, that the Tribune's eventual mix of revenue sources took a different path from the initial vision of drawing equal support from only three revenue streams—memberships, specialty publications, and corporate sponsors and events. As it turns out, sponsorships are generating more money than the Tribune's founders anticipated, while memberships and specialty publications have been slower to develop. Philanthropy continues to play a crucial role, and new sources of revenue (crowdfunding, for example) have emerged. The percentages constantly will change, but the Tribune's experience emphasizes the importance of constantly seeking a diverse mix of revenue sources.

- **Entrepreneurial creativity and customization.** The Tribune has been relentless in unearthing new ways to pay for its journalism. Over the years, its revenue experiments have included a sponsored "TweetWire" widget on the homepage that features curated Twitter posts by elected officials, newsletter sponsorships, podcast introductions on the weekly "TribCast," and even sponsored breaking news alerts. April Hinkle, the Tribune's chief revenue officer, said she considers the Tribune's media kit[22] to be more of a conversation starter than a take-it-or-leave-it menu. She works with prospective sponsors to develop customized packages—sometimes including event sponsorships—that suit the sponsor's needs. "Every single thing really becomes custom," Hinkle said. "I don't think we would be as successful today if we weren't willing to be flexible … People invest in what they need, and not what we want them to buy."

- **A shared sense of editorial and business mission.** The Tribune's organizational culture fosters collaboration between the editorial and business staffs, in contrast to the church-versus-state model historically followed by legacy media. Reporters and editors host and moderate panels during events, especially the annual festival, and are encouraged (but not required) to promote membership drives on their own social media accounts. Business-side employees sit in on weekly news meetings for a better understanding of what the newsroom is up to. When the Tribune launched its sister op-ed site, TribTalk,[23] in 2014, staffers from several departments—news, art, tech and business—worked together for months to design a site that would clearly distinguish between volunteer guest columns and "paid placement" advertorials. Over time, the newsroom and business side have developed a mutual sense of trust underpinned by the Tribune's nonprofit mission. "My first year here, I tiptoed through the newsroom," Hinkle said. "But I think we've kind of grown together."

## Best Practices in Revenue Strategies For Nonprofit News

Four principal revenue streams dominate today's landscape of nonprofit news: corporate sponsorships, events, philanthropy, and memberships.[24] The proportional weight of these revenue sources varies widely, depending on a news organization's particular scope, mission, and local circumstances.

"There's no one-size-fits-all approach when it comes to the right sources of revenue," the *Poynter Institute* **wrote**[25] in 2016 after spending a year visiting nonprofit news outlets around the country. "Test out different approaches and consider what opportunities are unique to your mission, audience and location."

## Sponsorships and Underwriting

One way to subsidize nonprofit journalism is by courting corporate and institutional sponsors who are looking to reach a more influential audience than a general-interest publication can offer. *The Texas Tribune* is widely regarded as a standout performer in this area—in 2016, the Tribune generated more than $3 million through corporate underwriting and sponsored events—but many other news nonprofits are pursuing similar strategies. The next section will consider specific revenue strategies for events, but here are some general sponsorship principles as practiced by the Tribune and several of its peers.

- **Know your audience and sell its value.** Nonprofit, mission-driven news organizations are uniquely positioned to connect sponsors with an educated and engaged audience. But to convert audience attention into sponsorship revenue, potential sponsors need evidence to be convinced that a site's readership is worth their money.

In May 2012, *The Texas Tribune* conducted its first audience identification survey,[26] which drew 872 responses in two days. The site found out that 91 percent of its readers are college graduates, 96 percent voted in the last election and 52 percent have a household income of more than $100,000. That's a smart, affluent audience that appeals to potential sponsors and advertisers, so the Tribune trumpeted the survey's results in its media kit.

"It's a very specific kind of audience, definite intellectuals," said Hilarie Houghton, executive communications consultant for BlueCross BlueShield of Texas, which through mid-2017 had spent nearly $800,000[27] on Tribune sponsorships, including events like the Texas Tribune Festival.

*VTDigger.org*, a political news site in Vermont, conducted a similar audience survey that quickly attracted more sponsors. By the end of 2013, corporate underwriting had risen to more than 40 percent[28] of *VTDigger.org*'s annual revenue. "It's made a huge difference for us, because we're able to show sponsors that our readers are very civically engaged," said founder and editor Anne Galloway, noting that the survey found her site's readers "are involved in their communities on many different levels—they're churchgoers, they're volunteers at schools, they're very politically active. More than 95 percent of them vote every year."

- **Provide ways for sponsors to make fuller arguments.** In Southern California, nonprofit organizations wanting to reach the *Voice of San Diego's*[29] civic-minded audience have long raised doubts that a banner ad could effectively get their point across. "It wasn't enough space for them to really explain and educate people about their mission," said Mary Walter-Brown, *Voice of San Diego*'s publisher and chief operating officer.

So in 2014, San Diego's pioneering online news startup quietly debuted a native advertising program[30] aimed at fellow nonprofits. The program, called Partner Voices,[31] publishes article-length "partner promos" that are either paid for by the nonprofits themselves, or on their behalf by a corporate sponsor. *Voice of San Diego*'s editorial staff has no role in producing the promos, which carry a monthly fee of $1,500 and are clearly labeled as sponsored content.

*Voice of San Diego* is one of several nonprofit news outlets to recently join the wider media world's adoption of sponsored content,[32] also called native advertising. Display ads are confined by the boundaries of the box, but sponsored content allows advertisers more room to make their case—an intriguing option for policy-minded organizations whose arguments and causes are difficult to boil down to a snappy slogan.

Making fuller arguments to an influential audience is a key selling point for *The Texas Tribune*'s op-ed site, TribTalk, which launched in 2014 and offers "paid placement"[33] slots to corporate sponsors. The Tribune charges $2,750 for a three-day run on the TribTalk.org homepage, although permalinks for sponsored content stay up indefinitely. April Hinkle, the Tribune's chief revenue officer, said she pitches TribTalk's paid placement as an opportunity "for thought-leading organizations to be able to post and lead a discussion" beyond what banner ads can provide.

When tapping into new revenue sources like native advertising, it is crucial for nonprofit news outlets to clearly explain how such initiatives support their mission, according to Kevin Davis, formerly the executive director of the *Institute for Nonprofit News*.[34] "Make very clear what type of organization you are and why you're doing this, because there is a different level of scrutiny for nonprofits," Davis said. "Go to the ends of the earth to say, 'We are a nonprofit, we are mission-driven, and this is an authentic way of furthering the mission—not just making money.'"

## Events

Live events have emerged as an increasingly popular revenue stream for both nonprofit and for-profit news outlets. Since 2013, events have generated more than $1 million[35] per year for *The Texas Tribune* while also building community and creating a library of video news content for its site. Here are some of the common event practices[36] followed by the Tribune and many of its peers.

### Seek out corporate sponsors.

You don't have to sell tickets to make money from events. In fact, nearly all Tribune events are free, other than its three-day festival.[37] Pitch events to corporate sponsors as a way to get their name in front of an influential audience. Underwriters, advertisers or donors who already support your site are a logical place to start, because your organizations already have a relationship. And think early, because corporate budgets tend to be planned months in advance. Keep in mind, however, that sponsors may be more interested in sponsoring a series than a single event. "It's much harder to go to someone and say, 'This is a one-off,'" said Tanya Erlach, the Tribune's founding director of events. "Their brand lives on if it's over and over again."

When determining sponsorship rates, Hinkle recommends first sketching out a tentative P&L (profit and loss) report that factors in the event's costs, likely attendance, and potential revenue. If, like the Tribune, you promote the event in advance and publish video or audio afterward, be sure to factor that into the calculations. Hinkle said the Tribune's event sponsorships range from $3,000 for a single event to six-figure amounts for a series of events that include custom topics. And before you book a pricey hotel ballroom, explore a partnership with a local university, museum, or nonprofit organization that might be willing to provide space.

## Build in a networking element.

Any successful event needs a compelling program, of course. But networking might be an even bigger draw. And for sponsors, Hinkle said, having the opportunity to invite clients and VIPs is an added plus. "You just have to make it so they have to be there—this is a can't-miss, it's a must-attend on their calendar," she said. Also, make every effort to gather attendees' contact information, whether through RSVPs or a simple box at the check-in table to drop off business cards. "If you can get an email address from somebody that's already showed up, that's your repeat customer," Erlach said.

## Consider virtual events, too.

NJ Spotlight,[38] a political news nonprofit in New Jersey, generates most of its earned revenue through a series of in-person roundtable events.[39] But the site collected an extra $20,000[40] in 2013 by hosting three sponsored webinars[41] on topics including offshore wind power, electricity and health care. Kevin Harold, NJ Spotlight's publisher, said the webinar format works best for a sponsor looking to make its case on a complex state policy issue that "begs a platform to get into the granular nature of it."

A reporter or editor moderates each webinar, which lasts about an hour. Sponsors present a slideshow, then answer questions posed by the moderator or the virtual, real-time audience. The pitch to sponsors, Harold said, goes something like this: "You have a content-rich story to tell. We have an independent flag. We will challenge you on things that you say, but we'll give you a platform to say them."

## Don't be afraid to monetize the fun factor.

For the past decade, pioneering nonprofit news site *MinnPost*[42] has hosted an annual variety show called MinnRoast,[43] during which the state's politicians and journalists "gently skewer" one another through songs, skits and stand-up comedy. In 2014, when I attended MinnRoast[44] at a historic theatre in downtown Minneapolis, the event raised roughly $160,000. Joel Kramer, *MinnPost*'s CEO and editor, noted that the Twin Cities region is saturated with serious events run by civic-minded organizations such as Minnesota Public Radio, the Citizens League and the University of Minnesota's Humphrey School of Public Affairs. From a strategic standpoint, Kramer said, MinnPost thought a fun-themed event had a better chance to attract sponsors and ticket sales than more straight-laced affairs. "You've got to find a spot that's empty, that's open," he said. "And nobody was doing it. … Most events in town are very serious. They talk about the mission, you know, they all have a silent auction. I go to many of them, and I believe in the causes, and we donate money. But they're a bit on the somber side. So we wanted to distinguish ourselves in that way."

## Memberships

Membership drives for nonprofit media have evolved far beyond volunteers taking pledges over rotary phones. Some public radio and TV stations still host on-air telethons, but today's nonprofit news outlets seek pledges through multi-channel membership drives that include websites, social media, e-mail, and in-person events. Memberships remain an important part of the revenue mix for nonprofit media. Running an effective membership program is a complex, never-ending endeavor, but here are some core strategies that have helped produce success.

## Define "the ask."

Are you asking people to join primarily based on benefits they will receive, or is their membership simply a vote of confidence in your mission? The Tribune offers modest benefits ranging from monthly newsletter updates to invitations to VIP events, but its membership strategy[45] mostly focuses on selling the value of the Tribune's public-service journalism. "It's really a philosophical ask: Please support our mission at the level that's most comfortable for you," Gilburg said.

*Investigate West*, a nonprofit news site based in Seattle, entices supporters to upgrade their basic, $10-per-month memberships by offering tiered benefits[46] including invitations to house parties with staffers for members who join the $25-per-month "Deadline Club."

## Plan ahead.

*The Texas Tribune* begins preparations for membership drives[47] months ahead of time. After settling on a campaign theme, messaging is catered to five modes of delivery: email, social media, direct mail, the site itself, and membership events. (Email tends to be most effective, because people on distribution lists have shown some form of previous support or interest.) The Tribune seeks buy-in from the entire organization, inviting employees to membership happy hours and circulating pre-written social media statuses that staffers can share.

While membership programs are a year-round commitment, the action heats up considerably as the calendar year comes to a close. "For nonprofit fundraisers, the entire fundraising calendar revolves around year-end campaigns and planning starts in the summer, if not sooner," advises[48] nonprofit news consultant Jason Alcorn. For example, the Maine Center for Public Interest Reporting begins formal preparations for its end-of-year fundraising drive in August, according to publisher Naomi Schalit.[49] By October, board members are jotting down personalized notes on appeal letters, which go out in late October and early November to allow time for follow-up before the year concludes.

## Push for automatic or multi-year pledges.

One-time donations are lovely and appreciated, but recurring donations are a golden goose. In 2015, monthly giving to nonprofits grew at a faster rate than one-time donations, a trend that Alcorn called[50] "great for nonprofits that can now plan around a predictable, stable revenue stream." The Tribune's membership program[51] defaults to recurring payments (annual or monthly) rather than one-time donations. Its "editor's circle" program, which asks supporters to pledge up to $5,000 annually for three years, also has proven to be a substantial revenue source.

## Evaluate the returns.

Cultivating and maintaining a membership base is a monumental task. For some nonprofit news organizations, the costs to staff, promote and maintain a membership program may not be worth the effort. It's important to weigh the expenses against the returns. "If you hire a person for X, and they bring in less than X, then it's not worth it," Gilburg said. One solution? Pooling resources. In late 2016 and early 2017, with funding from the Democracy Fund, five nonprofit newsrooms banded together to form the News Revenue Hub pilot[52] to manage their end-of-year membership drives together, led by the *Voice of San Diego*. The five newsrooms raised nearly $300,000 in addition to tens of thousands more in future commitments. The pilot was so successful that *Voice of San Diego* announced it would spin off[53] the Hub into a separate venture aimed at coaching and guiding news nonprofits through the membership process. "If all newsrooms do their part to address the crisis creatively, we can share lessons learned and build a new system that is more sustainable in the long term and more accessible and accountable to the people it's meant to serve," wrote Scott Lewis, *Voice of San Diego*'s CEO.

## Philanthropic Giving

Even as the nonprofit news sector finds creative ways to generate more of its own revenue, "the fact is, there's not a business model—definitely for nonprofits—without donations," said Brant Houston, board chair emeritus of the Institute for Nonprofit News. A 2017 data analysis[54] published by Columbia Journalism Review found that 10 foundations collectively donated $500 million to journalism nonprofits from 2009 to 2016. The Knight Foundation ($142 million) was by far the leading institutional donor for nonprofit news, followed by the Ford Foundation ($74 million) and the Bill and Melinda Gates Foundation ($64 million).

Foundation funding requires carefully cultivating and maintaining relationships, meeting the guidelines of specific grant programs, and many other interrelated factors.[55] When it comes to seeking major gifts from individual donors, here are a few commonly followed practices:

### Cultivate your community's network of business leaders.

This is especially important in the initial phases. The Tribune's initial $4 million fundraising campaign included a bipartisan list of high-profile donors, which brought the Tribune credibility while also funding its early operations. Joel Kramer, co-founder of *MinnPost*, said aspiring news entrepreneurs often focus entirely on the journalism, underestimating how important it is to recruit local business leaders to back their venture. "You do need connections in the community—and I'm talking now about business, revenue-side connections, not journalism connections," Kramer said.

### Persuade existing members to give more.

Once your news organization has established a track record, your next major donor may come from your own membership roster. The Tribune makes a habit of identifying existing members who may be willing to move up to a major donation. "We're developing a donor base, and we'll move those people down the line," Gilburg said. "From their earliest contribution, the connection deepens."

### Use donations to develop long-term sustainability.

Philanthropic donations probably always will constitute at least some part of the revenue mix for nonprofit news. But ideally, each grant or donation can help a news organization build business capacity that makes it more self-reliant. "As we got grant money in, we never saw that as a long-term proposition," said Anne Galloway, founder of *VTDigger*. "We saw it as, essentially, like venture capital—a way to get a certain distance with our project to attract a certain number of readers so we could get to a point that we could launch a strong membership campaign and attract enough underwriting to reach a level of sustainability." A grand experiment along these lines is now unfolding in Philadelphia, where newspaper owner Gerry Lenfest gave $20 million in 2016[56] to create a hybrid nonprofit/for-profit structure called the Institute for Journalism in New Media. Lenfest also donated the city's two main newspapers, the *Inquirer* and *Daily News*, to the new nonprofit institute, along with the $20 million in seed money. The goal behind the new structure is to stabilize the papers' finances (for now, anyway) while executives develop strategies for long-term sustainability.

## Supplementary Revenue Streams

In addition to the four central sources of funding for nonprofit news discussed above, a number of supplementary revenue streams also offer promise. Here are three areas where news nonprofits are generating some extra dollars:

## Crowdfunding

When looking to fund specific projects or staff positions, it's worth considering a crowdfunding campaign. During the fall of 2013, the Tribune's inaugural Kickstarter campaign[57]—for equipment to stream live video coverage of the 2014 Texas governor's race—tallied $65,310, plus a matching pledge of $10,000 from the Knight Foundation and another $10,500 in checks. Rodney Gibbs, the Tribune's chief innovation officer, said the campaign succeeded largely because it had a clear, focused call to action that was amplified on social media by employees and supporters. The Tribune turned to crowdfunding again in 2014 and 2015 to raise money for special investigative projects[58] and in 2017 to hire a new "community reporter"[59] to forge relationships with readers across the state.

The more novel the idea, the more likely it is to capture crowdfunders' attention. In 2014, fellow nonprofit *San Francisco Public Press* launched a Kickstarter campaign that more than tripled its original goal of $10,000[60] to expand its citywide network of bicycles to distribute the print edition of its newspaper.

For some digital news startups, crowdfunding has served as the initial spark for a more enduring, membership-driven business model, particularly in international settings. The *Hong Kong Free Press*[61] and Spain's *El Español*[62] both were created in 2015 as a result of successful crowdfunding campaigns that drew tens of thousands of supporters. And *De Correspondent*,[63] an investigative news site based in Amsterdam, launched in 2013 with a record-setting Kickstarter campaign, tallying $1.7 million in thirty days.[64] *De Correspondent* now boasts more than 50,000 members[65] who pay 6 Euros (roughly $7) per month to directly support a style of news that publisher and co-founder Ernst-Jan Pfauth calls "an antidote to the daily news grind." The site's business model is completely ad-free, which Pfauth says is liberating:[66] "Instead of viewing members as target groups for advertising, we can focus on serving our readers' interests. Instead of starting ad-heavy sections like travel and career, we can make editorial judgments based solely on the importance of a subject. Rather than hunting for page views, we hunt for great stories."

*De Correspondent* is a for-profit venture—it caps profits at 5 percent, reinvesting the remaining

95 percent back into its journalism—but its ability to convert an initial crowdfunding campaign into a thriving community of members[67] has drawn considerable interest from the nonprofit world. The site, which plans to expand into the United States in 2018, is working with New York University journalism professor Jay Rosen on a public research project[68] to develop and share best practices for news membership models. "The Correspondent knows things that local, nonprofit and specialized news sites in the U.S. can benefit from as they turn to readers to support them," Rosen wrote[69] in *Nieman Journalism Lab*. One of these lessons, international editor Maaike Goslinga told me, is that building trust with members can serve as its own "currency" to support journalism. "I'm not saying that *De Correspondent* has all the truths or that everyone should have our model," Goslinga said. "But we can sense that a lot of people read us because they trust us." The crowdfunded model, Goslinga said, builds trust with readers because "you are free from the pressure of corporate donors—and that means that you, as the journalist, have the complete freedom to write whatever you want, because we're not dependent on clicks."[70]

That degree of journalistic independence appeals to Kevin Smit, a 20-year-old Dutch college student studying biotechnology. Smit signed up for a monthly *De Correspondent* membership in June 2017 after following the site on Facebook for more than a year. "It's real journalism, like it's supposed to be," Smit told me, recalling several of the site's investigations, including an in-depth video analyzing the debt of the Dutch government. Smit said *De Correspondent*'s business model is, in fact, a major reason he has grown to trust the site. "How they're formed through crowdfunding means that you don't have one interest—you don't have that lobby, or this company supporting you," he said. "It's people paying 6 Euros a month for the articles."

## Syndication and Partnerships with Newsrooms and Universities

For four years, *The Texas Tribune* shared content with *The New York Times* as part of a syndication deal that brought in several hundred thousand dollars. That collaboration with the Times ended in 2014,[71] but the Tribune also has other syndication clients, including a textbook publisher. (The site's daily news content is offered for free to news organizations throughout Texas.)

The California-based *Center for Investigative Reporting* charges a yearly flat fee for the rights to republish its stories and videos. But when it comes to particular projects, syndication fees are determined according to a sliding scale based on audience size, platforms used (print, TV, online) and whether a syndication partner contributed editorial resources. "We have to kind of tailor it to the partner," said Meghann Farnsworth, *CIR*'s former director of distribution and engagement.

For news nonprofits with limited audiences, partnerships with commercial newsrooms can broaden the reach of their reporting while also generating revenue. *Investigative Post*, a nonprofit in western New York state, produces stories for Buffalo TV station WGRZ-TV in exchange for an annual fee ranging between $50,000 and $100,000, according to a 2017 report[72] published by the American Press Institute. As *Nieman Journalism Lab*[73] explains, partnerships like these "benefit both sides: The commercial publishers get expert reporting in specific areas that they don't have time to devote resources to in their own newsrooms, while the nonprofits get extended reach for their work (and, hopefully, money, too)."

Creative partnerships with public media organizations and universities also can help save money for news nonprofits. In San Diego, *inewsource*, an investigative news nonprofit, shares office space and resources with the *KPBS* newsroom on the campus of San Diego State University. In exchange, *inewsource* provides *KPBS* with news content but remains independent. "We operate as a self-standing investigative unit," editor Lorie Hearn told me in 2014. Such arrangements can invite scrutiny, however — in 2015, after *inewsource* published a series of investigative stories about a local attorney, a group affiliated with the attorney filed a lawsuit challenging the lease agreement between i*newsource*, *KPBS* and the university. The suit was dismissed,[74] but the episode highlighted the risk that a school can assume when allowing a news organization to operate on campus. Unflattering coverage of the host university can trigger tensions as well: In 2014, *The Lens*, a news nonprofit in New Orleans, lost its offices[75] at Loyola University after publishing a story critical of Loyola's president.

## Conclusion: Operating as a Mission-Driven Business

During the year I spent at *The Texas Tribune*, I found that in many ways it functions much like any metropolitan newsroom: Reporters spar on the phone with state agencies over public records requests, interns hustle to churn out quick daily stories, editors bug reporters about deadlines while shuffling between meetings.

But perhaps more than any other nonprofit news startup, the Tribune aggressively and unapologetically operates at all levels as a mission-driven business.[76] News, art, and tech staffers are mindful that their livelihoods depend on successful events and membership drives, so they actively promote the Tribune in person and on social media. Business staffers tout the Tribune's editorial content when making their pitch to potential sponsors, donors, and members. It's a bold, self-promotional mindset that sometimes borders on overconfidence, but it stems from an understanding throughout the organization that, ultimately, the Tribune needs more revenue to stay in business and carry out its public-interest mission.

This shared sense of purpose is important, because digital news startups need proactive financial strategies if they hope to survive. Another nonprofit news startup, the *Chicago News Cooperative*, shut down operations in 2012—partly because it failed to develop business capacity that could sustain its excellent journalism. "I think that was one of my mistakes, was not to invest in business management," editor and founder James O'Shea told me[77] in an interview, candidly admitting that he had overspent on journalism. "We've come to a point in journalism where the business side and the editorial side are much more 'one' than they used to be," O'Shea continued. "Journalists have kind of got to get with it and understand that, and begin practicing that and exercising their judgment in a way that really makes sure that if it's going to be done, it's done right and it's done under sound journalistic principles."

The same year O'Shea shut down his newsroom in Chicago, another high-profile experiment in nonprofit journalism — *The Bay Citizen* in San Francisco — merged with the *Center for Investigative Reporting*[78] after failing to build a sustainable business model despite an initial $5 million in startup funding from investment banker Warren Hellman.

For decades during the era of legacy media, the traditional church/state separation between editorial and business departments allowed journalists to insulate themselves from the financial realities of their profession. Today's news nonprofits cannot afford to subscribe to that worldview. They must, of course, behave transparently and ethically to maintain trust with the public. But by operating as mission-driven businesses, news nonprofits can enjoy the benefits of philanthropic support while simultaneously building out a diverse array of self-sufficient revenue streams that will ensure their long-term survival.

## Bibliography and Additional Resources

- 4 Lessons from the Launch of the News Revenue Hub[79]
- How News Partnerships Work: Commercial and Nonprofit Newsrooms Can Work Together to Benefit and Change Journalism[80]
- Lone Star Trailblazer: Will The Texas Tribune Transform Texas Journalism?[81]
- NewsBiz: Tracking Best Practices in the Business of Digital News[82]
- Texas Tribune Fellowship blog archives[83]
- Sustainable Strategies: Lessons From a Year at The Texas Tribune[84]
- Rethinking Philanthropy to Support Local News[85]
- 25 Ideas Nonprofit Newsrooms Can't Afford to Ignore[86]
- Institute for Nonprofit News Community Journalism Executive Training (CJET) online courses[87]
- Finding a Foothold: How Nonprofit News Ventures Seek Sustainability[88]
- Gaining Ground: How Nonprofit News Ventures Seek Sustainability[89]
- The Pleasure and Pain of Going Nonprofit[90]
- The Best Strategies for Generating Revenue Through Events[91]
- Nonprofit Journalism: A Growing but Fragile Part of the U.S. News System[92]

*Jake Batsell is an associate professor at Southern Methodist University's Division of Journalism in Dallas, where he teaches digital journalism and media entrepreneurship. His book, "Engaged Journalism: Connecting with Digitally Empowered News Audiences" (Columbia University Press, 2015) was one of three national finalists for the Tankard Book Award administered by the Association for Education in Journalism and Mass Communication. Reach him on Twitter at @jbatsell.*

## Leave feedback on this chapter.

## Notes

1. Jake Batsell, "Earning Their Keep," John S. and James L. Knight Foundation, April 2015, https://s3.amazonaws.com/kf-site-legacy-media/feature_assets/www/nonprofitnews-2015/pdfs/KF-NonprofitNews2015-Tribune.pdf.

2. "State of the News Media, 2016," *Pew Research Center,* June 15, 2016, http://assets.pewresearch.org/wp-content/uploads/sites/13/2016/06/30143308/state-of-the-news-media-report-2016-final.pdf.

3. *Institute for Nonprofit News,* https://inn.org/.

4. Nicholas Fandos, "Nonprofit Journalism Groups are Gearing up with Flood of Donations," *The New York Times,* December 7, 2016, https://www.nytimes.com/2016/12/07/business/media/nonprofit-journalism-groups-are-gearing-up-with-flood-of-donations.html?_r=1.

5. Mike Scutari, "It's Official: Donald Trump is the Best Thing That's Ever Happened to Nonprofit Journalism," *Inside Philanthropy,* March 30, 2017, https://www.insidephilanthropy.com/home/2017/3/30/trump-bump-an-vocal-opponents-foundations-give-nonprofit-journalism-a-boost.

6. U.S. law specifies eight specific purposes worthy of 501(c)(3) designation: religious, charitable, scientific, public safety testing, literary, educational, amateur sports and prevention of cruelty to children and animals. News nonprofits usually aim to convince the IRS that they fulfill an educational purpose by disseminating accurate, verifiable news content to the public. See Jeffrey P. Hermes, "Guide to the Internal Revenue Service Decision-Making Process Under Section 501(c)(3) for Journalism and Publishing Non-Profit Organizations," Berkman Center for Internet & Society, Harvard University, April 2012.

7. An earlier version of this chapter was published as "Earning Their Keep: Revenue Strategies From *The Texas Tribune* and Other Nonprofit News Startups," *Knight Foundation,* April 2015. The author has updated the current version with new information while editing for content and focus. Published with permission.

8. Jodi Enda, Katerina Eva Matsa and Jan Lauren Boyles, "America's Shifting Statehouse Press," *Pew Research Center,* July 10, 2014, http://www.journalism.org/2014/07/10/americas-shifting-statehouse-press/.

9. "T-Squared: Texas Tribune and ProPublica Win a Peabody," *The Texas Tribune,* April 25, 2017, https://www.texastribune.org/2017/04/25/t-squared-texas-tribune-and-propublica-win-peabod/.

10. Evans Smith, "T-Squared: Griggs, Batsell Will Be Tribune Fellows," *The Texas Tribune,* July 9, 2013, https://www.texastribune.org/2013/07/09/t-squared-introducing-our-tribune-fellows/.

11. Fiscal sponsorships also carry their own risk, both for sponsoring organizations and for fledgling nonprofits. See Rick Cohen, "Vanishing Act: Activist Groups Say Donations Disappeared with Fiscal Sponsor," *Nonprofit Quarterly,* February 3, 2012, https://nonprofitquarterly.org/2012/02/03/vanishing-act-activist-groups-say-donations-disappeared-with-fiscal-sponsor/; and Gene

Tagaki, "Fiscal Sponsorship: A Balanced Overview," *Nonprofit Quarterly*, January 19, 2016, https://nonprofitquarterly.org/2016/01/19/fiscal-sponsorship-a-balanced-overview/.

12. "Grants to Texas Tribune Support Online Journalism Launch," *Knight Foundation*, October 1, 2009, https://www.knightfoundation.org/press/releases/grants-to-texas-tribune-support-online-journalism.

13. Revenue figures cited in this chapter are drawn from internal budget comparisons used by Tribune managers to track year-by-year trends in revenue growth. These internal figures should not be confused with yearly financial reports to the IRS, also known as a Form 990, which are prepared according to Generally Accepted Accounting Principles (GAAP). The Tribune's internal figures deliberately exclude revenue associated with a large one-time foundation grant — for example, the Knight Foundation's $1.5 million grant to the Tribune in 2013 — in the interest of providing consistent ongoing comparisons to previous years.

14. Evan Smith, "T-Squared: TribuneFest by the Numbers," *The Texas Tribune*, October 7, 2013, https://www.texastribune.org/2013/10/07/t-squared-tribunefest-numbers/.

15. "The Texas Tribune: Corporate Sponsors," *The Texas Tribune*, https://www.texastribune.org/support-us/corporate-sponsors/.

16. Jim Moore, "The Trouble With the Trib," *Texas to the World*, February 16, 2014, http://www.texastotheworld.com/the-trouble-with-the-trib/.

17. "Jim Moore Calls For The Texas Tribune to Distance Itself From Funders," *Texas Observer*, http://www.texasobserver.org/close-comfort/.

18. Emily Ramshaw, "T-Squared: Trib Transparency, Continued," *The Texas Tribune*, February 28, 2014, https://www.texastribune.org/2014/02/28/t-squared-ethics-and-us/.

19. Emily Ramshaw, "T-Squared: Amanda Zamora is our Chief Audience Officer," *The Texas Tribune*, April 29, 2016, https://www.texastribune.org/2014/02/28/t-squared-ethics-and-us/.

20. *TribTalk*, https://www.tribtalk.org/.

21. Jake Batsell, "Lone Star Trailblazer," *Columbia Journalism Review*, July / August 2010, http://archives.cjr.org/feature/lone_star_trailblazer.php?page=all.

22. "Media Kit." *The Texas Tribune*, https://mediakit.texastribune.org/.

23. *TribTalk*, https://www.tribtalk.org/.

24. This portion of the chapter draws extensively from my *Texas Tribune* fellowship blog, *NewsBiz: Tracking Best Practices in the Business of Digital News*, in addition to more recent updates. The original, more detailed accounts of many of these strategies can be viewed in full at http://news-biz.org.

25. Katie Hawkins-Gaar and Ren LaForme, "25 Ideas Nonprofit Newsrooms Can't Afford to Ignore," *Poynter*. January 19, 2016, https://www.poynter.org/2016/25-ideas-nonprofit-newsrooms-cant-afford-to-ignore/391655/.

26. Jake Batsell, "Want an INNovation Fund Grant? Know Thy Audience," *NewsBiz*, http://news-biz.org/post/75146337062/want-an-innovation-fund-grant-know-thy-audience.

27. "The Texas Tribune: Corporate Sponsors," *The Texas Tribune*, https://www.texastribune.org/support-us/corporate-sponsors/.

28. Jake Batsell, "Corporate Sponsorships Fuel Revenue Growth at VTDigger," *NewsBiz*, http://news-biz.org/post/65689709104/corporate-sponsorships-fuel-revenue-growth-at.

29. *Voice of San Diego*, http://www.voiceofsandiego.org/.

30. Jake Batsell. "How Nonprofit News Outlets Approach Native Advertising," *NewsBiz*, http://news-biz.org/post/88677720443/how-nonprofit-news-outlets-approach-native.

31. "Partner Voices," *Voice of San Diego*, http://voiceofsandiego.org/partner-voices/.

32. Jeff Sonderman and Millie Tran, "Understanding the Rise of Sponsored Content," *American Press Institute*, https://www.americanpressinstitute.org/publications/reports/white-papers/understanding-rise-sponsored-content/.

33. Paid Placement, *TribTalk*, https://www.tribtalk.org/paid-placement/.

34. *Institute for Nonprofit News*, http://investigativenewsnetwork.org/.

35. Justin Ellis, "What Makes the Texas Tribune's Event Business so Successful?" *NiemanLab*, September 27, 2013, http://www.niemanlab.org/2013/09/what-makes-the-texas-tribunes-event-business-so-successful.

36. Jake Batsell, "Brass Tacks: Putting on Your First News Event," *NewsBiz*, http://news-biz.org/post/62161508693/brass-tacks-putting-on-your-first-news-event.

37. "The Texas Tribune Festival," *The Texas Tribune*, https://www.texastribune.org/festival/.

38. *NJ Spotlight*, http://www.njspotlight.com/.

39. "Roundtables," *NJ Spotlight*, http://www.njspotlight.com/roundtables/

40. Jake Batsell, "Turning 'Brand Equity' Into Earned Revenue at NJ Spotlight," *NewsBiz*, http://news-biz.org/post/69014211770/turning-brand-equity-into-earned-revenue-at-nj.

41. "Sponsored Webinars," *NJ Spotlight*, http://www.njspotlight.com/webinars/.

42. *MinnPost*, https://www.minnpost.com/.

43. "MinnRoast 2017," *MinnPost*, https://www.minnpost.com/inside-minnpost/2016/03/minnroast-2017.

44. Jake Batsell, "Monetizing the Fun Factor: How Upbeat Events Can Build Engagement and Boost the Bottom Line," *NewsBiz*, http://news-biz.org/post/84435323853/monetizing-the-fun-factor-how-upbeat-events-can.

45. Jake Batsell, "Brass Tacks: Strategies for Building a Strong Membership Base." *NewsBiz*, http://news-biz.org/post/73606745994/brass-tacks-strategies-for-building-a-strong.

46. "Membership," *Investigate West*, http://invw.org/membership/.

47. Jake Batsell, "Brass Tacks: Strategies for Building a Strong Membership Base," *NewsBiz*, http://news-biz.org/post/73606745994/brass-tacks-strategies-for-building-a-strong.

48. Jason Alcorn, "4 Lessons from the Launch of the News Revenue Hub," *Medium*, https://medium.com/@jasonalcorn/4-lessons-from-the-launch-of-the-news-revenue-hub-56c20570e8e9.

49. Naomi Schalit, "Presentation: #INNDay14 - Maine Center for Public Interest Reporting," *SlideShare*, June 23, 2014, https://www.slideshare.net/jbatsell/innday14-maine-center-for-public-interest-reporting-36206682.

50. Jason Alcorn, "4 Lessons from the Launch of the News Revenue Hub," *Medium*, https://medium.com/@jasonalcorn/4-lessons-from-the-launch-of-the-news-revenue-hub-56c20570e8e9.

51. "The Texas Tribune's Membership Program," *The Texas Tribune*, https://support.texastribune.org/.

52. Jason Alcorn, "4 Lessons from the Launch of the News Revenue Hub," *Medium*, https://medium.com/@jasonalcorn/4-lessons-from-the-launch-of-the-news-revenue-hub-56c20570e8e9.

53. Scott Lewis, "Voice of San Diego to Spin Off New Organization to Support Good Journalism Everywhere," *Voice of San Diego*, May 19, 2017, http://www.voiceofsandiego.org/topics/news/voice-of-san-diego-to-spin-off-new-organization-to-support-good-journalism-everywhere/.

54. Shelley Hepworth, Carlett Spike, Pete Vernon and Evan Applegate, "Who Gives to Journalism?" *CJR*, May 2017, https://cdn.cjr.org/wp-content/uploads/2017/05/funders2.png.

55. Molly de Aguiar and Josh Stearns, "Rethinking Philanthropy to Support Local News," *Local News Lab*, February 5, 2016, http://localnewslab.org/2016/02/05/rethinking-philanthropy-to-support-local-news/.

56. Jonathan Sotsky, "Could it be Sunny in Philadelphia? A New Report Explores Early Insights from the City's New Journalism Model," *Knight Foundation*, June 15, 2016, https://www.knightfoundation.org/articles/could-it-be-sunny-philadelphia-new-report-explores-early-insights-citys-new-journalism-model.

57. Jake Batsell, "Brass Tacks: Strategies for Your First Kickstarter Campaign," *NewsBiz*, http://news-biz.org/post/64527493737/brass-tacks-strategies-for-your-first-kickstarter.

58. Emily Ramshaw, "T-Squared: We're Crowdfunding Another Crucial Series," *The Texas Tribune*, February 9, 2015, https://www.texastribune.org/2015/02/09/t-squared-crowdfunding-crucial-series/.

59. "Help Us Hire our First-Ever Community Reporter," *The Texas Tribune*, https://www.texastribune.org/community-reporter-crowdfund/.

60. Lila LaHood, "Thanks to Our 1,016 Favorite People, We Got Our $10K Match!" *San Francisco Public Press*, July 2, 2014, http://sfpublicpress.org/blog/2014-07/thanks-to-our-1016-favorite-people-we-got-our-10k-match.

61. Ilaria Maria Sala, "Hong Kong to Get New Crowdfunded Independent Newspaper," *The Guardian*, May 20, 2015, https://www.theguardian.com/world/2015/may/20/hong-kong-to-get-new-crowdfunded-independent-newspaper.

62. Shan Wang, "Spanish News Startup El Español Carves Out a New Digital Space While Competing With Legacy Media," *NiemanLab*, October 29, 2015, http://www.niemanlab.org/2015/10/spanish-news-startup-el-espanol-carves-out-a-new-digital-space-while-competing-with-legacy-media/?relatedstory.

63. *De Correspondent*, https://thecorrespondent.com/.

64. Ernst-Jan Pfauth, "How we Turned a World Record in Journalism Crowd-funding Into an Actual Publication," *Medium,* November 27, 2013, https://medium.com/de-correspondent/how-we-turned-a-world-record-in-journalism-crowd-funding-into-an-actual-publication-2a06e298afe1.

65. Ernst-Jan Pfauth, "De Correspondent Now Has 50,000 Paying Members," *Medium,* January 23, 2017, https://medium.com/de-correspondent/de-correspondent-50k-members-59d1005ec9d3.

66. Ernst-Jan Pfauth, "Selling Ads is a Short-term Strategy. Here's Why Subscriptions Are the Future of Journalism," *Media Newsletter*, December 21, 2015, https://medianewsletter.net/selling-ads-is-a-short-term-strategy-here-s-why-subscriptions-are-the-future-of-journalism-6721226d52ca.

67. Jay Rosen, "Why Become a Member? This is What Readers of De Correspondent Had to Say," *The Membership Puzzle Project,* April 5, 2017, https://membershippuzzle.org/articles-overview/2017/4/3/why-readers-become-members-and-contribute-their-knowledge-to-the-correspondent.

68. *The Membership Puzzle Project*, https://membershippuzzle.org/about/.

69. Jay Rosen, "Jay Rosen: This Is What a News Organization Built on Reader Trust Looks Like," *NiemanLab*, March 28, 2017, http://www.niemanlab.org/2017/03/jay-rosen-this-is-what-a-news-organization-built-on-reader-trust-looks-like/.

70. *De Correspondent* also earns revenue through syndication, a speakers bureau, book publishing, grants, and extra donations from members beyond the standard membership fee. Even wildly successful crowdfunding campaigns eventually must evolve into a balanced business model with multiple revenue streams.

71. Evan Smith, "T-Squared: Trib, Times Will End Partnership," *The Texas Tribune*, October 31, 2014, https://www.texastribune.org/2014/10/31/t-squared-trib-times-will-end-partnership/.

72. Jason Alcorn. "How News Partnerships Work: Commercial and Nonprofit Newsrooms Can Work Together to Benefit and Change Journalism," *American Press Institute*, https://www.americanpressinstitute.org/publications/reports/strategy-studies/commercial-nonprofit-partnerships/.

73. Laura Hazard Owen, "'Won't Work for Exposure': The Financial Nitty-gritty of Commercial—Nonprofit News Partnerships," *NiemanLab*, May 18, 2017, http://www.niemanlab.org/2017/05/wont-work-for-exposure-the-financial-nitty-gritty-of-commercial-nonprofit-news-partnerships/.

74. Chris Young, "Judge Dismisses Lawsuit Against inewsource, San Diego State," http://www.kpbs.org/news/2015/sep/09/judge-dismisses-lawsuit-against-inewsource-san-die/.

75. "The Lens Criticizes Loyola Head, Loses Offices; and Other Area Political Notes," *The Advocate*, http://www.theadvocate.com/new_orleans/news/politics/article_3db0f3dd-ee5f-5a3f-9cab-e066342097b4.html.

76. Kevin Davis, "News Outlets Must Balance Capacity, Growth of New Revenue," *Knight Foundation*, November 14, 2013, https://www.knightfoundation.org/articles/news-nonprofits-must-balance-capacity-growth-new-revenue.

77. Jake Batsell, "Q&A With James O'Shea: Lessons From the Chicago News Cooperative," *NewsBiz*, http://news-biz.org/post/67379917415/qa-with-james-oshea-lessons-from-the-chicago.

78. "The Bay Citizen," *Nieman Journalism Lab Encyclo*, http://www.niemanlab.org/encyclo/bay-citizen/.

79. Jason Alcorn, "4 Lessons from the Launch of the News Revenue Hub," *Medium*, March 28, 2017, https://medium.com/@jasonalcorn/4-lessons-from-the-launch-of-the-news-revenue-hub-56c20570e8e9 .

80. Jason Alcorn, "How News Partnerships Work: Commercial and Nonprofit Newsrooms Can Work Together to Benefit and Change Journalism," *American Press Institute*, May 18, 2017, https://www.americanpressinstitute.org/publications/reports/strategy-studies/commercial-nonprofit-partnerships/.

81. Jake Batsell, "Lone Star Trailblazer: Will The Texas Tribune Transform Texas Journalism?" *Columbia Journalism Review*, July/August 2010, 39-43.  http://archives.cjr.org/feature/lone_star_trailblazer.php.

82. Jake Batsell, "NewsBiz: Tracking Best Practices in the Business of Digital News," http://news-biz.org/.

83. Texas Tribune Fellowship blog archives, available at http://news-biz.org.

84. Jake Batsell, "Sustainable Strategies: Lessons From a Year at The Texas Tribune," *Knight Foundation blog*, April 8, 2015, https://knightfoundation.org/articles/sustainable-strategies-lessons-year-texas-tribune

85. Molly de Aguiar and Josh Stearns, "Rethinking Philanthropy to Support Local News," *Local News Lab*, Geraldine R. Dodge Foundation/Democracy Fund, February 6, 2016. https://knightfoundation.org/articles/sustainable-strategies-lessons-year-texas-tribune

86. Katie Hawkins-Gaar and Ren LaForme, "25 Ideas Nonprofit Newsrooms Can't Afford to Ignore," *The Poynter Institute*, January 19, 2016, https://www.poynter.org/2016/25-ideas-nonprofit-newsrooms-cant-afford-to-ignore/391655/

87. Institute for Nonprofit News Community Journalism Executive Training (CJET) online courses, available at http://learn.inn.org.

88. Knight Foundation, "Finding a Foothold: How Nonprofit News Ventures Seek Sustainability," October 2013, https://knightfoundation.org/features/nonprofitnews.

89. Knight Foundation, "Gaining Ground: How Nonprofit News Ventures Seek Sustainability," April 2015. https://www.knightfoundation.org/features/nonprofitnews-2015/

90. Deron Lee, "The Pleasure and Pain of Going Nonprofit," *Columbia Journalism Review*, Spring 2017, 54-63. https://www.cjr.org/local_news/nonprofit-news-local-tulsa-frontier.php.

91. Kevin Loker, "The Best Strategies for Generating Revenue Through Events," *American Press*

*Institute* report, August 7, 2014, https://www.americanpressinstitute.org/publications/reports/strategy-studies/events-revenue/.

92. Amy Mitchell, Mark Jurkowitz, Jesse Holcomb, Jodi Enda and Monica Anderson, "Nonprofit Journalism: A Growing but Fragile Part of the U.S. News System," *Pew Research Center* report, June 2013, http://www.journalism.org/2013/06/10/nonprofit-journalism/

# FROM THE FIELD: THE KNOXVILLE EXPERIMENT

*Coury Turczyn*

## The Knoxville Experiment: A Footnote to Nonprofit Journalism

Attempting to launch a newspaper in the 21st century must be an awful lot like what entrepreneurs experienced starting up steam-powered-car companies[1] in the 20th—the product may still work, and even offer a few nice advantages, but it's not what most customers want anymore. So, being at odds with consumer trends (and, ultimately, the course of history), you're most likely doomed to failure. Why, then, did a small group of editors defy all logic with their 2015 launch of the *Knoxville Mercury*?

Well, not unlike those belated pioneers, we had a lot of passion for a crazy idea: Let's publish a newspaper owned by a 501(c)(3) nonprofit—that way, it would earn revenue with traditional advertising, but could also potentially benefit from tax-deductible donations to its parent organization. With two distinct revenue streams, we might just be able to pull off the anachronistic act of printing a weekly paper in the smartphone era.

Why even bother, you ask? That requires a little background: When the E.W. Scripps Company planned its merger[2] with Journal Communications in 2014 (creating the Journal Media Group, a publisher of newspapers that would in turn be sold off to Gannett[3] two years later), it decided against including one of its smaller, meagerly profitable properties: Knoxville, Tenn.'s *Metro Pulse*. Acquired by Scripps in 2007, the previously independent alt weekly had a steady client base of local businesses, particularly in arts, entertainment, and dining (not to mention multiple national awards for its stories and design). But Scripps' accountants did not deem the publication worth all the trouble of continuing under the new corporate scheme, so after 23 years *Metro Pulse*, along with its employees, suddenly got the ax.

Yet the paper's readers still existed, and they wanted it back. Furthermore, some of them were willing to pay to see a new publication launched—including a few large donors who specifically wanted it in print. So, the funds to start a newspaper were available—but how to sustain it once it was up and running? Everyone knows that print advertising is in a death spiral.[4] Meanwhile, the nonprofit models for journalism consist mostly of news-only websites—but our readers also wanted us to continue the alt-weekly staples of arts and entertainment coverage, plus opinion and comics and puzzles. Neither direction alone would appear likely to generate enough income to keep a weekly newspaper in business. But what if we combined them?

Thus, three of us former *Metro Pulse* editors decided to take a crack at devising a hybrid nonprofit model:[5] a taxable, not-for-profit publication owned by a local 501(c)(3) educational nonprofit called the Knoxville History Project.[6] (Not having to report to a disinterested, out-of-state corporate manager would be an added bonus.)

While unusual, this is not a completely unheard-of arrangement. *Smithsonian* magazine, for example, is part of Smithsonian Enterprises, which is a nonprofit division of the Smithsonian Institution. The nonprofit Poynter Institute, a journalism school, owns the *Tampa Bay Times* in Florida. However, those are both longstanding nonprofits that later started or acquired those subsidiaries; we were starting both entities at the same time, a more complicated process. Nevertheless, armed with an experienced tax lawyer and lots of paperwork, we were able to win the approval of the Internal Revenue Service.

We began our endeavor with a Kickstarter campaign[7] in December 2014 that raised over $60,000 for the paper's launch. Combined with larger private donations and other fundraisers, the paper began publishing in March 2015—and our plan for the future initially hinged on those two main revenue streams.

- Traditional ad sales: nonprofit media can't sell advertising with calls to action (live performances, happy hours, retail sales, etc.), which is the bread and butter of most alt-weekly papers. But by registering as a taxable not-for-profit with the state of Tennessee, we would be able to sell regular ads rather than just "sponsorships," such as those you hear on public radio. (And, of course, we'd pay tax on the income from those ads.)
- Tax-deductible donations: The educational nonprofit Knoxville History Project was established by former *Metro Pulse* columnist Jack Neely with a mission to research and promote the history of Knoxville. Its primary vehicle to fulfill that mission would be the *Knoxville Mercury*, which would often print columns and articles about Knoxville's history. KHP would launch the paper and help support it financially by taking out full-page educational ads that also presented Knoxville history.

So, the idea was this: We'd sell print and digital ads like any other newspaper, but we'd also make appeals to large donors who wanted to support independent journalism in Knoxville. These may be foundations or individuals who prefer their donations to be tax deductible—in which case, they could make them to the KHP, whose board would in turn decide how to best allocate the funds to the paper. And here's where we came to the tricky parts, a series of catch-22s that made continuing our existence even more difficult than we had expected.

First, the KHP's lawyer determined that only 25 percent of whatever it raised in funding could go to the paper, lest it appear to the IRS that the nonprofit was acting as a "front" for a for-profit business. One solution to that would be to raise a huge amount of money, enough that one-fourth of it would be sufficient to help fund the paper. This did not occur. So, instead, the KHP bought services from the *Mercury*: advertisements.

Second, explaining this ownership arrangement to potential donors was rather complicated: "A 501(c)(3) owns your newspaper?" "Yes, so if you want to make a tax-deductible donation to support the paper, it will have to go through the KHP first, and then its board of directors will decide what to do with it—most probably buying an ad contract with the paper." "Hmmmm...." And trying to describe this relationship in print was even more awkward—we couldn't simply say, "Support the paper with a tax-deductible donation to the KHP" because then it might appear that the nonprofit was just a conduit to the newspaper.

Third, avoiding those nonprofit hoops by asking readers for direct (non-tax-deductible) donations also became complicated. While we were able to spark the passion of readers to start the paper, it became much more difficult to constantly reignite that excitement year after year to continue the paper. Each fundraiser we held collected less money than the one before it. Unlike donating to public radio or TV, giving money to a newspaper is still a new, odd concept for most people, and we never figured out a good way to "normalize" it. (We really needed the services of a professional fundraiser, for which we had no budget; we were editors and designers and ad reps, not development directors.)

Fourth, paying your staff and your freelance contributors reasonable rates will require a good-sized budget if you're attempting to produce a professional, credible news source. (Unfortunately, many of our once-loyal advertisers from *Metro Pulse* opted out of supporting the *Mercury*—more than we expected.) While dropping the paper edition and going all-digital may sound like the easiest way to cut expenses, our printing and distribution bill was actually far less than our payroll. (We had six full-time employees and two part-timers.) And, in our experience, online ads for a niche website in a small market would not come close to paying for much of anything, let alone our payroll.

For two years,[8] we produced an excellent, award-winning local paper—just the sort that every commenter says we need to keep communities engaged in our democratic society. Unfortunately, there were not enough people who wanted to help pay for it. As a hybrid, we were neither fish nor fowl—not exactly a business that would interest investors (since all the profits would go to the KHP), and not exactly a nonprofit that would qualify for most national or regional journalism grants (since we were still a business rather than a nonprofit ourselves).

What's the solution for the industry? News as a for-profit business is becoming more and more difficult,[9] and most nonprofit models are still working themselves out. However, Philadelphia's newspapers have set themselves on a promising direction forward[10]—but it's predicated on finding a very wealthy person with a strong interest in local reporting to fund a multi-million-dollar endowment.

Know any rich people?[11]

*Coury Turczyn* is the former editor of the Knoxville Mercury *(2015-2017).*

**Leave feedback on this sidebar.**

## *Notes*

1. "List of Steam Car Makers," *Wikipedia*, https://en.wikipedia.org/wiki/List_of_steam_car_makers.

2. Michael J. De La Merced, "E.W. Scripps and Journal Communications to Merge, Then Spin Off Newspapers," *The New York Times*, July 31, 2014, https://dealbook.nytimes.com/2014/07/31/e-w-scripps-and-journal-communications-to-merge-then-spin-off-newspapers/.

3. Robert Mclean, "Gannett to Purchase Journal Media Group," *CNN*, October 8, 2015, http://money.cnn.com/2015/10/08/media/gannett-buying-journal-media-group/index.html.

4. "Newspapers' Circulation Revenue Climbs Steadily Even as Advertising Declines," *Pew Research Center*, May 31, 2017, http://www.pewresearch.org/fact-tank/2017/06/01/circulation-and-revenue-fall-for-newspaper-industry/ft_17-05-25_newspapers_revenue3/.

5. Tamar Wilner, "Laid-off Metro Pulse Editors Plan a New Publication in Knoxville," Columbia Journalism Review, December 12, 2014, https://www.cjr.org/local_news/knoxville_mercury_metro_pulse.php.

6. *Knoxville History Project*, http://knoxvillehistoryproject.org/,

7. "Knoxville Mercury Launch," *Kickstarter*, https://www.kickstarter.com/projects/789676771/knoxville-mercury-launch.

8. Knoxville Mercury, *issuu*, https://issuu.com/knoxvillemercury.

9. Michael Barthel, "Despite Subscription Surges for Largest U.S. Newspapers, Circulation and Revenue Fall for Industry Overall," *Pew Research Center,* http://www.pewresearch.org/fact-tank/2017/06/01/circulation-and-revenue-fall-for-newspaper-industry/.

10. Robinson Meyer, "Will More Newspapers Go Nonprofit?" January 14, 2016, https://www.theatlantic.com/technology/archive/2016/01/newspapers-philadelphia-inquirer-daily-news-nonprofit-lol-taxes/423960/.

11. Ed note: Having a wealthy owner doesn't guarantee success for a media outlet either. See William D. Cohan, "Journalism's Broken Business Model," The New Yorker, October 19, 2017, https://www.newyorker.com/news/news-desk/journalisms-broken-business-model-wont-be-solved-by-billionaires.

# EXERCISE: BEING A MEDIA NONPROFIT

## EXERCISE: BEING A MEDIA NONPROFIT

Learn more about the real-life logistics of being a media nonprofit.

One of the most common questions students have about nonprofit models is how they are different from a for-profit company. In both cases, an organization needs to make more in revenue than it spends. However, there are differences in that:

- The organization's mission and purpose are more important than profit.
- Ownership and leadership are different. (Unlike a business, no private person can own a nonprofit–they are led by a board of trustees or board of directors.)
- Any excess income at a nonprofit is not distributed to shareholders or owners, but rather reinvested in the organization's operation.
- When a nonprofit is a 501(c)(3), it may be exempt from certain taxes and it may also offer its donors the opportunity to make tax-deductible donations.
- A 501(c)(3) can't attempt to influence legislation or political campaigns.

*The Balance* does a great job of answering the question "How Is a Nonprofit Different from a For-Profit Business?"[1]

To learn more, read the IRS' requirements[2] in order for an organization to be tax-exempt as a 501(c)(3).

Then, pick a nonprofit news organization. Locate its 990, a public form nonprofits must file annually. (Guidestar[3] is one place to search for 990s.)

What does the organization's 990 tell you about their annual revenue and expenditures?

### For Instructors

Bring a media nonprofit founder into your class.

Have students interview them and complete a profile of the nonprofit explaining their revenue sources and budget.

*Thanks to the community of practice teaching Media Innovation & Entrepreneurship for these exercise suggestions.*

## Leave feedback on this sidebar.

## Notes

1. Joanne Fritz, "How is a Nonprofit Different from a For-Profit Business," *The Balance*, April 3, 2017, https://www.thebalance.com/how-is-a-nonprofit-different-from-for-profit-business-2502472.

2. "Exemption Requirements Section 501(c)(3) Organizations," *IRS.gov*, https://www.irs.gov/charities-non-profits/charitable-organizations/exemption-requirements-section-501c3-organizations.

3. *Guidestar*, http://www.guidestar.org/search.

# FREELANCING AS ENTREPRENEURSHIP AND CONSULTING AS BUSINESS MODELS

by Elizabeth Mays

## Summary

You don't have to create your own media outlet or technology company to be an entrepreneur in the journalism or communications space. You may want to sell your own services on a contractual basis to companies who need them.

Being a freelancer means you are responsible for marketing your services, finding clients, providing your services to them, billing them, and reporting on your activities to tax and governing bodies.

This chapter will talk more about the ups and downs of life as a freelance journalist or content producer, and how to navigate them.

### Learning Objectives

- Understand what it means to be a solopreneur-style consultant and how this is different from other models of entrepreneurship.
- Know steps you will typically need to take to set up your own business.
- Discover how to create value and exchange it for income.
- Learn how to market, price, and sell your services.
- Understand the downsides and risks to earning your income as a freelancer and learn ways to mitigate these, including bootstrapping a side hustle as a route to eventual full-time entrepreneurship.
- Get a sense of the day-to-day freelance lifestyle in firsthand perspectives from freelancers in the media and communications industry.

# Inside this Chapter

- Freelancing as Entrepreneurship and Consulting as Business Models
- From the Field: How to Get and Keep Gigs as a Freelance Journalist, by Georgann Yara
- From the Field: How I Ditched the 9 to 5 and Built a Business I Could Live With, by Lori Benjamin

*Elizabeth Mays' clients include the Canadian nonprofit the Rebus Foundation, software company Pressbooks and others. She is also an adjunct professor at the Walter Cronkite School of Journalism and Mass Communication who has taught audience acquisition, business and future of journalism, and editing. Reach her on Twitter at @theeditress.*

# FREELANCING AS ENTREPRENEURSHIP AND CONSULTING AS BUSINESS MODELS

*Elizabeth Mays*

*"You're gonna have to serve somebody." —Bob Dylan*

## Introduction

You don't have to create your own media outlet or technology company to be an entrepreneur in the journalism or communications space. You may want to sell your services on a contractual basis to companies who need them. Freelancing is one valid means of entrepreneurship that is ideal for those who don't want the commitment and rigidity of a full-time job, but want to work in the industry on their own terms.

---

### From the Field

#### My Freelancing Story

#### By Elizabeth Mays

When I graduated from grad school, I started my career as a freelance writer and editor, and for three years I did nothing else. My ability to sustain this line of business didn't just happen. I had laid the groundwork before graduating. While I was in grad school, in my spare time between work, school and homework, I sent lots of queries out to magazines (it was the 1990s). Occasionally, an editor would respond: "We're going to use your article, and we're going to pay you this much." I was studying to be an actor, and I had a professor who used to say "If you're working, you're good." I was working, I thought, so I must be good at this writing and editing thing. After graduation, I moved to New York. I was still straddling acting and publishing, until I was struck with a paralyzing health issue on the eve of an audition for "Rent." I was temporarily debilitated. Then, just after I'd recovered, I got a phone call from a New York magazine publisher I had pitched a story to while I was in grad school. "We're going to use your article, and we'll pay you this much," she said. "Oh, and can you do this

---

other story for us too?" In that moment, I knew I was a writer, not an actor. I eventually found some more writing and editing gigs, most of them much less glamorous (including a stint as a certified professional resume writer). Magazine work wasn't all that glamorous either–the jobs I got offered were sometimes 1- to 2-day turnarounds with a dozen interviews to coordinate. But for three years, I did nothing but freelance to earn my income as a sole proprietor. One of the many misconceptions I had about freelancing was the amount of control I would have have over my time. Yes, I got in my share of hikes in wine country. But ultimately, it was essential for me to be working on the client's timeline, and the highest paid jobs went to the earliest bird on call, so I made sure to be the earliest bird on call. Eventually I burnt out and I took my first "real job" in journalism, then another, moving up the ladder until I once again couldn't stand working for someone else anymore. I quit my job days after the crash in the late 2000s to do my own thing. I had once done an eloquent eulogy for a family cat that died, so at the time, I thought I would sell pet eulogies. As you can guess, that didn't pan out. However, that business turned into a successful business that I still own today. Before leaving my job, I had made my preparations and formed the business (an LLC this time) before jumping ship. I easily found my niche in two areas: editing (where there was less competition than in writing) and resume writing (a position that thrives when the economy crashes). Freelancing was a flexible career as I went back to school and earned a second master's degree, which added multimedia and digital media entrepreneurship to my skill set. I was offered a job before I graduated, and ended up in a stable education job for more than six years, during which I quickly realized that I wanted to work for myself again. Although I had a full-time job, I bootstrapped my business as a "side hustle," working four freelance gigs on the side at any one time. I worked nights, weekends and holidays, squirreling away every dollar I could as a cushion to go back out on my own. Finally, one of those gigs turned into a part-time client, with the same client offering me a second gig at a second business. Together, it was enough to venture back on my own. I've gone from sole proprietor to small business corporation, but I'm still a consultant. My next focus will be to figure out a "scalable entrepreneurship" piece of my business: that is, a product that does not rely on me performing a service, but that can be sold without my interference in the transaction. Think classes or books. The goal will be to provide a passive stream of revenue alongside all the consulting I do.

## Rules of Freelancing

I'm often asked how to keep a constant stream of incoming projects as a freelancer. The secret is delivering value. Put yourself in your client's shoes. What do they need from you? In my experience, these are some rules to live by, whatever your niche:

- **Deliver reliably (do what you say you will) on your commitments.**
- **Be on time.**
- **Be thorough, not sloppy.**

- Communicate.
- Don't be a pain in the butt to work with.
- Anticipate your client's needs.

## Creating Value: What's Your USP?

When I was a resume writer, I used to ask people, "What's your magic power?" By this, I meant the thing they did differently and better than everybody else who performed essentially the same work function. For a business, the term for this is "unique selling proposition."[1] A USP explains how your product is different from and hopefully better than the competition's. This is similar to a "unique value proposition,[2] which focuses more on the benefits people receive from working with you. As a freelance consultant, you are your business, and you'll need to figure out the USP or "magic power" that is your service offering. This can be a unique thing that you do, or the way that you do it. For instance, you might be a journalist with a certificate in programming; a broadcaster who knows how to do animated explainer videos; a communicator who specializes in conveying the messaging of clients in a certain industry; or a photographer who does two-hour turnarounds.

Why does anyone buy an iPhone over an Android? A certain brand of cereal or cleaning product over another? Because different brands vary in perceived strengths and weaknesses in the marketplace. You as a professional should have a brand too (and know what it is). To figure this out, do the following exercise.

### Exercise:

Mentally line yourself up alongside your professional colleagues like products on a shelf. Now, why would an employer reach out and choose you instead of them? Why would you choose you? Think about other individuals you know who do what you do professionally, or peers who are graduating from the same classes you took and are entering the same industry. Ask yourself: What do you do differently? Is there a facet of your approach or demeanor, or a specialized skill set you have that makes you more effective? Your USP or "magic power" can be a hard skill, a soft skill or a combination of skills.[3]

## How Freelancing Is Different

When you're a freelancer, you're almost always a consultant–a solopreneur or personal service corporation who takes on gig projects as they come to you. Example: You are a photographer who gets calls from the newspaper whenever a story comes up in your area and they need photos fast.

This doesn't mean you will be a sole proprietorship. You can still set yourself up as a corporation if you want to put another layer of distance between yourself and your business entity. As a company, it can still be just you performing services. In theory, this makes it less likely, albeit not impossible, for someone to sue you for personal assets if they perceive your company has wronged them. Business insurance is another worthwhile step. This is especially relevant if you do something risky. No matter how careful you are, a career in content comes with the potential for someone to accuse you of libel, privacy invasion, copyright violation, errors and omissions, or other hazards. Depending on your personal income situation (as well as whatever is decided in potential legislation on tax reform) being a business could have tax advantages, or if you have the wrong type of business, it could leave you paying higher taxes and/or double-taxed. A CPA and fiduciary are best to guide you through the ramifications and provide advice for your personal situation.

Consulting is the act of performing a service in your expertise in exchange for payment. While you may have expenses, you are generally being paid for your time and services.

This is different from a business in which you manufacture something and sell it to people. But even if you're mainly a consultant, you can still scale your business by adding ongoing streams of revenue that supplement your work for clients. Scalable entrepreneurship means you are creating something once and passively selling it numerous times, with no interference in the transaction. Example: You create a book once and place it into Amazon for sale. Royalties come in and begin to add up. Or, you create a software as a service. The system autobills people for a monthly subscription to use it.

Even a technology startup might still provide consulting services to other companies until it finds firmer footing and has regular SaaS (software-as-a-service) revenue coming in.

## Setting Up Your Business

Regulations vary from state to state, but generally, you will need to fill out some paperwork before you conduct business. This paperwork will vary regionally (check with your local chapter of SCORE or the commerce authority for specific requirements in your state). Here are just a **few** of the items you may need to file:

- A trade name or name you are "doing business as"
- Articles of incorporation
- State sales tax license
- City sales tax license(s)
- Tax licenses in other states where you may have nexus
- Federal EIN application (to get a federal employer identification number)
- Employer unemployment identification number
- Business bank account
- New hire paperwork (sometimes even if you're hiring yourself)

- You may need to publish documents like your articles of incorporation in a local newspaper.
- Professional licenses (for some occupations)
- Proof of insurance (sometimes required to get certain contracts)
- Your state or municipality may have additional requirements

Here is one example of what's necessary to start a business in the state of Arizona.[4][/footnote] There are likely similar resources available from the Commerce Authority, Corporation Commission, or similar governing body for your state.

A sole proprietorship is the simplest business structure, and in some states you don't even have to do any paperwork to become a de facto self-employed sole proprietorship. (Again check your local regulations.)

If you are not a sole proprietorship, you will need to decide on a structure for your business (S corp, LLC, C corp, etc.–see Chapter 6). There are many options to choose from and each has its own headaches and dramatically different ramifications as to the percentage of your revenue that will go to taxes and the legal distance between you and your business. There are tradeoffs on all these counts. I strongly recommend consulting an accountant or lawyer to help with your business formation. (Quality business setup services can run as little as $400-$700.)

If you are not a sole proprietorship, you will need to get an EIN from the federal government. This is an employer identification number that is used for things like corporate tax reporting, payroll and unemployment taxes, and more. You may also need this to set up a business bank account. Having it helps to separate your personal expenses from your business expenses too. Depending on your structure, you may also need to file articles of incorporation, and apply for state and local sales tax licenses in the regions where you do business. Local regulations may require you to have a professional license depending on the nature of your services. And you may need various types of insurance.

Once you're set up, you'll need to track your revenue and expenses and report and remit federal corporate taxes, federal personal taxes, state corporate taxes, state personal taxes, state and municipal sales taxes, federal and state payroll taxes for any employees you may have, and federal and state unemployment taxes. Plus, you'll pay into social security (the taxes the employer usually pays) on the income you receive.

If you don't have time for all this, or the confidence you can manage it accurately, it's wise to enlist an accountant. If you do something wrong as a business owner, you can't blow it off like a missed college assignment. Freelancing brings with it a big level of responsibility, and there can be serious consequences if you're not responsible. The good news is, for all this extra hassle and taxation, when you're your own boss, you are paying for some of the company overhead that is "the cost of doing business." Often, you can deduct legitimate business expenses and reduce the profit that you will pay taxes on. (Again, consult a CPA.)

---

**Exercise**

Research what's involved to legally set up a small business in your state. Produce a to-do list of the required tasks that must be done, in the order they must be completed.

---

## Pricing, Charging and Billing for Your Time

You might think that when you work for yourself, there are no limits to the income you can make. That's not exactly true. If you're the only person at your business, the hours you have available to work are finite. To get your maximum salary, multiply the number of hours you could feasibly work by how much you feasibly bill for those hours.

Do the math and you'll see you can't take on large projects that aren't worth your time. Also keep in mind that every freelance project has an administrative overhead that you may or may not be able to bill the client for. So you have to charge enough to make each hour worth your time.

When you're making those calculations, don't forget that the government could take at least 30% of your profits in taxes (the exact percent depends on your business structure as well as your other personal income–again, consult an accountant). So you may need to set your hourly rate higher than you would at a regular employer.

Here's how to calculate your hourly rate. If in the real world your time would be worth $15/hour, add an extra percentage of that based on the extra taxes you pay for being a self-employed business owner. Then, divide your monthly health insurance costs (which you'll have to pay yourself since you don't have an employer) by the number of hours you work each month to find each hour's portion of health insurance. Then do the same with any other overhead costs you have. Tack all those on to get your hourly rate.

Here is a great infographic[5] that portrays how to calculate your freelance rate. Or, use this calculator[6] to figure out your cost of doing business.

Speaking of billing, don't forget to do it. When I was an in-house magazine and website editor, I often found that I would have to remind freelancers to bill me. They were so busy doing their job as writers that they either forgot to bill me or couldn't find time. Or, they really dreaded billing because it dragged on their creative energies. This can be a recipe for disaster. You never know when the contact you work for within a company might move on, making it more effort for you to remind other people at the company of what you're owed. Don't forget to bill in a timely way!

---

### Exercise

- Figure out your freelance hourly rate, using the methods and calculators above.
- Design an invoice for your mock company.

---

## Contracts for Freelancing

One good way to make sure you get paid for your work, and to clarify expectations and minimize the potential for misunderstanding on either side, is to have a contract. They're a helpful reference point to protect you if something goes sideways–at least you have documentation of what both parties agreed to. If you ask for a contract and a company doesn't want to give you one, they're probably shady. Save your talent for another gig.

A good freelance contract will protect both you and the client. But it will probably be biased to whoever creates it. That's why even though the person commissioning your work will send you a contract in this business, it can be helpful to have your own to offer as an alternative. It's worth it to have a lawyer draft a template you can use repeatedly.

While I'm not a lawyer, I can tell you from experience handling freelance agreements as an editor (and having had my own drafted by a lawyer) that the following points (in addition to others) should generally be among those addressed in your freelance content contract:

- **Scope of Work:** What the work or project is that you're agreeing to, with enough specifics of the expectations to refer to later if there is a dispute. This is often referred to as the "scope of work." It can be helpful if a project runs longer than expected due to client delays, or if the client chooses to grow the project and wants you to do more than originally agreed to. Or if the client sells their company and the new owner suddenly expects you to do something more or different for the same price.
- **Compensation:** How much you'll be paid for the work, when, and how, and whether or not revisions or modifications they ask for are included in the fee, or additional. (Tip: You want them to be additional.) You might also include a clause re. terms for late payment–perhaps you charge interest or a late fee.
- **Independent Contractor Status:** The fact you are an independent contractor, not an employee, that you will pay taxes directly to the government on the income received, and that you have control over the when, where, and how of your work. (This is the employer's way of stating they don't owe you benefits, they won't lend you office space or equipment, they won't withhold taxes, and they don't have to pay employer taxes or insurance like unemployment or worker's compensation on you.) On your end, it gives you lifestyle control (in return for losing all these benefits and paying your own taxes–at a notably higher percentage on self-employment income).

- **Rights:** A contract will generally specify what rights you're selling–if you sell all rights, that means you can't re-release the content you produce somewhere else, whether that's for your own website or for someone else who'll pay you to republish it. And the publisher gets to keep reusing the content in ways that may gain them further revenue. So if you sign away all rights, make sure the fee is worth it. At minimum, you may want an exception that lets you put the work in your own online portfolio. Often you will be selling First North American Serial Rights, which give the publisher the right to be first in publishing your work in North America. Then the copyright reverts back to you.
- **No Infringement:** In the contract, you'll probably have to warrant that you're creating original content that doesn't infringe on anyone else's rights (copyright, etc.). You may also have to certify that you've ensured the information is accurate. Sometimes there will be a clause that says the company will not pay your legal fees if something you send them gets them sued. Sometimes there will be a clause that says you're not responsible. At minimum, it is good to have a clause that indemnifies you if the company edits something in a way that causes legal difficulty for them or you (an inexperienced editor changes something in a way that makes it defamatory, for example or adds a photo they took from the Internet without having the rights). Note that you can be held legally responsible for work you do as a freelancer. You should be extra careful to be accurate and abide by media law and ethics. And you may want to consider errors and omissions insurance depending on the nature of the content you produce.
- **Confidentiality:** You may have to agree to a confidentiality clause.
- **Non-Compete:** Some contracts will have a "non-compete" clause. I tell my students it's almost never worth it to sign one of these as a freelancer, unless it's at a major media brand. As an example, at a magazine I once worked at, most of the writers signed a clause that if they quit or were fired, they would never work at another lifestyle magazine in that metro. That meant if they left the company, they either had to find another profession, or move out of the state to find work. Don't put yourself in this position.
- **Non-payment:** What happens if they don't pay you, or don't pay you in a timely way? It's good to have a clause that reverts any rights to you if this happens so that you can try to sell the work to someone else.

Again, not a lawyer. But as a business owner, these are the bare-minimum things I expect to see in content-related freelance contracts.

## Marketing Yourself as Freelancer

We'll talk more about marketing in a future Chapter, so we won't go too in-depth here. But there are several things you will definitely need in your marketing arsenal as a freelancer:

- Website (You can build something cheap and easy on WordPress.com, or use a platform like Wix, Squarespace, or Weebly.)
- Opt-in (It's critical that people be able to give you their email when they land on your website, so that you can identify and communicate with the people–aka leads–who are potentially interested in your services.)
- Email marketing (You'll need a tool like MailChimp or similar to send emails to your audience.)
- Professional social media presence (People need to be able to research, find and connect with you — the professional you — on Twitter, LinkedIn, Facebook, and other networks.)
- Content marketing (Content could be anything from blog posts to emails to a podcast to YouTube videos or more as long as it's engaging, relevant, and effective at reaching and engaging your target audience.)
- Networking (If you get into freelancing because you don't like to interface with people, well, you may still have to do some of that in order to find clients.) Local industry groups are a low-pressure way to tap into a network if you're not naturally social.

### Ways to Fail at Freelancing

Freelancing isn't right for everyone, and there are plenty of ways to fail at it:

- As a freelancer your income threshold is capped at the number of hours you work times the amount you charge for them. So if you overcommit your hours and fail to deliver, or if you charge too little per hour and fail to bring in the necessary income, that can put you out of business.
- Taking on a bad contract that traps you in a situation that isn't a great deal for you (for instance, a non-compete or an exclusive contract) can be detrimental. Be careful about what you sign.
- Freelancing is the delicate balance of finding work and doing the work. If you spend too much time cultivating potential clients, you won't have time to do the work you have. Likewise if you spend too much time working alone, you won't have time or energy to add to your client roster.
- Every client you take on has an administrative cost. So shoot for steady clients rather than one-time gigs.
- You'll have periods of feast and famine as a consultant and you must be like the fabled ant, not the grasshopper[7] if you want to win the long game. Keep your monthly bills (business and personal) as low as possible and resist the urge to live large.

### Weathering the Lifestyle

You might think that freelancing will give you freedom. And it does, to a certain extent. But even though you're not necessarily out of work if your client fires you, it can be scarier in that you probably won't have the protections of unemployment insurance or a pool of vacation days to cash out for a few months off. If you're sick and can't work, you don't earn income. When you lose a client, you'll have to find a new one to replace them. And that process may or may not be instantaneous. When you're a freelancer, it's critical to have a financial cushion, which will help you weather the periods of feast or famine in freelance work.

The secret to longevity? Stay in it. I once had an acting professor who had had a more successful career than most. One of my friends asked him what the secret was to making it as an actor. His answer? Just stay in it long enough. You can't compete if you don't play. If you want to be a freelancer, stay in it. Your clients will come and go. That's okay. Keep looking for work, doing good work and billing for that work, and you'll be fine.

---

### Exercise

Pretend for a moment that you have no choice but to work for yourself. What would you sell as your product and service? (Tip: Think about this in the context of where you perceive a need, problem, or opportunity in the marketplace and where that opportunity aligns with your unique talents and passions.)

---

## Suggested Readings & Additional Resources

- SCORE.org[8] offers workshops, templates and resources, and can pair you with a mentor in your area.
- IRS small business and self-employed tax center[9] offers resources to help you start and structure your business and report taxes appropriately.
- Small Business Administration[10] has tips for getting started as a small business.

*Elizabeth Mays' clients include the Canadian nonprofit the Rebus Foundation, software company Pressbooks and others. She is also an adjunct professor at the Walter Cronkite School of Journalism and Mass Communication who has taught audience acquisition, business and future of journalism, and editing. Reach her on Twitter at @theeditress.*

## Leave feedback on this chapter.

## *Notes*

1. Unique Selling Proposition, "Small Business Encyclopedia," *Entrepreneur*, https://www.entrepreneur.com/encyclopedia/unique-selling-proposition-usp.

2. Value Proposition, *Investopedia*, http://www.investopedia.com/terms/v/valueproposition.asp.

3. Parts of this paragraph are from "What's Your Magic Power" by Elizabeth Mays and made available with permission under CC BY license here.

4. "Ten Steps to Starting a Business in Arizona," *Arizona Corporation Commission*, http://www.azcc.gov/Divisions/Corporations/Ten-Steps-to-Starting-a-Business-in-Arizona.pdf.

5. Ryan Robinson, "Infographic: How to Calculate Your Freelance Hourly Rate," *CreativeLive*, Oct. 2, 2017, http://blog.creativelive.com/how-to-calculate-freelance-hourly-rate-infographic/.

6. "NPPA Cost of Doing Business Calculator," *NPPA*, https://nppa.org/calculator.

7. "The Ants and the Grasshopper," *Library of Congress Aesop Fable*, http://read.gov/aesop/052.html.

8. *SCORE*, Score.org.

9. *IRS Small Business and Self-Employed Tax Center*, https://www.irs.gov/businesses/small-businesses-self-employed.

10. *Small Business Administration*, https://www.sba.gov/.

# FROM THE FIELD: HOW TO GET AND KEEP GIGS AS A FREELANCE JOURNALIST

*Georgann Yara*

## From the Field

### My Story

You can take the freelance plunge soon after tossing your cap in the air or envision it as a future turn in a semi-seasoned journalism career. My path was the latter.

After 12 years in daily and weekly newspapers, I was looking for something new. I loved what I did and freelancing gave me the opportunity to continue doing that with the perks of flexibility with regard to the kind of writing I'd be doing and the topics I'd cover.

By the time I went freelance, I had been in the Phoenix journalism market for 10 years. Word got out about my career decision quickly and I got offers immediately. That was in 2006, and I've been busy ever since. My experience covering just about every beat from movie and restaurant reviews to breaking news and courts came in handy and expanded my potential client pool, which includes newspapers, magazines, online publications, and special print projects, i.e. coffee table books and bios for award luncheon programs. None of this work, however, has been in public relations or marketing.

First, the good stuff: I love calling the shots, from the hours I work and when I work them to the kind of jobs I take and leave on the table. The commute from my bedroom to the living room couch, patio, or wherever I want my headquarters to be can't be beat.

It feels good to skip the full makeup and hair routine every morning, and keep the grown-up clothes in the closet. My dry cleaning bills decreased immensely, as did stress amped up by occasional rush hour road rage. Running errands on a Tuesday mid-morning is definitely more relaxing than battling the crowds on a Saturday afternoon.

Of course there are a few comforts I miss. A steady and predictable paycheck is one of them. Paid vacations are another. If I'm not working, essentially I'm not getting paid. In a newsroom, I was compensated for downtime spent chatting with co-workers, perusing the Internet, the cake celebrations for co-workers' birthdays or last day at the office, and pretty much every non-work activity that consumed 15 minutes or less. That compensation no longer exists. I do budget time into my day for non-work tasks — checking my social media channels, dentist appointments, laundry — but I maintain an efficient schedule that allows me to complete all my assignments on deadline each week. Is this perfect? No. But it has worked just fine for me for more than a decade. Here are some tips to make freelancing work for you.

## Getting Gigs

Look for new magazines or newspapers around town or in your neighborhood. Those stands outside of grocery stores and local magazines in the waiting room at medical offices are filled with potential clients. Also, search writing websites that offer jobs. The neat thing is that you can take work based in any city as long as the company will allow you to work remotely.

Being new on the freelance scene, I felt the need to generate clips and credibility as a solo writer and get on people's radars. Taking as many jobs as possible to get your name out there is key. I took pretty much any gig that was offered to me, regardless of the pay, for the first two years or so. Also, pitching ideas does the same. Often, one leads to another. And never underestimate the power of word-of-mouth. When you do good work, word travels. When you do bad work, word travels.

Be open-minded. You may think you know exactly the kind of stories or projects to which you want to dedicate your career, but leave the door open to discovering something new. It may be a subset of a topic you initially don't care for that you discover excites you. It could be something you never thought of that requires you to indulge a creative or pensive side. Being willing to do anything is an asset to any writer, especially at the start of a freelance career. Stretching your limits also keeps you learning, while keeping burnout at bay.

Network with other freelancers in the industry — writers or PR people. Your peers are a great resource for jobs, support, and skills. They also know what you're going through and, if need be, can commiserate with you about wacky editors or demanding clients. I can't tell you how often a fellow freelancer has provided insight and talked me off the ledge.

These connections also can create a positive job domino effect. An example: a fellow freelancer did occasional work for *US Magazine*. One day, an editor there needed a Phoenix-based writer for an assignment but she was unavailable. My colleague gave her my contact info and the next day I was scouring the Valley on a hunt for Tiger Woods. My searching came up empty, but I got paid well for my work and it led to more assignments chasing down leads and rumors involving celebs, which was a fun — although frustrating at times — new experience. When that editor left the magazine and took over at an online publication, she needed writers. She reached out to me and I was able to do more projects that paid equally well.

## Keeping Gigs

There are two really important things you can do to please your editors.

Deadlines — always, always meet them. I cannot stress this enough. About halfway through my freelance career, I was surprised to hear from editors that a significant number of freelancers did not meet their deadlines. I thought this would be the easiest requirement to meet since it is really the only factor completely within your control from the start. I believe that my ability to meet deadline — I only blew it once and it was by 30 minutes — has been a huge factor in keeping jobs and getting new ones. An editor can always clean up copy or ask you to tweak the project, but their hands are tied if they don't have anything to work with.

Deliver clean copy. If deadlines are the most important, this is second. Learn what style your publication wants — AP style or one developed just for the company, for example — and follow it to the T. If it's their own style, take a good look at their published articles so you have an idea of what it entails. And this may sound like a given, but you'd be surprised at how many people overlook spelling (beware of auto-correct), punctuation, and basic grammar before hitting "send."

## The Business Side

OK, here's the practical reality check.

If your spouse has employer-provided benefits, then you can skip this paragraph. If not, employer-provided health insurance is one thing that freelancers miss. Quality healthcare is tough to get on your own without a steep price tag. If you're healthy or have a hefty savings account that you can access if needed, you may be OK. If not, you may need to consider taking a job that offers benefits until your freelance business is up and running on all cylinders.

Figuring out a monthly budget seems like a no-brainer, but having one that's specific that you will stick to is crucial when you're not guaranteed a paycheck. It also gives you an idea of what you'll need to make each month and therefore a rate to offer potential clients. About half of my clients come to me with a rate, but the other half ask for one. Coming up with a standard rate that made me happy without scaring off potential clients was one of the most difficult aspects of settling into being my own boss.

You may not be receiving a set amount every two weeks, but it's possible to generate a base income. Try to get regular assignments that provide steady income that you can count on. If you know that you'll be getting at least $800 a week for two or three assignments then it'll be easier to craft a monthly budget and determine what other jobs you can and should take. For the last five years or so, I've had three assignments that are due every week, which gives me a predictable minimum "salary" through the busy and slow times.

## The Long View

Speaking of money and success, determine what that means for you on a priority scale. Over the years, I found that money has moved down from the top priority position in my life to the fourth — after enjoyment, fulfillment, and time and effort. If pay remains at the top for you, that's perfectly fine. Just know that you'll discover how that affects the rest of your priority list.

That said, try to get a diverse project folder going that is balanced with jobs that pay well and those that may not pay as well but that you find fulfilling. Throwing in a pro bono job for a cause that you believe in or for a good friend every now and then will give you a fresh perspective too.

Try not to pack your schedule so tight that if a neat opportunity comes along that you would love, you are unable to take it. Early on, I wasn't comfortable keeping a workload with wiggle room. But after a couple of years of kicking myself over opportunities lost because I simply didn't have the time, I managed to find that sweet spot between steady busy and not too hectic. Eventually, you'll find that sweet spot too.

*Georgann Yara has been a freelance writer in Phoenix since 2006. Reach her on Twitter at @georgannyara.*

## Leave feedback on this sidebar.

# FROM THE FIELD: HOW I DITCHED THE 9 TO 5 AND BUILT A BUSINESS I COULD LIVE WITH

*Lori Benjamin*

## From the Field

### My Story

I started working as a freelance content marketing writer after about 15 years of work in traditional marketing and advertising, mostly in the business-to-business software field. So, I come to it from a business rather than a journalism lens. Content marketing felt like an enormous (and obvious) breakthrough. For years, I'd been asked to write product-focused emails and online ads designed to interrupt busy people with a sales pitch. Now suddenly, I had clients who wanted to produce things that people would actually seek out and read. What a concept!

I discovered content marketing after leaving my ad agency job in the city behind and moving to an island about two hours north of Seattle and an hour by ferry from the mainland. Commuting was not an option. After five years of writing emails for Microsoft clients, I needed to update and sharpen my skills. It was 2012, and new ideas, voices, and technologies occasionally broke through the ad agency bubble, but were usually rejected in my commercial, business-to-business niche.

From my first Skype interview as an islander, it was clear I had a lot to catch up on. I began investigating marketing blogs in earnest, and found sites like *Copyblogger*, *HubSpot*, *Seth Godin*, *Content Marketing Institute*, and *Convince and Convert*. I had a decent portfolio, but not much for bylined articles, and I was competing against writers much younger than me. At first, all I found were clients asking me to work for less than minimum wage: To type fast and think very little.

Ultimately, LinkedIn turned out to be my most valuable tool. As an "early adopter," I had started collecting recommendations around 2007—a great way to establish credibility in a field where almost nothing I wrote had my name on it. I began applying for any and every job I felt qualified for, no matter where it was based geographically. Unless the job description said specifically, "This is an onsite position," I sent an application. If it seemed like a perfect match, sometimes I applied anyway, ending my cover letter with a polite, "I hope you'll consider me as a remote candidate for this position or alternatively, for any project work I may be able to help you with."

After a few months of this, I started picking up work that paid reasonably well. Within the first 18 months, I was making a decent living writing ebooks and ghostwriting guest blog posts on the very content marketing websites I'd been reading. I was over the moon.

The content marketer's motto: Be helpful.

"Content marketing" is nothing new, of course. John Deere has been publishing its brand magazine, *The Furrow*, since 1895. Today however, every brand in the world is up against the overwhelming information overload that we all experience in our multi-screen, multi-tasked lives. Audience attention is the holy grail.

Because of the Internet and social media, the corporate decision-makers who've been my target audience for most of my career increasingly choose to do their own research, reaching out to sales only after they're close to reaching a decision. It makes sense for software companies to offer insight and context as a part of that research conversation. Not many executives have the time or patience for traditional direct mail gimmicks and other interruption advertising tactics.

Marketing is an exciting field to be in now, because it's changing so rapidly. It's much more customer- and data-focused than it was even a couple of years ago—which means that good, effective work rises to the fore more consistently. Formats change constantly—in the past year, podcasts and video have surged. Virtual reality is on the horizon. But words will always be essential to communication, whatever the medium. If you're a disciplined writer with a curious, creative bent and a basic understanding of business, you can make it work.

A few tips, for starters:

- **Take a creative writing workshop (or three).** If I had a stronger technology or business education, I'm sure that would be valuable, but I cannot imagine a better preparation for my work than the many creative writing workshops I took in college and graduate school. Sitting in a room with my peers, I learned how to give and receive constructive feedback. To listen even when the critique I heard caused a spike in my blood pressure. To respond with thoughtful, creative rewrites that, as often as not, turned out better than the original. There's more than one way of nailing it.

- **Choose unpaid work wisely.** If you're starting with no portfolio or experience, it may make sense to write for people who expect you to work for next to nothing. But it may make even more sense to write on a topic of your own choosing and develop credibility and a following that way. Go ahead and build expertise in an area with high income potential—but make sure you also feed your personal passions. That well of sincere interest and curiosity is where the best insights and writing come from.

- **You are your client's voice.** In high-demand fields, you can make upwards of $100 an hour as an established marketing writer, but never forget: Your client is in charge. Don't like the feedback you're getting? Take a deep breath and open your ears. Your work is not only about whether you can put together sentences that make people sit up and take notice. It's most essentially about doing it in a way that accomplishes your client's goals.

- **Professional courtesy is crucial.** In building client and team relationships, you'll find a collaborative mindset and a positive, pragmatic attitude much more effective than quick criticism or competitive maneuvering.

- **It's okay to fire a client.** There's nothing worse than a client who doesn't seem to respect your time and effort (unless it's the client who flat-out refuses to pay at all). You will come across those people, unless you're very lucky. Set your boundaries early, and keep a list of the qualities you expect from clients. Professional courtesy goes both ways.

- **You are the boss of you.** Don't feel like working? Think you can fudge that deadline and go skiing with your friends? As an independent consultant, you have a lot of leeway around when and how much you work. But if you commit to a deadline and don't make it, you risk losing a client, pure and simple.

- **Print it out and proofread it before you hit send.** Deliver a document full of typos and repetition, and your client will be predisposed to ripping it to shreds, metaphorically speaking. Read the print-out one last time before you send it. You'll be amazed at what you didn't catch onscreen. Aim for perfection, so your client can focus on the message rather than the misplaced apostrophe.

- **Client relationships are your lifeblood.** When you work remotely, it can be hard to connect with people and maintain relationships. But one great connection can truly make or break your career. In my industry, people move from company to company constantly, which means two things: 1) My contact at Client XYZ could jump ship at any time and I could lose the business, and 2) My contact at Client XYZ could bring me many additional clients during her career. To develop a stable freelance business, treat people with respect and loyalty always. If you sense any issue, head it off immediately by reaching out personally.

- **Save your pennies.** Every freelance business has its ups and downs—cycles of 80-hour weeks, mixed with ones where things seem eerily quiet. Make sure you build a good buffer to get you through the slow times. That way, you can relax and hit the beach, rather than checking your email every five minutes, praying for work.

*Lori Benjamin writes for technology and marketing companies, mostly in the startup community. She has an M.A. in creative writing from Purdue University and a B.A. in English from the University of Redlands. Contact her at www.loribmedia.com.*

## Leave feedback on this sidebar.

# LOOKING AHEAD

## Looking Ahead

You have an entrepreneurial idea, plus some thoughts on who will be your customer and what you'll charge them for. Do you need initial funding to get your business, project or product started? Startup Funding will explain the types of funding available to startups and help you understand which might be best for you.

# STARTUP FUNDING

by CJ Cornell

## Summary

What is funding? Why do you need it? Where should you seek it? Which types are best for you? This chapter will answer these and other questions you may have as you launch your media enterprise.

| Learning Objectives |
| --- |
| • Learn the different funding types (choices) available for startup ventures. |
| • Determine which of the funding types are most appropriate for a particular kind of startup. |
| • Learn about the sources of the funding—the funding organizations and individuals—and about their expectations. |
| • Learn what your company must do—preparation and activities—to attract and secure funding. |
| • Get an overview of many of the critical issues, terms, and metrics you'll have to know when pursuing outside funding for your startup. |

## Inside this Chapter

- Introduction
- Why Funding?
- Traditional Venture Funding
- Nontraditional Funding Sources
- Crowdfunding
- From the Field: Friends, Family and Fools Funding, by Francine Hardaway
- From the Field: The Journey from Listening to Leader, by Chris Dell
- From the Field: Your Kickstarter Campaign is a Story, Interview with Daniel Zayas

*CJ Cornell is a serial entrepreneur, investor, advisor, mentor, author, speaker, and educator. He is the author of the best-selling book: The Age of Metapreneurship—A Journey into the Future of Entrepreneurship[1] and the upcoming book: The Startup Brain Trust—A Guidebook for Startups, Entrepreneurs, and the Experts that Help them Become Great. Reach him on Twitter at @cjcornell.*

# STARTUP FUNDING: INTRODUCTION

*CJ Cornell*

## Overview

In modern entrepreneurship, "funding" is mentioned so often that it almost seems like a required step in the process. New companies, particularly companies that are developing brand-new products, often don't have customers or revenues when they start. These startups need money for product development, and to support the company's operations until revenues (sales) pay the bills. Often, the more innovative the product, the longer it will take to develop, or to reach a large market. So a new company needs money to develop and survive during this innovation startup period.

Anyone who has been exposed to entrepreneurial success stories of the past fifty years—from Apple, Microsoft and Amazon to Google, Facebook, Uber, and Airbnb—is familiar with the vital role <u>angel investors</u>, <u>venture capitalists</u>, and <u>initial public offerings</u> played in funding these multi-billion-dollar success stories. But it wasn't always this way. Prior to the twentieth century—unless you were starting a new railroad or oil or steel company—most likely your new business was a small retail business or farming business. For small businesses, there really was no "product development" and your market was easily identifiable: they were your neighbors.

In those earlier times, if your business made a profit then you might have some extra money to expand. Today we call this "organic growth": funding the growth of your new company from revenues from sales (to customers).

 **Discussion/Assignment:** *Can you identify any modern, successful companies that did not use outside funding to develop their product or service before becoming successful?*

Most "small businesses" fall into this category: right from the very beginning they have a product or service they can sell to customers who are very accessible. They don't have to develop any new product innovations, hire a large team, or spend a lot of money trying to find customers. Thus, most small businesses don't need outside funding. These businesses can be started with the founder's personal savings or credit, and grow as revenues grow.

But if your startup is developing something brand-new or cutting edge, or you are trying to reach brand-new customers or markets, then it is likely you will need external funding—i.e., funding that does not come from the entrepreneur's personal money, or from the company's revenues. Venture capital, angel funding, debt, grants, and crowdfunding are the most common sources of funding for early-stage companies.

## The Language of Funding

Before we dive into the world of startup funding, you will need to learn some of the language. Even studying the common funding lingo provides a good introduction and insights into the startup funding landscape.

**Note:** The list below is not exhaustive, just some of terms we will use in the next sections.

## A. Stage/Type of Company

| Term | Definition | What This Means to You |
|---|---|---|
| **pre-Startup** | An idea-stage company—just an idea on paper (no product or service yet) | Usually never funded by an external funding source, except for "friends and family" and certain grants |
| **Startup** | A founder or team who have identified a technology, market, and business and are in the process of developing a product or service, or in the process of commercializing one | The term varies from a very early-stage product or team, to one that is operating and releasing products. Usually a startup is still trying to find a sustainable business model, for a relatively new market, and expecting significant growth. |
| **Small Business** | An operating business that already has customers and a product/service. Usually it is selling a proven product or service to an existing market. | Small businesses already have a proven business model but differ from startups in that they are already operating, and are not structured for rapid growth. |
| **Early Stage Venture** | Often synonymous with "startup"—but usually implies a startup that has made progress with developing a product and attracting customers. | |
| **Growth Company** | A company, that for the moment, is more concerned with attracting a large customer base (market share) than with profitability | Many modern tech companies—particularly in brand-new markets, or new technologies—focus on growth first. This way they can grow fast and dominate the market (and |

| | | eliminate competition), then they can focus on profitability. |
|---|---|---|
| **Social Entrepreneurship / Social Venture** | A company whose primary concern, primary service or product is focused on advocating or advancing a "social cause" or some other kind of advocacy (eg. saving journalism, improving trust in media)—rather than profits | The ultimate measure of these companies is not in revenues or profits—but in some other kind of success metric. This usually places these ventures outside the interest of typical funding sources (who need to see a return on their investment). |
| **Investment** | Money given to a company, in return for a percentage ownership (shares of stock) | Investors are part owners, and have some say in the strategy and decision making of the company, and (ultimately) share in the profits. |
| **Institutional Funding** | Funding from venture capitalists (can also refer to bank loans and investments from large corporations) | Generally, institutional funding means that the investment decisions are made by professional money managers—as opposed to the "owner" of the money. |
| **Angel Capital / Angel Investor** | Investments made by (relatively) wealthy individuals—usually they are investing in startups as part of their overall investment portfolio. | Angels are "accredited" investors (who meet certain SEC criteria for net worth and income). Angels usually have little personal relationship with the founders. |
| **Venture Capital / Venture Capitalist** | A VC is a professional fund manager. They aggregate investment funding from large institutions then make investments in high-growth companies for potential high returns. | VCs need their funds to make an extraordinary return on investment. |
| **Debt** | Loans—usually from banks—who seek low risk | Debt funding almost always must be "secured" by collateral (or assets). If a company owns a building or has equipment, then they might qualify for a bank loan. Most startups lack the collateral to qualify for a loan unless the founders personally guarantee the loan. |
| **ROI** | Return on investment—usually stated in financial terms (i.e., percentages) | Most investors in the startup ecosystem are looking to make back huge returns—many times their original investment—in order to offset the risk. Some investors, however may be |

| | | looking for other forms of ROI—such as gaining access to new technology or new markets. |
|---|---|---|
| **Exit/Exit Strategy** | An "event" (or transaction) when shareholders are first able to sell their shares for cash (a.k.a. "liquidity"). Usually this means either the company is sold to a larger company, or the shareholders are allowed to sell shares on the stock market (IPO). | Investors usually need an exit in order to see a return on their investment (i.e., someone needs to buy their shares of stock at a much higher price than what they originally paid). Investors want some sense of the company's "exit strategy" before investing. |
| **Due Diligence** | The background checking that investors will do before investing: technical, marketing, financial, legal, and personal (about the entrepreneurs) | |
| **Corporation (S, C)** | Only corporations can issues shares of stock. Corporations also provide some levels of legal protection to the managers and founders. Corporations have tax liabilities (and other similar ramifications). | Almost all investors need to invest in a corporation, not other forms of a company. |
| **LLC (Partnership)** | A form of a company that is very easy and inexpensive to establish. LLC = limited liability corporation | LLCs are in, in effect, partnerships. There are no "shares of stock" and it is difficult to include investors or incentivize employees or even confounders. |
| **Sole Proprietorship** | "The owner is the business." Often consulting businesses and freelancers are sole proprietorships. | For tax and legal liability, the owner is the same as the company. Sole proprietorships rarely have outside investors. |
| **Board of Directors** | A group of individuals elected by the shareholders of a corporation to oversee the management of the company, and to make major decisions for the corporation, on behalf of the shareholders | |
| **Scale / Scalable Growth** | To grow fast (in market share, and/ or revenues)—particularly the ability to grow exponentially, while only using incremental resources | Venture investors usually look for businesses with the potential to scale. E.g., with $1M investment, can the company grow to $200M in 5 years? |
| **(Market) Traction** | Evidence that customers are buying and using your product or service—enough such that investors | |

| | | |
|---|---|---|
| | believe that this customer adoption can continue and grow | |
| **Market Validation/ Customer Validation** | Evidence from customers that your product/service will gain wide acceptance. Market validation is different than traction in that this evidence doesn't have to come from customers. Partnering with a large or credible company could constitute validation (e.g., a partnership with Google or Facebook). | Market validation (and traction) are important pieces of evidence that investors look for when deciding to invest. Most startups lack a solid track record of revenues and profits, thus investors look for other evidence of future success: traction and market validation. |

## B. Round of Funding

| Term | Meaning | (implication) |
|---|---|---|
| **Bootstrap** | All money / funding comes from the founders' own savings, credit, etc. | Many tech and media startups can initially be bootstrapped because of the plethora of free/cheap resources for product development and marketing. |
| **Organic Funding** | Money for new product development/marketing comes from the company's revenues (not from outside funding). | Often startup founders will perform consulting services or sell other products in order to fund the product development of the company's primary product. |
| **FFF** | A.k.a. "Friends Family and Fools"—funding of the startup by sources close to the founders | Usually these funding sources are investing due to their personal belief in the founders, or because they want to support the founders (or cause) for emotional reasons—rather than for purely financial reasons. |
| **pre—Seed** | A relatively new term for funding that does not fall within the FFF/ bootstrap definitions, and is not quite seed funding | |
| **Seed Funding** | Refers to the first "outside money" a startup attracts. Usually this money is to establish proof of concept (product development) and/or proof-of-market (market validation). | |
| **Series A** | Usually refers to the first "institutional" funding round for a startup | By this stage, the startup usually has some customers and revenue, and the funding is to help the company achieve significant growth, and expansion of operations. |

| Series B, C, D | Subsequent rounds of institutional funding, to further help the company expand and grow | |
|---|---|---|
| IPO / Initial Public Offerings | When the company (and investors) first sell shares to the public (e.g. the stock market), the company can raise significant amounts of money to fund operations, growth or new products. | This also offers the investors (and founders) a chance to sell some of their stock for (sometimes significant) cash. |

There is no set funding path for entrepreneurial startups. The path depends on two factors: What the startup needs (funding requirements) and the potential return on investment.

- **Funding requirements of the startup:** May vary wildly, depending on the type of company, product, product development costs, and expected time until break-even
- **Funding sources:** The preferred investment size, industry sector, expected ROI, and the total they have available

Many small businesses, and service businesses never need outside funding since they are able to generate revenue right away. Other startups need significant funding to develop a product and to grow fast—to dominate a market.

For the former, bootstrap or self-funding may be enough to sustain the operations until revenues can support the company. For the high growth (usually high-tech) ventures, they will need significant external investment—in the millions, tens of millions or even hundreds of millions of dollars. For these companies. the funding path is usually pre-seed/seed funding to prove the idea or market; then successive Series A, B, C investments to fully launch the product, market, and expand and grow the company.

## Resources

7 Ways to Fund Your Startup[1]

From Accelerators to Venture Capital: What Is Best for Your Startup[2]

*CJ Cornell is a serial entrepreneur, investor, advisor, mentor, author, speaker, and educator. He is the author of the best-selling book: The Age of Metapreneurship—A Journey into the Future of Entrepreneurship[3] and the upcoming book: The Startup Brain Trust—A Guidebook for Startups, Entrepreneurs, and the Experts that Help them Become Great. Reach him on Twitter at @cjcornell.*

## Leave feedback on this chapter.

## Notes

1. "7 Ways to Fund Your Startup," *Visual.ly*, https://visual.ly/community/infographic/business/7-ways-fund-your-startup.

2. "From Accelerators to Venture Capital: What Is Best for Your Startup," *Gust.com,* http://blog.gust.com/from-accelerators-to-venture-capital-what-is-best-for-your-startup/.

3. Cornell, CJ, *The Age of Metapreneurship*, (Phoenix: Venture Point Press, 2017). https://www.amazon.com/dp/069287724X.

# STARTUP FUNDING: WHY FUNDING

*CJ Cornell*

First, let's define funding, in the context of entrepreneurship and startup companies. For the purposes of this chapter we are referring to external funding.

As an entrepreneur, you might think you need external funding. External funding usually means:

- Funding (money) exchanged in return for stock in the startup company (equity), loan payments (debt), or for a series of payments (e.g. royalties).
- Funding is not the result of the sale of a product or service.
- The startup receives cash (money that can be deposited into the startup's bank account)— as opposed to other products/services the company needs. (For instance: If an organization provides your startup with office space, laptops, or servers, this is not considered funding).
- Funding is from a person or organization not officially affiliated with the company (i.e.,—not an employee, founder, or major customer).

Most other forms of funding would be "internal" or organic funding—from the founder's family, or from consulting or other revenues. While these are valid and common forms of funding for startups, they don't require formal or deliberate fundraising activities and preparations—and the money is not dependent or controlled by sources unrelated to the company.

When entrepreneurs think about funding, usually their first thoughts are "How much do we need" and "How do we get funding for our project or company?" And then "Where can we find funding?" or "Who can we ask for funding?"

And these are the right questions—but in the wrong order. There are more important questions that need to be asked, and answered, first:

- Why do you need (external) funding?
- What is the unique product or service?
- What specific value will you offer to customers? That is, what is your "value proposition"?
- What is your industry category, or product category?

- What is your mission?
- What are the risks?

Asking those first questions is more than just an exercise, or soul-searching. The answers will, in part, dictate "who" you should be asking for funding. The "who" should be aligned with the "what." Only then should you work on the "how" to secure funding.

Before we focus on the details of startup funding sources, and how to attract and secure funding, let's first focus on the "why"—but from the perspective of the funding sources. Knowing why they want to fund a company or project is vital. Your reasons need to be aligned with their reasons. It the reasons are not aligned, then nothing else matters.

If you need funding to pay yourself a salary, pay back loans, or to merely make sure the business can pay its current bills then the chances are you will never obtain outside funding. But if you need funding to advance your product development efforts, launch a new product, to enter new markets, or to grow and expand then your reasons may be more aligned with funders' reasons.

 *Discussion/Assignment:* Can you think of reasons why people, companies, and organizations with money would want to be the source of funding for startups and new projects?

## Reasons for Funding (from the Other Side of the Table)

When anyone provides support, resources or money to someone else, there is always an "agenda," or motivation. This is not as devious or as mercenary as it sounds. A parent pays their child's tuition because they want their child to have a better chance at being happy and successful. When a person sends money to a political campaign, or for a climate change awareness group, it's because they feel these organizations will advance a viewpoint or cause on their behalf. It's still an investment; it's just that the return on investment is not explicitly a financial gain.

As a founder of a new venture, new startup, or a new project that might become a new company, your objectives need to be aligned with those of the potential funding source. Talking about how your revolutionary new blockchain technology is going change the quality of life in underdeveloped countries is not going to resonate with a local bank that only cares about loans, interest rates, and collateral.

Every funding source has an intention, motivation, or some kind of potential benefit they expect as a result of providing the funding. They also want to maximize the chances of success and minimize risks of failure. In other words, they want to allocate their funding to projects or companies that have the best chance of advancing their interests.

Here are some of the most common reasons why people and organizations fund new ventures:

| | |
|---|---|
| **Profits Only** | A pure financial ROI—usually looking for "windfall" profits (significant financial gains—better than almost any other) |
| **Profits, within an "Investment Thesis"** | While financial ROI is the simplest motivation, it is usually not without other interests. For instance a venture capital firm wants windfall profits, of course, but they also may want to invest in companies that advance certain industries or technologies. Or they may invest in companies that demonstrate a culture of diversity, for example. |
| **Economic Development** | The funding organization wants to support new companies that will create new jobs within their region. |
| **Ecosystem Development** | The funding organization wants to ensure there are many companies innovating around a new technology or platform. |
| **Strategic** | The funding organization is looking for startups working on products or technologies, or penetrating markets, that are aligned with the organization (usually a corporation)'s goals. |
| **Charitable, Altruistic** | The funding organization is looking for startups that embrace principles (social, business, etc.) that are aligned with the organization's charitable mission (e.g., advancing women's health care issues). |
| **Industry Development** | Because the funding organization's mission is a combination of economic development and ecosystem development, it is designed to fund projects that will advance help an entire industry (e.g., Knight Foundation supports Journalism projects). |

### In-Class Exercise

**Web Search:** Can you name some funding organizations focusing on ecosystem development? e.g., Bitcoin/Blockchain, Mobile/Android funds. Facebook app funds(s); or, other funding initiatives and organizations that are not strictly for profit.

Now, let's look at the most common reasons why entrepreneurs seek outside funding for their projects and companies.

# Reasons for Funding (from the Entrepreneur's Perspective)—a.k.a. "Use of Proceeds"

| Reason | Description | Investor/Funder perspective |
|---|---|---|
| Establishment | Funding for essential legal work, website, physical location | Usually of very little interest (as the sole reason for funding) |
| Research | Activities exploring new product, marketability, customer demand, etc. | Usually of very little interest (as the sole reason)—may be of interest if combined with other reasons |

| Development | Substantial and tangible product development, or market development | Of interest to seed-stage or early stage funders—though they will need evidence of market viability, and other evidence that reduces risk |
|---|---|---|
| Growth | Rapidly expanding sales, or customer acquisition, or market share—via hiring and accelerated product development or distribution. | Of high interest—particularly to the profit-focused funders |
| Operations, Salaries | Paying for day-to-day expenses, such as rent and salaries | Of little interest to any funding source, unless combined with other primary reasons |
| Expansion | Creating new products or entering new markets—once the startup is established with a product and a market | Of interest to many kinds of funding sources depending on the market and category |
| Purchase of Assets | Such as manufacturing equipment, patents, exclusive IP rights, inventory | Of primary interest to banks and other lending institutions. Medium-low interest from other funding sources unless combined with other reasons |
| Debt, Prior Expenses | Paying off loans, paying back founders for costs incurred. Paying back credit card debt | Of little interest to any funding source, and a detriment ("turn off") if mentioned |

 **Discussion:** *Can you think of reasons why a company—particularly a startup—might want to raise money—even if they \*have\* money?*

Before embarking on the funding journey, it's critical to be very self-aware of your reasons for needing funding, the kind of company you are, and what value you offer. Only then can you start pursuing potential funders whose methods and mission are aligned with yours. Otherwise, it's a long, painful, and frustrating exercise in futility—a path many entrepreneurs take on the road to failure.

## Preparation

All funding requires some preparation and pre-requisites (even winning the lottery requires buying a ticket). Applying for loans requires forms, documentation, and collateral.

Most funding sources for startups require a set of presentation materials, or a deliberate application.

Generally all will require:

- Description of a clear market problem/pain you are solving (or a new market opportunity you are addressing)
- Clear descriptions of the company and idea (product or service)
- A solid and capable management team
- Customer/market validation:
  Evidence that you are addressing a big market problem or opportunity
  Evidence of a market, and evidence of customer traction
  Any external validation or endorsements
- Product/service innovation (USP)
  Evidence of product viability (that the innovation will translate into a product)
- Financials—estimates/forecasts of costs, revenues and profits
- ROI potential, growth potential
- Funding request/requirements, use of proceeds

If you're starting a social entrepreneurship venture, then the ROI or financials might not be a requirement, but there may be more requirements about describing the social impact. Very early stage companies (idea stage) won't have most of this information. Idea-stage companies typically seek funding that will help them develop the idea to the point where they will be able to answer that list of questions.

## Resources

Here are some examples and recommendations as you prepare your pitch.

- Sequoia Capital  Pitch Deck Template[1]
- The Only 10 Slides You Need in Your Pitch[2]
- Lessons From A Study of Perfect Pitch Decks[3]
- Funded Pitch Decks[4]
- All the Public Startup Pitch Decks in One Place[5]
- The Ultimate Startup Funding Pitch Deck[6]
- Free Templates for Great Startup Pitch Decks, Direct from VCs[7]

| Key Takeaways |
| --- |
| 1. The startup should be clear on the reasons they need outside funding. |
| 2. The startup should understand the different sources of funding available (and the motivations of each kind of funding source). |
| 3. The startup should make sure that their reasons are aligned with the funding source's reasons. |

*CJ Cornell is a serial entrepreneur, investor, advisor, mentor, author, speaker, and educator. He is the author of the best-selling book: The Age of Metapreneurship—A Journey into the Future of*

*Entrepreneurship*[8] *and the upcoming book: The Startup Brain Trust—A Guidebook for Startups, Entrepreneurs, and the Experts that Help them Become Great. Reach him on Twitter at @cjcornell.*

## Leave feedback on this chapter.

## *Notes*

1. "Sequoia Capital Pitch Deck Template," *Slideshare*, https://www.slideshare.net/PitchDeckCoach/sequoia-capital-pitchdecktemplate.

2. Guy Kawasaki, "The Only 10 Slides You Need in Your Pitch," *GuyKawasaki.com*, https://guykawasaki.com/the-only-10-slides-you-need-in—your-pitch/.

3. Kim-Mai Cutler, "Lessons from a Study of Perfect Pitch Decks," *TechCrunch.com*, June 8, 2015, https://techcrunch.com/2015/06/08/lessons-from-a-study-of-perfect-pitch-decks-vcs-spend-an-average-of-3-minutes-44-seconds-on-them.

4. "Funded Startup Pitch Deck Repository," https://www.fundedpitchdecks.com/.

5. Andy Sparks, "All the Public Startup Pitch Decks in One Place," *Medium*, Jan. 10, 2017. https://medium.com/startup-grind/all-the-public-startup-pitch-decks-in-one-place-7d3ddff33bdc.

6. Chance Barnett, "The Ultimate Startup Funding Pitch Deck," *Medium,* Aug. 12, 2016, https://medium.com/@chancebar/the-ultimate-startup-funding-pitch-deck-1c1565eeb324.

7. David Beisel, "Free Templates for Great Startup Pitch Decks, Direct from VCs," *Traction*, February 3, 2015, http://nextviewventures.com/blog/free-startup-pitch-decks-template/.

8. Cornell, CJ, *The Age of Metapreneurship*, (Phoenix: Venture Point Press, 2017). https://www.amazon.com/dp/069287724X.

# STARTUP FUNDING: TRADITIONAL VENTURE FUNDING

*CJ Cornell*

## Traditional Funding

Recently, the Ewing Marion Kauffman Foundation (the world's foremost organization focusing on entrepreneurship and education), posted some data on the most common sources of funding for new companies:[1]

| Source | Amount | Share |
|---|---|---|
| Banks and Other Loans | 38,059 | 34.09% |
| Personal Savings | 32,658 | 30.00% |
| Friends and Family | 6,910 | 6.30% |
| Credit Cards | 6,756 | 6.20% |
| Angel Investors | 6,350 | 5.80% |
| Venture Capital | 4,804 | 4.40% |
| Government Related | 2,129 | 2.00% |
| Other | 11,350 | 10.40% |
| **TOTAL** | **109,016** | **100.00%** |

But this data needs some interpretation: It appears that Angel and VC funding (the kinds most commonly associated with new ventures) barely total 10 percent of all startup funding.

This can be misleading. First: "new company" is not the same thing as a "startup" in the entrepreneurial sense of the word. The vast majority falling under the broad definition of "new company" are really *small businesses*—those that are not developing a new product or service, nor addressing new markets. Thus, the level of risk and investment needed is much lower than typical high-technology ventures.

In addition, the chart does not differentiate between the stage of company seeking funding. In other words, a startup's founder might use personal savings, credit cards, and loans from family to get started—but once the startup becomes a company with a more definable product and market, it's time for other forms of funding.

## Venture Funding

In the context of startup ventures and entrepreneurship, funding equals external resources (usually money), plus some support. *External* means the resources are being controlled by individuals, groups, companies or organizations that are not officially connected to the startup venture. *Resources* means cash/money (usually), but in many cases resources are other instruments of value for the new company: a line of credit, office space, retail or manufacturing space, equipment, supplies, or access to distribution channels.

And since the funding source has a vested interest in seeing the new startup succeed, the funding often comes with support—in the form of advisors, board members, connection to key customers or markets, etc.

## Attracting and Securing Funding

This is the big question on the minds of most new entrepreneurs. In the beginning, most aren't too discerning. The type of funding needs to match the type of startup company, and its situation. For instance, if a startup company feels they can guarantee payback of a $500,000 loan within two years with 20 percent interest—but they approach venture capital firms—it will be a futile quest. Regardless of if it's a good deal, financially, venture capitalists, as a general rule, just don't loan money to startups.

---

Money is money, right? And this is the moment when entrepreneurs begin to waste a lot of time and effort chasing the wrong kinds of funding.

---

So, in the following sections, we'll explore the different funding types typically available to entrepreneurs, and to the companies they create. We'll dive in a little as to "who" the funding sources are (who controls the money), what interests them, what motivates them, and where you can find them—so you can understand which sources are appropriate for your company, how to prepare, attract, and secure the funding.

If you are a student entrepreneur, or someone with just a raw idea (and not a company), then many of the funding sources described will not apply—at least not yet. But entrepreneurs who understand the language of funding and the broader landscape will have a distinct advantage over those who only focus on their short-term needs.

[Ed. Note: Use the slider to navigate the chart below in the web book. This will get better soon!]

## Traditional Funding Sources for Early Stage Ventures[2]

| | Self—funding / Friends and Family | Angel Investors / Angel Groups | Super Angels | Venture Capital |
|---|---|---|---|---|
| **Overview** | Usually has no added value to the venture other than cash | Accredited investors investing as individuals or in groups | Accredited individual investors who have significant investing experience and take active roles | Institutional funding (managed by professional investors) |
| **Typical Range** | Less than $20,000 | $150,000- $1.5 Million | $250,000- $1.5 Million | $5 Million- $50 Million |
| **Annual $$ Invested (approx)** | $50 Billion | $20 Billion | $0.2 Billion | $20 Billion |
| **Stage** | Idea, seed, pre-seed | Seed, Series A. Mostly for startups and growth stages | Seed, Series A. Startup and growth stages | Startup, mostly for growth and later stages |
| **Obstacles and Issues** | Younger entrepreneurs lack sufficient self-funding or resources from friends. | Requires evidence of market validation and traction; often requires "aggregating" small investments from many angels | Requires evidence of market validation and traction. Super Angels are rare, but they can add significant value to a startup beyond money (connections, introductions, and significant help securing additional funding). | Fund companies, not ideas. Requires significant commitment (an issue for student entrepreneurs) |

# Venture Capital

When it comes to funding entrepreneurial startups—especially high-tech, high-growth companies—most people think of venture capital. Take any modern, startup-to-billion dollar success story, and you'll find that the company had significant investment, and help, from venture capitalists.

## The Venture Capital Industry

Venture capital firms typically manage money on behalf of large institutions (e.g. pension funds, university endowments) and sometimes on behalf of corporations and extremely wealthy individuals. VC firms then try to identity and invest in high-growth companies that will transform the investment into windfall returns. Some quick facts:

- VC fund sizes range from the small (under $150M), medium ($250M to $1B) to large (>$1B).
- As a general rule of thumb, VCs know that 4 out of 5 of the companies they invest in will fail (i.e. not provide an acceptable ROI), so:
- VCs need companies that are capable of (or have the potential) to generate 20, 50 or 100 times the original investment in 5-10 years.
- VCs are looking for companies that can scale.

During 2016[3], total invested: $59.3 Billion in 4,799 deals—broken down as follows:

- Seed Stage: $2.07B in 1,428 deals
- Early Stage: $10.48B in 1,272 deals
- Expansion Stage: $20.65B in 985 deals
- Later Stage: $20.84B in 429 deals

The total invested—$59.3 Billion—is quite a large number—and that is just in one average year. But looking at the details we see:

- VCs funded fewer than 1,500 seed stage companies (i.e., their first money in).
- And even if you look at all of the "startups," they only invested in 2,700 companies. Given the number of companies formed each year seeking funding, it doesn't take much to figure out how rare attracting venture capital really is.

But let's take a look at where venture capital is being invested, into what industries and what kinds of companies, so you can determine if there is alignment with your objectives:

## Sectors Invested by VCs—in Seed/Early Stage Companies[4]

| Year | Traditional Media Investment | Total Investment |
|------|------------------------------|------------------|
| 2012 | $742,020,000 | $32,692,900,000 |
| 2013 | $186,070,000 | $35,949,570,000 |
| 2014 | $280,900,000 | $58,743,560,000 |
| 2015 | $287,560,000 | $74,405,520,000 |
| 2016 | $209,540,000 | $62,750,350,000 |

| | | |
|---|---|---|
| 2017 (Q1, Q2 only) | $27,380,000 | $32,811,520,000 |

| Year | Number of Deals (Traditional Media) | Total Number of Deals |
|---|---|---|
| 2012 | 9 | 4,605 |
| 2013 | 15 | 5,021 |
| 2014 | 9 | 5,710 |
| 2015 | 11 | 5,650 |
| 2016 | 8 | 5,004 |
| 2017 (Q1, Q2 only) | 6 | 2,358 |

VCs predominantly invest in Internet, mobile/telecom and software companies—both in the number of deals and the amount invested. Note that out of 4,799 total deals in 2016, only 8 of them were in media. Media received an infinitesimal amount–not even 1 percent–of the total dollars invested.

## Where VCs Invest (Regionally)[56]

The top five regions for VC investment in 1Q 2017 were San Francisco, New York metro, Silicon Valley, New England, and the Southeast, according to a recent PwC MoneyTree Report. National Venture Capital Association and PitchBook Data[7] shows that more than half of the value of first-quarter VC deals was invested on the West Coast.

Not surprisingly VCs invest within the top regional entrepreneurial ecosystems in the U.S. While not a hard rule, the prevailing wisdom is, if you want VC funding, prepare to move to Silicon Valley, New York, or Boston.

## How to Find VCs

It's easy to search the Web for venture capital firms—most belong to the NVCA (National Venture Capital Association)—NVCA.org. And VC firms' partners and associates can be found speaking at local venture/entrepreneur events, sitting on panels, blogging, or writing articles. Identifying VC firms and partner names is usually not that hard.

### In-Class Exercise

Look up the top five venture capital firms and identify one of their partners in your region.

But, as we'll find with almost every kind of investor—the most common (and preferred) method of connecting to an venture capitalist (or angel investor) is through a personal introduction. Cold calls or unsolicited emails usually won't get any response.

The most common complaint among young entrepreneurs is that they don't know anyone who would provide an introduction. But introductions to busy VCs aren't impossible, even for brand-new entrepreneurs. Many VCs participate at local entrepreneurship events, panels, or contests and are fairly easy to meet. Entrepreneurs usually interact with other entrepreneurs, advisors, mentors, lawyers, accountants etc., all of whom may be able to provide an introduction—directly or indirectly—to a venture capitalist.

### How to Determine if VC Funding is Appropriate for your Company

VCs generally like the following conditions for investing in a company.

- Solving a clear market pain, problem (or opportunity)—the bigger the better
- A strong team with clear track record—that can execute on the plan
- An "unfair advantage" over potential competition
- Demonstrating customer traction
- Demonstrating market validation (product-market fit)
- If your startup is weak on any of those conditions, either VC funding may night be the right path, or you need to demonstrate how you will address the weaknesses.

---

**Instructor Resource**

- Look up successful companies that got their initial, external, funding from angel investors vs. VCs. Discuss the origin stories of Google and / or Facebook.
- Look at case studies where the presence of too much venture capital was cited as the cause of *failure* for a well-known venture. Examples include Webvan, Kozmo, Pets.com, Flooz, Color.com, and others. Use this list[8] as a starting point.

---

# Angel Funding

For earlier stage startups, angel investors are the more likely alternative to VC funding.

Some metrics for angel funding for the year 2016:[9]

- A total of 64,380 entrepreneurial ventures received angel funding,
- from 297,880 active investors,
- for a total of $21.3 billion,
- with an average deal size of $330,185.

## How to Find Angels

Given the number of angel investors (or potential angels) out there, finding an angel is a lot easier than finding a venture capitalist.

In his popular blog "Startup Professionals" blogger, advisor and angel investor Martin Zwilling offers some concise advice for finding and engaging with angel investors:[10]

- Angels invest in people, more often than they invest in ideas. That means they need to know you, or someone they trust who does know you (warm introduction). For credibility, they need to know you BEFORE you are asking for money.
- Angel investors are people too. Investors expect you to understand their motivation, respect their time, and show your integrity in all actions. They probably won't respond well to high-pressure sales tactics, information overload, or bribes.
- Angels like to "touch and feel" their investments, so they are generally only interested in local opportunities. It won't help your case or your workload to do an email blast and follow-up with 250,000 members around the world.
- But angel investing is risky and time consuming—so more and more, angels are pooling their money and joining groups.

## Angel Groups

In 2016, direct investments reported from U.S. angel groups more than doubled from the year prior:[11]

- The median size of investment (where angel groups co-invest with other investors) in first-round deals was $950,000.
- Groups located in the Northeast make roughly 7 percent of their investments outside of their region, while California groups make 43 percent of their investments outside their state. Having access to the necessary resources and tools is crucial for the success of angel groups looking to invest outside of their region.
- California accounted for 30 percent of all angel-funded early stage deals in 2016, followed by the Southeast, New York, and the Northeast, all of which hovered around 10 percent. Angel groups invested in software (34.3 percent), health care (17.3 percent), B2B (13.0 percent), Internet and mobile (11.2 percent), and B2C (10.3 percent). No other industry or sector generated more than a 2 percent share in funded deals.

The most active angel groups with multiple locations or networks included Keiretsu Forum, Tech Coast Angels, Investors Circle, Golden Seeds, and Astia Angels.

## Resources for Finding Angel Groups:

- **Gust** [12] **(formerly AngelSoft)**
  This is perhaps the most widely used source of information on angel investor groups. Gust claims to have facilitated over $1 billion of investments in 500,000 startups to date, via connection through their platform to over 70,000 angel investors in 190 countries.
- **AngelList** [13]
  AngelList has featured over three million businesses for potential investors in a format that is, effectively, a social network for entrepreneurs and angels. They claim to have already raised over $560 million for 1,400 startups, primarily in the U.S. and Europe. In addition, they serve as a jobs available site for 24,000 startups.
- **Keiretsu Forum** [14]
  This site claims to be the world's largest single angel investor network, with 2,500 accredited investor members throughout 52 chapters on three continents. Since its founding in 2000, its members have invested over $800 million dollars in over 800 companies in technology, consumer products, health care and life sciences, real estate, and other segments with high-growth potential.
- **USA Angel Investment Network** [15]
  This group claims to be the largest angel investment community in the world. They have already raised $300 million for startups in the U.S. and across the world.
  The reach is very broad, with a network has 30 branches extending to 80 different countries. They have over 785,000 registered members with 140,000 investors and 650,000 entrepreneurs.
- **Angel Capital Association (ACA)** [16]
  The ACA is the angel industry alliance, which now includes a directory to more than 240 angel groups and 13,000 individual angels across North America. ACA member angel groups represent more than 10,000 accredited investors and are funding approximately 800 new companies each year, and managing an ongoing portfolio of more than 5,000 companies throughout North America.

## Angel Funding

Angels invest in far more early stage companies than venture capitalists. And while the *average* investment is approximately $330,000 (for individual angels) and $950,000 for groups—angels often invest as low as $10,000, $20,000 or $50,000—making them a very attractive source of funding for early stage ventures.

# Further Reading

- 8 Simple Rules of Angel Investing[17]

# Resources

- Term Sheet Series Wrap Up[18]
- Angel Investing: Term Sheet Economics.[19]
- VC Nomenclature and the Investor Spiral[20]
- How to Read a Term Sheet[21]
- Corporate Venture Capital[22]
- Term Sheets: The Definitive Guide[23]

*CJ Cornell* *is a serial entrepreneur, investor, advisor, mentor, author, speaker, and educator. He is the author of the best-selling book: The Age of Metapreneurship—A Journey into the Future of Entrepreneurship[24] and the upcoming book: The Startup Brain Trust—A Guidebook for Startups, Entrepreneurs, and the Experts that Help them Become Great. Reach him on Twitter at @cjcornell.*

## Leave feedback on this chapter.

## *Notes*

1. Arnobio Morelix, "Insights from the Fastest Growing Companies in America," *Slideshare,* March 2015, https://www.slideshare.net/arnobiomorelix1/kauffman-sxsw-4-insights-from-the-fastest-growing-companies-in-america www.kauffman.org. The Kauffman Foundation is based in Kansas City, Mo., and is among the largest private foundations in the United States with an asset base of approximately $2 billion. They are focused on entrepreneurship—education and research.

2. Bill Payne, "The Funding Gap," *Gust Blog,* December 6, 2011, http://blog.gust.com/the-funding-gap/.

3. "PwC Moneytree Report 2016 Final," *PwC,* https://www.pwc.com/us/en.htm.

4. "PwC Moneytree Report 2016 Final," PwC, https://www.pwc.com/us/en.htm.

5. "Venture Monitor," *National Venture Capital Association* and *PitchBook Data, Inc.,* http://nvca.org/research/venture-monitor/, and https://pitchbook.com/news/reports/1q-2017-pitchbook-nvca-venture-monitor.

6. "PwC / CB Insights MoneyTree(™) Report, Q1 2017," *PwC,* https://www.pwc.com/us/en/moneytree-report/assets/MoneyTree_Report_Q1_2017_FINAL_F. pdf

7. "Venture Monitor," *National Venture Capital Association and PitchBook Data, Inc.,* https://pitchbook.com/news/reports/1q-2017-pitchbook-nvca-venture-monitor.

8. "111 of the Biggest, Costliest Startup Failures of All Time," *CB Insights Blog,* June 22, 2017, https://www.cbinsights.com/blog/biggest-startup-failures/.

9. Liisa Rajala, "Angel Market Sharnk in 2016," *NH Business Review,* June 23, 2017, http://www.nhbr.com/June-23-2017/Angel-market-restructures-in-2016-to-focus-to-seed-and-startup-funding/.

10. "If You Can't Find an Angel Investor, Look Again Here," *Startup Professional Musings,* June 11, 2017, http://blog.startupprofessionals.com/2017/06/if-you-cant-find-angel-investor-look.html.

11. "Angel Resource Institute Halo Report (2016)," *Angel Resource Institute,* http://angelresourceinstitute.org/research/report.php?report=106&name=2016 percent20Annual percent20Halo percent20Report and http://angelresourceinstitute.org/.

12. *Gust,* Gust.com.

13. *AngelList,* https://angel.co/.

14. *Keiretsu Forum,* http://www.keiretsuforum.com/.

15. *Angel Investment Network,* https://www.angelinvestmentnetwork.us/.

16. *Angel Capital Association,* http://www.angelcapitalassociation.org/.

17. CJ Cornell, "8 Simple Rules of Angel Investing," *Academia.edu,* https://www.academia.edu/172159/_8_Simple_Rules_on_Angel_Investing_.

18. Brad Feld, "Term Sheet Series Wrap Up," *Feld Thoughts*, August 2005, https://feld.com/archives/2005/08/term-sheet-series-wrap-up.html.

19. "Angel Investing: Term Sheet Economics," *Women Invest*, March 25, 2013, https://womeninvest.nyc/2013/03/25/angel-investing-term-sheet-economics/.

20. "VC Nomenclature and the Investor Spiral," *Fortune*, May 16, 2011, http://fortune.com/2011/05/16/vc-nomenclature-and-the-investor-spiral/.

21. "How to Read a Term Sheet," *Hyde Park Angels*, July 21, 2015, https://medium.com/hyde-park-angels/how-to-read-a-term-sheet-3c4204ab1c0f.

22. The Most Active Corporate VCs in Q1/Q2 2016," *Plug and Play*, November 14, 2016, http://plugandplaytechcenter.com/2016/11/14/corporate-venture-capital/.

23. Todd Miller, "Term Sheets: The Definitive Guide," *Capshare blog*, https://www.capshare.com/blog/term-sheets-guide/.

24. Cornell, CJ, *The Age of Metapreneurship*, (Phoenix: Venture Point Press, 2017). https://www.amazon.com/dp/069287724X.

# STARTUP FUNDING: NONTRADITIONAL FUNDING SOURCES

*CJ Cornell*

## Introduction

These are coined "nontraditional" only because their prominence as viable funding sources has skyrocketed in the past 10 years. They are indeed becoming mainstream, and even the norm, for startup funding:

- Incubators and Accelerators
- University Programs and Corporate Programs
- Economic Development (government) Programs
- Grants
- Crowdfunding

[Note: Use the slider to navigate the chart below. This will get better soon!]

| | Incubators | Accelerators | University Programs |
|---|---|---|---|
| **Distinguishing Features** | Are usually physical locations with shared office space (and office resources) for new businesses. They charge rent and other fees. Usually incubators are more efficient for "operating" companies (small businesses) as opposed to startups just developing their first products.<br><br>Incubators offer individual workspaces (cubicles) or offices | Accelerators usually offer a small amount of equity funding and have an intensive program (a few weeks or months) that is designed to prepare the entrepreneurs, their product, and company for seed investment. Accelerators are usually "cohort" programs (a group of entrepreneurs are accepted and participate during the same timeframe).<br><br>"Graduates" usually pitch before investors affiliated with the accelerator. | Almost exclusively for students or for faculty trying to commercialize research.<br><br>University programs may offer a combination of incubator facilities and programs similar to accelerators—with the funding being more in the form of small grants. |

| | | | |
|---|---|---|---|
| | with shared use of conference rooms, receptionists, common areas, etc. | Accelerators don't necessarily have buildings or facilities. | University programs often offer an extensive network of advisors and mentors. |
| **Funding** | None. | Usually in the $10,000-$50,000 range. Often VCs and prominent Angel investors participate so they can invest in the promising graduates. | Varies. Usually in the $5,000-$20,000 range and/or free but with use of other university resources. |
| **Participants** | Usually businesses that already have a need for an office presence to conduct business, small businesses. | Usually (but not always), younger teams of entrepreneurs—who can collectively survive for 3-4 months on the accelerator's funding, while participating in the program. | Students (affiliated with the university) and faculty researchers. |
| **Duration** | Varies, but in the 1-5 years range | 3-6 months | Varies but often coinciding with the academic year: 1 semester or 2 semesters |
| **Selection Criteria** | No specific criteria, other than to be able to afford the monthly rent/charges. Some incubators will take equity in return. | Usually highly competitive. Startups/entrepreneurs apply, must go through intensive vetting processes. Usually accelerators also have a preferred type of company they want in the program (e.g., health care ventures only, or mobile app ventures only). | Varies. Most students and faculty are permitted to participate in the programs, but may need to apply (or compete) for funding awards. |
| **Education** | None | Varies. Some offer educational programs but don't require them, while other accelerators have specific startup training programs. | Usually has lots of courses, workshops, seminars and other instructional programs for brand-new entrepreneurs. |
| **Mentorship** | Minimal. Often none—but some incubators affiliate with a list of mentors. | Specific and intensive | Broad. Varies in quality and in type (from small business |

mentoring to
growth venture
advising)

In any geographic region, accelerators and university programs compete for startups and entrepreneurs, so it's not surprising when they each seem to imply that they offer all of the benefits that the others offer. Yes, there are hybrids—but they still primarily fall into one of the categories above.

# Incubators

Incubators don't offer funding as part of their business model. A rare few (like Plug and Play) have separate funding programs as part of their Incubators. Co-working spaces, incidentally, are like very short-term versions of incubators. A rare few (like HubSpot) have some funding programs along with many other programs for startups. So while there are a few hybrids, as a rule, incubators are not a source of funding for startups. They are only included on the chart because entrepreneurs sometimes mistake incubators for accelerators—based on how many incubators decide to market themselves.

# Accelerators

## What Are Startup Accelerators?[1]

Susan Cohen[2], a professor of entrepreneurship at the University of Richmond and a leading scholar on startup accelerators, provides a comprehensive definition of the concept:

> Broadly speaking, [accelerators] help ventures define and build their initial products, identify promising customer segments, and secure resources, including capital and employees. More specifically, accelerator programs are programs of limited-duration—lasting about three months—that help cohorts of startups with the new venture process. They usually provide a small amount of seed capital, plus working space. They also offer a plethora of networking opportunities, with both peer ventures and mentors, who might be successful entrepreneurs, program graduates, venture capitalists, angel investors, or even corporate executives. Finally, most programs end with a grand event, a "demo day" where ventures pitch to a large audience of qualified investors.

Brad Feld, a co-founder of TechStars, a global accelerator program, likened the accelerator experience to immersive education, where a period of intense, focused attention provides company founders an opportunity to learn at a rapid pace.[3]

Learning by doing is something that all company founders eventually go through, but it's a highly inefficient process that drags out over time. The point of accelerators, suggest Feld and others, is to accelerate that process—speeding up the learning cycle in a time-constrained format. In this way, founders compress years' worth of learning into a period of a few months.[4]

## Startup Accelerators in the United States

Y Combinator[5] launched the first accelerator program in 2005, followed closely by TechStars[6], founded in 2006. Both programs have evolved over the years—Y Combinator consolidated its bicoastal programs to a single Silicon Valley location in 2009 (and in fact as of recently[7], has transformed into a later-stage investor), and TechStars has grown to 21 programs[8] worldwide since first launching in Boulder, Colorado. Still, they remain arguably the two premier accelerator programs[9]—or at least among the very best[10].

Growth in U.S.-based accelerators took off after 2008. They grew from 16 programs that year to 27 in 2009 and to 49 in 2010, before eventually reaching 170 programs in 2014 and holding mostly steady. All told, the number of American accelerators increased an average of 50 percent each year between 2008 and 2014.[11]

During the 2005 to 2015 period, these 172 U.S.-based accelerators invested in more than 5,000 U.S.-based startups with a median investment of $100,000.

These companies raised a total of $19.5 billion in funding during this period—or $3.7 million per company on average—reflecting both the relatively small investments made in these early stage companies by accelerators, and the fact that many go on to raise substantial amounts of capital later on.[12]

## Where Are the Accelerators?

In terms of their geography, accelerator programs are unsurprisingly concentrated in the well-known technology startup hubs and major cities of San Francisco—Silicon Valley, Boston—Cambridge, and New York. These three regions account for about 40 percent of all accelerators in the United States, and almost two-thirds of accelerator-funded deals between 2005 and 2015.[13]

However, a good amount of activity is occurring outside of these prime tech hubs. In fact, fully 54 metropolitan statistical areas and four nonmetropolitan regions spread across 35 states and the District of Columbia have accelerator programs today. A number of surprises show up in terms of cities with more than two accelerators, including Chattanooga, Nashville, Cincinnati, Milwaukee, and Honolulu.

## The Down Side to Accelerators

Accelerator funding can be very attractive for young companies (or founders with a new idea)—but it can take a lot of work to prepare and apply—and most of them are extremely competitive. Not only do they take a lot of work (and even more work, if you get accepted)—the funding from the accelerator is designed only to last as long as the program (the bootcamp). Be prepared to drop everything for the next three to six months to participate. When it is over you will be much better positioned to attract traditional angel or venture funding, but there are no guarantees.

## University Programs

For most students, university funding programs are the best (if not, only) option for funding their startup ideas, projects and companies. Most larger universities (and many smaller ones) have specific programs for educating and funding student entrepreneurs. They vary widely—from grants and competitions, to accelerator-like programs just for students. Usually the funding is relatively low ($5,000-$10,000 or so), plus other resources—just enough for students to develop their idea, business model, maybe a prototype, and a pitch.

For students, this remains, by far, the most efficient and effective option for funding early stage ideas.

|  | Corporate Programs | Economic Development | Grants |
|---|---|---|---|
| Distinguishing Features | Larger companies (usually established leaders in their industries)—who have formal programs to encourage new ideas for using their technologies, or improving their business | State, city, or regional governments who want to encourage job-creating companies to move to the area, or to foster new high-growth startups in the region | Awards (gives) money to people or companies who will advance the organization's mission |

| | | | |
|---|---|---|---|
| **Funding** | A very wide range. From $5K—to $25K in grant-style funding to $100K or more in equity (investment funding)<br><br>*Corporate Venture Funding* is a separate department that invests in companies just like a venture capital firm. | Varies depending on the level of government. Often in the form or small equity investments, tax breaks or grants | Varies widely from small grants of a few thousand dollars for those who apply online, to special one-time million-dollar grants |
| **Participants** | Often early stage startups, or founders about to become a startup company | Usually new, but established businesses, or small businesses already making revenues<br><br>Recently, many are offering funding for startups. | Varies, but usually for social entrepreneurs (individuals) or small very early stage companies |
| **Duration** | Usually very short, 3-6 months, often part-time or "virtual" | Funding is awarded (or invested) and often with a specific "use of proceeds" mandated over the course of 1 or 2 years. | Funding is awarded (or invested) and often with a specific "use of proceeds" mandated over the course of 1 or 2 years. |
| **Selection Criteria** | Usually they have an application process and participants are chosen by a committee.<br><br>(For *Corporate Venture Funding*—see Venture Capital.) | Usually they have an application process—but for a contest or competition—where the winners are chosen by a panel of judges. | Usually they have an application process and participants are chosen by a special advisory board or similar committee. |
| **Education** | Some—specific to the corporation's field | Usually none, unless they partner with a university or experts to offer workshops and seminars | None |
| **Mentorship** | Varies | Often will match entrepreneurs will local mentors or SCORE. Quality varies. | None |

# Corporate Programs

Corporate programs often resemble accelerators—but often in a highly focused domain, industry, or market. For instance, AT&T Aspire Accelerator specifically focuses on educational ventures (usually in technology) and they initially provide grant funding, and a virtual acceleration/development program with mentors. As one example, the Walt Disney Company accelerator states[14], "The Disney Accelerator is looking for technology—powered startups from around the world with innovative ideas for products and services in the consumer entertainment and media space."

## Economic Development (Government)

Economic development programs usually focus on attracting growing companies to the region via tax incentives. But more and more states and cities are instituting programs to educate, incubate, accelerate, and grow new venture with funding incentives, and funding programs.

## Grants

Grants are (from Wikipedia):[15]

> Grants are nonrepayable funds or products disbursed by one party (grant makers), often a government department, corporation, foundation or trust, to a recipient, often (but not always) a nonprofit entity, educational institution, business, or an individual. In order to receive a grant, some form of "grant writing," often referred to as either a proposal or an application is required.

> Most grants are made to fund a specific project and require some level of compliance and reporting. The grant writing process involves an applicant submitting a proposal (or submission) to a potential funder, either on the applicant's own initiative or in response to a Request for Proposal from the funder. Other grants can be given to individuals, such as victims of natural disasters or individuals who seek to open a small business. Sometimes grant makers require grant seekers to have some form of tax-exempt status, or be a registered nonprofit organization or a local government.

More and more, grants are becoming a viable source for startup funding. A few grant-giving entities are specifically devoted to entrepreneurship and funding startup companies. Usually their ultimate goal is economic development for a region or for a specific demographic: e.g., funding startups in underdeveloped nations in Africa, or funding inner-city small businesses, or funding startups founded by minorities. Others provide grants because they have a mission to support an industry or a cause, and believe that supporting innovative startup ventures is the best way to advance that cause—as is the cause with the Knight Foundation grants for journalism and technology.

# Journalism's Foundations

(*Adapted from* The Age of Metapreneurship)[16]

Right now, thousands of independent entrepreneurial projects are helping to rebuild journalism's future. Some are experiments in new techniques and products, meant to replace outdated methods. Other projects are addressing brand new issues, like "fake news" which are byproducts of our times.

All around the world, entrepreneurs are working on components of new journalism, in areas such as:

- New payment models like advertising, syndication, paywalls
- Tools for easier, more accurate and higher quality investigative reporting
- Richer election reporting, polling, and prediction technology
- Richer data journalism tools
- Advanced fact checking
- "Drone journalism," machine learning, artificial intelligence
- Better tools for citizen journalists, and for integrating with professional journalists
- And of course, social media tools for better reporting, distribution, and reader engagement

## Knight Foundation

The Knight Foundation, as you might expect from its name, traces its lineage to the founders of the Knight-Ridder news empire. Today, it is the nation's leading funder of journalism and media innovation. In fact, many of the university programs in journalism innovation and entrepreneurship owe their existence (and their names) to the Knight Foundation.

The Knight Foundation is not working on some kind of "moonshot" to save journalism. Instead, they are placing many small bets on vital experiments—any one of which could start a chain reaction.

Each year, it sponsors The Knight News Challenge[17], which awards several million dollars in small grants to promising projects in different areas of journalism, or that impact communities. This is not merely a contest with a prize. The News Challenge is a transparent, collaborative process of vetting great ideas, funding them—and then sharing the results with the industry. Some winners become companies, while others are one-off projects or products. All results—including technology and code—are made available for use and reuse by anyone.

Since 2007 Knight Foundation has reviewed more than 10,000 News Challenge applications and provided more than $37 million in funding to 111 projects. Winners include leading Internet entrepreneurs, emerging media innovators, and traditional newsrooms. Their projects have been adopted by large media organizations and are having an impact on the future of journalism.[18]

Here's just one example of a recent grant opportunity from Knight Foundation, the Knight Prototype Fund,[19] to address the spread of misinformation and increase trust in journalism.

Knight Foundation is not alone in offering funding for journalism endeavors. Other foundations that fund journalism projects include Ford Foundation, MacArthur Foundation, Scripps Howard Foundation, and the Democracy Fund, among others. Some foundations with similar missions are included in this spreadsheet[20] of national grants and competitions for journalism ventures.

Programs like New Voices and New Media Women Entrepreneurs, funded by the McCormick Foundation, as well as professional programs like NewU offered through UNITY, Journalists of Color and with funding from the Ford Foundation, offered startup funding and coaching for media founders from underrepresented and diverse communities. These programs, now defunct, were the precursors to the growing accelerator programs in corporations, in regional spaces and pitch competitions that help get visibility to new media innovations and founders.

Foundations support ventures, individuals, and ideas that align with their mission. If you're going to seek funding from a foundation, it pays to do the deep dive into a foundation's recent awards and see what has been funded. Is collaboration a feature of all of the grants? Do they focus on technological innovation? What are upcoming deadlines? Who is the program officer? Have a conversation with the program officer well in advance of the deadline expressing your interest and asking of any additional thoughts they have on what is of particular interest to reviewers who will be rating the grant. You might ask what they learned from their last round of funding and whether you can get access to it. All this intelligence will help you open the door to a dialogue with the foundation officers and offer you a better understanding of whether your idea aligns with the foundation's goals.

# Resources

- Incubators:
    NBIA —The National Business Incubation Association[21]
    State Level Business Incubation Associations[22]
    International Incubator Associations & Organizations[23]
- Accelerators:
    Comprehensive Accelerator Database[24]
    Global Accelerator Network[25]
    Seed Accelerator Rankings Project (SARP)[26]
    Seed—DB — World—wide Database of Seed Accelerators[27]
    30 Best Startup Accelerators in the U.S. Ranked[28]
- Corporate Programs:
    Corporate Accelerator Database[29]
    Corporate Venture Capital[30]
- Economic Development Programs:

Startup New York[31]
Startup Washington[32]
Arizona: Startup, Arizona Commerce Authority[33]
Arizona Innovation Challenge[34]

***CJ Cornell*** *is a serial entrepreneur, investor, advisor, mentor, author, speaker, and educator. He is the author of the best-selling book: The Age of Metapreneurship—A Journey into the Future of Entrepreneurship[35] and the upcoming book: The Startup Brain Trust—A Guidebook for Startups, Entrepreneurs, and the Experts that Help them Become Great. Reach him on Twitter at @cjcornell.*

## Leave feedback on this chapter.

## *Notes*

1. Ian Hathaway, "Accelerating Growth: Startup Accelerator Programs in the United States," *Brookings,* February 17, 2016, https://www.brookings.edu/research/accelerating-growth-startup-accelerator-programs-in-the-united-states/.

2. "Susan Cohen," *University of Richmond,* http://robins.richmond.edu/faculty-staff/scohen2/.

3. Ian Hathaway, "Accelerating Growth: Startup Accelerator Programs in the United States," *Brookings,* February 17, 2016, https://www.brookings.edu/research/accelerating-growth-startup-accelerator-programs-in-the-united-states/.

4. Ian Hathaway, "Accelerating Growth: Startup Accelerator Programs in the United States," *Brookings,* February 17, 2016. https://www.brookings.edu/research/accelerating-growth-startup-accelerator-programs-in-the-united-states/.

5. *Y Combinator,* https://www.ycombinator.com/.

6. *TechStars,* http://www.techstars.com/.

7. Douglas MacMillan, "Tech Incubator Y Combinator Takes New Tack With Venture Capital Fund," *Wall Street Journal,* October 23, 2015, https://www.wsj.com/articles/tech-incubator-y-combinator-takes-new-tack-with-venture-capital-fund-1444938590.

8. "TechStars Accelerator Programs," *TechStars,* http://www.techstars.com/programs/.

9. Jonathan Shieber, "These are the 15 Best Accelerator Programs in the U.S.," *TechCrunch,* March 10, 2014, http://techcrunch.com/2014/03/10/these-are-the-15-best-accelerators-in-the-u-s/.

10. "These are the Top Accelerators in the U.S.," *Seed Accelerator Rankings Project 2017,* http://www.seedrankings.com/

11. Ian Hathaway, "Accelerating Growth: Startup Accelerator Programs in the United States," February 17, 2016, *Brookings,* https://www.brookings.edu/research/accelerating-growth-startup-accelerator-programs-in-the-united-states/.

12. Ian Hathaway, "Accelerating Growth: Startup Accelerator Programs in the United States," *Brookings,* February 17, 2016, https://www.brookings.edu/research/accelerating-growth-startup-accelerator-programs-in-the-united-states/.

13. Ian Hathaway, "Accelerating Growth: Startup Accelerator Programs in the United States," *Brookings,* February 17, 2016, https://www.brookings.edu/research/accelerating-growth-startup-accelerator-programs-in-the-united-states/

14. *Disney Accelerator,* https://disneyaccelerator.com/.

15. "Grant (money)," *Wikipedia,* https://en.m.wikipedia.org/wiki/Grant_(money).

16. CJ Cornell, *The Age of Metapreneurship* (Phoenix: Venture Point Press, 2017), 278—279.

17. *Knight News Challenge,* http://www.knightfoundation.org/challenges/knight-news-challenge.

18. *Knight Foundation,* http:www.knightfoundation.org.

19. Chris Barr, "20 Projects Will Address the Spread of Misinformation through Knight Prototype Fund," *Knight Foundation,* https://knightfoundation.org/articles/20-projects-will-address-the-spread-of-misinformation-through-knight-prototype-fund.

20. "National Grants and Competitions for Journalism Ventures," https://docs.google.com/a/rebus.foundation/spreadsheets/d/1-1h8aAHIcERKjzBFLSyBxrsXcPchGT2i7LQD7S7rqVs/edit?usp=drive_web.

21. "Information for Entrepreneurs," *NBIA,* http://www2.nbia.org/for_entrepreneurs/.

22. "U.S. State Incubation Associations," *NBIA,* http://www2.nbia.org/links_to_member_incubators/state.php.

23. "International Incubator Associations & Organizations," *NBIA,* http://www2.nbia.org/links_to_member_incubators/international.php.

24. *Acceleratorinfo.com,* http://www.acceleratorinfo.com/see-all.html.

25. *Gan.co,* http://gan.co/.

26. "These Are the Top Accelerators in the U.S.," *Seed Accelerator Rankings Project 2017,* http://www.seedrankings.com/.

27. "Seed Accelerators," Seed-DB, http://www.seed-db.com/accelerators.

28. Conor Cawley, "30 Best Startup Accelerators in the U.S., Ranked," *Tech.Co,* https://tech.co/30-best-startup-accelerators-us-2017-06.

29. "Database of Corporate Accelerators," *Corporate Accelerator DB,* https://www.corporate-accelerators.net/database/.

30. "Corporate Venture Capital," *Plug and Play Tech Center,* November 14, 2016, http://plugandplaytechcenter.com/2016/11/14/corporate-venture-capital/.

31. *StartupNY,* https://startup.ny.gov/.

32. *Startup Washington,* http://startup.choosewashingtonstate.com/.

33. "Arizona: Startup," *Arizona Commerce Authority,* http://www.azcommerce.org/start-up.

34. "Arizona Innovation Challenge," *Arizona Commerce Authority,* http://www.azcommerce.com/programs/arizona-innovation-challenge.

35. Cornell, CJ, *The Age of Metapreneurship,* (Phoenix: Venture Point Press, 2017). https://www.amazon.com/dp/069287724X.

# STARTUP FUNDING: CROWDFUNDING

*CJ Cornell*

Crowdfunding, which barely existed a few years ago, spread to every aspect of society—from funding creative projects, local civic projects to causes and charities, and of course—funding startup companies. Today, crowdfunding is an essential part of every entrepreneurship conversation.

Modern <u>crowdfunding</u> has the following haiku-like definition:[1]

- An individual or organization,
- on behalf of a cause, a project, a product, or a company,
- solicits and collects money,
- usually in relatively small amounts,
- from a large number of people,
- using an online platform,
- where communications and transactions are managed over electronic networks.

Crowdfunding is one of the great movements of the twenty-first century, and one of the most powerful. Still in its infancy, crowdfunding moved beyond Kickstarter-like passion projects and became a major new and disruptive force in investment funding. And just in the last few years, the crowdfunding movement impelled the U.S. Congress, state legislatures in all 50 states *and* the Security Exchange Commission to overhaul investment laws that existed since 1934.

Broadly defined, crowdfunding is collecting small amounts of money from a large number of people. With the advent of social networks (abundance of people on the network), crowdfunding only recently became practical. But the concept has been around for centuries—except that with crowdfunding, the people willingly contribute money for a project, product, or cause that they believe in.

## Crowfunding—a Little History

The concept of crowdfunding is old. What's new is applying technology—social networks—to the process. This allows interested supporters from around the globe to support any project, anywhere, as long as they share passion and see merit in the project's goals.

In the early 1880s, France gave the United States a gift: the Statue of Liberty. It was shipped to New York City where remained packed in crates for over a year. Why? The New York state government would not allocate the $200,000 required to build and mount the statue onto a pedestal (today this would be over $2.5 million). Newspaper mogul Joseph Pulitzer ran a fundraising campaign through his "New York World" tabloid—offering to publish the name of everyone who donated, to the front page. Donors also would get little rewards: $1 got you a 6-inch replica statue and $5 got you a 12-inch statue. The campaign went viral. Within six months of the fundraising appeal, the pedestal was fully funded, with the majority of donations being under a dollar.

But this was not the first crowdfunding campaign. For centuries, book authors have appealed to the crowd for funding. Kickstarter (the largest crowdfunding site) proudly recounts one of the earliest examples:[2]

> In 1713, Alexander Pope (the poet) set out to translate 15,693 lines of ancient Greek poetry into English. It took five long years to get the six volumes right, but the result was worth the wait: a translation of Homer's Iliad that endures to this day. How did Pope go about getting this project off the ground? Turns out he kind of Kickstarted it.
>
> In exchange for a shout-out in the acknowledgments an early edition of the book, and the delight of helping to bring a new creative work into the world, 750 subscribers pledged two gold guineas to support Pope's effort before he put pen to paper. They were listed in an early edition of the book.

## A Boon for Entrepreneurs

Entrepreneurs discovered crowdfunding as an efficient and exciting method of funding innovative product ideas that were too early for investors. Instead, they reached out to like-minded supporters, early adopters, and technology fans, who were enthusiastic about backing early stage ideas. The crowd not only contributes money to develop the product—but the crowd offers something just as valuable: early market validation for the product, and a chance for the entrepreneur to build reputation and credibility.

Backers embraced rewards-based sites like Kickstarter and Indiegogo because they offered a model that was both engaging and lower risk. Potential contributors discussed the merits of the project or product with each other and with the founders; they were allowed to pre-commit to donations at specific, nominal levels—typically $5, $25, $100, $250—with each level of contribution receiving different rewards. This pre-commitment was important. It amounts to a binding pledge. The entrepreneur sets a funding goal and a time limit. If the pledges meet the funding goal within the time limit, everyone gets charged. Otherwise, no money changes hands. For early backers, this was a critical feature getting them to embrace crowdfunding.

Later, as backers get more comfortable with crowdfunding, other methods of contributing proliferated.

[Note: Use the slide bar to navigate the below chart on the web book. This will get better soon!]

## The Many Facets of Crowdfunding

| | Donation Crowdfunding | Rewards-based Crowdfunding | "Pre-order" Crowdfunding | Debt Crowdfunding | Equity Crowdfunding |
|---|---|---|---|---|---|
| **Overview** | Charities and causes. Usually for individuals and smaller organizations | Donors get token rewards as part of their contribution. Usually used for projects in the arts, entertainment and community/ civic projects | Similar to rewards-based crowdfunding, except the donations are made with the expectation that the backers will receive early versions of the product that they are funding | A.k.a. "peer to peer," "P2P," "marketplace lending," or "crowdlending." Funding is aggregated into a loan, that will be paid back to the contributors. | The general public invests small amounts in return for stock. |
| **Typical Range** | Under $10,000 (often under $2,000) | Varies widely. Average $7-10K per project. But many attract $50-$100K | Varies widely; many projects attracting over $100K, to $1-$5M | From "microloans" for small business >$2,500, to traditional loans in $10k – $500k range subject to personal credit approval. | Brand-new SEC regulations. While companies can raise as little as $100k this is really only practical for over $500K to $5M or greater given the level of fees and preparations required. |
| **Prominent Platforms[3]** | GoFundMe, CrowdRise | Kickstarter, Indiegogo | Kickstarter, Indiegogo | Funding Circle, Lending Club, Prosper, Kiva | AngelList, Crowdfunder, CircleUp, Gust4, Seedrs, Fundable, Indiegogo |
| **Typical Candidate Projects** | Charitable causes, events | Creative projects, events | New product innovations | Small business | Established startups (post-seed) |
| **Advantages (for entrepreneurs)** | Allows entrepreneurs to efficiently solicit funding from friends and family (who primarily want to help | Solicits funding from advocates passionate about the idea, as well as feedback and advice | Pre-order (advance sales) provide valuable market validation as well as product funding. | Funding for small businesses that otherwise would not qualify for bank loans | Circumvents the venture capital industry and allows for raising significant funding by going directly to the public |

| | | | | | |
|---|---|---|---|---|---|
| | | | | | the entrepreneur, personally) |
| **Disadvantages (for Entrepreneurs)** | Practical for small amounts only | Practical for nominal fundraising, but does not always prove customer demand for a specific product. | Pre-order commitments can be very risky (selling a product that does not yet exist). | P2P lending requires repayment, and usually personal guarantees. | Significant overhead costs in preparing. Regulations still in flux |

Hundreds of crowdfunding platforms emerged since the early success of Indiegogo (2008) and Kickstarter (2009). It is not necessary to use a third-party platform. Individuals or organizations can raise funds using their own websites, but they still need to incorporate tools for sophisticated payment processing, managing contributors—and attracting a crowd.

Hybrids and new categories are emerging: royalty-based crowdfunding—allowing backers to receive royalties from the product they funded, and litigation crowdfunding—allowing backers to fund a lawsuit in return for a stake in any resulting monetary judgments.

Today, the latest numbers show worldwide crowdfunding raised approximately $35 Billion in 2015 with the vast majority, approximately $25 Billion, being debt. Crowdfunding followed by over $5 Billion for donation/reward-based crowdfunding.[5]

But those figures are for all kinds of crowdfunding campaigns—including those that are for charity, community, and personal projects. To get a sense, realistically, of the kind of projects that are funded through the most popular crowdfunding platforms, let's take a look at Kickstarter—who publishes their data, real-time, for all to see:

## Kickstarter Stats

Kickstarter provides raw stats about projects funded on its platform, representing the site's all-time figures since it launched in 2009, and updates this data every day. View the data at https://www.kickstarter.com/help/stats[6]. Below is a summary of the data as of June 12, 2017:

| | |
|---|---|
| Total dollars pledged to Kickstarter Projects | $3,096,331,221 |
| Successfully funded projects | 126,396 |
| Total backers | 13,043,973 |
| Repeat backers | 4,185,194 |
| Total pledges | 38,692,691 |

| Category | Successfully Funded Projects | Less than $1,000 Raised | $1,000 to $9,999 Raised | $10,000 to $19,999 Raised | $20,000 to $99,999 Raised | $100 K to $999,999 Raised | $1 M Raised |
|---|---|---|---|---|---|---|---|
| **All** | **126,422** | **15,418** | **71,392** | **18,139** | **17,374** | **3,863** | **236** |
| Music | 25,624 | 2,542 | 18,295 | 3,351 | 1,368 | 66 | 2 |
| Film & Video | 23,012 | 2,635 | 13,065 | 3,616 | 3,347 | 343 | 6 |
| Publishing | 11,298 | 1,676 | 7,082 | 1,480 | 987 | 73 | 0 |
| Games | 10,849 | 848 | 4,312 | 1,982 | 2,753 | 874 | 80 |
| Art | 10,580 | 2,452 | 6,571 | 946 | 561 | 45 | 5 |
| Design | 9,132 | 591 | 3,126 | 1,600 | 2,772 | 993 | 50 |
| Theater | 6,275 | 884 | 4,566 | 532 | 275 | 18 | 0 |
| Technology | 5,759 | 349 | 1,592 | 800 | 1,827 | 1,110 | 81 |
| Food | 5,719 | 607 | 2,397 | 1,352 | 1,292 | 64 | 7 |
| Comics | 5,117 | 660 | 3,177 | 644 | 560 | 75 | 1 |
| Fashion | 4,854 | 544 | 2,193 | 917 | 1,026 | 170 | 4 |
| Photography | 3,122 | 594 | 1,754 | 440 | 316 | 18 | 0 |
| Dance | 2,232 | 209 | 1,748 | 208 | 66 | 1 | 0 |
| Crafts | 1,887 | 647 | 990 | 148 | 96 | 6 | 0 |
| Journalism | 962 | 180 | 524 | 123 | 128 | 7 | 0 |

## Successfully Funded Projects

According to Kickstarter, the majority of successfully funded projects raise less than $10,000, but a growing number have reached six, seven, and even eight figures. Currently funding projects that have reached their goals are not included in this chart—only projects whose funding is complete.

In other words—while there are indeed several multimillion-dollar crowdfunding success stories, most campaigns—particularly first-time crowdfunding campaigns—bring in a far more modest figure. For entrepreneurs seeking crowdfunding, well, expectations should be aligned with reality.

| Category | Successfully Funded Projects | Less than $1,000 Raised | $1,000 to $9,999 Raised | $10,000 to $19,999 Raised | $20,000 to $99,999 Raised | $100 K to $999,999 Raised | $1 M Raised |
|---|---|---|---|---|---|---|---|
| All | 126,422 | 15,418 | 71,392 | 18,139 | 17,374 | 3,863 | 236 |
| Music | 25,624 | 2,542 | 18,295 | 3,351 | 1,368 | 66 | 2 |
| Film & Video | 23,012 | 2,635 | 13,065 | 3,616 | 3,347 | 343 | 6 |
| Publishing | 11,298 | 1,676 | 7,082 | 1,480 | 987 | 73 | 0 |
| Games | 10,849 | 848 | 4,312 | 1,982 | 2,753 | 874 | 80 |
| Art | 10,580 | 2,452 | 6,571 | 946 | 561 | 45 | 5 |
| Design | 9,132 | 591 | 3,126 | 1,600 | 2,772 | 993 | 50 |
| Theater | 6,275 | 884 | 4,566 | 532 | 275 | 18 | 0 |
| Technology | 5,759 | 349 | 1,592 | 800 | 1,827 | 1,110 | 81 |
| Food | 5,719 | 607 | 2,397 | 1,352 | 1,292 | 64 | 7 |
| Comics | 5,117 | 660 | 3,177 | 644 | 560 | 75 | 1 |
| Fashion | 4,854 | 544 | 2,193 | 917 | 1,026 | 170 | 4 |
| Photography | 3,122 | 594 | 1,754 | 440 | 316 | 18 | 0 |
| Dance | 2,232 | 209 | 1,748 | 208 | 66 | 1 | 0 |
| Crafts | 1,887 | 647 | 990 | 148 | 96 | 6 | 0 |
| Journalism | 962 | 180 | 524 | 123 | 128 | 7 | 0 |

Journalism and media entrepreneurs should notice that, since Kickstarter's inception, a total of 962 journalism projects successfully raised money through crowdfunding, with the majority of those raising less than $10,000.

Technology products fare better—but those are usually consumer hardware (electronic) products. Arts projects (Film, Video, Music, Art, Design, Theater and photography) garner the lion's share of the crowdfunding donations on Kickstarter.

For entrepreneurs, it's important to note:

1. Crowdfunding is usually most effective for startup companies who are able to deliver a tangible product. Backers donate money in return for "rewards" are really pre-orders for a physical product.
2. Service businesses and consulting businesses have little chance of being funded on typical crowdfunding sites.

Regardless of the risks and limitations, crowdfunding remains a powerful new way to fund new companies and new projects. But it's not free money or easy money. Attracting money from the crowd takes significant preparation and significant work. However, unlike other forms of funding, the steps are largely under your control.

# Basics of a Crowdfunding Campaign

- Kickstarter, currently the most popular crowdfunding platform, enables "project creators" to post project or product descriptions and videos in order to solicit funding (in the form of "pledge" contributions).
- Project creators set a fundraising goal and a deadline, usually 30-90 days (with the average being 45-60 days).
- Using social media and other promotional techniques, the project owners attempt to engage advocates and supporters who pledge relatively small amounts of money.
- The project creators offer token "rewards" as incentives for contributors to donate to the project. If the total amount of the pledges meets or exceeds the goal, before the deadline, then the "pledges" are automatically collected from the donors.
- Kickstarter crowdfunding campaigns are "all or nothing": If the target funding goal is not met by the deadline, then no money changes hands.
- Indiegogo is a platform that allows for an all-or-nothing campaign, or a "flexible funding" campaign: where the money pledged is awarded to the campaign at the end of the time limit, regardless if the goal was met.

## Notable Crowdfunding Campaign Techniques and Tips

Indiegogo CEO Slava Rubin offers a few critical tips and tricks for those looking to crowdfund successfully.[7]

- Rubin notes how important pitch videos are to campaigns: "Campaigns that feature videos—about the startup and the products—typically raised 114 percent more money on Indiegogo compared to those that don't."
- Discussing how "word of mouth" is important to campaigns, Slava shared: "Get your inner circle of friends, family and customers to fund you and to spread the news about the campaign. This will get the momentum going."
- Noting that organizers should stay in contact with backers, the CEO and co-founder of the platform stated:
- "Campaigns that provide updates every five days raised twice as much as those that update every ten days or more."

Yancey Strickler, CEO of Kickstarter, points out that Kickstarter campaigns that reach the 20 percent mark have an 82 percent success rate. If you reach 30 percent, you have a 98 percent chance of reaching your goal.[8]

"Think about that: with less than a third of your goal funded, you have a 98 percent chance of success. These inherently lopsided results require a lopsided approach: you should be putting the vast majority of your efforts on the early or even very—early portion of your campaign."[9]

The implication here is that you shouldn't promote a campaign with 10 percent or 12 percent funding to strangers. This also includes Facebook fans, blog readers, or your existing user base. This sounds counterintuitive, but even a die-hard fan can be off-put by poor crowdfunding performance. It's one thing to mention your new campaign, with one or two small posts, but don't waste these high-quality leads early on. Save them for when they'll help the most: maybe before 50 percent, but definitely after you've reached a respectable 20-25 percent."[10]

- Your first step is to figure out your target audience at least a month before your campaign is scheduled to go live.
- Campaign owners often try to target everyone around them (friends, family, co-workers, etc.) because they don't invest enough time to identify their target audience which gives them vastly expanded reach.
- This lack of focus is certainly not the most efficient way to market a crowdfunding campaign. In order to determine the target audience for your campaign stop and think about WHO can benefit from your product or your service.[11]

Then zero in on key demographics of this audience by considering the age range, gender, income, and education level (as applicable) of the pool of potential crowdfunders who could or would back your project."

## Lessons for Entrepreneurs from Crowdfunding

Kauffman Dissertation Fellow Ethan Mollick at the University of Pennsylvania's Wharton School examined almost 47,000 projects on Kickstarter that raised a combined revenue of $198 million.[12] Mollick concluded that several factors influence whether a project will succeed or not:

- The greater the size of the founder's social network, the greater the chance for success (particularly Facebook in this case; this is also known as the "be popular" strategy).
- The underlying quality of the projects—those with high-quality, polished pitches are more likely to be funded (e.g., use a video; as Kickstarter's website states, "Projects with videos succeed at a much higher rate than those without").
- A strong geographic component tie-in seems to increase success (pitching country music in Nashville, film in Los Angeles, etc.).
- A shorter Kickstarter duration is better (35 percent chance of success for 30-day pitches, 29 percent for 60-day pitches). Mollick noted that a longer duration implies a lack of confidence in the project's success.

- Being highlighted on the Kickstarter website is hugely beneficial (89 percent chance of success vs. 30 percent for unfeatured projects).
- A large number of creative individuals in the city where the project is based is associated with greater success (target these kinds of people).

### Research Study from Indiegogo: Crowdfunding Campaign Stats

Indiegogo took a look at the numbers and statistics behind 100,000 Indiegogo campaigns to see what's working and what's not. They offered several tips for campaigns.[13]

- They suggest 30-day campaigns. Of successful campaigns they analyzed, roughly a third lasted between 30 and 39 days.
- Keep updating your campaign page throughout your campaign with progress updates, newly added perks and other successes. Contributors get notified by email when you update the campaign, so this is an important way to keep your funders engaged. Indiegogo suggests updating your campaign at least four times.
- Indiegogo found that of the 100,000 campaigns they looked at (including those that didn't meet their goals), 42 percent of funds were raised in the first and last three days. Be ready to start and finish strong.
- Their stats showed that successful campaigns added an average of 12 new perks to their campaigns after they launched.
- Don't go solo—campaigns with a team behind them and therefore many networks to leverage were more successful.
- Stats showed that campaigns with video raised four times the funds as those without. So be sure to include this crucial marketing element.
- Don't limit your efforts to a U.S. audience. The United States, Canada, United Kingdom, Australia and Germany were the top five contributing countries to the campaigns analyzed.

---

*Assignments / Discussion: What are the most successful crowdfunding campaigns of all time? What do they have in common? Search for current and successfully completed crowdfunding campaigns in journalism and media. Discuss what works and what doesn't work. Discuss specific strategies that would improve the success of journalism and media crowdfunding campaigns.*

---

# Equity Crowdfunding

Until very recently—under antiquated U.S. securities laws—it was illegal to offer equity (stock) to anyone in the crowd. But then the crowd became a movement, and made history.

Now, crowdfunding is also poised to become a growing source of earliest stage equity financing following passage of the JOBS Act in April 2012. The JOBS Act enabled investors to use the Web and social media to make investments in entrepreneurs and small and medium companies.

On April 5, 2012 President Barack Obama signed the Jumpstart Our Business Startups Act (JOBS Act)—a bipartisan bill that was specifically designed to open the floodgates of funding for emerging growth companies. After nearly four years of regulatory wrangling, the Securities and Exchange Commission released the final rules, taking effect on May 16, 2016.

Equity crowdfunding is the category with all eyes watching. Not only does the new law allow for just about anyone to *invest in*, not just donate to an emerging startup company—it allows startups to publicly solicit from the crowd. Until May 2016, all this was illegal. Until then, startups had to make the rounds with VCs and Angels, educate them about their industry, pitch, get "warm" introductions. Up until then, an engineer, for instance, who might have recognized the unique potential of a nascent Kickstarter product, could not invest because she wasn't an "accredited" investor. The VCs and Angels were allowed to become millionaires, but experts who could spot the early potential were not.

The World Bank forecasts a global crowdfunding market of $96 billion by 2025[14]—far more than venture capital and angel funding combined.

---

## Spot.us—Honorable Mention

Before Kickstarter or Indiegogo existed, there was Spot.us.

Founded in 2008 by a young—but experienced—journalist named David Cohn[15], Spot.us was an online product and a company. It no longer exists, yet Spot.us was one of the most important experiments to emerge from the Knight News Challenge.

Spot.us pioneered *community funded reporting*: crowdfunding for journalism. Today, this is an easy concept to digest—but in 2008 a lot of people had a hard time understanding the concept. It's the innovator's curse.

Stories began as tips from the public giving an issue they would like to see covered, or pitches from a journalist to create a story, including the amount of money needed. Visitors to the website could then donate to fund the pitch.[16]

If, for instance, a local citizen wanted to see an investigative story on the mayor's past business ties with a contractor, they would post the idea to Spot.us. A journalist browsing the site might be intrigued, and would agree to research and write the story, for an estimated $5,000. People in the community would pledge or donate $20 or $50 each. When the total was met, the journalist would write the story. News organizations could obtain exclusive rights by contributing greater than 50 percent of the funding.

Without this kind of mechanism, important stories and investigative reports might never have seen the light of day. Many services today for freelance writers and creatives—particularly crowdfunding sites—owe their existence to the trailblazing efforts of Spot.us.

## Resources

- KickTraq[17]

### Instructor Resources

For faculty wanting to bring first-hand expertise on funding into their classroom, consider inviting guests including:

- outside speakers
- angel investors / a local angel group
- local VCs
- a local startup entrepreneur—who has raised venture funding (... try to avoid lawyers, consultants, accountants etc ... )

Require students to make a grant application to a journalism foundation or set up a Kickstarter campaign during the course of the semester.

*CJ Cornell is a serial entrepreneur, investor, advisor, mentor, author, speaker, and educator. He is the author of the best-selling book: The Age of Metapreneurship—A Journey into the Future of Entrepreneurship[18] and the upcoming book: The Startup Brain Trust—A Guidebook for Startups, Entrepreneurs, and the Experts that Help them Become Great. Reach him on Twitter at @cjcornell.*

## Leave feedback on this chapter.

# Notes

1. Cornell, CJ, *The Age of Metapreneurship*, (Phoenix: Venture Point Press, 2017), 197—199. https://www.amazon.com/dp/069287724X.

2. Justin Kazmark, "Kickstarter Before Kickstarter," *Kickstarter,* July 18, 2013, https://www.kickstarter.com/blog/kickstarter-before-kickstarter.

3. Note that many platforms allow for more than one type of crowdfunding type: e.g., Kickstarter allows for rewards and pre-orders; Fundable allows for equity and rewards.

4. Gust, founded by super-angel David Rose, was originally a platform exclusively for angel investors and angel groups, but has recently expanded into equity crowdfunding, fortified by a host of support services for companies and investors—including due diligence, financials, and cap tables.

5. "Crowdfunding Industry Statistics 2015-2016," *CrowdExpert.com,* http://crowdexpert.com/ crowdfunding-industry-statistics/. and Anthony Zeoli, "Crowdfunding: A Look at 2015 & Beyond!" *Crowdfund Insider,* January 05, 2016, http://www.crowdfundinsider.com/2015/12/ 79574-crowdfunding-a-look-at-2015-beyond/.

6. Kickstarter Stats, Accessed June 12, 2017, *Kickstarter,* https://www.kickstarter.com/help/stats.

7. Samantha Hurst, "Brief: Indiegogo's Slava Rubin Offers up Tricks for Crowdfunding Success," *Crowdfund Insider,* August 27, 2015, https://www.crowdfundinsider.com/2015/08/73438-brief-indiegogos-slava-rubin-offers-up-tips-tricks-for-crowdfunding-success/.

8. "How to Reach Your Crowdfunding Tipping Point," *Trustleaf on Medium*, April 30, 2014, https://medium.com/on-small-businesses/how-to-reach-your-crowdfunding-tipping-point-d418aa1a2853.

9. "How to Reach Your Crowdfunding Tipping Point," *Trustleaf on Medium*, April 30, 2014, https://medium.com/on-small-businesses/how-to-reach-your-crowdfunding-tipping-point-d418aa.

10. "How to Reach Your Crowdfunding Tipping Point," *Trustleaf on Medium,* April 30, 2014, https://medium.com/on-small-businesses/how-to-reach-your-crowdfunding-tipping-point-d418aa1a2853.

11. "Build the Crowd Before Starting Your Crowdfunding Campaign," *Crowdfund Buzz,* June 4, 2014, http://www.crowdfundbuzz.com/build-crowd-starting-crowdfunding-campaign.

12. Ethan R. Mollick, "The Dynamics of Crowdfunding: An Exploratory Study," *Journal of Business Venturing* 29, no. 1 (January 2014): 1-16. https://papers.ssrn.com/sol3/ papers.cfm?abstract_id=2088298.

13. Amy Yeh, "New Research Study: 7 Stats from 100,000 Crowdfunding Campaigns," *Indiegogo Blog,* https://go.indiegogo.com/blog/2015/10/crowdfunding-statistics-trends-infographic.html.

14. "Crowdfunding's Potential for the Developing World," *Information for Development Program infoDev / The World Bank*, November 18, 2013, http://funginstitute.berkeley.edu/wp-content/ uploads/2013/11/Crowdfundings_Potential_for_the_Developing_World.pdf.

15. *Digidave*, http://blog.digidave.org/about.

16. "Spot.us," *Wikipedia*, https://en.wikipedia.org/wiki/Spot.us.

17. *KickTraq*, https://www.kicktraq.com.

18. Cornell, CJ, *The Age of Metapreneurship*, (Phoenix: Venture Point Press, 2017). https://www.amazon.com/dp/069287724X.

# FROM THE FIELD: FRIENDS, FAMILY AND FOOLS FUNDING

*Francine Hardaway*

## From the Field

Friends, family, and fools. That's who usually funds very early startups. After all, who in their right mind would invest money in an unproven product with an unsubstantiated market, often with a single inexperienced person at the helm? Think about it: Would YOU give hard-earned money to a stranger?

I am often contacted by startups who know I've been an angel investor and think if they email me a pitch deck and ask me if I want a follow-up meeting that I will enthusiastically reply in the affirmative.

I never do. And here's the reason. I only invest in people I know. Why? Because that slightly minimizes the risk. Only slightly, however. When I make an investment in a startup, I kiss the money good-bye. I might as well have lost it in Las Vegas gambling, for the number of times I get a return on my investment, and over time I have come to know this. Every person (relative, friend, or just random risk-taker) who invests in your venture should be aware of this.

There are three risks every early-stage investor must know, and every entrepreneur should ignore: the product risk, the market risk, and the people risk. If entrepreneurs focused on the risks, they'd never start companies. But if investors *didn't* focus on risk, they'd be broke and on the street.

The product risk consists of the unknowns surrounding whether the proposed product can be created or built at all. Think virtual reality, which has been announced for two decades without becoming a product accessible for the average user. To make virtual reality accessible would mean making the glasses look like real glasses, and not like something only a dork would wear. And making the focus good enough so ordinary people don't get sick after a half hour. And bringing the price down to an affordable number. For most of us, $2,500 for a fast computer and another $1,500 for glasses is not affordable for an entertainment device.

Then there's the market risk. Let's go back to the highly-touted virtual reality. Suppose we could afford

$4,000 for the setup. What would we actually DO with it? With every product, there must be a product market fit. We must *need* the product for something to make us overcome our desire to save our pennies. Food is one of those products.

And last there's the people risk:

- Will this founder be able to make a go of this business?
- Will she stick with it when the chips are down?
- Will this product scale enough to make a return on investment?
- Will a competitor come out of the woodwork before I, the investor, make the 10x return on investment that I want to make?
- Will the founders continue to get along well enough to be able to work together? Will the product become a business and the business become a company?
- Will the founder create a corporate culture that develops and nurtures new employees?

I always invest in someone whose capabilities for business I think I know well. My first investment, in one of my former students, was because I knew how tenacious this guy was as a student, and also how ethical he was as a human being. That investment paid off about 50 to 1. That's extremely rare. But the next time he started a company, I invested in him again. That's why experienced investors seem to invest in experienced entrepreneurs.

These three risks — product, market, and people—together constitute the investment risk. Since you can't minimize the product and market risk involved in an as yet untried product, the only one that can be minimized is the people risk.

And that's why investing in strangers almost never happens, and as a startup, you should only look to people who know you and would bet on you no matter what you did. That's where your family comes in. Moms want their children to be successful, so they'll gamble where others will not. Sometimes friends are like that, too. The third group are fools. They don't realize all the risks, and the problem with taking their money is that they're likely to contact you every day to see if their investments are getting more valuable.

That is unless they are a special kind of "fool," an early customer. A customer is someone with a pain so intense that she's willing to take any kind of risk to have it relieved, even the risks described above. Early stage companies just aren't appropriate for other kinds of investments beyond friends, family, and fools. Or beta customers.

Truthfully, customers are the best people to fund your startup. They've already got the need, so you don't have to prove the market to them. And their need is so intense that they're willing to take a chance on an unproven technology. You can sell them an early version of the product and they will appreciate it so much that they'll pay for it in advance, which generates the funds for product development. Kickstarter works this way. People who contribute to Kickstarter campaigns aren't looking for a 10x return on their investment. Instead, they want the product. That's why crowdfunding took off—because people truly interested in products like home robots and fitness watches were willing to take the gamble that an entrepreneur they didn't know could deliver those products.

When I teach my classes, I make my students all start a business during the semester. And I ask them to find an investor—even if it's a parent and a miniscule investment, just so they learn how to pitch and what a great responsibility it is to take another person's money. Or I ask them to find a customer: someone who will pay for the product. They panic. But they produce. Which ultimately is what real entrepreneurs must do.

*As the founder of Stealthmode Partners, **Francine Hardaway** is a nineteen-year advocate and resource for entrepreneurs and intrapreneurs. She has consulted with more than 1,000 startups and blogs about technology, entrepreneurship, and health-care policy issues at* Huffington Post, Medium, *and* http://blog.stealthmode.com. *Reach her on Twitter at @hardaway.*

## Leave feedback on this sidebar.

# FROM THE FIELD: THE JOURNEY FROM LISTENING TO LEADER

*Chris Dell*

---

## From the Field

*Contest funding helped Chris Dell to get his venture, Go Baller, off the ground, but the road to sustainability involved some pivots.*

### Pivot #1 – From Listening to Questioning (2006-2010) "The College Years"

During my undergraduate years I had seemingly every person in the world telling my classmates and I that we had picked the wrong career path. It was a four-year-running journalism joke that forced about half of my class to change majors between 2006 and 2010. My college professors would literally go on hours-long rants trying to convince us to leave the journalism field for something else, whether it be public relations, marketing, economics, or something more "financially friendly." I took it personally, more as a challenge to succeed against all odds. In a profession when many others were getting fired or quitting altogether, I added it as a chip to my shoulder and started asking questions back. Why were people always asking me "Do you think newspapers will die?" It wasn't the right question to ask, yet so many remained stuck on it, as though there were no other options to consider. The answer was easy. Just like I had realized about my resume and bachelor's degree: A piece of paper means nothing without results clipped and attached. Resumes won't die with paper. They move online to LinkedIn. Storytelling and news won't die with paper, either. They will move to Facebook, Instagram, Snapchat and the next craze. It's crazy to think storytelling could die or news could die. This motivated me to wonder why these old ways of thinking even existed in the first place, and how much pushback was needed in the media industry against this legacy media mindset.

### Pivot #2 – From Questioner to Practitioner (2012-2014) "Grad School"

In 2012 I left my family and lifelong home in Florida and moved to New York City to pursue my M.A. at the CUNY Graduate School of Journalism. It was a decision that not many around me endorsed.

Less than a year earlier I told my favorite undergrad professor of my intentions to pursue journalism in grad school, and he swiftly "sat me down" for a talk. So much for validation from others, whether that meant my professors, parents or even best friends back home! I had to trust my gut. I wasn't simply going to NYC to get another degree – this time there was a purpose and a strategy, a "light at the end of the tunnel" so to speak. This light was the Tow-Knight Center for Entrepreneurial Journalism, which for me meant three semesters of grad school before I could even be eligible for the program.

### Pivot #3 – From Practitioner to Founder (2014-2015) "Accelerators & Incubators"

It is now spring of 2014, and at the Tow-Knight Center each week we visit budding tech startup offices and new media company headquarters all throughout NYC, often sitting down with their CEOs and top C-level leaders (executives like CEOs, COOs, CTOs, etc.). A month later I attended a Google Startup Weekend NYC pitch competition, and my "idea" received the minimum amount of votes (six) out of all the pitches needed to move to the next round of the "team-building phase." Then, the minimum of two people (out of hundreds) actually decided to join my team and work with me for the weekend on "Baller," a new sports app that aggregated viral sports content in one place from every social network. After Google Startup Weekend, I applied for and was accepted into "3-Day Startup," an invite-only startup weekend unlike Google's where anyone could attend. I took this as my next challenge to better improve my pitch and vision for "Baller" as a future tech CEO. My new pitch earned more team member requests (seven) than any other pitch that Friday night at 3-Day Startup, just a month after the Google event, and we hustled all weekend to put together a final pitch, survey potential users and receive mentoring from top marketers and tech founders in the area. "Always be pitching" is the motto I adopted from the founder of the program and a future advisor. A few weeks before 3-Day Startup I had also applied and pitched successfully to General Assembly's "Client UX Projects" program where they choose startups to partner with their students and UX designers to build a prototype and new product design. I took this mobile app mockup into our 3-Day Startup weekend/ pitch and also leveraged it to apply to Bizdom, a seed fund accelerator specializing in sports and entertainment technology startups owned by none other than NBA owner Dan Gilbert of the Cleveland Cavaliers. The only reason I even knew about Bizdom was from my friend Brendez, whom I had met at 3-Day Startup when she was the first to join my team and then actually pitch with me on that Sunday. Brendez told me about her organizing an entrepreneurship event in Columbus where there was also a "Shark Tank" open casting call pitch happening that same weekend. Not being able to afford a roundtrip plane ticket and hotel room for the weekend (I was still living off student loans at the time during the Tow-Knight program!) I bought a roundtrip bus ticket instead, arriving there at 5 a.m. and leaving at 5 p.m. the same day, using my friend's hotel room to quickly shower and change/practice between pitches. Little did I know my pitch would bomb in the sixty seconds I got in front of a table trying to convince one of the Shark Tank "TV show producers" of my app's potential. Little did I also know that following my bombed pitch, my new friend and colleague Brendez would introduce me to an investor who would sit down one-on-one with me to hear my pitch. Then after passing on my idea (it was too early stage for him) he recommended that I apply to Bizdom and said he'd personally recommend me to their team. Two months and a rugged application process later, and I had been invited as a finalist to Cleveland to pitch in front of the Bizdom accelerator/investor team at the Quicken Loans Arena, home of NBA's Cleveland Cavaliers in hopes of earning $25K for my startup "Go Baller," which had undergone a name change and product pivot in becoming "a social discovery app for sports fans." Go Baller become one of ten startups to join Bizdom's 2014-15 cohort, and a month later I was loading a Penske truck moving my entire life from Brooklyn, New York to Cleveland, Ohio.

### Pivot #4 – From Founder to CEO (2015-2016) "Episode 2: Reality Strikes Back"

Within a few short months my Go Baller pitch and presentation deck was completely ripped to shreds by the program's investment team. My startup was a "ripoff of X company they had already invested in," or "It's just a version of X that doesn't make money." The feedback was brutal, and I took it more personally than I should have. Pitch after pitch I was denied the chance to appear at Demo Day, the end event of the program where we present to big-time VCs and investors in the area for follow on funds, etc. It was the whole point of doing an accelerator program in a sense, and I felt like a failure because I was only one of two founders in the cohort who weren't allowed to pitch there. What I didn't appreciate then was the direction in which those failed pitches would take Go Baller. The day after Bizdom's demo day I won a $20K grant competition for new media startups from the NewU program funded by UNITY: Journalists for Diversity and the Ford Foundation. The same pitch trounced by Bizdom advisors was the same pitch that won us another $20K in funding. The rollercoaster took a turn for the better, right? With no revenue in sight as a free sports app and with limited cash on hand, we had to rethink our product and recreate our value point from a B2C to B2B platform, going from a standalone sports app to an enterprise social media software platform. On the app we aggregated viral sports social media content all in one place. On the platform we did the same exact thing, but for other businesses on their apps and websites. "Let's do for them what we only wanted to originally do on our own app, giving others value, to put all of their social media/viral content in one place," we decided.

### Pivot #5 – From CEO to Leader (2016-Present) "Go Baller Media"

Soon after earning the $20K grant money for Go Baller's pivoted pitch and new focus, the money had dried up. While we had secured commitments and non-verbal letters of intent from top players and teams in the sports industry, we did not have a finished product to integrate and could only beta test with them. Then reality actually sunk in. Money was gone. Rent was due. Then two months rent were due. Those "888" collection calls started piling up and flooding the phone. I had to suspend all Go Baller operations, move to back to Florida, and live on couches while looking for a job to pay my damn phone bill. The struggle was real, both financially and psychologically. Had I failed in my quest to become the sports media version of Mark Zuckerberg? Unfortunately I had allowed myself to sink into negativity. A few weeks later I received a job as a social media marketing manager and a month later was promoted to the company's digital director. A month after that I introduced two new revenue streams into this ad agency's business model with mobile website development and A.I./logic-based digital forms to turn offline form processes into automated digital smartforms. The mental low I had hit only a few months prior to this taught me to be more self-aware than ever before. It taught me that it's just as important not to get caught up in the hype of successes than it is with the hype of failures. In reality, they are both learning lessons and part of the overall journey of entrepreneurship. At Go Baller, we are now a mobile app-turned-media agency that helps brands *on the go* with mobile websites, mobile ecommerce and full-service digital strategies. We currently have four monthly agency clients ($2,000+ monthly recurring revenue in total) compared to our past life of being a pre-revenue sports app or a social media software company with a beta-phase platform and no cash on hand. "Pivoting" is not just about changing your revenue model or mission statement, it is most often about challenging your own ego, assumptions and ideas against the feedback of the world. It's about thinking for a snap second, then doing and doing and iterating and iterating for the long haul. Patience and action must be at the utmost focus, in addition to the self-awareness needed to admit your own mistakes and change. If you can create value for someone and maintain that value, then you can truly build something people will not only want to use but want to pay you for, for a very long time. Patience and action. Action and patience. They might appear to be opposites but are the true two skills you need to be able to constantly pick yourself up from failure and move on to the next day, to the next pivot. This what being an entrepreneur is all about.

*Chris Dell is a veteran sports journalist and news editor turned entrepreneur. He has published work and managed news sites for the* New York Daily News, The New York Times *and Yahoo!'s* Rivals.com. *In 2015 he launched Go Baller, a sports social media app, with backing from serial entrepreneur Dan Gilbert and the Ford Foundation. Reach him on Twitter at @maddjournalist.*

## Leave feedback on this sidebar.

# FROM THE FIELD: YOUR KICKSTARTER CAMPAIGN IS A STORY

*Interview with Daniel Zayas by Elizabeth Mays*

## From the Field

Daniel Zayas is a Verified Kickstarter Expert[1]. He has run numerous crowdfunding campaigns as the marketing director for board game publisher Eagle-Gryphon Games, has a prominent weekly blog[2] about successful Kickstarter campaigns and consults regularly to optimize campaigns. Three years ago, Zayas was studying at the Walter Cronkite School of Journalism and Mass Communication, where he took two classes on journalism entrepreneurship, much like the ones you may be in now.

While the road post-graduation led to roles in his field of passion, tabletop board games, Zayas says the media entrepreneurship courses prepared him well for what he's doing today.

He says this was not only because they imparted a foundation in how crowdfunding works for digital ventures, but because one of the keys to crowdfunding is storytelling—a central tenet of journalism education. Helping your audience understand the value proposition quickly is crucial to converting them into funders, Zayas says. "The storytelling aspect of it—the inverted pyramid—that specifically, as a broad concept of 'hook them early,' is 100 percent applicable to what I do today."

Zayas says board games make the most money on Kickstarter as a group, which may be because crowdfunding in this context is one form of pre-ordering. But Zayas says some core keys to success are the same for any Kickstarter project: namely, a clear and compelling story of how your product will benefit the funder.

He offers these tips for media outlets seeking crowdfunding on Kickstarter:

"The number one rule in crowdfunding is that you need a crowd," Zayas says. "You already need someone to care about you or your project." This might be friends and family, your audience from a previously successful campaign, or a celebrity voice in the industry who might give you testimonials and a shout-out. If you don't have a network already that can bring about 70 percent of the funding for your campaign, Zayas says, you'll need to reach out to some tastemakers who can lend their following.

To fully fund your campaign, Zayas says, you'll need to also attract the "scrollers" who are searching for projects on Kickstarter—and capture them very quickly with storytelling hooks. "The idea is that people know immediately what they are getting and why it's important," he says. "Not everyone is your customer but if you can capture your customers through an ease of understanding, then you will be in better shape."

With media projects, Zayas says there are two models that work the best:

1. Fund your season of content; or
2. Fund a specific project.

Zayas advises against trying to fund your whole business or company as it's too nebulous for the funder to care about. "People need to know when they're giving you money what they are getting as concretely as possible," Zayas says. "When you say I am funding my business, that is too many steps removed from 'how am I benefiting?'" Businesses don't lend themselves to stories well enough, he says, whereas with a project, you can show how your coverage is going to benefit the potential funder directly. The exception might be a media company whose whole operation could be considered a project—for instance, coverage of a niche topic or a certain geographical location.

Zayas notes there are usually some costs to do a successful project. It's important to have great visuals, so you may need graphics designed. In addition, a minor investment (even $100) in highly targeted paid social media marketing campaigns can pay off exponentially if you are effective in targeting it specifically to the types of people who will want your product. Social media marketing, using A/B testing, retargeting and optimization, is a low-cost way to do this. If this isn't your specialty, you may want to hire someone, but make sure they're an expert in your niche.

Finally, while your mother may give to your campaign no matter what, remember that you should be targeting an audience that will benefit from your project in some way. There's some altruism in being a crowdfunder, Zayas says, in that you are helping someone make something that didn't exist before, but there's also always self-interest. "You're also needing to see some verifiable proof that it's going to exist and that I'm going to 100 percent benefit from this," he says. You have to convince contributors that you're "going to do good work that will benefit (their) life.'"

*Elizabeth Mays is the operations and marketing manager for Canadian nonprofit the Rebus Foundation, which is building a new, collaborative model for open textbook publishing through the Rebus Community. She is also an adjunct professor at the Walter Cronkite School of Journalism and*

*Mass Communication, teaching its first online course in audience acquisition. Reach her on Twitter at @theeditress.*

## Leave feedback on this sidebar.

## Notes

1. "Kickstarter Experts," *Kickstarter,* https://www.kickstarter.com/experts.

2. *Board Game Badger,* http://dzayas.com/board-game-badger/.

# LOOKING AHEAD

| Looking Ahead |
| --- |
| You know the types of entities you plan to approach for funding. Now you'll need to develop a pitch. Pitching Ideas will show you how to develop one. |

# PITCHING IDEAS

by Mark Poepsel

## Summary

Want to get funding for your j-startup? You'll need to learn how to pitch.

---

### Learning Objectives

In this chapter, you will:

- Learn how to take ideas for media startups and turn them into professional pitches following a suggested template.
- Learn the components of a good media pitch presentation.
- Use tools and materials for pitch development.

---

## Inside this Chapter

- Pitching Ideas
- From the Field: The Perfect Pitch, by Amy Eisman

*Mark Poepsel, Ph.D., is an assistant professor at Southern Illinois University in Edwardsville in the Department of Mass Communications. He researches media sociology and leadership in journalism organizations and teaches courses in media management, media entrepreneurship, graduate research methods, broadcast writing, introductory writing, and introductory theory. In 2016, he was a fellow at the Scripps Howard Journalism Entrepreneurship Institute, and he was a Scripps Visiting Professor in Social Media. Reach him on Twitter at @markpoepsel.*

# PITCHING IDEAS

*Mark Poepsel*

***To pitch a journalism or media product is to make the case for your idea to an individual or group in exchange for financial or some other kind of support.*** Pitching is a dynamic process that requires you to be of two minds. On the one hand, you need to believe in the value of your idea and in your team's ability to make it viable. On the other hand, you must also demonstrate a capacity for change and perseverance as your idea evolves over time in response to feedback from potential customers and investors. Your pitch must demonstrate that you have a great product idea, that you have done market and competition research, and that you are willing and able to scrap key features, even ones you love, if feedback from customers or investors makes it necessary. Developing a pitch is more than coming up with a great idea for a media product and shopping it around to investors. It involves ideation, key feature identification and testing, market research, design and branding work, redesign, and pitch performance practice. At the heart of the pitch is your promise to develop a successful product, even though you may not yet know all of the variables that will influence its success.

Let's freeze the conversation for a second for students who are not necessarily interested in being entrepreneurs. "Why should we study ideation, research, project management, and pitching?" You should study this because every job involves pitching. Journalists make story pitches every day and to a growing extent they are expected to provide evidence of engagement on previous similar stories to justify their pitch. For example, they may need to pull data from CrowdTangle or Chartbeat to show that stories about a particular bridge under construction garner a lot of attention and engagement. Stories may not seem sexy at first, but engagement numbers can help a journalist close the deal.

If nothing else, you will need to pitch yourself and your skills on the job market. If you treat your career search as a product to be managed, you will ideate potential outcomes in terms of workplace, location, and job description. You will go into job interviews with a well-researched plan, good-looking supplementary materials including your resume website, and you will know what the competition looks like. You need to understand what your "key features" are as a potential employee. You can refine those and present them well and find a good market fit for the product, i.e. your professional labor.

Studying how to ideate and to pitch is also fun. It's not a lecture series or a knowledge dump. It's a guided tour through a process of self discovery, group relationship building, and global market awareness. Even if you never take your own new endeavor to market, learning how to ideate and to pitch could and should change your life.

Pitching can happen formally or informally. An <u>elevator pitch</u>, a short two- or three-sentence description of your idea, is a pitch format you might use to describe your project to a stranger in casual conversation or to a potential team member at a meetup. It is similar to the log line in a film project. This chapter is designed for students who are developing formal pitches for ideas seeking seed funding. For best results, you should already be acquainted with the lean startup model of product development prior to creating your pitch. Developed by Eric Ries,[1] *The Lean Startup* stresses the value of customer development as its central thesis. In essence, the book states that the business of lean startups is to *learn*. You learn by practicing a sort of customer service science. Lean startup teams hypothesize about what product changes might work, and they test those changes on real consumers, a.k.a. users, so that the product is always improving, always moving closer to perfect product market fit. It's an ideal that's not often attained, but that's the goal, and you need to be able to explain that you understand this concept and can put it into practice.

You may have begun (for real or in mock exercises) by self-funding the development of a prototype, a.k.a. bootstrapping, and you should have continued through the "friends and family" stage of financing where you have sought funding via personal networks, i.e. your parents, friends, perhaps a rich uncle.

This chapter assumes you have worked through the ideation phase of product development (see chapter on Ideation) and that you'll continue to make improvements to your product even as you work on your pitch. Your team demonstrates leadership and change management skills by showing how your product has already evolved in response to customer development efforts. Customer development includes doing essential market research, testing features, and gathering and analyzing design feedback. The best pitches impart these nuts-and-bolts elements by demonstrating that your team has learned from this feedback and also convey the team's passion, ingenuity, and perseverance. When your team has done as much product development and customer development as you can afford, or as time allows during a class session, you build toward a "big ask," which may be a meeting with investors, a presentation to a startup competition committee, or a pitch contest, etc. This chapter focuses on preparing you for that big presentation, but it also briefly covers preparing an elevator pitch and writing a prospectus paper.

To narrow the scope of the discussion, this chapter identifies six presentation elements that serve as a starting point for pitch preparation. They are:

- **Element 1: Brand identity image and tagline**
- **Element 2: Problem-solution narrative**
- **Element 3: Key features and your value proposition**
- **Element 4: Product-market fit description**

- **Element 5: Competitive analysis**
- **Element 6: Financial projections**

These are the must-haves for a pitch about ten to fifteen minutes long. Each may be represented by one or more slides if you are crafting a slide deck or by one or more sections if you are writing a prospectus. Depending on your product, presentation type, preferences, and priorities, you should feel free to customize around this framework.

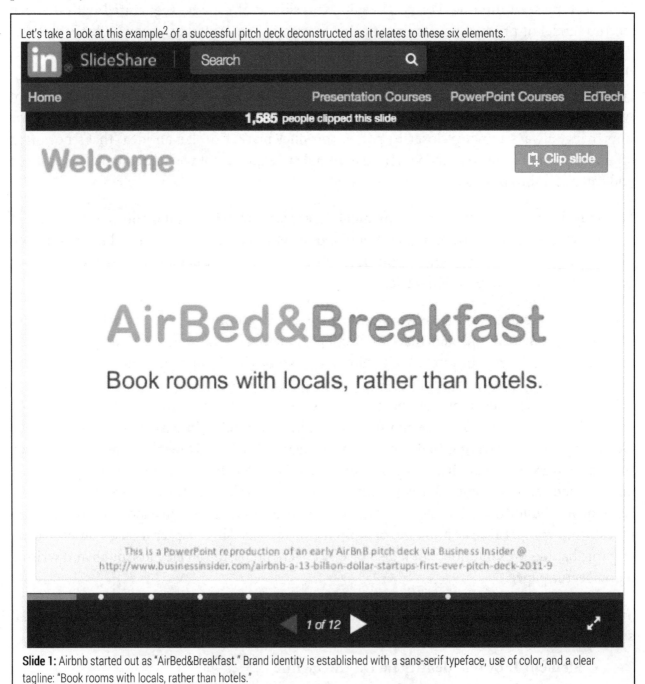

Let's take a look at this example[2] of a successful pitch deck deconstructed as it relates to these six elements.

**Slide 1:** Airbnb started out as "AirBed&Breakfast." Brand identity is established with a sans-serif typeface, use of color, and a clear tagline: "Book rooms with locals, rather than hotels."

**Slide 2:** The problem statement is straightforward: Travelers need an affordable alternative to hotels.

Slide 3: The solution statement focuses on the nature of the product, i.e. that it's a web platform, and on key features and how they create value, both financial and cultural capital. Note that key features and the value proposition are already addressed through three simple slides.

**Slide 4:** To establish product-market fit, you first have to have a market. The Airbnb pitch deck notes that at the time there were 630,000 users on couchsurfing.com and that there were 17,000 temporary housing listings on Craigslist in San Francisco and New York combined in one week. Thus, there existed a large potential traveler pool and a large pool of people with rooms for lease, but these groups were in need of a unified platform.

**Slide 5:** The fifth slide details the size of the market and Airbnb's share, showing potential for growth.

**Slide 6:** Completing the case for product-market fit, this slide shows the attractive user interface and provides a mini-narrative for how the product works.

**Slide 7:** This slide shows four years' of revenue totals as simple math: 10 million + trips x $20 average fee = about $200 million in revenues. This is evidence of product-market fit and whets the investor's appetite for potential future earnings.

**Slide 8:** This slide shows how Airbnb has already beaten its competition to own the market for certain events and to create partnerships.

**Slide 9:** Here, investors get the full picture of the competition.

**Slide 10:** The financial expectations are pretty well established by this point and were explained verbally. What this shows are the barriers to competition expected to help preserve Airbnb's position and future earnings and growth expectations.

This chapter focuses first on developing the six presentation elements. When the time comes to build slide decks, the order, breakdown, and prioritization of elements is up to you. You are not expected to finish your product before developing your pitch. Rather, it is strongly suggested that you develop your pitch and your product in parallel.

# PRESENTATION ELEMENT #1: Brand Identity Image and Tagline

Your presentation slide deck should begin with a memorable brand image. It can be a logo representing your product in a stylized way, or it could be a screen grab of your product if you are particularly happy with the design. It's often a good idea to create a tagline as well. It helps drive the message home for investors who want to know right away if they see a marketable idea. From a persuasive standpoint, all you are trying to establish with your first slide is that this is a great product that many people need that's easy to understand and remember.

Your brand introduction should be kept to one slide and should set the aesthetic tone for the rest of the presentation. Establish a color palette and stick with it. If you're going to use design elements such as borders, background colors, or shapes, use them in your introductory slide. Go with clean, simple design elements. If something doesn't add to your presentation, leave it out and keep it out in subsequent slides.

As you present the brand image and tagline visually, your talking points should include a brief description of the team. Don't feel the need to introduce every member right away. The project manager should introduce the concept and herself or himself, and as the presentation moves on other members of the team can introduce themselves when it's their turn to speak. There's no correct way to divide up presentation responsibilities. Different courses and competitions will set requirements for the minimum and maximum number of speakers or group members you should have. Just be sure to keep the introduction slide focused and brief. Whenever it is your turn to speak, identify yourself. Mention your role and very briefly discuss your background as it pertains to your role on this project. Holding off on team introductions will keep your pitch moving.

You should start working on branding at the same time you begin product ideation. Establishing your brand identity is like selecting your best photo and description for a dating app. Put only your best face forward. Give investors a single, interesting, lasting image that they can connect to the rest of your pitch.

## PRESENTATION ELEMENT #2: Problem-Solution Narrative

Every product solves a problem. Many entrepreneurial media products solve problems that users didn't know they had. It's your job to help the investor identify a media-related problem that many people share and then clearly explain in a story or short anecdote how your product solves the problem or, if it is not an outright solution, how it alleviates pain associated with the problem. Look at other problem-solution narratives in advertising and in corporate origin stories for examples of how to craft a quick, compelling problem-solution narrative.

---

**Classic Problem-Solution Narratives**

- A young man starting high school lacks muscle mass. He drinks milk and gets stronger, earning the respect of his classmates.
- Young people, pictured in silhouette, walk around a city looking bored with life. Then, they turn on their new MP3 players and start dancing in the streets. Their world is set ablaze in color and sound.
- A man literally turns into Joe Pesci when he gets hungry. He eats a candy bar and turns back into his normal self.

---

These may not be the greatest stories ever told. You're not going to get a National Book Award for a Snickers commercial, but these are memorable narratives about people who have a problem that the product in question can solve.

You may want to personalize the narrative as it relates to you or someone on your team. This is common practice, but don't force it. Often, student media entrepreneurs are caught in a quandary. They tend to come up with products suitable for their demographic that may not be massively appealing, or they come up with products for general audiences (read: people of a different generation). Then students may have difficulties crafting a relatable narrative. Your preference should be for creating a viable product and telling the product's story as well as you can. Use your research and communication skills to craft narratives with a great problem-solution story. If your product is not for people like you, simply identify the type of person who has this problem or this pain point. Create user or customer personas (see Customer Discovery chapter[3]): "fictional, generalized representations of ideal customers." Explain how your product is a feasible, meaningful solution for her or him. What motivates them to adopt your product? Tell the story in thirty seconds or less, in three slides or fewer.

By the time you create your pitch, you may have developed a concept and wireframe or some other mockup of a minimum viable product (MVP). Often the best way to present this narrative is to tell the problem-solution story verbally while simultaneously demonstrating on a couple of slides precisely where users need to tap or click to fix the problem. If this is a semester project for class, you may not have a prototype ready yet, but you should work to make your mockup look as much like the "real thing" as possible.

Try out different narratives on potential customers as part of your customer-development research. Keep internal records of which narratives work best. Ask people why these resonate more than others. You usually do NOT want to spend precious time delving into bullet points about key features at this stage. You can tell investors how the product works later on in the pitch. At this point you are simply a brand that solves a problem a lot of people have. Strive to make the narrative relatable and fun.

## PRESENTATION ELEMENT #3: Key Features and Your Value Proposition

During your pitch, consider introducing investors to your key features, your value proposition and, where applicable, your user interface (UI) at the same time. Key features are the specific jobs your product or service accomplishes or assists with. A most basic example is that a bowl is innovative in relation to a plate. Both share the key feature that they hold food. A bowl adds another feature by holding liquids comfortably. Many innovative media products add several key features to solve nuanced problems. Limit yourself to developing a small handful of key features at first. Figure out how they will look and feel and be able to show users how your product's design is easy to use.

One way to think of your value proposition is as the sum of your key features. How exactly are you solving problems, addressing pain points? The bigger the problem and the simpler the solution set, the more impressive your value proposition is likely to be.

At its core, a value proposition is a statement about why someone needs your product or service. How are you making their life better or making them more wealthy, with "wealth" being broadly defined?

Answer this question in your presentation visually while stating it verbally. Show investors your product or your UI and walk them through two or three tasks that can be accomplished easily. This is a chance to show off your key features and to make your potential investors understand your value proposition so well they become excited to invest and to bring this product with these, or similar, key features to audiences.

Demonstrate your UI or your product's design in two or three slides. You may prefer to simply show a mock-up against a monochrome background so that the product's design is all that investors notice. This will make the value proposition pop. Alternately, if you want the slides to carry over an existing set of design elements from the rest of your presentation, try to make the color palette, shape, and line selections for your slide background complement your product's design elements.

Do not feel the need to introduce every feature or to narrate every design choice, but you should show that you have a good sense of design and that your design will make your key features easy to find and use.

A popular tool for creating wireframes is Balsamiq.[4] You can create mobile and/or web app wireframes that incorporate realistic design elements such as buttons, menus, and media players. You can build a wireframe mockup of your application or web application that users can actually click through and try out. If you work with a clickable wireframe, though, double and triple check that it functions properly on the device you will be using during your "big ask." If you're not completely sure that the functions will work, use a static mockup and sell it with your enthusiasm and with evidence of thoughtful, thorough research. If you are pitching a tangible media product, e.g. a wearable, you should bring a physical prototype for investors to try out.

Whatever your combination of digital mockup and tangible prototype is, it is preferable to show something basic that helps investors understand key features rather than show an elaborate mockup on which little or nothing works. Stick to the minimum viable product and keep the mockup clear and simple; however, note that certain startup competitions or investors may require working prototype sites or apps.

Tips for crafting great-looking, useful user interfaces are abundant online. They usually come with collections of colors in "color kits"[5] that serve as pre-determined palettes, and they will also include button and menu design styles for you to choose based on the tone and function of your product. Try out completely different approaches to UI on potential customers. Once you have narrowed down their basic color and design preferences using stock design elements, try creating your own color combinations, button styles, and menu designs. Stay within your users' stated preferences, but apply your own creativity so that you can truly brand your product as your own.

I allude to the term "iterative development" throughout this chapter, but it merits definition here. Iteration in innovation refers to building out prototypes again and again–first for the developers themselves, then for beta testers, and then for a (hopefully) growing audience. At the root of the concept is repetition, which means the process of designing, building, testing, seeking feedback, re-designing, etc. continues indefinitely. Think, for example of a common platform such as Facebook and how many times it has been redesigned since you or the people you know have been using it.

If you spend even a few months using a favorite platform or app, you will likely see iterations of its development. What you need to know during the entrepreneurial pitch process is that iterating can happen while the pitch is being developed. This is normal and expected. You should seek to iterate based on user data and feedback. Iteration is not guesswork, and it's not merely trial and error. It's an informed repetitive development process meant to develop a product-market fit by molding the product to an existing market.

## PRESENTATION ELEMENT #4: Product-Market Fit Description

In your team's pitch so far, you have established a brand, demonstrated through storytelling how it solves a problem, and shown that your team is capable of designing an MVP with a combination of user input and your own creative design skills. You have shown investors that you and your team have a valuable idea and the skills to work in a lean startup environment using an iterative process. Now you must demonstrate how you are going to make money.

The next few slides in your deck should present a brief discussion of product-market fit. In two to three slides, show how big the market is, show where your product fits, and show evidence of iterative development according to customer preferences. Your goal is to quickly show the investors where there is an underserved mass market. Then, you must show that your product can tap that market and reach real customers. Every aspect of the market you are entering is fair game for questions from investors. You can head off killer questions by showing a depth of understanding about the market. There may be many solutions in the marketplace. Do not ignore them. Explain why your solution fits best. Explain that you're working harder than anyone else to serve customers by directly testing their preferences.

Marc Andreessen of investment firm Andreessen-Horowitz calls product-market fit "the only thing that matters."[6] Specifically, his commentary is about successful startups and whether team, product, or market matters more. He argues it's the market. Andreessen says: "In a great market — a market with lots of real potential customers — the market *pulls* product out of the startup [original emphasis]."[7] None of your creative ideation or inspired design work matters if you can't demonstrate knowledge of the marketplace. Practicing customer development, then, is establishing a process where you allow consumers to pull great products out of your efforts.

Fit your market research into your presentation in under a minute. Emphasize the size and strength of the potential market in a slide. Then, demonstrate that you have conducted careful customer research to learn what potential users want. You should have data from testing general product ideas, key feature combinations, and design elements. You should be able to show quantitative data, probably from surveys, and qualitative data, probably from focus groups. Present the highlights of customer development in a couple of slides.

Investors only want the summary of this data. Present it in a narrative form. For example: "We have found that our users prefer our social media app because their friends are using it, and as the number of friends using our app increases a certain amount, the amount users spend with the app increases in correlation." If you're not able to show that level of correlation in your data, at least be able to show that you are building the most popular version of your idea with key features that users preferred over all other potential features they were shown.

The visuals you use are up to you, but you must establish that there is a market for this kind of product and that you've sought to achieve product-market fit by developing a product with direct user feedback. That's what customer development is all about. For the lean startup, it cannot be stressed enough how important customer development is. It's not enough to show that you have had some good ideas. You need to show that you can bring your product and its customers together. Products evolve, and so do customer tastes, so you need to show that your team can already work on this product in response to user feedback data.

## Market Research

Your first task in conducting market research is to define the scope of the media market where your product will compete. If you are working on a journalism startup, define a news niche in terms of geography and topic. If your news product focuses primarily on one topic, you will probably need to cover a wide geographical area, perhaps a national market.

If you are planning to bring news to a geographical region, limit it in a logical way. You might determine a reasonable driving radius around your community and cover the counties and cities within, which is essentially what defines a Designated Market Area (DMA) in broadcast news. You might wish to focus more narrowly on a single metro area or suburb.

Use census data to learn everything you can about the people who live in your coverage area. Read broadly about the history of the area, its economic background, and its economic future. Plug into the local entrepreneur scene long before you launch your media startup because understanding the startup market is your key to understanding the economic future of your area.

Most mass media startups that do not focus on journalism serve as communication platforms, games, or information curation/aggregation services. Service-logistics apps of the so-called "sharing economy" help people providing specific services to coordinate with others who need those services. If your team is pitching this type of app, avoid calling your product the "Uber of" something. Uber has become synonymous with corroded corporate culture,[8] and it has proven to be a high-stakes global gamble for investors. The sharing economy model is a difficult sell because the ideas are cheap and execution is expensive. Whatever your product is, you will need to demonstrate that this particular shared service is needed. You can't expect to rely on sharing economy research in another sector to justify your concept. Nobody needs the "Uber of toothbrushes," or do they?[9]

# PRESENTATION ELEMENT #5: Competitive Analysis

After working through the first four presentation elements, students sometimes think that their product's value is self-evident based on its key features, its design, and the strength of the marketplace. There is a tendency to think that because the processes of designing a product and strategizing about customer development are labor intensive those elements should be enough to demonstrate a product's value, but investors will look for something more. They will want to know that your media product is not already available elsewhere, offered by someone with more experience and an established customer base. You must demonstrate that your product is unique.

Describe your competition as clearly and directly as possible. Name names. Cite links. Clearly and accurately describe their relevant products and their features. Describe in some detail what they do and don't do. Know your competitors as well as you know your own brand. In the context of where your targeted markets overlap, know them better than they know themselves. Show that you have looked at trade industry publications detailing your competition's strategies. Show that you have read, synthesized, and summarized up-to-date industry blogs' take on your competition, and, most important, show that you understand your competitors' strategy based on their About Page and design blog, if they have one.

Competitive analysis should be presented in about two slides. Pretending not to notice major players in the field will get you laughed off the presentation stage. You need to note in one slide who your key competitors are in the marketplace. You need to explain how your product or service is unique. What key features do you offer that no one else does? When you have similar features, how do you prioritize them or present them in ways that are unique or more affordable or more tailored to a target audience than the options that already exist? Answer these questions for each competitor.

Demonstrate this knowledge in clean, carefully crafted slides with straightforward storytelling. Neither overestimate nor underestimate the competition. When organizing this section of your slide deck, you are going to have to make executive decisions about what to leave in the presentation and what to cut. Use the "iceberg principle." Present about one-tenth of the research you have done and be prepared to tailor the competitive analysis of your presentation for each investor or competition keeping in mind that competitors and markets are in flux.

Keep the pace quick and have a strategic counter for beating or at least competing with competitors' strategies. It's not enough to list their related products and the key features of those products. Identify the brand strategies so that you can anticipate where your competition is headed. You should be able to answer what you would do if someone new entered the marketplace doing the same thing you're doing. Explain if this can be prevented. If it can't, explain with substance how you're performing better than the competition at delivering a similar product. If that is not possible, you need to come up with a different product. Pivot to target a different market or develop a different feature set. It's essential that you don't try to pitch a product that's already available in the same marketplace (potentially from multiple sellers with more resources and experience).

You can present your competitive analysis by going through one competitor at a time and explaining how you will beat each one, or you can go topic by topic, such as "feature set," "target market," "user interface," "supply chain," "development costs," "outcomes," "branding," etc. and explain how you will best your competitors on each item. This element of your presentation can easily get convoluted. You may not wish to address all of these elements. If you do good customer development work, you can prioritize which of these aspects of the product matter most to them and limit your competitive analysis discussion based on that research. In this way, customer development is doubly important. It tells you how to focus your own product and tells you where to focus your competitive efforts.

Your competitive analysis needs to evolve as you go through the customer development process. Each time you add or remove a key feature from your product, you must research who else is doing something similar and alter or amend your presentation to show that you're aware of them and have a plan to beat them.

## PRESENTATION ELEMENT #6: Financial Projections

In about three slides, explain your revenue model, that is, what your customers, advertisers, underwriters, etc., will be paying and what will they be paying for, as well as the costs to deliver those products or services. One of the best ways to express your revenue model is to work with the Business Model Canvas (BMC) (see Business Models chapter for more on this)[10] to map out how money will flow through your organization. The BMC helps you to picture how your startup fits into its financial ecosystem. It enables or forces you to think about who you're going to work with and how you're going to work with them to get the resources you need to provide valuable products or services. It helps you to plan to whom exactly you will deliver those services and how you will deliver them, and it demands that you understand what your costs are and where your revenue will really come from. The BMC will inform your estimation of startup costs and operating costs. From those (revenues, startup costs, and operating costs), you can determine your breakeven analysis according to what your class syllabus or competition guidelines require. Groups in media entrepreneurship class often go through a dozen business model canvas drafts, or more, as they plan and develop their product and as they conduct customer development. The BMC will help you to decide on a revenue model and express it in visual form, though the actual visualization should be tailored to suit your product.

You must indicate how much of your startup funds you have already contributed, if you plan on seeking other funding sources, and what proportion of the business you are going to hand over to investors for the amount of funding you request. You should probably share only a summary of your plan. Spend no more than three minutes presenting realistic, well-thought-out financial estimates. Again, the iceberg approach may be the best approach.

Investors will want to know what basis you have for your financial estimates and claims. Often, this is the part of the presentation that generates the most questions from the audience. Document your sources for any financial assertions you make and be prepared to hand over more detailed business plans if asked. Make the case that your product is a great investment. Practice with mentors, friends, family members, and your professors so that you can make the strongest possible feasible case for funding.

## Pitch Deck Examples

An example of a successful pitch is CardLife featured on this[11] blog post of the 35 best pitch deck examples. It is a tracking company that communicates to users, usually business, how much they are spending on subscription software services. Businesses have a problem. They subscribe to many software solutions. They do so at different times for different amounts for plans that may renew automatically year over year or that may increase in price, sometimes without review. CardLife helps track this expense in order to make it easier for businesses to balance budgets. This is a business that serves other businesses, yes, but it's also media-related because it gathers, tracks and presents information in a service that's designed to be easy to use. It's a time saver and potentially a stress reducer. The slide deck established that this is a problem for businesses by keying in on one number: 93%. That's the percentage of businesses that fail to keep track of their software and other subscription expenses. In their pitch, they note that 1,000 businesses signed up for their service within six weeks of launch, and they note that they are connecting to a $10 billion industry. Though they cannot plan on receiving a portion of that particular pie, by being connected to such a large market with continued growth potential, they easily make the case that their business is positioned for future growth. Please review their presentation video and slide deck. It's No. 15 on this list, which includes several other examples of solid slide decks accompanied by videos of each as they were given by the entrepreneurs themselves at Y Combinator 2017.[12]

## Mobile Development Costs

Let's start with an anecdote: In our entrepreneurial media management course at Southern Illinois

University in Edwardsville, guest judges came one semester and quoted wildly different costs for app development. One estimate was based on an alert app that let students know when on-campus athletic events are being held. Students budgeted tens of thousands of dollars in their plan to build a fully functional app, but the guest judge said he had proposals for similar alert services on his desk that would cost the university about $2,000.

At a pitch competition later the same semester, a different team proposed to a different set of judges to build a new social media platform that would visualize posts and group audiences into "cliques" enabling social media managers to send targeted message to only certain "cliques," in real time. One judge happened to have served as an adviser to a military contractor who wanted to develop its own social media platform. He had a front-row seat to the proposal, and his company quoted a base price (with a development team of dozens of software developers) at $20 million. Thus, the class was left with a range of costs for "app development" somewhere between $2,000 and $20 million. The best way to estimate costs for an app is to look for something with a similar feature set and find out how much seed money it got in its earliest round or rounds of funding.

# FOLLOW UP

## Question and Answer Preparation

Preparing for question and answer sessions with potential investors is something of a challenge because every investor is different. You should anticipate likely questions and be prepared for "wild card" questions by having an open mind and by practicing your pitch in front of different audiences. Vary the age of your pitch audience. Get test audiences that vary in income level and education. Sometimes you are not pitching to the investor but to the investor's idea of who the consumer for this product must be. Once you have practiced presenting in front of various audiences, you should identify a few likely questions and prepare well-researched answers. You need not promise the world to an investor. But you must be prepared to indicate your plans for improvement, or be able to explain why something that seems like it should be done is not yet done. You should identify known weaknesses in your pitch and prepare reasonable answers regarding your plans to improve upon shortcomings. You may plan to conduct further research where more information is needed, or you may have identified key features that need to be altered or replaced. If you have identified something that needs doing and that isn't done yet, that may not be a deal breaker as long as you have a reasonable plan for making changes and you show that you are prepared for change.

## Staying Connected

You should also strategize for staying in touch with any potential investors. Task a point person with collecting and organizing investors' contact information. Make note of each investor's investing background and interests and take detailed and careful notes about their feedback regarding your pitch. Do your research. You should know any potential investor's history and strengths and weaknesses. Treat an investor's individual concerns as the most important keys to your success. Making it work with one real investor ready to cut a check is more important than developing a perfect product pitch for future potential investors.

Generally, cold calls to angel investors are not appreciated. Work carefully immediately after an investor expresses interest in your proposal to open a line of communication. Follow the investor's preference, which may be for asynchronous communication such as email or SMS, or they may prefer to speak via video chat or by phone.

One goal, perhaps the goal of an initial pitch is to gain enough interest on the part of an investor that she or he wants to hear a second, personalized pitch in the near future.

You are not going to meet your "soulmate" investor the first time out or in any of the first ten times making your pitch. Shoot for a 1 in 100 rate of success at setting up a meeting with a funder. That means that for every 100 contacts you make, one of them might consider funding your business.

There is often a two-step flow to reach an investor. You may need to pitch a surrogate who can get you a meeting with the right investor. As a baseline, you, as a representative of your startup, ought to have an up-to-date LinkedIn profile. You should have a professional Twitter account where you follow and connect with investor networks, and you should plan on attending events with investors and other entrepreneurs through Eventbrite and Meetup.

Show up early to events. Stay late. Strategically attend paid events where investors are the invited speaker for a better shot at meeting the right investor. The "right" investor is the one who shoots you down but who knows three or four other investors who are more likely to be interested in your idea or your brand.

Be where other startups are, such as co-working spaces, and consider creating a recruiting profile for your startup on AngelList. You need to be easy to find and ready to meet.[13]

If you make your pitch informally 100 times, you will have the opportunity to refine your idea and your informal narrative. You will learn what gets investors excited, how to pace your informal pitch, and you will learn to move away from all-or-nothing formal pitches on the stage to the kinds of informal conversations with connected people who can get you a meeting with the right investor. It is important to learn who the connectors are, who are "all hat and no cattle," and ultimately you must know what you are asking for: a sit-down meeting with an angel investor who will listen to your idea.

The informal pitch may include a ballpark figure funding goal, but above all else should communicate capability and passion for the idea.

Your first pitch to an investor, according to the odds, will not result in an offer of funding.

The investor will often tell you why she or he is interested in your pitch. Keep this in mind and ask if there are any portions of the pitch that they would like to know more about. Be straightforward and be open to change. Know when to stop selling and listen. Know that you need not point out any flaws in your product when discussing a possible investment. A solid, experienced investor will have noted many or all of the potential flaws, conflicts, and stress points in your product pitch by researching your business before the meet.

Gauging investor interest is important. It is subjective. It takes time and regular, professional communication. You can change mockups and make prototypes with investor input in mind, but you must consider your costs and recognize when an investor is not serious. You do not want to spend more than your startup can afford to alter your product for an investor who is only testing the waters.

How often you communicate with a potential investor depends on their availability, their willingness to communicate, and how many resources you have at your disposal for cultivating relationships. One thing is for sure: You must follow up with potential investors. They will expect you to do so if they have expressed an interest in your proposal.

A few somewhat universal goals you might pursue for communicating with interested investors:

- Establish a pattern of regular communication.
- Encourage the investor to use your prototype.
- Encourage her or him to ask questions and make suggestions.
- Expect to pitch to a potential investor again and again. Expect to make follow-up pitches and progress reports consistently and professionally regularly even after she or he has bought in.
- As you work to secure and reassure investors, your work will likely evolve to include two difficult but essential facets: 1. You will have to be the communicative connector between your customers and investors. 2. You will need to keep innovating even after investors have thrown their weight around.

## OTHER TYPES OF PITCH

There are a few other types of pitch you may wish to prepare or that you may be assigned to develop besides the somewhat standard ten- to fifteen-minute slide deck proposal. The following are examples of longer-form and more brief pitch types: elevator pitches, three-minute pitches, prospectus writing, and nonprofit pitches.

## Elevator Pitches

The elevator pitch, or Twitter pitch, should land somewhere between a branding statement and a problem-solution narrative. It should take no longer than a minute to deliver, and in most cases it ought to be memorized. The point of an elevator pitch is to earn a chance to make a longer pitch at a later date at the time and place of the investor's choosing. Giving an elevator pitch is an art. It's often done informally at networking events. In movies, these types of pitches are given in bathrooms, on the street, in the firm's lobby as a courtesy, or, yes, in elevators. In reality, you never know when you might need to give an elevator speech. That's why you always have it memorized.

Be able to tell a potential investor precisely what your product does, why a mass audience would be interested, and where mass revenues are going to come from. All other aspects of the pitch will be in response to questions—if you can manage to get an investor interested. If you're asked to write one, make it two to three sentences, or a tweet. Write one that's easy to memorize so that any member of your team can deliver it and any potential investor can comprehend what the brand is, what you do, and how you plan to make money.

## Three-Minute Pitches

Two- or three-minute pitches are often used at "pitch days" or "speed dating" events where many entrepreneurs and many potential investors or well-connected people meet to hear what's being developed. Rather than tailoring a deck for a potential investor or for a competition and then reading the audience during the pitch performance, you may need to take a Swiss Army Knife approach and develop a handful of different short, *completely scripted* pitches to present to different people depending on their role (e.g. investor or journalist), their field (e.g. tech, advocacy, PR), or their attention span.

When startups attend pitch days in front of prospective investors, there is a formulaic approach to the ask. While you may not need to adhere to a script for a slide deck, a solid three-minute pitch can help you attract vendors and suppliers, woo landlords and advertisers, recruit employees, and win over other advocates. And, yes, maybe even investors someday (at which point you'll revisit that pitch deck).[14]

Craft pitches that are long enough to incorporate a narrative without missing the essentials of the elevator pitch. Joanne Cleaver, writing for Entrepreneur.com, suggests that the three-minute pitch can be tailored to an audience according to this formula: "Get their attention, tell them the right story, and keep 'em on the hook."

## Prospectus Writing

A successful pitch presentation might end with an investor asking for your prospectus.

"Prospectus" is a tricky term in the startup world. Prospectus.com spells out all of its potential meanings:

> "A prospectus is somewhat used as an interchangeable term. Often a business plan is referred to as a prospectus, as is the private placement memorandum (PPM). In many cases, the prospectus is a public disclosure document that, like the PPM, is used to disclose the company's data prior to a public listing of securities (with the goal in mind to raise capital publicly). However, prospectuses are also used in the private placement market and often the term itself is employed in lieu of an offering memorandum or a PPM. Referring to your business plan or your private placement memorandum as a 'prospectus' is not inaccurate, but it may not be precise [edited for spelling and clarity]."[15]

Be sure you know what's being asked of you if someone asks for a "prospectus." Have your complete business plan ready in case that's what an investor really wants to see. It's much more feasible to break down a business plan into different types of prospectuses depending on who's making the request than it is to try to turn a legal prospectus into a complete business plan.

"Whether you are raising private capital or set to launch a publicly listed company on a stock exchange, a business plan and a disclosure document is required."[16] Per prospectus.com, the document needs at a minimum the following information:

- Terms of the Offering: The terms should be directed to a targeted audience of appropriate investors.
- Regulation Disclosures: Whatever regulations exist for raising funds need to be indicated and addressed.
- Management Team: Describe who is leading this organization, what each person's background is, and where they are getting their help from in terms of outside organizational or institutional support.
- Risk Factors: In particular, note any risks associated with the specific field you are trying to enter.
- Subscription Procedures: You need to write up a legal document to explain the terms of the stock or other security your startup is offering.[17]

For this text, a prospectus refers to a summary of a business plan put in writing that might be used as a disclosure document. There are online aids available that can help you write a business plan, which can be streamlined and used as a prospectus. You should make contact with a lawyer before you make any serious pitches to investors. The best advice may be to use the U.S. Small Business Administration's tools for crafting a business plan as completely as you can, and then based on a thorough examination of the marketplace and your plans, you can then craft a prospectus.

## Nonprofit Pitches

Nonprofit startups need to make pitches to request funds, and they may still go through the process of bootstrapping, asking friends and family for money, and eventually going to larger investors (i.e. donors, foundations, grantors, etc.) to try to get their business off the ground. In the vast majority of cases, nonprofit organizations will need to identify various revenue sources apart from the initial grantor or foundation if they plan to stay afloat. Thus, nonprofits often have to be grant-managing machines and great pitch developers too. Other ways that nonprofits bring in revenues beyond getting grants include signing up small donors in person at community events, hosting fundraising galas, crowdfunding, making direct mail requests, and sending phone, email and text requests.

Potential sources of revenue must be described in great detail in any documentation explaining your nonprofit business plan. Other elements should still be included: branding, a problem-solution narrative, communications plans and tools demonstrating your design sense, an analysis of the "competition," and financial plans. They need to be addressed in terms of terminology and tone to donors and grantors, but at the end of the day the pitch for a nonprofit business has a lot in common with a startup pitch.

## TOOLS TO IMPROVE YOUR PLAN AND YOUR PITCH

The Business Model Canvas mentioned earlier can be used to develop the components of your pitch; however, it shouldn't be used as a checklist. The sections of the canvas flow into one another and should be considered a strategic whole.[18] Write and edit multiple versions of your business model so that you could make it into a flipbook and animate it if you wanted to.

If your company or university would pay for it, Strategyzer costs $299 per year and allows you to electronically build within the BMC framework and to generate reports based on what you have proposed.[19] *The Value Proposition Design* text zeroes in on two points of the BMC—the value propositions and customer segments—and breaks down your analysis and development into smaller units that can be profiled, anticipated, and measured to try to achieve the best product market fit *as you further develop your actual product and test it with users.*[20]

Canvanizer[21] and BMFiddle[22] allow you to digitally build the BMC over and over again. With some practice, either can be a useful tool for applying virtual sticky notes to the BMC. Neither does your thinking for you, but if you're looking for inspiration, BMFiddle shares the Skype BMC example.[23]

Regardless of the tool you use, it is essential not to be boring. Present your slide deck to new people consistently. Present it to people with no knowledge of investing or entrepreneurial pitches to see how they respond to the design and the flow of your presentation.

Guy Kawasaki offers good guidelines for using PowerPoint in his 10/20/30 rule.[24] You may have to adjust your presentations for each pitch setting, but these are solid guidelines to start with. Kawasaki says that a slide deck should have 10 slides, the presentation should take about 20 minutes, and the type size should be at least 30-point. Follow these rules to have easily understood PowerPoint presentations that don't drone on and that conform to investors' expectations when dealing with startups. The 10-slide structure presented by Kawasaki is a good alternative to the structure presented in this chapter.

## PITCHING PRACTICES – WHAT RESEARCH SAYS

Scholars study the art and (social) science of the startup pitch. The discussion here includes brief analyses of research on the use of rhetoric in pitches, the role gender plays in pitch success, and analysis of how entrepreneurs can dress to win. Useful academic research focusing narrowly on entrepreneurial pitches has been done, but the body of pitch research is not nearly as robust as work delving into other aspects of entrepreneurial business management and success.

Plenty of articles have been written about how to pitch. Some may prove useful to you in planning and delivering your pitches, but they usually lack academic rigor. This section is a synthesis of carefully conducted social science research that has gone through peer review. Assumptions were tested. Findings are backed by detailed evidence, and limitations are acknowledged directly in detail.

### Successful Presentation Language: Framing the Pitch

Research regarding rhetoric in pitch presentations covers a variety of areas. This is an interesting area of study for scholars of rhetoric because pitch competitions and television shows are fertile ground for looking at what works in contemporary persuasive speech. One key concept is "impression management."[25] In a recent publication in the *Journal of Business Venturing*, Parhankangas and Ehrlich examine down to the word "How entrepreneurs seduce business angels." They looked at what words or types of words helped entrepreneurs actually secure funding and found that there may be optimal points in terms of numbers of words to put in your pitch deck for employing "positive language" (nine words), for self-promotion regarding your ability to innovate (2.8 words), for referencing your own weaknesses (3.5 words), and for "blasting" the competition (3.3 words). This serves as a reminder that these things – referencing your innovativeness, your weaknesses and your competition's failings – are good to do in a pitch, but you probably shouldn't overdo it. There seems to be, at least based on one study, a "Goldilocks"[26] point beyond which you don't want to step.

Stay positive, and reference your skills and failings and your competition's major weaknesses without overdoing it. Another paper on rhetoric and the entrepreneurial pitch looks at how Korean entrepreneurs reconfigured their pitch decks when participating in a competition designed to bring *already successful* Korean products to American markets. The entrepreneurship program studied here is intense. Program organizers and their staff do "actual market research for each company's product, and the competition's winners receive actual business development that has historically led to actual deals."[27] The authors of this paper probably use the word "actual" so often because they want to stress that this is not a paper about "merely academic" concepts.

They analyzed initial pitch decks and final decks of fourteen teams that completed the program: "a full cycle of activity: application to the program, initial pitches, initial feedback from program personnel, detailed feedback from representative stakeholders in the target market, and revised pitches." Product claims changed as teams went through the program: "There is a change in wording or details to provide more evidence-based and benefit-oriented language." At times, questions raised in the feedback process were directly addressed in rebuttal slides showing an engagement in the process that reached beyond trying to perfect the pitch deck. When entrepreneurial pitch development programs are running at top speed, so to speak, entrepreneurs show they can think strategically about their product, their market, and how to communicate to all types of audiences the value of their solution *and their approach to solving problems*.

Another article, published in *IEEE Transactions on Professional Communication*, analyzed frames used by entrepreneurs and how they are developed.[28] Here, "frame" is a way of talking about something that helps connect your understanding of an object, product, or event with other people's understanding and values. The article states, "The entrepreneur acquired the most influential frames through stakeholder discussion, applied these frames in a way that stacked and made salient multiple frames beyond the problem-solution frame, and judged frame fit by considering the degree to which catchers took up the frames." The author calls investors and stakeholders in this study "catchers" to stress that they are the ones pitches are directed to. It's important that they understand, so it can help to use multiple frames.

Problem-solution is *just one frame you can use*. What this means for students is that the way you describe your product will probably evolve as you talk about it with stakeholders, and it should probably evolve in ways that are meaningful to them. It's okay to stack frames if you need to. You can work to come up with different, specific terms that help define your innovation in different contexts for different groups. The example in this paper framed the innovation – a nonprofit organization called Hacker Gals – as a collection of hackers who know about computers, makers who get things done, and women who have unique perspectives in the startup world. The combination of frames helped the paper's author, who also runs the startup, to communicate better with more stakeholders. Ultimately, more specificity emerged as she reworked her pitches: "Specificity and salience appeared to be, in other words, directly proportional." Thus, one thread tying all these rhetorical analyses together is that specificity is important in entrepreneurial pitches, but it doesn't come only from the minds of the pitch team. It comes as a result of working and reworking the pitch with stakeholders and mentors.

## Gender and Pitch Success

Lakshmi Balachandra, Anthony Briggs, Kimberly Eddleston, and Candida Brush studied how gender affects the way entrepreneurial pitches are perceived.[29] They did not find that being female absolutely precluded an entrepreneur from finding funding, but they did find that "gendered expectations do make a difference as women entrepreneurs who present masculine behaviors are more likely to be evaluated positively than those who do not." The authors continue, "Interestingly we find women entrepreneurs have stronger communication skills, but rates of women's entrepreneurial participation remain weaker than men's." The authors suggest that this is because investors, generally speaking, are males who prefer to see so-called "masculine behavior," characterized as "bold," "attentive," "[demonstrating] self-assurance," "calm" and "confident," in women giving entrepreneurial pitches.

The authors go on to say: "Consistent with liberal feminist theory, women do face bias in terms of the masculine stereotype held by the majority of the male-dominated investment community: During the pitch, women should 'act' like men and indicate masculine behaviors or they may be penalized by investor audiences to not have the qualities they believe to be consistent with entrepreneurship."[30]

Students shouldn't interpret this article simply as a plea to female entrepreneurs to "Pitch Like a Man" in early-stage pitch presentations, to reference the title of this article. Social structures setting the norms for pitch analysis need to change. Investors must become aware of their own biases and retrain themselves to analyze pitches on their own merits rather than on the gender of the people making the pitch. Scholars and advocates are better positioned to demand these changes than entrepreneurs begging for startup funds in an environment where the success rate is very low.

## What to Wear

The quality of a pitch presentation is subjective. Investors and judges will notice when a pitch lacks quality, but they might not care to or be able to discern if it was the style of dress or style of presentation that spoiled the deal. Your dress and your performance can obviously influence whether or not your pitch is successful, but there are not many hard and fast rules. Web resources are filled with advice on how to dress and whether or not you should wear formal business attire, business-casual attire, or even casual attire. What's essential is that you research what pitch competition calls for or what the investor prefers. Just ask how formal the context of the presentation is and dress accordingly. If it's a competition, look for media from previous events showing how previous winners were dressed.

There's not a deep pool of academic research on what to wear to your pitch presentation, but scholars have shared a clear idea of what *doesn't* work: "Casual dress and nonchalance have a negative influence on investors' evaluations."[31] Do the research that allows you to dress to suit the occasion. When in doubt, wear a business suit and jacket. You can always set the jacket aside and lose the tie or your most formal accessories, e.g. Mom's pearls, if needed.

## The Importance of Performance

There is a better body of work on performance and what works. Jeffrey Pollack, Matthew Rutherford, and Brian Nagy reviewed 113 successful pitches from the TV shows *Shark Tank* and *Dragons' Den* (Canada's answer to *Shark Tank*).[32]

They had students rate these successful pitches and noted that those who were more prepared received more funding, and they found that perceptions of legitimacy had to be present for this relationship to work. This suggests that merely being over-prepared isn't enough to secure the most funding. An entrepreneur must be prepared and legitimate to survive the sharks. What comprises legitimacy? In this study, it was a wide variety of concepts ranging from the founder's level of experience to the business' likelihood of gaining good media attention. Additionally, showing strong management skills, existing resources, and likelihood of gaining endorsements helped.

## Digging Deep Into Performance Types and Practices

Even if investors don't want to acknowledge it, the quality of the pitch makes a difference. Studies show that investors often say their decisions are based on rational elements of the business and the plan presented to them. However, an article titled "The Impact of Entrepreneurs' Oral 'Pitch' Presentation Skills on Business Angels' Initial Screening Investment Decisions" suggests otherwise:

> "Presentational factors (relating to the entrepreneurs' style of delivery, etc.) tended to have the highest influence on the overall score an entrepreneur received as well as on business angels' level of investment interest. However, the business angels appeared to be unaware of (or were reluctant to acknowledge) the influence presentational factors had on their investment-related decisions: the stated reasons for their post-presentation intentions were focused firmly on substance-oriented non-presentational criteria (company, market, product, funding/finance issues, etc.)."[33]

How do you show preparedness? Melissa Cardon, Cheryl Mitteness, and Richard Sudek suggest that it's essential the pitch team demonstrates that it understands the larger context of the market and social conditions for their product. "Not surprisingly, our results confirm that entrepreneurs seeking funding from angel investors need to have a strong opportunity and be perceived as competent. More important, beyond these factors, entrepreneurs appear to be able to increase their chances of receiving funding if they are able to signal to potential investors that they are prepared, meaning they have thought through the big picture and impact of their product or service and are able to answer questions with confidence and without appearing defensive."[34]

This suggests that for your pitch performance to land, you need to demonstrate not just that you understand how your business model works but that you understand how all similar business models work, what the economic conditions in the related field need to be, and whether those conditions are present.

The research of Sean Williams, Gisela Ammetller, Inma Rodríguez-Ardura, and Xiaoli Li finds (based on a study of a small sample) that different cultural values are evident in the entrepreneurial pitches made in different countries.[35] Even if you're not presenting outside of your most comfortable cultural sphere, it may be in your best interests to learn about the values of the organization, angel or judges you'll be pitching to and speak to those values to maximize your success. These scholars considered entrepreneurial values in pairs, e.g. some entrepreneurs tend to focus on the motivation of profits while others focused more on autonomy. Some tend to promote individualism while others show the strength of their networks. Some focus on learning while everyone (in this small study) discussed action. The country-by-country breakdown in this study's results is somewhat murky, but these pairings ought to be helpful for you to consider what kind of entrepreneur you are. Identify your values and communicate them. Look for investors and competitions that are trying to achieve the same things with their entrepreneurial efforts.

## PRESENTATION TOOLS

There is more to life than PowerPoint, but Prezi gives people headaches. If you must use PowerPoint, generate a branded deck format or, perhaps better yet, let the product design lead the way and have a plain deck background. Avoid extensive use of bullet points. Illustrate every number that appears in your presentation. A dollar amount belongs in context. You should either demonstrate expected growth or expenditures or represent your target market, for example, as a small piece of a relatively large mass media pie.

Alternatives to the traditional deck include Perspective by Pixxa, which allows you to represent and animate data, and Haiku Deck, which includes lots of propriety art elements and a startup pitch template — not for professionals but perhaps good for novices getting right to work. Slidebean is good for producing pitches and testing online because it has built-in support for analytics and tracking. Wideo, an animation development app, can be used to completely stack and time a deck with various animations within and between sides.

Spinuzzi, et al. developed another paper on pitch deck development and noted that in intensive pitch competitions entrepreneurs are quite limited in how they can adjust their decks. Consider yourself lucky if you can develop your product and your pitch at the same time so that feedback on your pitch is simultaneously feedback on your innovation. In the same article, authors identified three ways pitch decks are most often altered. The **structure** of the deck may change—slides can be added and deleted. The **claims and evidence** may be clarified or strengthened, and the level of <u>audience engagement</u> may be tweaked. Consider judging yourself on these three areas as a good, overarching, holistic approach to determining what, if anything, you can improve on as you work to perfect your pitch.

## Resources

See Startup Funding: Why Funding[36] for resources on pitching.

*Mark Poepsel, Ph.D., is an assistant professor at Southern Illinois University in Edwardsville in the Department of Mass Communications. He researches media sociology and leadership in journalism organizations and teaches courses in media management, media entrepreneurship, graduate research methods, broadcast writing, introductory writing, and introductory theory. In 2016, he was a fellow at the Scripps Howard Journalism Entrepreneurship Institute, and he was a Scripps Visiting Professor in Social Media. Reach him on Twitter at @markpoepsel.*

## Leave feedback on this chapter.

## Notes

1. Ries, Eric. *The Lean Startup: How today's entrepreneurs use continuous innovation to create radically successful businesses.* (New York: Crown Business, 2011).

2. "Airbnb First Pitch Deck," *Pitch Deck Coach on Slideshare*, https://www.slideshare.net/PitchDeckCoach/airbnb-first-pitch-deck-editable.

3. Ingrid Sturgis, "Customer Discovery," *Media Innovation and Entrepreneurship*, https://press.rebus.community/media-innovation-and-entrepreneurship/chapter/customer-discovery/.

4. *Balsamiq*, https://balsamiq.com/.

5. Alex Ivanovs, "Top 35 Free Mobile UI Kits for App Designers 2017," *colorlib*, March 9, 2017, https://colorlib.com/wp/free-mobile-ui-kits-app-design/.

6. Marc Andreessen, "The PMARCA Guide to Startups. Part 4: The Only Thing That Matters," *Pmarchive*, June 25, 2007, http://pmarchive.com/guide_to_startups_part4.html.

7. Ibid.

8. Mike Isaac, "Inside Uber's Aggressive, Unrestrained Workplace Culture," *The New York Times*, February 22, 2017, https://www.nytimes.com/2017/02/22/technology/uber-workplace-culture.html.

9. Julie Schott, "Is Quip the Uber of Toothbrushes?" *Elle*, August 7, 2015, http://www.elle.com/beauty/reviews/a29700/quip-toothbrush-subscription/.

10. *Strategyzer*, "Business Model Canvas Explained," *YouTube*, September 1, 2011, https://www.youtube.com/watch?v=QoAOzMTLP5s.

11. "35 Best Pitch Decks That Investors Are Talking About," *Konsus*, https://www.konsus.com/blog/35-best-pitch-deck-examples-2017/.

12. "35 Best Pitch Decks From 2017 That Investors Are Talking About," *Konsus*, https://www.konsus.com/blog/35-best-pitch-deck-examples-2017/.

13. Hernan Jaramillo, "11 Hacks to Get Meetings With Investors in Silicon Valley," *HackerMoon*, January 12, 2015, https://hackernoon.com/11-hacks-to-get-meetings-with-investors-in-silicon-valley-14b4851ab3e8.

14. Joanne Cleaver, "3 Steps to the Perfect 3-Minute Pitch," *Entrepreneur*, March 20, 2015, https://www.entrepreneur.com/article/242523.

15. Ibid.

16. "Business Plan vs. PPM vs. Prospectus," *Prospectus.com*, https://www.prospectus.com/business-plan-vs-ppm-vs-prospectus/.

17. Ibid.

18. Alex Osterwalder, "Tools for Business Model Generation," *Stanford eCorner,* February 2012, https://www.youtube.com/watch?v=8GIbCg8NpBw.

19. *Strategyzer App*, https://strategyzer.com/app.

20. "Value Proposition Design," *Strategyzer,* https://strategyzer.com/books/value-proposition-design.

21. *Canvanizer,* https://canvanizer.com/new/business-model-canvas.

22. *Business Model Fiddle,* https://bmfiddle.com/.

23. Example from Business Model Generation, *BMFiddle,* https://bmfiddle.com/f/#/local.

24. Guy Kawasaki, "The 10/20/30 Rule of PowerPoint," *GuyKawasaki.com*, https://guykawasaki.com/the_102030_rule/.

25. Annaleena Parhankangas and Michael Ehrlich. "How Entrepreneurs Seduce BusinessAngels: An Impression Management Approach." *Journal of Business Venturing.* Vol. 29.4. July 2014. https://doi.org/10.1016/j.jbusvent.2013.08.001.

26. "Goldilocks Principle," https://en.wikipedia.org/wiki/Goldilocks_principle.

27. Clay Spinuzzi, Scott Nelson, Keela S. Thomson, Francesca Lorenzini, Rosemary A. French, Gegory Pogue, Sidney D. Burback, Joel Momberger, "Making the Pitch: Examining Dialogue and Revisions in Entrepreneurs' Pitch Decks." *IEEE Transactions on Professional Communication* 57 no. 3, September 2014. http://hdl.handle.net/2152/25712.

28. Stacy J. Belinsky and Brian Gogan, "Throwing a Change-Up, Pitching a Strike: An Autoethnography of Frame Acquisition, Application, and Fit in a Pitch Delvelopment and Delivery Experience," *IEEE Transactions on Professional Communication,* 59 no. 4. October 2016, http://ieeexplore.ieee.org/document/7592403/.

29. Lakshmi Balachandra, Anthony Briggs, Kimberly Eddleston, and Candida Brush, "Pitch Like a Man: Gender Stereotypes and Entrepreneur Pitch Success," *Frontiers of Entrepreneurship Research*, 33 no. 8, June 2013, http://digitalknowledge.babson.edu/cgi/viewcontent.cgi?article=2634&context=fer.

30. Ibid.

31. Louis F. Jourdan Jr., "The Relationship of Investor Decisions and Entrepreneurs' Dispositional and Interpersonal Factors," *Entrepreneurial Executive*, 17 no. 1, January 2012.

32. Jeffrey M. Pollack, Matthew W. Rutherford, and Brian G. Nagy, "Preparedness and Cognitive Legitimacy as Antecedents of New Venture Funding in Televised Business Pitches," *Entrepreneurship Theory and Practice*. 36 no. 5, September 2012, https://www.researchgate.net/publication/233733878_Preparedness_and_Cognitive_Legitimacy_as_Antecedents_of_New_Venture_Funding_in_Televised_Business_Pitches.

33. Colin Clark, "The Impact of Entrepreneurs' Oral 'Pitch' Presentation Skills on Business Angels' Initial Screening Investment Decisions," *Venture Capital: An International Journal of Entrepreneurial Finance,* 10 no. 3, July 2008.

34. Melissa S. Cardon, Cheryl Mitteness, and Richard Sudek, "Motivational Cues and Angel

Investing: Interactions Among Enthusiasm, Preparedness, and Commitment." *Entrepreneurship Theory and Practice,* October 2016, http://www.effectuation.org/?research-papers=motivational-cues-angel-investing-interactions-among-enthusiasm-preparedness-commitment.

35. Sean D. Williams, Gisela Ammetller, Inma Rodríguez-Ardura and Xiaoli Li. "A Narrative Perspective on International Entrepreneurship: Comparing Stories From the United States, Spain, and China," *IEEE Transactions on Professional Communication,* 59 no. 4, December 2016, http://ieeexplore.ieee.org/document/7736039/.

36. CJ Cornell, "Startup Funding: Why Funding?" *Media Innovation and Entrepreneurship*, https://press.rebus.community/media-innovation-and-entrepreneurship/chapter/section-2-why-funding/.

# FROM THE FIELD: THE PERFECT PITCH

*Amy Eisman*

*How to avoid the dreaded blank stare during a live presentation. 'Good ideas die all the time,' one expert reminds us.*

## From the Field

What makes a compelling, memorable presentation? What will make investors sit up and take notice?

Most experts say the first thing a startup presenter should do is tell a good story. You have to be engaging, even entertaining, explains Tom Davidson, former senior director of PBS Digital, now in product development at Gannett.

Executive coach and author Peggy Klaus calls that "painting images about how this product or company could impact the audience."

Klaus, president of Klaus & Associates, has seen thousands of presentations — from executives and entrepreneurs, to private bankers and nonprofits. She tells clients to keep the audience in mind by embracing fictional radio station *WIFT-FM* — where the call letters stand for *what's in it for them?*

"Most people who start a speech or presentation think about what *I* want to say, what is *my* point," Klaus says. "That is a narcissistic way of looking at it. What are *their* goals and objectives?"

Insiders admit the soul of a good pitch presentation is really common sense. Don't dare read your slides. Be confident and concise. And of course practice, practice, practice.

"People think they can wing it because they've been verbal since 18 months," Klaus says. "This results in a terrible meltdown situation."

Below, the experts weigh in on the perfect pitch:

### Your parents were right.

"Maintain eye contact with your audience," says Jan Schaffer, who has funded 220 media entrepreneurship and innovation projects as Executive Director of J-Lab: The Institute for Interactive Journalism. "Walk around. Be at ease. Show some personality without being obnoxious."

### They were right about this, too.

Introduce yourself, says Schaffer, who teaches media entrepreneurship at American University and the CUNY Graduate School of Journalism. Don't forget to tell your listeners who you are. Your audience won't always be classmates.

### Be armed.

Have one or two sentences that show that you, as the founder, have a firm grasp of the opportunity, says Ju-Don Marshall Roberts, startup advisor and coach and now Chief Content Officer for *WFAE.FM*. Convey enough passion to show you are the one to pull this off.

Davidson emphasizes that you simply can't let the investors, humans like the rest of us, get distracted. If you don't know an answer, tell them an exact time you will get back to them with the response.

### Define your opportunity.

Will the market sustain the product? Have you explained how your idea is different from a similar one? "Good ideas die all the time," Roberts says.

Equally critical: Convince funders that this is a business, not a hobby, Schaffer says.

### Bring a solid team.

"I've seen a lot of pitches where you think, 'This is a great idea, I wish someone else was doing it,'" Roberts says.

### Memorize your pitch and don't read your deck.

"Likewise, don't read from your laptop or cell phone," Schaffer says.

Klaus has seen so many presentations that a question about biggest mistakes momentarily stumped her. "There are so many. Where do I begin?"

She identifies some of the top presentation mistakes as using jargon, causing death by PowerPoint, speaking longer than seven minutes before interacting with the audience, and being condescending or arrogant.

Klaus also warns against promising future results and cautions that conditional language is preferred. "With our numbers, we see a future where we can … "

Klaus warns that young people's nerves often get the best of them. They end up talking quickly or speaking with an upward inflection (making statements sound like questions). They fidget. They twist their hair. They slap their thighs.

Klaus says young presenters have a particular challenge that interferes with the enthusiasm our experts say is critical. "A lot of young people feel if they show passion and excitement they will come off as too exuberant or too young," says the author of *Brag! The Art of Tooting Your Own Horn Without Blowing It*. "It is actually the inverse — that young people feel, 'If I am really serious, they will think I am really smart.'"

In the end, make a video of yourself while practicing your pitch. Yes, we know you hate seeing yourself perform. But if even you can't stand watching you, why should an investor have to listen?

For examples and pitching resources, see this chapter.[1]

*Amy Eisman* is director of media entrepreneurship at the School of Communication at American University in Washington, D.C. An innovator in journalism education and consultant, she held previous editing positions at AOL, USA Today, USA Weekend, and others. She is a former Fulbright lecturer and chairs the MJ Bear Fellowship Committee for ONA. Reach her on Twitter at @aeisman.

## Leave feedback on this sidebar.

## *Notes*

1. CJ Cornell, "Startup Funding: Why Funding," *Media Innovation and Entrepreneurship,* https://press.rebus.community/media-innovation-and-entrepreneurship/chapter/section-2-why-funding/.

# LOOKING AHEAD

## Looking Ahead

You're in business! Now, how to connect with your target market efficiently? Read Marketing Your Venture to Audiences for an overview of content marketing and analytics, an important and low-cost component of any startup's marketing efforts.

# MARKETING YOUR VENTURE TO AUDIENCES

by Jessica Pucci and Elizabeth Mays

## Summary

Content marketing and social media marketing level the playing field for new ventures, allowing them to reach and engage users and customers organically, with minimal investment. This chapter will provide an overview of key concepts in content marketing, including how to develop a marketing strategy to move people through your conversion funnel and leverage content tactically to execute your plan. In addition, the chapter will give an overview of some of the metrics used to measure success of content and social marketing endeavors in terms of reach and engagement.

---

### Learning Objectives

- Understand what content marketing is and why it's particularly important to new digital ventures (or your personal brand if you're a solopreneur).
- Identify types of content that might be used for marketing your venture (email marketing, blogging, video, podcasting, events, social media, etc.).
- Understand how basic social and website analytics can help make marketing decisions, measure success, and pivot.
- Differentiate between reach and engagement strategies, and why you might pursue one over the other.
- Develop conversion-focused objectives, strategies, and tactics marketing your venture.
- Strategically optimize your content to be discoverable in search engines.

---

## Inside this Chapter

- Marketing your Venture to Audiences, by Elizabeth Mays
- Engagement and Analytics, by Jessica Pucci

*Jessica Pucci is a professor of practice at the Cronkite School, specializing in data analytics and audience engagement. She leads social media and analytics for Cronkite News, the news division of Arizona PBS, and also teaches a course in analytics and engagement. Reach her on Twitter at @jessica_pucci.*

**Elizabeth Mays** *is the operations and marketing manager for Canadian nonprofit the Rebus Foundation, which is building a new, collaborative model for open textbook publishing through the Rebus Community. She is also an adjunct professor at the Walter Cronkite School of Journalism and Mass Communication, teaching its first online course in audience acquisition. Reach her on Twitter at @theeditress.*

# MARKETING YOUR VENTURE TO AUDIENCES

*Elizabeth Mays*

## Overview

You've identified a problem, need or opportunity and you've developed your solution to it as an entrepreneurial venture. You now have a minimally viable product or service. This chapter will talk about how to market that product or service to your target audience in order to find users and customers.

## Your Audience: Users vs. Customers

The first thing to keep in mind is that media entrepreneurship is different from traditional entrepreneurship. You may be marketing to two distinct groups—users and customers—and you may want them to take different actions.

Think of a restaurant you frequent. The people who go in to eat are the end users of the product and also the people who pay for that product. The restaurant's users are also its customers, so it only needs to market to one audience.

Now think about a technology venture like Facebook. Facebook makes its platform free to its users but charges advertisers to market to those users. This is much more similar to the traditional model for content and media businesses in which the core product (news) is given away free to an audience whose attention is then sold to the advertisers.

That's not to say that as a media startup you can't charge your users—you might have premium news or subscriptions, branded tchotchkes, events they can attend and hopefully countless other streams of revenue.

Your users may be just users of the product, or they may also be both users and customers to you.

The point is, if your customers and your users are different, you may need to reach them with different approaches and messaging.

For the purposes of this chapter, though, we're going to focus on marketing your business in a way that attracts and engages an audience that uses your product, because whether that audience is paying you or inspiring others to pay you, without an <u>audience</u>, you can't monetize.

## Audience Acquisition

You might ask, why do you need an audience if they are not paying you directly, or not paying you yet? Traditionally, in media, the size of an outlet's audience is important because it determines how much it can charge for advertising. Nowadays as a media startup, you probably want to also charge the audience for something–whether that's a membership, events, a subscription to premium content, or something else. Either way, the larger your audience, the more revenue potential. Even if you're grant-funded, you'll want to prove to funders that your work matters and is worthy of more funding. The size of the audience that sees your work is one measure you can use to demonstrate impact.

Quantifying your audience is a measure of reach. The depth of their interest in you (which may be measured in terms of the length of time they spent with your content, whether they shared it, and other metrics) is known as engagement.

When you're marketing your venture, it's important to know whether it is more useful to your business goals to get a large quantity of audience members, or audience members who are passionate about your business and engage deeply.

In either case, it's important to find an audience that is a match for your brand. This is called your target audience. The Customer Discovery for Content and Tech Startups[1] chapter discusses how to identify and target your intended "market segment," whether that is demographic, psychographic, behavioral, or geographic. It also discusses how to perform market research and develop user personas, or buyer personas.

## AIDA Models and Conversion

Ever heard of an AIDA model? The initials stand for attention, interest, desire, and action. The terms were originally used to describe how advertisers moved prospects or consumers down a pipeline or sales funnel from hearing about your product to being interested in knowing more about it, to wanting to get it, to actually buying it. For many businesses nowadays, including content businesses, this journey happens online. It's called a "conversion funnel" in the e-commerce context.

Even as a journalist, your media outlet has an AIDA funnel that should matter to you. Ideally you probably want readers and visitors to subscribe to the media outlet as their conversion. But even if a user or audience member is not making an actual purchase or if your story doesn't advance that end goal, chances are there is an action you want them to take (sign up to receive

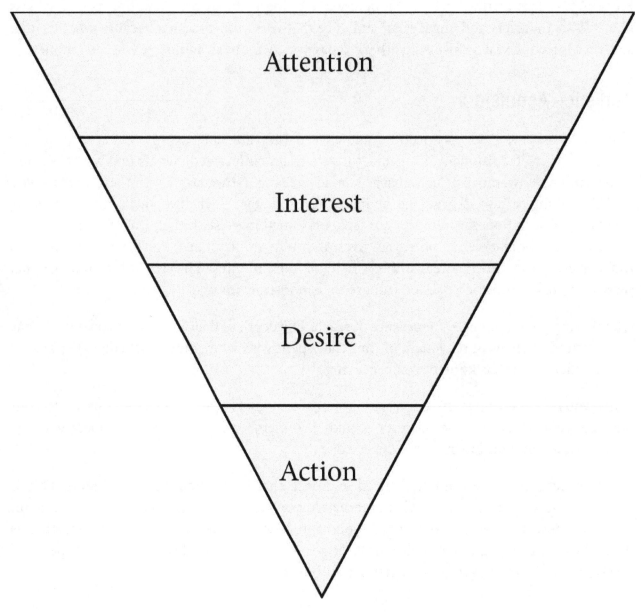

AIDA funnel

your column in their inbox each week, for instance). That action is still called a conversion even when it doesn't involve a purchase.

Conversion, whatever form it takes, is a "bottom of the funnel" activity. A user is unlikely to do a bottom of the funnel activity without being aware of your company and becoming increasingly interested first. Sometimes, this does all happen in the span of a moment, in which someone comes to your landing page and converts by signing up to your email list. More often, movement through the funnel happens through multiple contacts with your company over time. For example, someone might see a boosted post from you on Facebook, but not take the action to go to your website. Another day, they might see another post and this time click through to go to your site, an investigative reporting site. There, they fill out the opt-in form to join your email list. They forget all about you for awhile, but now they get your biweekly emails. A few weeks later, they click on a link from one of them to a really good story about something that impacts them directly. In this action, they realize why you are important to them. A few weeks later, they get another email from you with information about a crowdfunding campaign you are running. They click to make a small donation.

Figuring out what conversion means for your organization and how to move audiences through the funnel should be the goal of your marketing.

# Content Marketing

The great thing about a digital business is that all you need to start off is some talent, a great business idea, some paperwork, a website, a way to transact business, and some content marketing. You don't have to be rich to start a business nor do you have to spend thousands on advertising to get people into your physical doors. If you sell to people online, you can market to them there too. Content marketing is one of the main ways digital organizations acquire audiences. And content marketing costs only your time if you know how to do it yourself. Content marketing is a common way to avoid needing a million-dollar advertising budget.

Content marketing is the David to advertising's Goliath. And the Internet is the great equalizer. Today, you as a startup media organization and *The New York Times* have equal opportunity to acquire an audience because the Internet allows you to reach a niche audience in ways previously not possible.

Content marketing can be even more effective than advertising at growing a digital audience. Think about the advertisements you see–they're often an unwanted interruption pushing you to want to buy something. Content is different. It pulls you into something you are already interested in, reminds you of your needs and wants, and subtly markets a solution to those needs in an enjoyable, soft-sell package, complete with a call to action.

The type of content you do will be different if you are a news outlet, in which case you will probably rely on amazing news content to market your outlet, than if you are a consultant, in which case you will probably produce content that positions you as an expert in the type of work you do, or if you are marketing a platform, in which scenario you'll probably do content that helps your target audience solve problems they have that your platform can help them solve.

## Marketing Strategy, Competitive Analysis and Content Strategy

Once I've said the word content marketing, it's tempting to take that to mean, "Okay, I just need to create some blog posts." But that's going straight to tactics and bypassing strategy, and marketing starts with strategy. You have to first ask and answer the following questions:

- Who are you trying to reach?

- What are their needs and problems?
- What content might you provide that meets those needs?
- Where is your potential audience now?
- How will you distribute it through channels that reach them?
- And how will you measure / know whether your marketing was effective and iterate if not?

NewsCred offers one methodology for content marketing programs. It breaks down content marketing into five steps:

- documenting strategy
- producing and distributing content
- refining based on insights gleaned through producing and distributing content
- converting visitors to leads and customers
- and connecting metrics to business outcomes

You can read more in their white paper[2] (free if you sign up to their site).

Even though some people find creating content fun, that's not why you're doing it. You should be doing it to meet the business objectives. Content as marketing inevitably involves research and data to help you with decision making.

How do you decide what type of content to do? After all, if you're launching your own startup, chances are you have lots of other core things you need to be doing (building the product, building a revenue model around it, etc.) in addition to marketing it. So you've got to decide where to put your resources.

Here's a process that will help you decide where to put your efforts.

- First, develop an overall marketing strategy that takes into account your Goals, Strategies, Measurable Objectives and Tactics, as well as KPIs (key performance indicators by which you will measure success).
- Conduct a SWOT analysis to help you understand your brand's strengths, weaknesses, opportunities and threats in the marketplace.
- Then, conduct a Competitive Analysis of your competitors' content to see what your closest competitors are doing.
- Finally develop a Content Strategy that shows where you might compete.

Let's say you are creating a brand-new political news outlet targeted to progressive millennials.

- Your goal might be to become the go-to political news source brand with this audience.
- Your measurable objective might be to get X # of subscribers to your outlet's daily newsletter.

- Your <u>strategy</u> to do that might be to do things that make your brand prominent on college campuses.
- One <u>tactic</u> might be to do paid social that markets your newsletter signup to a targeted audience on an appropriate social network. Another tactic might be to sponsor relevant events on college campuses and give away cool swag with your brand on it in exchange for on-site email signups.
- Your key performance indicators (or KPIs) in this example would be the number of signups to your newsletter.

| Exercise |
|---|
| Put together a one-page marketing plan for your venture. Include high-level goals for the marketing you do, strategies, measurable objectives (X number of new users, X percent growth each week, X new followers on Twitter, etc.), and the tactics you will pursue to achieve these goals. |

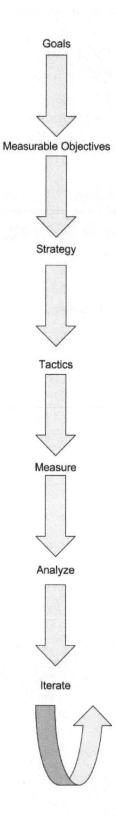

Now that you know what you're focusing on and why, check out what the competition is doing and conduct a competitive analysis. There are two levels of competition here: the peer competitors you know about who do something very similar to what you do (other professional political news outlets in the example above), and the competitors you might not have thought of as competitors, but who are competing for your audience's attention in search results on the Internet (for instance, a random but hugely popular blogger you may never have heard of).

You can use a program such as SEMRush or SpyFu to compare yourself to the competitors you know about and discover the competitors you weren't aware of.

Use such programs to:

- Discover which topics in your expertise are popular and what topical niches are not being filled by your competitors.
- Unearth the search terms that commonly land people on your website or blog and your competitor's.
- Surface other websites that also compete for those same search terms.
- See which variations of relevant search terms draw the highest number of searches.
- See what Google adwords terms your competitors have paid for and presumably find valuable from in attracting an audience.

Knowing the terms that are relevant to your enterprise that a good swath of people are searching for will give you the insights you need to develop a content strategy–i.e., what niche are you going to write about, that people are interested in but that is not already well-served by a similar competing company.

Here are some questions to ask as you approach this:

- What relevant search terms are your competitors ranking for?
- What does that information lead you to believe about what their audience is interested in and the demographic characteristics and interests of that audience?
- How does that match or diverge from the audience you want to reach?
- Which of your competitors' words do you also want to rank for?
- Which of those are most difficult to compete for? Are they worth it given your budget and goals?
- What other words get traffic and provide an opportunity they haven't considered or capitalized on?

These and similar lines of inquiry should lead you to some preliminary conclusions about the content that might engage your target audience–what topics do they care about and seek out, what information do they need, and most importantly, which of those are not covered ad nauseum elsewhere. Where can you provide a fresh and needed perspective?

If your venture is a content business, these questions would be used to hone the direction of the content that is your product, and marketing that product would become more of a question of how to distribute that content you're doing as a product into the right channels to reach people who might be interested in it.

If your <u>venture is a technology startup</u>, this process would help you learn about the needs of the marketplace and where your competitor's blog is providing value and where there might be a new niche opportunity to compete.

If you're a <u>freelance consultant</u> providing a service to a certain type of business, this process will help you shape content your target clients might need and want that differentiates your brand and keeps it top of mind.

# SEO

SEO is the topic of countless blog posts, by countless so-called gurus. What follows is an attempt to give an overview of generally agreed-upon principles that content producers should be aware of, not a comprehensive deep dive into the controversial nuances.

Here are the basics of what you need to know.

There are two facets to getting an audience for your (presumably great) content: distributing it into channels where your audience already is; and ensuring its discoverability in the places where audiences might be searching for it: in this case, search engines.

The first thing to understand is that search engines want to show people the most relevant results for whatever they're searching for. By doing this, they gain eyeballs and become the most trusted authority, and can leverage that status to monetize their engines through advertising and other methods. So they've built a variety of complicated proprietary algorithms to ensure they only show the content they think people will find most relevant. This calculation includes the behaviors other people have had on the content–did they linger or did they bounce; did they share it; did reputable experts in the same topical space link to it?

This means that the best way you can optimize your content to be found is by doing amazing content on a top that people are searching for because they want to know. Ideally your posts will also be so good that influencers–leaders in their/your field with large audiences–will link to them. This is the ultimate compliment as they are endorsing you to their audience, and in a way, sending a quality signal to the search engines.

There are lots of search engine marketers who use "black hat" tactics to fool the algorithms into thinking your content is relevant, but using these is dangerous and can get you demoted in rankings. Two examples of black hat techniques are keyword stuffing, packing content full of irrelevant but high-traffic keywords; or cloaking, hiding such keywords in a way where search engines see them but humans don't.

Again, the best thing you can do to show up in the search results to the right audience, is to create amazing content that is needed or wanted by that audience. What is amazing content? To start with, that means content that solves a problem or serves a need for its audience, content that's more than just what you had for dinner, content that's long enough to be worthwhile, and content that delivers on its promises.

The other thing you can do that is within your control is to optimize that content in several ways.

The first is in your meta description. This shows up in search results and when you post on social, and it may encourage or discourage someone from clicking on your post, so it's an important component of acquiring audience in the first place. When people engage with your content by clicking or lingering on it, that sends a signal that your content is authoritative.

If you use WordPress, you'll need a plugin like Yoast or similar to edit this area of your post to be tantalizing.

The next is by making sure you use the terms (aka keywords) your audience is searching for (in a natural and relevant way) when you're writing.

Remember that competitive analysis you conducted? In it, you found out what people were searching for on sites similar to yours and how many people were searching for various relevant topics? You also found out the many variations of relevant terms, and which were most commonly used. Note that similar phrases might have vastly different search volume—"hiking in Phoenix" might get 10,000 searches a month whereas the variation "Phoenix hiking" might only get 500. Even if something gets a million hits a month though, that doesn't mean it's a great thing to build your content strategy around. It may have too much competition.

Hopefully you've found some words that have a decent audience, but that your competitors aren't yet leveraging well, that you can use to optimize your strategy. (These should also help you find your outlet's niche subject matter.)

Here are some of the places you may want to include the keywords you've decided to target:

- in your post URL
- in page titles
- in subheads
- near the top of the post
- in image alt tags, image title tags
- in the metadescription

Of course, you never want to overuse or "stuff" keywords into your content, and you certainly shouldn't hide them (known as "cloaking"). These are black-hat tactics that will get you penalized by search engines.

But if your post is about a certain niche topic or specific person, it should say so, prominently. Save cutesy or abstract headlines or ledes for print. You should also research which variations of terms people are searching for around the topic and be strategic about which ones you use.

The above description focuses on "text" types of content. Of course, there are numerous types of content, such as video and multimedia, and there are different ways to leverage these for SEO. If you're doing video or audio, optimize the title and description, and consider including a transcript. Also, realize that video and multimedia formats are great for getting other reputable sites to link to your content. But if you're hosting the videos on YouTube or similar, you will need to think about how to get people back to your site.

There are also some technical things you can do to your site, especially if you are starting out. These include:

- You may need to install a plugin to help you control page titles and your search and social meta description.
- Avoiding having a bunch of 404 errors on pages that have been deleted. (Redirect any such pages to avoid this. Also redirect pages where you've changed the URL.)
- Enable an XML sitemap and submit it to Google Webmaster Tools. This will allow you to see when Google thinks your site is giving people a bad experience.
- Use SSL.
- Have good navigation (breadcrumbs) and URL structure.

You can get far more into the weeds with this (and people do), but following these best practices is a good start.

## Types of Content

There are many types of content you can deploy as part of a content marketing strategy. Here are just a few of the types of content that can be used for marketing.

- Blog posts
- Videos, 360 video or virtual reality
- Social posts
- Email messaging
- Events, webinars and conferences
- Games
- Podcasts
- Ebooks, books
- And more (See Beyond 800 Words: New Digital Story Formats for News[3] for a list.)

Note that content is not always the same as distribution. For instance, you might have a blog post that is designed to be distributed on social, a video designed to be distributed through

YouTube, messaging written to be distributed via email, a lecture designed to be delivered at a conference, a podcast for iTunes, an ebook for Amazon, and so forth.

Social media can be a platform on which you create content. But it is also a distribution method for content housed elsewhere.

Each piece of content will be designed to fit the appropriate format for the platform(s) it will be distributed on, leaving lots of room for the same message to be repurposed into different content formats and then distributed into different channels where you can connect with different parts of your audience.

# Social Media

## Organic Social Media

The Internet is saturated with blog posts on how to use each social media network to best effect. We will not replicate those here. Instead, we'll give an overview of how to use social media, generally, in the context of a broader marketing strategy for your venture.

Of course, you can create content that is solely meant to live on a social network. Instagram is a great example of a network that lends itself to this. People post awesome images and links are not clickable by default, which decreases the value of using this network to promote things you're doing elsewhere.

However, when you're using someone else's network to post content, you don't own your audience.

The social network owns the data about that audience, which decreases the value to you in building an audience on social media outlets like Facebook, Twitter, etc. These are what we call "borrowed channels."

In addition, these borrowed channels all have different algorithms, some of which are specifically designed to demote content that is too obviously promotional rather than personal.

Furthermore, as a social media manager colleague of mine likes to say, social media is like throwing a pebble in the ocean. The odds of people seeing your efforts here at scale are low (if you don't have lots of resources to devote to this).

For all of these reasons, in the content marketing context, social media is more often used to:

- Distribute, amplify, and bring attention to content that lives elsewhere on your "owned channels" and encourage people to subscribe to your owned channels.

- Expand the audience you reach on your owned channels by targeting a similar audience that wasn't connecting with you previously.
- Listen to your audience and find out about their needs so you can serve them better.
- Foster engagement with your audience for your brand.

In my experience, when student teams pitch an entrepreneurial idea, they focus on social media as the main way to market their product. But posting on social media in itself does not comprise a marketing strategy. Social media is but one tactic or tool in a much larger toolbox. And the tools you employ should be tied to your venture's business goals and marketing strategy, with some eye to the resources you have to deploy.

## Paid Social Media

Why pay to reach your audience through social media networks? When you pay, you reduce the chance your efforts will be ineffective. For instance, by paying to advertise on these networks, you can ensure that your content reaches a larger audience, reaches more of the right niche audience or gets the right audience to engage with your content, if that's your goal. Sometimes, you even get better analytics to track the effectiveness of your efforts.

Social advertising offers important advantages over conventional advertising:

- It lets you target a niche audience. It leverages the social network's data about its users to show your ad only to the people most likely to care about your product, rather than the most eyeballs.
- It's usually far less expensive than other types of advertising.
- It often allows you to pay only for the people you reach or engage (depending which you choose to optimize your ad for), so there is less waste.
- It gives you clear data and analytics about how your ad performed and lets you A/B test different variables–paid social will show you everything from the numbers of people who saw it and the actions they took on it to the ad variation they preferred. This allows you to optimize your efforts and minimize your expenses in the future.

Social media outlets typically let you choose which goal to pursue with your advertising, which can include:

- Get people to your website.
- Get people into your physical location.
- Get people to buy something from you.
- Build your email list.
- Get people to subscribe to other content you offer.
- Increase your followers, or followers of a certain demographic.
- Target your competitors' followers and bring them into your fold.
- Get people to engage with your content.
- Generate leads.

- Target a very specific niche.
- And more.

Across most networks, when placing a social ad, you can choose between goals of reach, engagement or conversion. You will be charged accordingly:

- CPM, the cost per 1,000 views, is a measure of reach. This is great if you care mainly about awareness.
- CPC, the cost per click, is a measure of engagement. This is a better metric if you want people to go to a specific link. However, if your website or landing page—wherever you send people from the ad—isn't set up well to get people to move down your funnel, this is a waste.
- CPA, the cost for an action that you specify, is a measure of conversion. This could include buying something, downloading an app, signing up, or similar.

## When Brands Go Social

Social media has a down side too. Whenever you use it as a brand, you should think, "Who might not appreciate this message I'm going to put out?" And think about how those parties might co-opt your content to put out a counternarrative. You should also ask yourself, "Is there anything remotely potentially offensive in this piece of fun creative content I'm about to do?"

Perhaps you heard about Dove's recent ad fail—a campaign on Facebook depicting a black woman turning white—and its mea culpa afterward.[4]

Or Ghost in the Shell's backfired viral marketing campaign. The movie put out a hashtag and an image generator to encourage fans to make "I am Major" images that identified with the main character. However, people ended up using the hashtag and generator to call attention to what they saw as whitewashing on behalf of the movie, which cast a white woman in an Asian role, and renamed the character.[5]

## Testing, Measuring and Iterating

Once you've executed your strategy, it's important to determine whether it was successful, and how it might be adjusted in the future to better meet your goals.

This is where analytics come in to answer questions like which blog post topics or story topics performed better, which brand imagery did people respond best to, and which CTA (call to action) messaging was most effective in getting people to sign up / subscribe / etc.?

Here are just a few things you can and should test on your landing pages, in your marketing emails, on social, and in paid advertising:

- Text

- Visuals
- Headlines
- CTAs
- The relative performance of different landing pages

So how do you measure the effectiveness of your content efforts? Read on! The next chapter, Marketing Your Venture: Engagement & Analytics,[6] goes further into depth on how to set goals and objectives, measure success, and decide which analytics make the most sense to track and care about.

## Resources

- *Content Inc.*[7]
- *Epic Content Marketing*[8]
- *The Hubspot Marketing Blog*[9]
- *The Buffer Social Blog*[10]
- *Yoast SEO Blog*[11]
- *Growthrocks Growth Hacking Marketing Blog*[12]

## Training

- How to Use Twitter Ads: The Complete Guide for Business, Hootsuite[13]
- How to Advertise on LinkedIn, LinkedIn[14]
- Snapchat's Ad Manager: A Beginner's Guide, AdEspresso by Hootsuite[15]
- Instagram for Business, Facebook Blueprint Course[16]
- Facebook Ads Manager, Facebook Blueprint Course[17]
- Targeting Core Audiences, Facebook Blueprint Course[18]
- Targeting Lookalike Audiences, Facebook Blueprint Course[19]
- Targeting Custom Audiences, Facebook Blueprint Course[20]

*Elizabeth Mays is the operations and marketing manager for Canadian nonprofit the Rebus Foundation, which is building a new, collaborative model for open textbook publishing through the Rebus Community.[21] She is also an adjunct professor at the Walter Cronkite School of Journalism and Mass Communication, teaching its first online course in audience acquisition. Reach her on Twitter at @theeditress.*

## Leave feedback on this chapter.

# Notes

1. Ingrid Sturgis, "Customer Discovery for Content and Tech Startups," *Media Innovation & Entrepreneurship*, https://press.rebus.community/media-innovation-and-entrepreneurship/chapter/customer-discovery/.

2. "Whitepaper: Newscred Methodology: Five Elements of Content Marketing Success," *Newscred*, https://insights.newscred.com/whitepaper-newscred-methodology-five-elements-of-content-marketing-success/.

3. Tristan Ferne, "Beyond 800 Words: New Digital Story Formats for News," *BBC News on Medium*, https://medium.com/bbc-news-labs/beyond-800-words-new-digital-story-formats-for-news-ab9b2a2d0e0d.

4. Anita Balakrishnan, "Dove Apologizes After Social Media Users Skewer Soap Ad as Racist" *Cnbc.com*, Oct. 8, 2017, https://www.cnbc.com/2017/10/08/dove-ad-dove-apologizes-after-social-media-calls-ad-racist.html.

5. Michelle Jaworski, "'Ghost in the Shell' Viral Marketing Campaign Backfires," *The Daily Dot*, March 14, 2017, https://www.dailydot.com/parsec/ghost-in-the-shell-viral-marketing-backfire/.

6. Jessica Pucci, "Marketing Your Venture, Engagement and Analytics," *Media Innovation & Entrepreneurship*, https://press.rebus.community/media-innovation-and-entrepreneurship/chapter/marketing-your-venture-engagement-and-analytics/.

7. Joe Pulizzi, *Content Inc.*, (New York: McGraw-Hill Education, 2015) http://contentmarketinginstitute.com/content-inc/.

8. Joe Pulizzi, *Epic Content Marketing*, (New York: McGraw-Hill Education, 2013), http://epiccontentmarketing.com/.

9. *The Hubspot Marketing Blog*, http://blog.hubspot.com/marketing.

10. *The Buffer Social Blog*, https://blog.bufferapp.com/.

11. *Yoast SEO Blog*, https://yoast.com/seo-blog/.

12. *Growthrocks Growth Hacking Marketing Blog*, https://growthrocks.com/blog/.

13. "How to Use Twitter Ads: The Complete Guide for Business," *Hootsuite*, https://blog.hootsuite.com/twitter-ads/.

14. "How to Advertise on LinkedIn," *LinkedIn*, https://business.linkedin.com/marketing-solutions/how-to-advertise-on-linkedin.

15. Snapchat's Ad Manager: A Beginner's Guide, *AdEspresso by Hootsuite*, https://adespresso.com/academy/blog/snapchat-ad-manager/.

16. "Instagram for Business," *Facebook Blueprint*, https://www.facebookblueprint.com/student/home/show_enrollment/43448847.

17. "Facebook Ads Manager," *Facebook Blueprint*, https://www.facebookblueprint.com/uploads/resource_courses/targets/340588/original/build/index.html.

18. "Targeting Core Audiences," *Facebook Blueprint*, https://www.facebookblueprint.com/uploads/resource_courses/targets/339376/original/build/index.html.

19. "Targeting Lookalike Audiences," *Facebook Blueprint*, https://www.facebookblueprint.com/uploads/resource_courses/targets/340891/original/build/index.html.

20. "Targeting Custom Audiences," *Facebook Blueprint*, https://www.facebookblueprint.com/uploads/resource_courses/targets/341016/original/build/index.html

21. Rebus Community, https://about.rebus.community/.

# MARKETING YOUR VENTURE: ENGAGEMENT AND ANALYTICS

*Jessica Pucci*

Far too often, entrepreneurs focus squarely on conversion and forget about the rest of the funnel.[1] It can sound tempting to measure the success of your business solely by tickets sold, apps downloaded or T-shirts shipped. But evaluating a venture that way neglects the value and impact of your audience—the audience you have now, and the audiences you want but don't have yet. Is your company really successful if it sells 750 hats at a music festival? To really say one way or the other, you'd need to know what your audience opportunity was first: Did 1,000 people attend the festival (if so, you sold hats to 75% of them, and that's excellent!), or did 50,000 people attend (if so, you sold hats to only 1.5% of them, and that's not so excellent, assuming everyone at the festival had a head)? And what about the 200 festival-goers who came to browse your hat booth but didn't buy anything... yet? What about the 450 attendees who saw your hats around the festival and started following your brand on Instagram? Shouldn't we include them when we tally up our successes? Don't they count for something?

Your job as an entrepreneur is not just to make a single sale: It's to build relationships with audiences who will grow your company. Focusing on a one-time sale will get you just that: one sale. But focusing on audience development—strategic growth and engagement of likely, long-term customers—creates a sustainable business.

Growth and engagement go hand-in-hand. Tomatoes don't just grow: They need a particular patch of dirt with at least six hours of sun; they need a trellis; they need regular water, pruning and support—and that's just tomatoes. Other veggies need different care. The point is, you don't toss down some seeds and expect a harvest. Growth takes research, planning, hands-on care, and recognition that no two crops need the same thing. Gardening isn't so far from digital audience growth. Just like produce, digital audiences are all different, and all require different forms of nurturing and nourishment to thrive. The way we feed and care for our digital audiences is engagement.

## Engagement

Broadly, entrepreneurs and marketers use the term "<u>engagement</u>" to capture the many ways people and organizations identify, listen to, interact with, and activate digital audiences. When a company states it wants to "ramp up engagement," it usually wants to increase discussion and activity around its brand, content or product. When a company hires an "<u>engagement manager</u>," it usually intends for that person to manage the connections to and conversations with its audiences, on digital platforms or otherwise.

More specifically, however, engagement is defined as any action taken on digital content. A <u>tweet</u>, for example, is a piece of digital content; engagements with tweets include likes, retweets, and replies. A page on a website is a piece of digital content; engagements on web pages include scrolls, clicks, taps, video views, cursor or mouse movements, and form submissions.

Music is digital content, too; engagements include downloads and listens. All of these engagements are tangible and quantifiable. When we speak of "engagement" in the general sense, we can include face-to-face community outreach, magazine ads, and garage-sale posters. When we talk about "engagement" in the digital sense, we're referring only to measurable content interactions.

Most organizations recognize that digital engagement is a critical marketing channel, though not all companies engage well. To work effectively—that is, to not only increase conversions, but to build a thriving customer pipeline—engagement has to occur at every stage of the funnel, and every stage requires strategy. Businesses should engage with users who are new to their brand differently than they engage with customers who have been brand-loyal for years. Companies selling baby products should engage with customers differently than a political organization engages. Here are four examples of companies with vastly different identities using digital engagement to achieve organizational success:

## Engagement Example 1: Brand Discovery

https://www.instagram.com/p/BWam9YmDzTI/?taken-by=minimalistbaker

Your audience can't engage with you until they know you exist, and brand discovery is one of the things Instagram does best. Here, the gluten-free food blogger Minimalist Baker, aka Dana Shultz, is showing off a vegan taco recipe. Shultz wants to sell cookbooks, of course, but she knows that to do that, she must first build awareness and authority within the food content market by forging and nurturing relationships with audiences who enjoy eating and looking at pretty pictures of food. Shultz has almost 1 million followers, but even a robust Instagram account isn't likely to directly drive too many users to her blog, or to Amazon to buy her book. It is likely to reach Shultz's target audiences: people who like to cook, particularly vegan and gluten-free folks. Users will discover the Minimalist Baker account if someone they follow mentions @minimalistbaker, but more likely, they'll discover the brand by clicking a hashtag in another post—say, #tacos. If someone I follow shares a photo of family taco night and uses #tacos, I may tap that hashtag to see more tacos… and then I'd see @minimalistbaker's droolworthy photo. As soon as I tap it, I'd find myself suddenly aware of the Minimalist Baker brand. From here, any action I take is an engagement. If I like, save, or comment on any Minimalist Baker post, that's an engagement. If I share a Minimalist Baker post with my sister, that's an engagement. If I tap another hashtag—say, #vegan—on any Minimalist Baker post, or if I click on the link in her profile, those are engagements, too, even though performing those actions take me away from Minimalist Baker. None of those engagement actions made Minimalist Baker any money. There were no conversions in this scenario. But what did happen is that I became aware of the Minimalist Baker brand, and perhaps I began to take some small actions with the brand's content, which officially makes me part of the Minimalist Baker audience, at the top of the Minimalist Baker funnel.

## Engagement Example 2: Content Consumption

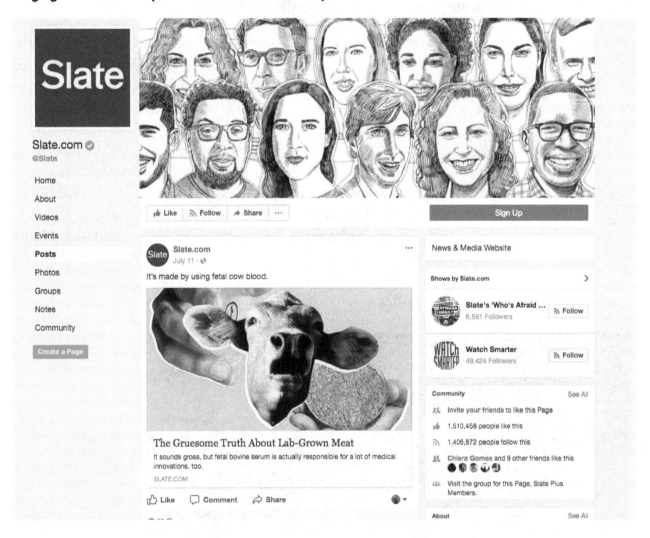

*This image is linked to, not embedded. It is not CC BY.*

Here, online magazine Slate wants something a bit more than the typical social media engagement. Slate produced a story about lab-grown meat that the company would like its audience to read. But they can't see the story in Facebook—they have to click. So Slate combined an eye-catchingly bizarre image with a text hat-trick of novel post, practical headline, and a story description that teases the story (but doesn't tell all!) to persuade users who view this post to click the cow for more. Now, Slate would absolutely love for readers to like, comment about, and share this article within Facebook—those engagements are great, because they help put this story in front of more people—but it's also very important to the organization to get users to take the specific "click" engagement action. Doing so brings the user away from Facebook and onto Slate.com, which brings that user further down Slate's funnel toward conversion. (Conversion, for Slate, may be subscriptions to SlatePlus, its membership-only content experience.)

## Engagement Example 3: Group Discussion

https://www.facebook.com/groups/yourmoneyandlife/

NPR hosts a personal finance podcast called Your Money and Your Life, but the star of the show might just be its corresponding Facebook group of the same name. Originally intended as a forum where listeners could ask questions and swap ideas (and NPR could promote the podcast), the group has taken on a life of its own and boasts more than 30,000 members. Within the group—which anyone can join—members join in rich discussions on money advice, credit scores and retirement planning. NPR still shares podcast episodes within the group, but some of the group's loudest conversations have nothing to do with NPR[2]... which is fine by NPR, because all of the engagement happens within an NPR-created and -facilitated environment. Robust online communities—just like offline groups—are excellent spaces to create or join as an organization. They're where you can listen, research, network—and build a captive audience for your content.

## Engagement Example 4: Video Views and More

This video is linked to, not embedded. It is not CC BY.

This video, a creative PSA on gun violence awareness with a shocking twist, has a clear objective: raise awareness of the warning signs of at-risk behavior. But you only get that message if you complete the entire video—and getting digital audiences to actually complete a video they begin is no small feat. You may notice that Sandy Hook Promise, the organization that created and posted this video, turned off comment functionality. So, truly, the only digital engagements a user can make with this video are to watch it, like or dislike it, or share it. Those are the only physical actions audiences can take. However, it's Sandy Hook Promise's hope that engagement around this video will go far beyond those three digital actions: After watching it, viewers can talk it about it at the dinner table, or initiate deeper discussions at school. And hopefully, because of this video, a viewer may be able to prevent a violent tragedy. Those are all engagements, too—and they may be more impactful than a like or a share.

Indeed, there are many types of engagement that are important, but not necessarily digital or measurable: A shoe company can count when a user likes a Facebook post, clicks an ad or actually buys a pair of sneakers, but the company cannot count when the shoes are worn. Wearing a brand is engaging with that brand!

In-person engagement is valuable, too: If you see a band play, you may choose to download their music, follow them on Twitter, or buy a ticket to their next show. You attending the concert wasn't a digital event, but you and the band were absolutely engaging with each other as they rocked and you listened. Reading a vendor's poster, seeing a choir sing, clipping a mailbox coupon, and reading a paper newsletter are all forms of engagement. However, some engagements are just easier to track—and thus, easier to grow strategically—than others.

Indeed, offline engagement is still alive and well. There's an entire discipline of marketing dedicated to physical experiences; "experiential marketing" seeks to connect a brand to audiences directly via physical experiences such as flash mobs, taste tests, competitions, performances, art installations, and other events designed to evoke emotion and interaction. You may have seen the 2012 viral video "A Dramatic Surprise on a Quiet Square[3]," which captured an offline experiential marketing event. The cable channel TNT was launching in Belgium, and to encourage audiences to feel drama—in line with TNT's tagline, "We know drama"—the channel placed a big, red button in the middle of a quiet town square and waited for a brave soul to push it. When the button's finally pushed, drama ensues! The bystanders didn't know it was a stunt at the time, and you can see their expressions of surprise; it was TNT's hope that participants in the marketing event would forever connect their feelings to the brand, and that the campaign would grow its Belgian audience.

Even good, old-fashioned word-of-mouth is more important than ever: While academics have tuned focus to digital word-of-mouth (think Yelp reviews, comments and sharing), offline word of mouth can still grow and engage audiences. If I recommend my plumber to you in conversation, that's engagement—and meaningful, high-quality engagement at that!

Engagement for engagement's sake is fine if engagement alone is your goal. But if you have another goal—that is, if you need to get an audience to do or buy something—you have to use engagement as a stepping stone, one that builds and ushers potential and existing customers through your marketing funnel. It can be difficult to do all of that in a bubble: How do you know if you're reaching your target customer? How do you know if all the time you spend on engagement is making your organization money? For those answers, we turn to analytics.

## Analytics

Digital analytics are the data organizations use to measure the audience's interactions with, quantify the impact of and inform the messages of our content and brand. Analytics is a collection of individual numbers called metrics that, when analyzed, tell the story of how far our brand or content reaches, how users engage with it, who those users are, where they are in the funnel, and when they take conversion actions. Nearly every digital activity can be recorded and counted, and analytics is the quantitative and qualitative analysis of that activity.

Analyzing your company's digital performance is a critical step in understanding your overall business performance; understanding when, where and why users convert and how they interact with your brand adds necessary context to more traditional business data like revenue and supply-chain analysis. Analytics also help understand how our products and messages resonate with our audience, and suggest how to pivot our content to build stronger audience connections. But companies also use analytics to understand how digital audiences engage with their competitors—called "competitive analysis"—which helps businesses understand why, say, one furniture brand outsells another. Marketers also use analytics to identify audience opportunity. Before we ever start trying to feed audiences into our funnel, we can use analytics to determine what audiences we should target for our funnel in the first place.

**Assignment:** Facebook Audience Insights

You can use Facebook Audience Insights—the same tool all companies use to target specific audiences in Facebook—to research audience opportunities.

STEP 1: To access Facebook Audience Insights, you'll need to be an editor or an administrator of a public Facebook page (a page is different from your regular profile). Don't have a page? Make one! Visit facebook.com/pages/create and follow the directions to create a page of your own.

STEP 2: Visit Facebook.com/ads/audience-insights to access the Insights tool. Select "Everyone on Facebook" from the initial options; this ensures you can research Facebook audiences from scratch. Right away, you see data that represents all Facebook users; at the top, Facebook explains that the data you see represents all 150 to 200 million monthly active Facebook users in the United States.

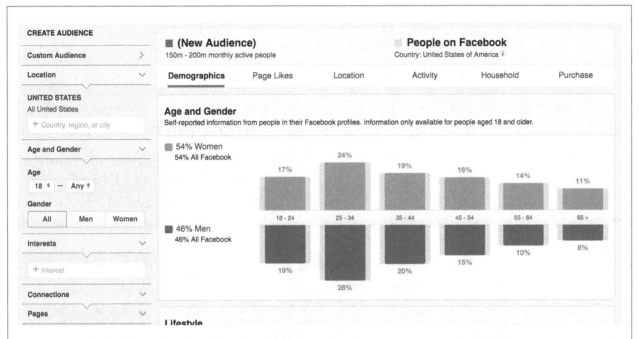

STEP 3: Make your potential audience more specific by narrowing it down. Instead of looking at everyone in the country, select a state. Type a state into the "Location" box in the left-hand menu; here, we've selected Arizona. Immediately, we see that the data changes a bit: Now, the Insights tool tells us that the data we're examining represents the 4 to 4.5 million monthly active Facebook users. You'll also notice that the demographic data has shifted; the blue bars represent data for Arizona users, but the gray bars behind the blue ones represent the same United States Facebook users you started with, so you can compare your new audience to the "typical" Facebook user.

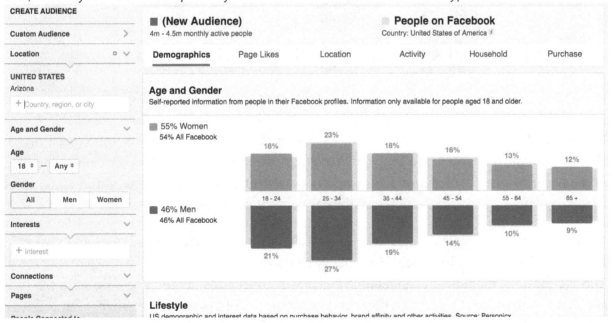

STEP 4: Now, narrow down your audience even further by selecting an age group, a gender or an interest from the options at left. Here, we've selected 18- to 30-year-olds with an interest in fitness and wellness;

*the Insights tool tells us that there are 600- to 700,000 Arizonans ages 18 to 30 who have indicated an interest in fitness.*

*STEP 5: Now that you've identified a "target" audience, explore it. Stay within the Demographics tab and scroll down to reveal information about the lifestyle, relationship status, job type, and education of your audience; think about what learnings you can take from this to apply to your overall marketing strategy. Then, go back to the top and click through the insights in the Household, Purchase, and Location tabs. Which of this data is helpful to you? Do you notice any major differences between "typical" Facebook users and your niche audience?*

*STEP 6: Finally, click on the Page Likes and Activity tabs. What other pages does this audience like? How can you replicate the success of those pages on your own? In the Activity tab, determine whether the audience you chose is more or less likely to engage on Facebook in the following ways. How can you turn these insights into action and audience growth? Our sample audience tends to comment, like, and click ads more often than typical Facebook users; this is a good opportunity for an Arizona fitness company!*

**Frequency of Activities**
The number of times the selected audience performed these actions on Facebook. Based on Facebook user activity and environmental data.

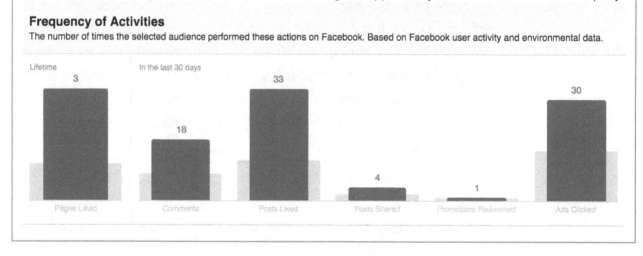

Most of the digital metrics available to analyze can be parsed into two buckets: reach metrics and engagement metrics. Generally, reach metrics explain how widely a piece of content (or a website, or an entire brand or message) was distributed and to whom, while engagement metrics explain how users interacted with that content once they saw it.

Social media metrics make for easy examples. To analyze the performance of a single tweet, we first have to understand its reach: How many times did Twitter serve it to users? How far did it "go"? That data, then, puts engagement metrics in context. What did users do with the tweet once it was shown to them? In twitter, and across most other social networks, the following core reach and engagement metrics are at the heart of social media analytics:

- **<u>Reach:</u>** Reach defines the number of accounts or users a piece of content was served to.
- **Impressions:** Impressions represent the number of times a social network has served

a piece of content to its users. One person can see a single Instagram, say, four times; that's four impressions, but a reach of only one.

- **Engagements:** Social media engagements are any action taken on a piece of social content. Likes, retweets, shares, comments, taps, video views, poll responses—all of these are engagements.
- **Engagement rate:** Divide the total number of engagements by the total number of impressions for an engagement rate, which describes how "engaging" a piece of content is. In other words, engagement rate describes how likely users are to interact with the given content.

Site and app data are quite different than social metrics, but they're close cousins. Just as we can divide social content into "reach" and "engagement" boxes, we can do the same with site and app metrics—the numbers are different, but they still help us organize our thinking and analyses around to who is receiving our content and what they're doing with it. To understand who our site content or app reaches, organizations examine metrics such as:

- **Pageviews:** A pageview is counted when a user visits a page. It's that simple! Be careful, though: A pageview is not a user. One person or one user can view a page more than once, and visit several different pages.
- **Unique pageviews:** Technically, Unique Pageviews (or "uniques") are the number of sessions during which a specified page was viewed at least once. Uniques are not synonymous with "people" or "users"; one person can view a page on a laptop and the same page the next day using a mobile device… that's two unique pageviews, but only one user.
- **Sessions:** A session is a single visit to your site or app; it's the group of interactions made by a single user within a given time frame. A single session can contain multiple pageviews, clicks, events, transactions, and more. Knowing how many sessions or visits our audience initiates is a critical piece of the puzzle:
- **Video views:** A video view is counted whenever a user clicks "play" on a digital video—or when a social network or video platform auto-plays a video.
- **Geography:** Are your users actually from the state, region, or country you hope to do business in? Geography reports help explain whether the people interacting with your content are in your target markets.
- **Device:** If you know what kind of device—desktop, mobile, or tablet—your audience uses to access you, you can better tailor your website's design and content to their needs.
- **Source:** Knowing your audience's acquisition source—or where your site or app traffic comes from—is as important as knowing who's showing up. Users can access your site by typing the URL into a browser or clicking a bookmark, or they can find your site via a search engine, a tweet, a Facebook post, an ad, an email, or a link on another website. Source breakdowns tell organizations which of these avenues are

driving users to particular pages, which helps organizations understand where to spend their marketing energy.

Understanding who is getting to our site or downloading our app with those reach-related metrics is a critical step in evaluating digital performance—not only do they provide interesting business insights alone, but they set the stage for many other metrics, including engagement metrics. We can't begin to understand, for example, how many users abandoned an ugly web page until we first know how many people arrived there. Sessions, pageviews, and unique pageviews—as well as segments of those, such as mobile sessions, or pageviews acquired by search engines—are building blocks for engagement metrics that explain how users behave with digital properties once they get there. Engagement or behavior metrics include:

- **Average time on page:** Time on page metrics help marketers understand how long users spend on each piece of content. It's often safe to assume that the more time users spend on a page, the more highly engaged they are with that page's content; therefore, time on page (and, similarly, session time metrics) are good indicators of how engaging content actually is.
- **Entrances:** Entrances are the number of times users entered a site or app through a particular page; in other words, entrances represent the number of sessions for which the specified page was the first page in a session. It's one thing for people to view a page at some point during the course of a session, but it's quite another for a user to actually arrive at the site on a particular page. Entrances help organizations understand what products (or blog posts, or photos) attract users to the site or app in the first place.
- **Exit rate:** Close to (but not exactly) the opposite of entrances, exit rates tell the story of pages in terms of how often they exit. To calculate exit rate, analytics platforms divide the number of exits from a page by that page's total pageviews. Essentially, exit rate is a measure of how likely users are to leave a site from the given page.
- **Conversions:** Think back to your digital marketing funnel. A conversion is the action users take that moves them from potential customer to actual customer. Sometimes the point of conversion is a completed sales transaction, but other times it's an app download, a form submission, a series of steps taken—say, viewing four articles. Marketers can configure their analytics program to report on when and where most conversions take place.
- **Completion:** Just because a user arrives on a web page or plays a video does not mean they'll consume every word or frame of content. Completion tells us how many users watched through to the very end of a video, or scrolled all the way down to the bottom of a page. When completions are divided by pageviews or video views, the metric becomes a "completion rate," which suggests how likely the audience is to complete the content.

Alone, any of these metrics can reveal snippets of content performance: How many times that

Instagram post was seen, how many users downloaded that app, how long they watched that video. But taken together, they tell the audience narrative. Individual metrics combine in the art and science of audience analytics to help organizations reach their goals efficiently—and identify who to reach next.

---

**Exercise**

## TRY IT: TWITTER ANALYTICS

Below is a tweet from Cronkite News, the news department of Arizona PBS; it's goal is to get users to click on the link and get to the full story. Use the tweet's corresponding analytics to answer the following questions:

- How many impressions did this tweet earn?
- How many total engagements did this tweet earn?
- Calculate the engagement rate (remember: that's total engagements divided by impressions).
- Is the engagement rate above or below the account average of 2%?
- Do the types of engagement this tweet received make this tweet a success? Why or why not?
- What would you change about this tweet to increase its impressions?
- What would you change about this tweet to increase the desired engagement types?

**Cronkite News** ✔
@cronkitenews

.@FootballASU's #SunDevil Stadium is getting a major upgrade, including a new big & bright video display. STORY: ow.ly/3Sto30cCzfF

5:15 PM - 21 Jun 2017

**20** Retweets  **42** Likes

Impressions                                        12,751

Total engagements                                   650

Media engagements                                    403

Link clicks                                          121

Detail expands                                        52

Likes                                                 42

Retweets                                              20

Profile clicks                                        10

Hashtag clicks                                         2

Tweet's Analytics

## TRY IT: STRATEGIZING WITH CONTENT & ENGAGEMENT

Imagine that you are the founder of MartianAde, a new lemonade company. It's not your average lemonade: Your lemonade is made with lemons grown on Mars. You create a gorgeous 20-second video that highlights your out-of-this-world (literally!) lemons and the red earth they grow in; then, you create a second video showcasing the lemons' space journey from Mars to your factory on Earth. You plan to share the videos in social media, as well as on your website above text that details your unique lemonade-making process.

Answer the following questions:

- Describe your target audience for the videos. What characteristics, interests, or behaviors do they share?
- How will you reach your target audience?
- How will you measure the videos' success in social media?
- How will you measure the success of the videos on your website?
- What steps can you take to encourage people who watch the videos to actually buy the lemonade?
- What can you do to build loyalty with customers who have already purchased MartianAde at least once?

## TRY IT: PERSONAL SOCIAL MEDIA AUDIT

Select your personal Twitter account or Facebook page (note: this only works with a Facebook page, not a Facebook profile). Download your data. IN TWITTER: Navigate to analytics.twitter.com. Select Tweets from the top menu. Find the button near the top right that reads "Last 28 Days." Click it and change the date range to the past 60 days. Click "Export Data" to download the data in spreadsheet format. IN FACEBOOK: Navigate to the Facebook page and select "Insights" from the top menu. On the Overview page, locate "Export Data" near the top right. Under "Data Type," select "Post Data." Under "Date Range," select the past 60 days. Click "Export Data" to download the data in spreadsheet format.
Open your data, and read, sort and analyze it to answer the following questions.

- What is your average number of posts per day?
- What is the post with the highest reach or impressions? Why?
- What is the post with the lowest reach or impressions? Why? How could you change the post to improve its reach/impressions?
- What is the post with the highest engagement rate? Why?

- What is the post with the lowest engagement rate? Why? How could you change the post to improve its engagement rate?

Select an engagement type (likes, shares, retweets, comments, replies, reactions, or link clicks). What is the post with the highest number of your selected engagement type? Why?

- What do the posts with the top 10 engagement rates have in common?
- What do the posts with the lowest reach/impressions have in common?
- Does there seem to be a pattern to the days on which your reach/impressions are higher than others? Discuss.

Using your answers above, and other knowledge of your account, answer the following questions:

- How many page likes or followers does your account have?
- What are your account's greatest strengths and weaknesses?
- What kind of content should you CREATE for this account?
- What kind of content should SHARE from this account? (As in, what content created by others does it make sense to curate/share with your audience?)
- What conversations should you join to grow and engage your audience?
- Going forward, what will you change about your posting habits to reach and engage more users with this account?

## Resources

- *NPR*'s Private Personal Finance Facebook Group[4]
- The Content Strategist, *Contently*[5]
- Whiteboard Friday, *Moz*[6]

*Jessica Pucci is a professor of practice at the Cronkite School, specializing in data analytics and audience engagement. She leads social media and analytics for Cronkite News, the news division of Arizona PBS, and also teaches a course in analytics and engagement. Reach her on Twitter at @jessica_pucci.*

## Leave feedback on this chapter.

## *Notes*

1. Elizabeth Mays, "Marketing Your Venture to Audiences," *Media Innovation and Entrepreneurship*, https://press.rebus.community/media-innovation-and-entrepreneurship/chapter/marketing-your-venture-to-audiences/#aidafunnel.

2. Ricardo Bilton, "NPR Built a Private Personal Finance Facebook Group That Now Has More Than 10,000 Members," *NiemanLab*, April 6, 2016, http://www.niemanlab.org/2016/04/npr-built-a-private-personal-finance-facebook-group-that-now-has-more-than-10000-members/.

3. TNT, "A Dramatic Surprise in a Quiet Square," *YouTube*, https://www.youtube.com/watch?v=316AzLYfAzw.

4. Bilton, Ricardo. "NPR Built a Private Personal Finance Facebook Group That Now Has More Than 10,000 Members." *Nieman Lab*. April 6, 2016. Accessed July 14, 2017. http://www.niemanlab.org/2016/04/npr-built-a-private-personal-finance-facebook-group-that-now-has-more-than-10000-members/.

5. "The Content Strategist," *Contently*, https://contently.com/strategist/.

6. "Whiteboard Friday," *Moz*, https://moz.com/blog/category/whiteboard-friday.

# LOOKING AHEAD

| Looking Ahead |
| --- |
| What does entrepreneurship look like around the world? The next chapter provides an overview of Entrepreneurship Abroad. |

# ENTREPRENEURSHIP ABROAD: CULTURAL AND INTERNATIONAL PERSPECTIVES AND CHALLENGES

by Betty Tsakarestou

# Summary

In this chapter, we explore international perspectives in entrepreneurship, how the startup "fever" captured the minds and souls of innovators across Europe and around the globe, and how leading cities are growing as startup and innovation ecosystems.

While this section is titled entrepreneurship abroad, the preliminary chapter focuses on entrepreneurship in Europe. (This chapter will be expanded to other continents for Version 2.)

We also look into how Silicon Valley has provided the prototype of scalable success and startup ecosystems which others in the world have tried either to differentiate from or emulate. This U.S. West Coast model built a world-leading innovation ecosystem attracting talent, funding, and resources.

Media innovation and entrepreneurship initiatives and startups are presented in the context of the broader global focus on entrepreneurs leading both change and solutions to global and local challenges that impact twenty-first-century interconnected societies.

Activities will help you to take the lead in implementing and learning more from your own experience and experimentation.

## Learning Objectives

- Gain a wider global perspective of entrepreneurship outside the U.S., with a focus in Europe.
- Learn about the key structural and cultural drivers that help or create barriers to building successful startup cities-based ecosystems around the world, with a focus on the European tech-startup scene.
- Learn the key players and stakeholders shaping and scaling up startup ecosystems across Europe.
- Explore what it takes to build an entrepreneurial mindset in regions with a weak enterprising culture.

- Learn current challenges and dilemmas that face different regions and cities in the world as they choose between inventing their own approaches to entrepreneurship or trying to emulate the Silicon Valley model.

# Inside this Chapter

- Entrepreneurship Abroad: Cultural and International Perspectives and Challenges
- A Short History of Silicon Valley, by Francine Hardaway

*Betty Tsakarestou, Ph.D., is assistant professor and head of the advertising and public relations lab at Panteion University, in Athens, Greece. She is co-initiator of Connecting Cities,[1] an exchange scholar of Study of U.S. Institutes (SUSI) on Journalism and Media at Ohio University (2015), branding officer and European co-liaison of the International Communication Division of The Association for Education in Journalism and Mass Communication (AEJMC) and a Startup Weekend on Entrepreneurial Journalism[2] organizer. Reach her on Twitter at @tsakarestou.*

# ENTREPRENEURSHIP ABROAD: CULTURAL AND INTERNATIONAL PERSPECTIVES AND CHALLENGES

*Betty Tsakarestou*

Journalists, legacy media, digital publishers and platforms, communicators, branded content creators, and social innovators have reinvented the profession by creating and testing new business models as niche and specialized journalism startups. In so doing, they have offered novel news experiences and publishing environments, served underserved communities, empowered contributors to build their own digital brands, offered more relevant content to their communities, and explored new opportunities for audience engagement. They have advanced new storytelling approaches with the help of big data; have integrated immersive virtual reality and Internet of Things (IoT) technology; and have designed journalistic new products and services related to key questions and challenges such as fact checking for non-specialists, filter bubbles, and the impact of personalization of the Internet.

While in many European countries legacy newsrooms are still laying off journalists, online publishers and some legacy media companies are revamping for growth and diversifying their strategies by investing in digital startups according to a Financial Times analysis.[1]

"Following the examples of Time Warner and Comcast, European companies have sought to structure their venture arms like independent funds – with partners judged on the financial value of the portfolio companies, rather than on looser strategic value to the parent company."

At the same time, across Europe, journalism startups are creating the first "pockets of innovation" by introducing alternative business models, getting public attention, and raising or crowd-sourcing funds.

Take a first glimpse of some notable cases:

In Germany, *Republik,*[2] an open-source cooperative digital magazine to be launched in January 2018, reclaims the role of journalism to reinforce Democracy. *Republik* co-founder Christof Moser, a journalist and professor, succeeded in raising $2 million.[3]

Innovative Journalism Startups from Netherlands[4] are focusing on quality journalism. *Blendle* employs an "iTunes" model for news.[5] *De Correspondent*[6] is getting ready for its U.S. presence while more media startups are taking tech press influencer Charmaine Li's attention: *Piano Media* in Austria, *PressPad* in Krakow, *Sellfy* in Riga/ Latvia, *Movellas* in Copenhagen and London, *Ghost*, *ShareWall*, *ReadWave*, and *Reedsy* in London, *Liberio* in Berlin. In Athens, Press Project [7] is one of the few independent investigative journalism and data reporting startups that fill the vacuum of failing legacy media.

When you look at the global heat maps of the emerging dynamic startup ecosystem, innovation starts to be geographically and culturally diverse and unevenly distributed. We can get an overview and a very informed perspective of the emerging and dynamic startup ecosystems all over the world through the lens of Startup Genome the Global Startup Ecosystem Report 2017.[8] In 2011 a devoted team of researchers, entrepreneurs, and data mavericks launched the Startup Genome project. Inspired and driven by the mission to help building the entrepreneurial ecosystem, they conduct and publish annually primary research with 10,000+ startups and 500 partnering companies to inform local startup leaders about success factors to measure the ecosystem's lifecycle, to provide in-depth insights by continent or startup city, and to produce a global startup ecosystem ranking.

Startup Genome examines nine factors that determine how cities become key players[9] and catalysts into enabling vibrant startup ecosystems:

1. funding,
2. market reach,
3. global connectedness,
4. technical talent,
5. startup experience,
6. resource attraction,
7. corporate involvement,
8. founder ambition and
9. strategy

As the CEO of Startup Genome states in their mission statement: Startup founders are driven by their pathos to create a positive change in our world, to participate in a world movement and a revolution in search of innovative solutions, and to experiment with the new business model canvases for making a great idea into an impactful service to people and to their communities. This entrepreneurial ethos is representing a cultural shift about the potential of startup entrepreneurship to bring positive change, to have a desirable impact by the communities, cities, and people in producing solutions.

Says J.F. Gauthier, Founder and CEO of Startup Genome:

"There is a revolution going on — the global startup revolution. We are changing the world together. All of us startup leaders, and all of us working in different parts of the ecosystem. We are challenging the status quo, putting new ideas to work, and holding fast to the belief — the knowledge — that anyone, anywhere should be able to participate in this revolution. The work of startup leaders in spreading this culture of meritocracy and equality is never finished and we are all helping each other, paying it forward, and expanding boundaries of startup culture."

Let's see the panorama of the top 20 global startup ecosystems to learn more about the cities and continents that are closer to your own interest and entrepreneurial journalism focus. The Startup Genome Top Global 20 Startup Emerging and Established Entrepreneurial Cities and Ecosystems List allows you to compare 2017-2015 rankings for each city.[10] Here's a snapshot of the 2017 rankings.

## Startup Genome Top Global 20 Startup Emerging and Established Entrepreneurial Cities and Ecosystems

|  | 2015 | 2017 |
|---|---|---|
| 1 | Silicon Valley | Silicon Valley |
| 2 | New York City | New York City |
| 3 | Los Angeles | London |
| 4 | Boston | Beijing |
| 5 | Tel Aviv | Boston |
| 6 | London | Tel Aviv |
| 7 | Chicago | Berlin |
| 8 | Seattle | Shanghai |
| 9 | Berlin | Los Angeles |
| 10 | Singapore | Seattle |
| 11 | Paris | Paris |
| 12 | Sao Paulo | Singapore |
| 13 | Moscow | Austin |
| 14 | Austin | Stockholm |
| 15 | Bangalore | Vancouver |
| 16 | Sydney | Toronto – greater Waterloo area |
| 17 | Toronto – greater Waterloo area | Sydney |
| 18 | Vancouver | Chicago |
| 19 | Amsterdam | Amsterdam |
| 20 | Montreal | Bangalore |

1. Silicon Valley (unchanged)
2. New York City (unchanged)

3. London (up from #6)

4. Beijing (new entry)

5. Boston (down from #4)

6. Tel Aviv (down from #5)

7. Berlin (up from #9)

8. Shanghai (new entry)

9. Los Angeles (down from #3)

10. Seattle (down from #8)

11. Paris (unchanged)

12. Singapore (down from #10)

13. Austin (up from #14)

14. Stockholm (new entry)

15. Vancouver (up from #18)

16. Toronto – greater Waterloo area (up from #17)

17. Sydney (down from #16)

18. Chicago (down from #7)

19. Amsterdam (unchanged)

20. Bangalore (down from #15)

While Silicon Valley keeps its leadership above any other ecosystem, it is no longer the number one pool of talent, losing its long-uncontested dominance over the Asia-Pacific region and Europe. Government initiatives are playing a significant role in both Singapore and Beijing by creating a friendly entrepreneurial business and cultural environment.[11]

According to Gauthier:[12]

"For the first time we can all see the comparative strengths of Beijing and Shanghai with the rest of world. Beijing's amazing performance at creating large scale-ups is confirmed with its second place in our performance factor, and third place overall, but the lack of global connections of its startups was also clear. Shanghai takes a surprising eighth place overall with its strong early-stage funding, how it attracts talent and resource from all over the world, and how globally connected its startups are."

African startup cities are on the rise. Even though they have not made it to any of the prominent ranks of the Global Startup Eccosystem report, they are competing for their share in tech, innovation, and sustainable startup solutions. Cape Town in South Africa is the largest startup ecosystem in the continent, which still needs to build up its global networking and connectedness, followed by Johannesburg and Lagos in Nigeria.

## Innovators and Startup Entrepreneurs in Europe: Are They Lagging Behind Silicon Valley?

If you are a regular reader or visitor to *TechCrunch*, a leading technology website founded in 2005 to cover news about startup companies, founders and investors, then you might as well be following a recurring topic, the comparisons of the U.S. and European startups and innovation ecosystems. Back in 2010, Alan Gleason, a guest contributor to the *TechCrunch* European startup section gives his theories on why Europe lags the U.S. in technology startups"[13]

Gleason writes as an insider, who has gained a considerable experience in consulting with U.S. startup entrepreneurs. He asserts that there is an uncontestable structural gap, a disparity, between the two continents when considering their capacity to enable and scale up globally-successful technology-led innovative startups and develop tech giants like Google, Facebook, YouTube, or Apple. He takes the Silicon Valley model (see sidebar) as the benchmark to assess the dynamism and the potential success of entrepreneurial ecosystems that follow a different path of development outside of United States. In 2010, the U.S. enjoyed a "semi-monopoly" position worldwide in generating startup companies.

Let's follow Gleason's analysis from 2010 about the structural and cultural triggering factors that created this capacity gap for innovation in entrepreneurship between the U.S. and Europe.

Gleason identifies six structural and cultural factors that are at play:

> 1. **Location**: Europe seems to lack the "hub network effect" of Silicon Valley's model as an ecosystem attracting innovating entrepreneurs from all over the world, venture funds, and top engineers. Europe has mainly developed "pockets of innovation" in metropolitan cities across the continent.
> 2. **Talent:** Silicon Valley's model as an ecosystem that attracts a diverse pool of talent of innovating entrepreneurs immigrating from all over the world is compared with European mobility of talented and highly skilled people that in the latter case are not translated into a critical mass of successful startups.
> 3. **Market Size**: Gaining traction as a startup and making profitable new product launches is considered a safer venture in the U.S. market rather than Europe on the basis of perceived cultural homogeneity (language, culture) and common currency versus a more culturally diverse Europe despite the fact the European overall population is almost double the United States' size.
> 4. **Support Systems:** Compared to the West Coast ecosystem in the U.S., Europe lags in creating access to capital ranging from early-stage funding, seed and angel funds to venture capital funding rounds, along with a supportive business environment offering multiple options for legal and communication advice and professional services along with a pro-entrepreneurship strong media presence. Most notably,

compared to the U.S., in Europe there are fewer investors and funding schemes to help tech startups go to market and scale up.

5. **Attitude to Risk and the "Fail Fast" Mindset:** Risk-taking or risk-aversion is one of the most culturally debated issues in the startup ecosystems and hubs all over the world. The United States fosters a more entrepreneurial mindset, open to more risk, to experimentation, and to "failing fast." This entrepreneurial mindset becomes a pivotal point in Europe as it attempts to develop global reach and impact.

6. **Media**: Media and blogs covering technology, entrepreneurship, startup news and innovation topics, founders and funders' thinking and methodologies have created a new positive and forward-thinking public imagery and culture that encourages new ventures and initiatives. Again, the most influential blogs mentioned such as Mike Arrington, serial entrepreneur and founder of *TechCrunch* or Jason Calacanis (who defines himself as a serial entrepreneur, angel investor, podcaster, and writer) are featuring the fervent U.S. entrepreneurial scene while Mike Butcher has been one of the more influential voices writing for the *TechCrunch* European section.

Another difference between the European mature ecosystems and Silicon Valley is that that European startups are mainly (55 to 75 percent) B2B oriented while in U.S. the vast majority (two out of three startups) are consumer-oriented businesses.

In conclusion, European tech startups and entrepreneurs must overcome some structural limitations in three key areas:

1. Take smart money only as an investment to scale and expand into your investors' global networking capacity and/or their ability to successfully address "go-to-market" challenges.
2. Focus hard on gaining market traction through the creation of awareness of key influencers.
3. Locate your business activity or networking in one of the emerging European hotspots.

## The European Commission Seeds Startup Growth

Even with the growth of entrepreneurial ecosystems across the European Union, many entrepreneurs at major tech events such as the Web Summit question whether Europe's startup culture truly exists. In "Does Europe lack a Startup Culture"?[14], the authors compare the dollars being transferred in the different markets, however, dollars may not provide a fair comparison.

"Debating Europe", [15] a bottom-up platform co-initiated by multiple partners[16] to bring together European citizens' voices directly to European policy makers, published in December

2016 an infographic (see Figure 1) based on data issued by Eurostat, OECD, Google, and Forbes. The graphic provides some insight into this recurring question.

According to this graphic: In 2014 venture capital investment in computer and consumer electronics was more than $24 billion for the United States and $959 million for Europe. This is the chasm that Europe anticipates as it rapidly builds its own startup culture. In 2015, five European countries attracted the highest venture capital investments in companies developing new products and technologies, as percentage of GDP: Denmark, Luxembourg, Finland, Ireland, and Portugal. Google for Entrepreneurs, a network of 40 tech hubs worldwide, provides financial support, mentorship, and education to European entrepreneurs and facilitates the access to a network of startup hubs across 125 countries all over the world. From "Debating Europe":

> "Young entrepreneurs are quick to identify the factors holding Europe back. Lack of finance tops the list, particularly the venture capital needed to move from startup to scale-up. Then comes red tape – too many European countries impose too many regulatory and administrative burdens; Europe's digital-single market has failed to overcome fragmentation. Taxes are too high and too complicated. Then there are underlying cultural problems – from a multiplicity of languages to a fear-of-failure mentality."

To address the funding concern, during Web Summit in 2016, the European Commission announced a "fund of funds"[17] designed to trigger at least €1.6bn in venture capital for startups." The European Fund for Strategic Investments for small and medium-sized enterprises[18] is one of the many European funding opportunities to mobilize finance in a collective and coordinated way seeking to reverse the low level of investment since the global economic crisis.

> "The programme, which was presented today at the Web Summit, has been sponsored by the European Union and set up in cooperation with EIF. Under the Pan-European VC FoF programme EIF is looking to invest, using resources of the Horizon 2020 InnovFin Equity facility, EFSI Equity Instrument, COSME Equity Facility for Growth and EIF's own resources, in private-sector-led, market-driven Pan-European VC Fund(s)-of-funds (the Fund(s)-of-Funds)."

## Startup Europe

The European Commission is taking the lead in this global and networked-innovation-driven world where entrepreneurship and innovators address and provide entrepreneurial solutions. These startups are often aligned with the United Nations' 17 interconnected Sustainable Development Goals[19] (SDGs) to address effectively the challenges they entail "to end poverty, protect the planet and ensure that all people enjoy peace and prosperity." These goals are at the

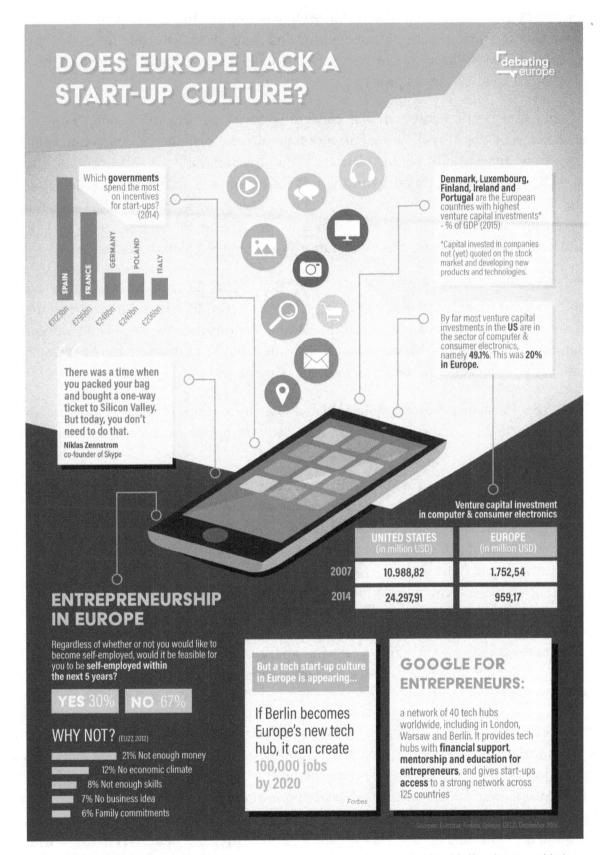

Figure 1. Infographic copyright Debating Europe. All Rights Reserved. Included with permission here. Download the original here: http://www.debatingeurope.eu/2016/12/15/europe-lack-start-culture/#.WWl-KoqQw0r

core of twenty-first-century societies for making positive and impactful change by 2030. The European Commission, by actively contributing and supporting SDGs and the 2030 agenda,[20] strategically positions Europe to pursue a leading role in the new reshuffle of dynamics among global financial and tech robust players.

The twenty-first century international consensus advanced also by United Nations (UN) SDGs seems to be that it is all about entrepreneurship and sustainable innovating solutions-makers around the world. A United Nations "Solutions Summit"[21] in 2015 brought together policy makers, innovators, investors in the private sector, and civil society leaders, together with technologists and scientists to partner and co-create impactful "solutions-in-progress." Entrepreneurs and cross-disciplinary innovators are taking the lead across the world to imagine and develop impactful positive solutions to the biggest global challenges.

> "Everyone has a role to play in advancing the Global Goals, and innovators and entrepreneurs are central to finding the solutions needed to achieve these goals," said Kathy Calvin, president and CEO of the United Nations Foundation. "The Solutions Summit is a catalytic gathering of some of the best and brightest who have developed innovative approaches to the world's most vexing issues."

In 2011, the European Commission initiated Startup Europe[22] as a "One Stop Shop," providing information, tools, legal advice, and networking for startups in Europe with the goal:

- To connect all European Startup Ecosystems based in different cities and key players and ecosystem builders such as investors,[23] accelerators,[24]female entrepreneurs,[25] corporate networks, universities,[26] and *#EUTech Writers*[27]
- To help startups to enter other markets such as Silicon Valley, Africa, The United Arab Emirates, and India[28]
- To celebrate entrepreneurial successes by launching awards and other events such as Tech Allstars, Europioneers,[29] and StartUp Europe Awards[30]

The EU response[31] has prioritized catalyzing a risk-taking and experimentation culture in Europe by launching the project "FACE Entrepreneurship" and EXCEL, a European Virtual Accelerator to address local limits on access to co-founders, resources, expertise, and markets.

One of the key factors in forming successful and sustainable innovation startup ecosystems that will incubate and support world-leading ventures is to establish strong synergies and collaboration between the universities and the innovation startup hubs. Stanford University and its role in building Silicon Valley[32] has been one of the most influential paradigms around the world, a benchmark that inspired both scholarly research[33] and extensive media coverage in the quest of replicating Silicon Valley model[34] in other regions and cities in the world.

In Europe, a longstanding barrier to creating continental cities as startup hubs has been the weak or missing collaboration between the academic community and the business-startup ecosystems. The European Commission, by launching the Startup Europe Universities Network,[35] is aiming to connect academic institutions and community to the business and scientific parks setting the framework for enabling collaborative forums, sharing of information and resources, and catalyzing synergies and collaborations.

And taking a it step further, Erasmus+ Program[36] provides more funding opportunities to help teachers prepare primary and secondary pupils to be entrepreneurial and creative. The Exchange programs for Young Entrepreneurs[37] nurtures the entrepreneurial mindset at an early age in an attempt to change the cultural paradigm to funding.

What might be the impact of combined institutional initiatives taken by the European Commission[38] to "Startup Europe" in creating a more innovation- and startup-friendly environment? Through tax incentives, startup visas, legal context, and advisory services infrastructures built by the European Commission, along with the bottom-up initiatives of the startup ecosystem leaders, entrepreneurs and policy makers hope this European mix will attract more talent, venture funding, and help create global startup brands. The European Startup Initiative[39] takes an active role in facilitating the debate around where Europe's hottest startup hub is evolving by designing the first data-driven report on startup locations and mobility in Europe as well as a startup heatmap on the perceived quality of the startup hubs in Europe.

## Cities as Startup Ecosystems

In the last decade, entrepreneurial ecosystems are proliferating across Europe. Cities such as London, Paris, Berlin, Amsterdam, Barcelona, Madrid, Dublin, Manchester, Milan, and Copenhagen were listed according to Social Media Week as the top "10 European Cities to Watch in 2017". [40]

These cities are emerging as pockets of growth[41] in different European regions, competing for the innovative local and international talent, for digital and mobile creative class, and for investors' money.

A 2016 Venture Beat article makes a good point when it stated that "So While Europe Might be a Single Market, It's Definitely Not a Single Tech Scene."[42] This is a challenge for Europe to invent and establish a sustainable innovation and entrepreneurship model.

Many of Europe's unicorn startups,[43] a term coined by Aileen Lee, founder of Cowboy Ventures[44] that describes companies that are valued at $1 billion or more, are based in London. Collectively they raised $2.9 billion in 2015, according to London & Partners. "That's 75 percent of all VC money in the UK"[45] and even Brexit has raised concerns that a startup exit will follow. Yet, London still has a competitive advantage as it offers a lighter regulation[46] framework. Analysts estimate that even post-"Brexit," London will continue to be one of the flourishing startup scenes. Paris is emerging as the second European metropolis investing in startups. The French Government has been the most active venture investor in small and medium digital businesses within their broader strategy for digital "France 2030."[47]

Paris is getting ready to impress the world by revamping and launching in 2018 Station F[48] (formerly known as la Halle Freyssinet), a 34,000-sq-meter startup campus and co-living space with the goal to gather the whole entrepreneurial ecosystem in the same space. This ambitious project seeks to create the "world's biggest campus."[49]

"We're talking about a startup campus because we're actually very similar to a university campus," Station F director Roxanne Varza[50] said in an article in *TechCrunch*. "We're expecting about one thousand startups in this space."

The city of Paris and the French Government, not Berlin, are set to become the beneficiary of any post-Brexit startup fallout, according to some analysts. The government is aiming to make France a "Digital Republic"[51] by supporting digital startups and providing the "French Tech Ticket"[52] to attract international startups.

Germany's capital Berlin has for many years been considered a European mecca for startups.[53] The city has successfully appealed to international professional and artistic creative class talent, converting this success into a booming startup hub. The city is a great example on how to be "inviting" to international talent to relocate, by offering a reasonable cost of living combined with an open culture[54] to learning, to experimentation, to change,[55] to sharing knowledge and to collaboration that can attract and retain diverse entrepreneurial and creative talent. Compare this aspect of Berlin city culture to the rising costs of living in Silicon Valley, where exorbitant housing costs make it inaccessible to new talent, whether international or domestic. Berlin is also investing into lively community meetups that can "help foster individual success." Government and political support[56] created with a "grassroots inclusive feel" supported by "The German Startup Association–The Voice of Startups in Germany" [57] make the case for Berlin startup ecosystem.

Stockholm in Sweden[58] is a new entrant in the startup cities world, earning a reputation as a "unicorn factory" and in a league of its own with unicorns such as Skype, Minecraft, Klarna, Spotify, and King. And who doesn't know MySQL, Kazaa, uTorrent, and Piratebay?

According to the article, *"The country is leading the 2016 ranking in a number of industries, including gaming, music-tech, and sport-tech, giving much bigger economies such as Germany, UK, Spain, Italy, and France a run for their money."*[59]

Looking at the South of Europe, Spain is becoming a considerable leading startup player, with two cities in the forefront. Barcelona and Madrid are both attracting international investment and global digital players like Google and Amazon who are establishing their presence in the innovation-driven cities.

Besides the capital cities, we also see vibrant and scalable and high-performing ecosystems growing fast in Lausanne (Switzerland), in Ghent (Belgium), in Krakow (Poland), and in Porto (Portugal).

Will these distinct cities-based tech and innovation hubs operate independently or will they become a collaborative network of connected hubs? This is a real bet and challenge for Europe. We will have to see in coming years how these European "pockets of growth" across multiple cities and regions will establish an entrepreneurship model that will fare and compete successfully with the Silicon Valleys or emerging Asian ecosystem(s) as analyzed in Startup Genome Global Startup Ecosystem Report 2017[60] and the Asia Startup Ecosystem[61] accelerator.

If you wish to explore more in depth the commonalities and what differentiates the unicorns from around the world, take 15 minutes to read a very well-documented post on *Startup Grind* by Alex Stern, published on February 27, 2017 on "Revisiting the Unicorn Club."[62] In it, he covers all continents, all countries, and sectors.

## The Digital News Initiative Innovation Fund (DNI Fund)

In an attempt to further explore the emerging media innovation hubs around Europe and the corporate actors that take action to enable such an approach, it is worthy to look into The Digital News Initiative Innovation Fund (DNI Fund).[63] The fund is a partnership between Google news publishers in Europe to support high-quality journalism through technology and innovation with the goal to enable and nurture sustainable news ecosystems, collaboration and dialogue between the tech and news industries. Among the founding members are prominent legacy media companies such as *The Guardian, The Financial Times, Die Zeit, El País, Les Echos, La Stampa,* and organizations such as Global Editors Network, European Journalism Centre, and NRC Group.[64] DNI Fund was launched in 2015 andhas invested more than €70m to more than 350 projects in 29 European countries.[65] DNI seems to have a quite balanced distribution of its fund among the participating countries. As an indication, here are the number of funded projects by country: Austria (9), Belgium (10), Czech Republic (7), Denmark (6), Finland (9), France (9), Germany (9), Greece (7), Sweden (9), Switzerland (9), and the United Kingdom (9).

The DNI Fund Projects offer innovative journalism and media entrepreneurial solutions to a wide spectrum of media-related challenges.

- In Austria, De-Escalation Bot[66] is figuring out how to de-escalate negative emotions online.
- In Belgium, Wave[67] offers interest-based listening experiences through connected cars, virtual assistants, and other smart technology devices. Likewise, in Greece, the Connected Cars, Connected Audience, News Ecosystem[68] Project is a prototype developed at Aristotle University. It's investigating the ways connected and self-driving cars will impact news organizations. In Switzerland, NZZ Companion App[69] will provide personalized, geotargeted, niche news based on a user's preferences.

- In the Czech Republic, Mural[70] makes visual storytelling easier for online journalists.
- In Denmark, PoliWatchBot[71] helps citizens better understanding their political process through public data.
- In Germany, Tagesspiegel Causa[72] is a website for debates.
- In the United Kingdom, Project Arete[73] is developing a highly transparent "digital advertising trading platform."
- In Finland, Woodpecker Findings[74] employs gamification to serve millennials.

And there are others. You can tour more DNI FUND projects at https://digitalnewsinitiative.com/dni-projects/ (filter by country and then DNI Fund Projects).[75]

## Media Entrepreneurship Education Around the World

One key lesson for building successful entrepreneurial ecosystems both from Silicon Valley as well as from the European Commission strategy is to actively involve the academic, scientific, and research communities as co-creators and enablers.

This is the path that many leading academic institutions in the U.S. have followed very actively over the last ten years by introducing entrepreneurial journalism and media innovation programs[76] into their journalism, media, and communication programs to help students as well as to train professionals in entrepreneurial thinking, skills, tools, and methodologies…and to innovate.

Initiatives to introduce media entrepreneurship compared to those in U.S. are modest.[77] The journalistic traditions in Europe that separate journalism production from the business and market side of media companies are still strong in many countries. European academics are still skeptical of the new "hybrid" and porous concept of bringing both editorial and financial sides together into collaborating and re-defining the purpose and the impact of journalism.

According to one article,[78]

> "In attempting to create an overview corralling the various outlooks and initiatives related to entrepreneurial journalism in Europe, one thing remains clear: There is no common understanding of the phenomenon and its ramifications. Some view the transformation as a new window of opportunity for ambitious journalism, while others merely consider it a new name for the old game of freelancing."

In 2012, the entrepreneurial journalism U.S. educational model found its first early advocates in Britain and Baltic countries' universities. Entrepreneurial journalism courses are offered as part of journalism academic programs or professional training initiatives in France, Germany, Switzerland, and the Ukraine.

As an indication of the growing international interest and demand for media entrepreneurship education, a post on Quora, a question-and-answer, crowd-sourcing knowledge and information platform, asks "Which colleges and universities offer entrepreneurial journalism programs?"[79]

In response to this request, Pierre France, Quora community member, posts a document with a list of entrepreneurial journalism courses offered in their U.S. Universities, with a few in Europe, in Canada, and in Mexico (list updated 21 July 2014).[80]

## Greece: An Emerging Ecosystem

*"Create more value than you capture"- Tim O'Reilly*

Athens, Greece, even though is not featured in any of the top startup cities rankings, has gained publicity for succeeding in building a vibrant startup culture and ecosystem in a crisis-ridden economy[81] that has been retracting since 2010, despite a long period of political and financial uncertainty and the unemployment rate climbing around 25%.

The last ten years, Athens has enjoyed the bottom-up birth, growth, and impact of enabling disruptive change and innovation out of the vision and the passion of a very small group of techies and bloggers, who are well connected locally and internationally with pioneering tech communities.

### Open Coffee Club Greece- Greek Startups Are Here[82]

In 2007, a new generation of Greek tech startup entrepreneurs and digital innovators self-organized as a movement around the Open Coffee Club Greece to take action and support. Their goals were to:

- Create a network of people with common interests to support relationship building and collaboration.
- Cultivate a culture of innovation and entrepreneurship.
- Spread new technologies with an emphasis on the web.

Adopting the model of the global Open Coffee Club Network they kept organizing with great success.[83] Monthly Open Coffee meetups in Athens bring together "nerds and marketers, bloggers and journalists, venture capitalists and developers, entrepreneurs and [public relations practitioners], who shape and help shape the Greek startup scene" and invite participants to "create [their] own network and become part of this new informal and interactive community."[84]

These pioneers followed closely the three waves of the Internet revolution[85] and the emerging startup movement and were familiar with the global debates and developments, particularly in Silicon

Valley. They became the first ambassadors for disruptive startup innovation during the second wave of the app economy and mobile revolution (2010-2015) building their own startups. They purposefully collaborated, in a non-collaboration-friendly culture, to building a very active Athens startup ecosystem. They worked to connect the hubs of innovation and they launched the first funding schemes (Open Fund,[86] Marathon VC[87]) and tools to enable the first promising local founders with the potential to scale their businesses internationally. They invested in building trust and social proof[88] (a psychological principle marketers use to build trust around brands and products) as the most important currency for impact and success.

Within a turbulent political and social landscape and an anti-entrepreneurial mindset prevailing for decades in both the political class and the society at large, Athens startup founders created a strong case of disruptive and impactful innovation where they were able to reverse the current attitudes and trigger a "startup fever" among youth, business, and institutions, followed by the reluctant political class.

Startup incubators, co-working spaces and innovation labs, Startup Weekend events, and hackathons were initiated by startup founders, social entrepreneurs, foundations, philanthropic and cultural institutions, NGOs, museums, embassies (the U.S. Embassy and the Embassy of Netherland being among the most active ones), business associations, international initiatives, digital leading companies such as Google or Microsoft, and companies that invested in empowering young startup entrepreneurship as part of their sustainability policies to spark innovation in their own sectors and supply chains.

The majority of Greek startups are aiming to serve international markets and customers. The local market is very small to sustain a viable startup venture that scales up internationally and has a successful exit.

In 2013 *TechCrunch Europe* and its editor, Mike Butcher, held their second meetup in Athens, showcasing how the Greek startup community could break the local financial and cultural boundaries and enable some international players.[89]

"In many ways Greece faces the quintessential problems of many European countries: plenty of talent, but a dearth of sources of funding for startups; limited markets at home and the difficulty of reaching out to large international markets like the U.S. Time and again panelists pointed out some of the obstacles that need to be overcome, such as a mismatch in university computer science courses with modern tech startups, and a moribund academic world. That said, it also acted as a showcase for success stories emerging from Greece that hope to show that there is plenty of talent just waiting to be unleashed."

In the World Bank high-ease-of-doing-business ranking for 2017 indicating if the "regulatory environment is more conducive to the starting and operation of a local firm," Greece is ranked in the 56th position for starting a new business and fell to 61st for the ease of doing business.[90]

In this unfriendly regulatory environment, international media positive coverage of the successful Greek startups[91] with the potential to turn Greece into a startup hub has been juxtaposed against the counternarrative of all the financial and political coverage about the prospects of the never-ending crisis-torn country.

> "It's been easy to overlook Greece's tech scene since the country's recent economic woes eclipsed most of the other news," wrote Itai Elizur in *The Next Web*.

> "The debt crisis sent most businesses reeling, and, despite declared over in 2015, its negative effects still linger today. The rest of Europe still keeps a close eye on the government's management of the economy and unemployment still is at 23.6 percent in Q4[92] of 2016.

> But despite this grim outlook, I was pleasantly greeted by an energetic tech scene composed of ventures that aim to bring some luster back into Greek entrepreneurship. Greece has at least a couple of major tech success stories that they can be proud of."[93]

"Could the Greek tech sector save the Greek economy?" asks Cate Lawrence, a contributing writer at *Readwrite*.[94] How did we reach this high point of expectations of the Greek startup innovators to make such change ,and impact in a country plagued by one of the worst financial and social crises in her recent history?

With an educated and innovative workforce, and great traction with angel investors through structures like EVEA Business Angels Network,[95] Angels Group by StartTech Ventures Incubation Fund,[96] and more recently by Marathon VC,[97] it's clear that Greece's startup sector is healthy. With its reputation growing, we soon might see entrepreneurs emigrating *to* Greece to join the burgeoning tech scene. As a first evidence-based estimation of the size and investments in the Greek startup technology market for the period between 2010-2016, Marathon VC conducted a short study[98] researching available data from public and private sources to track the dynamic and potential of the market.

The study shows that "the [Greek tech startup] market has grown to more than 40 investments taking place every year starting from 2013, with 137 companies receiving 214 rounds in total." As a general pattern they observe that "local funds and angels participate early, followed by international investors taking the lead in later stage rounds. This also suggests that, as more companies mature, more investments by international players are to be expected."

## Higher Education: Taking the Lead to Teach and Mentor Startup Founders on Media Entrepreneurship

In 2015, I introduced a graduate course on Entrepreneurial Journalism[99] in a newly launched program on Journalism and New Media at my home institution Panteion University. The curriculum change developed as a result of my participation on the Study of U.S. Institutes on Journalism and Media at Ohio University the same year, which focused my personal research project on developing a curriculum in the field after studying, benchmarking, and creatively adapting the best U.S. academic and training practices in this innovative field in my local academic and professional journalism context.

In 2016, with the support of U.S. Embassy Athens and in collaboration with the Tow-Knight Center for Entrepreneurial Journalism, we organized the first Athens "Startup Weekend on Entrepreneurial Journalism"[100] as a community outreach activity. We invited mid-career journalists in legacy media and online publishers, communications professionals who are experimenting with introducing intrapreneurial-branded journalism, and native advertising projects as well as university students.

Both initiatives have so far offered valuable insights:

- Value creation and the quest to make a positive change by engaging students, the startup ecosystem, legacy media, and online media into collaborating to imagine and design innovative journalism startups, proved a stronger transformative experience to overcome long-standing suspicious attitudes to entrepreneurship and to empower people to start their own journalism independent or intrapreneurial projects.
- The co-creation educational and learning model of inviting key stakeholders from the local and international ecosystems to contribute as mentors at the core of the program is creating an "accelerator effect" and a fertile environment where all partners and participants are sharing and testing new ideas.
- Local market conditions and academic cultures, despite harsh critics, have been proved to be more fluid and adaptive in embracing a bold entrepreneurial mindset and course of action as the way out of current financial crisis as well as the path for bold https://www.youtube.com/watch?v=65NgOzCk1aA exponential growth and innovation.[101]

## Exercises

### Try This!

- Organize an international meetup for young journalism entrepreneurs and make an impact in your community.
- Consult an easy-to-read Mashable article to guide you step-by-step on how to organize a Successful Meetup".[102]
- Create a meetup[103] now and get into action!

### *Discussion Questions:*

1. Is Silicon Valley or should it be a replicable model for developing successful innovation and startup ecosystems around the world?

2. Discuss how a model of "pockets of innovation" like the one we explore in Europe can provide an alternative "connecting the hubs" approach for scalable innovation.

3. Why might mobility and diversity of talent in the U.S. and Europe have had different impact on developing and scaling up comparable numbers of successful startups?

4. Building on the previous question: What other factors might be critical to help the talent and innovation pools around the world to make their mark? Consider booming innovation and startup ecosystems also in Africa, Asia, and Latin America.

5. Discuss the assumption that U.S. market and society is more homogeneous in terms of culture and subsequently, is more attractive and promising for new ventures and investments.

6. Imagine what does not yet exist by working as a team on "What If" questions about the possible futures for media innovation hubs across different cities and regions of the world.

## Exercises

### Team Activity

Choose a city/region of the world where you want to launch a scalable journalism startup. Organize a discussion and reach an informed decision with your team, all simulating the roles of journalism startup co-founders.

- In this project, you will scale up internationally a journalism startup that taps into the opportunities of the third wave of the Internet revolution (Internet of Everything) with your base in a major city in Europe, Asia, Africa, or Latin America.

- Decide on the city and continent where you will launch your journalism startup, based on what will best enable you to scale up internationally.
- Discuss and evaluate global startup ecosystems and markets.
- Meet and consult with startup ecosystem experts in journalism innovation to get market and investment insights.
- Create alternative options and scenarios based on your assessment of opportunities and risks for each ecosystem.
- Reach an informed decision.

## Suggested Readings

- Briggs, Mark. "What Makes a Successful News Startup?" *The Quill* 99, no. 6 (2011): 27-30.
- "Britain Needs Scale-up Businesses as Well as Start Ups." *Business Review Europe*, 2015, Business Review Europe, Nov 26, 2015.
- Chimbel, Aaron. "Introduce Entrepreneurship Concepts Early in Journalism Curriculum." *Newspaper Research Journal* 37, no. 4 (2016): 339-43.
- CIOL Writers. "Berlin May Replace London as the Startup Capital of EU after Brexit," *CIOL*, June 25, 2016.
- "Commission Gives Boost to Startups in Europe." *European Union News*, November 23, 2016.
- Dvorkin, Lewis. "Inviting the Rise of the Entrepreneurial Journalist: True/Slant Is Modeling the Newsroom of the Future by Empowering Contributors to Build Their Own Digital Brands — and by Changing the Role of the Editor." (Building Community: Journalists' New Journey)(Viewpoint Essay)." *Nieman Reports* 63, no. 3 (2009): 22.
- Estrin, Saul, Mickiewicz, Tomasz, and Stephan, Ute. "Entrepreneurship, Social Capital, and Institutions: Social and Commercial Entrepreneurship across Nations.(Statistical Data)(Abstract)." *Entrepreneurship: Theory and Practice* 37, no. 3 (2013): 479.
- Fullerton, Romayne Smith. "It's Time to Find a New Business Model ... Because without Journalism, Our Democratic System Will Fail." *Media (Canadian Association of Journalists)* 17, no. 6 (2016): 8-11.
- Gerosa, Andrea, and Tirapani, Alessandro NiccolA2. "The Culture of Entrepreneurship: Creating Your Own Job.(Report)." *European View* 12, no. 2 (2013): 205-214

- "Germany: EU Monitor: Startups and Their Financing in Europe." *Mena Report*, September 30, 2016.
- Grant, Adam. Originals. How Nonconformists Move the World. Penguin Books. Reprint Edition. 2017.
- Hunter, Anna, and Nel, Francois P. "Equipping the Entrepreneurial Journalist: An Exercise in Creative Enterprise." *Journalism and Mass Communication Educator* 66, no. 1 (2011): 10-24.
- "Investment Plan for Europe: EIF and KfW Bankengruppe Sign Agreement in Germany to Provide EU1 Billion to startups." *European Union News*, September 18, 2015
- Johnson, Steven. Where Good Ideas Come From.The Natural History of Innovation. Riverhead Books, 2011.
- Kelly, Kevin. The Inevitable. Understanding the 12 Technological Forces that will Shape our Future. Penguin Books. Reprint Edition, 2017.
- Maisonnave, Fabiano. "Covering the Waterfront: Despite a Fraught Political and Economic Environment, Entrepreneurial Brazilian Journalists Are Striving to Revitalize Coverage." *Nieman Reports* 70, no. 1 (2016): 14.
- McAfee, Andrew, and Erik, Brynjolfsson. Machine, Platform, Crowd: Harnessing our Digital Future. W.W. Norton & Company, 2017.
- Sarasvathy, Saras D., and Venkataraman, Sankaran. "Entrepreneurship as Method: Open Questions for an Entrepreneurial Future." *Entrepreneurship: Theory and Practice* 35, no. 1 (2011): 113.
- "Tech Trailblazers Tech Startup Index Highlights Social Media and Promotional Divide between Europe and US Startup Culture." *M2 Communications*, July 09, 2014.
- Vega, Tanzina. "New Journalism Degree To Emphasize startups." *New York Times (1923-Current File)* (New York, N.Y.); September 20, 2010.

## Additional Resources

- *Both Sides of the Table*[104] blog on Entrepreneurship Venture Capital and by Mark Suster
- *BuzzMachine* by Jeff Jarvis[105] blog on journalism innovation
- *Fast Company*[106] section on technology, apps, startups
- *Calacanis.com*[107] blog
- *PressThink*,[108] a project of the Arthur L. Carter Journalism Institute at New York University written by Jay Rosen
- Revisiting the Unicorn Club. Get to know the newest crowd of billion dollar startups:[109] All media-related unicorn startups are under the category "Consumer Internet."
- http://startupeuropeclub.eu/about-us/>Startup Europe[110] and Startup Europe Map Ecosystem[111]

- Startup Genome. The Global Startup Ecosystem Report 2017[112]
- *TechCrunch*[113]
- Media Startups | @mediastartups[114] Twitter account on news about innovation and startups in the media and entertainment industry

**Betty Tsakarestou**, *Ph.D., is assistant professor and head of the advertising and public relations lab at Panteion University, in Athens, Greece. She is co-initiator of Connecting Cities,[115] an exchange scholar of Study of U.S. Institutes (SUSI) on Journalism and Media at Ohio University (2015), branding officer and European co-liaison of the International Communication Division of The Association for Education in Journalism and Mass Communication (AEJMC) and a Startup Weekend on Entrepreneurial Journalism[116] organizer. Reach her on Twitter at @tsakarestou.*

## Leave feedback on this chapter.

## Notes

1. "European Media Bet on Tech Start-ups," *Financial Times*, https://www.ft.com/content/4e8abfa0-2958-11e4-8b81-00144feabdc0?mhq5j=e2.

2. *Republik*, https://www.republik.ch/en.

3. Alison Langley, "Startup That Promises 'No-Bullshit Journalism' Nets Serious Cash," *Columbia Journalism Review*, May 3, 2017, https://www.cjr.org/innovations/news-startup-crowdfunding-switzerland.php.

4. "Three Innovative Journalism Startups From the Netherlands," *Dutch Review*, https://dutchreview.com/dutchness/the-dutch-perspective/three-innovative-journalism-initiatives-netherlands/.

5. *Blendle*, https://launch.blendle.com/.

6. *de Correspondent*, https://thecorrespondent.com/.

7. Roy Greenslade, "Greek Media in Crisis - But Online Start-ups Fill the Vacuum," *The Guardian*, February 19, 2013, https://www.theguardian.com/media/greenslade/2013/feb/19/downturn-greece.

8. "The 2017 Global Startup Ecosystem Report," *Startup Genome*, https://startupgenome.com/report2017/.

9. Mar Masson Maack, "Silicon Valley Is No Longer #1 for Talent Says Huge Global Startup Report," *TheNextWeb*, April 2017, https://thenextweb.com/insider/2017/05/01/global-startup-ecosystem-report-2017/#.tnw_JGGttFU2.

10. "The Startup Genome Top Global 20 Startup Emerging and Established Entrepreneurial Cities and Ecosystems List," *Startup Genome*,  https://startupgenome.com/report2017/.

11. Michael Tegos, "In 2017's Top 20 Ecosystems, Beijing Leads in Startup Experience, Singapore in Talent." *Tech in Asia*, March 14, 2017, https://www.techinasia.com/startup-genome-startup-ecosystem-ranking-report-2017.

12. Mar Masson Maack, "Silicon Valley Is no Longer #1 for Talent Says Huge Global Startup Report," *TheNextWeb*, April 2017, https://thenextweb.com/insider/2017/05/01/global-startup-ecosystem-report-2017/#.tnw_JGGttFU2.

13. Alan Gleason, "Guest Post: Why Europe Lags the U.S. in Technology Startups," *TechCrunch*, Sept. 17, 2010, https://techcrunch.com/2010/09/17/guest-post-why-europe-lags-the-u-s-in-technology-startups/.

14. "Does Europe Lack a Start-up Culture?" *Debating Europe*, December 15, 2016, http://www.debatingeurope.eu/2016/12/15/europe-lack-start-culture/#.WXoNSNPyuqD.

15. *Debating Europe*, http://www.debatingeurope.eu/about/.

16. "Partners," *Debating Europe*, http://www.debatingeurope.eu/partners/.

17. Thomas Ohr, "European Investment Fund & the European Commission Launch New 'Fund of Funds' initiative to boost VC investments in Europe," *EU Startups*, November 8, 2016, http://www.eu-startups.com/2016/11/european-investment-fund-the-european-commission-launch-new-fund-of-funds-initiative-to-boost-vc-investments-in-europe/.

18. "EU Funds and Support," *Startup Europe*, http://startupeuropeclub.eu/eu-funds-and-support/.

19. "Sustainable Development Goals," *UN Development Programme*, http://www.undp.org/content/undp/en/home/sustainable-development-goals.html.

20. "The 2030 Agenda for Sustainable Development," *European Commission*, https://ec.europa.eu/europeaid/policies/european-development-policy/2030-agenda-sustainable-development_en.

21. "Solutions Summit Live from the UN at 6 p.m. ET Features Global Goals Innovators from Many Continents," *United Nations Foundation*, September 27, 2015, http://www.unfoundation.org/news-and-media/press-releases/2015/Solutions-Summit-Live-from-the-UN.html.

22. "About Us," *Startup Europe*, http://startupeuropeclub.eu/about-us/.

23. *Startup Europe Partnership Investors Forum*, http://startupeuropepartnership.eu/investor-community/sep-investors-forum/.

24. *Startup Europe's Accelerator Assembly*, http://www.acceleratorassembly.eu/.

25. *Women Web Entrepreneur Hubs*, http://wehubs.eu/.

26. *Startup Europe University Network*, http://welcomepro.webfactional.com/startup-europe-university-network/.

27. #EU Tech Writers, http://startupeuropeclub.eu/eu-tech-writers/.

28. *Startup Europe India Network*, https://startupeuropeindia.net/.

29. *Europioneers*, http://europioneers.info/.

30. *Startup Europe Awards 2017*, http://startupeuropeawards.com/.

31. "Startup Europe Projects Impact and Results," *Startup Europe Club*, http://startupeuropeclub.eu/startup_europe_impact/.

32. Ritika Trikha, "The Interdependency Of Stanford And Silicon Valley," *TechCrunch*, September 4, 2015, https://techcrunch.com/2015/09/04/what-will-stanford-be-without-silicon-valley/.

33. David Huffman and John M. Quigley, "The Role of the University in Attracting High Tech Entrepreneurship: A Silicon Valley Tale," *The Annals of Regional Science*, 36 (2002): 403-419. https://urbanpolicy.berkeley.edu/pdf/HQ02PB.pdf.

34. Barry Jaruzelski, "Why Silicon Valley's Success Is So Hard to Replicate," *Scientific American*, March 14, 2014, https://www.scientificamerican.com/article/why-silicon-valleys-success-is-so-hard-to-replicate/.

35. *Startup University Europe Network*, http://welcomepro.webfactional.com/startup-europe-university-network/.

36. "Helping Teachers Support Pupils to be Entrepreneurial," *Erasmus+*, May 31,

2017, http://ec.europa.eu/programmes/erasmus-plus/updates/20170531-helping-teachers-support-pupils-entrepreneurial_en.

37. "The European Exchange Programme for Entrepreneurs," *Erasmus for Young Entrepreneurs,* http://www.erasmus-entrepreneurs.eu/.

38. "Startup Europe," *European Commission,* https://ec.europa.eu/digital-single-market/en/startup-europe.

39. *European Startup Initiative,* http://www.startupheatmap.eu/.

40. Katie Perry, "10 European Startup Cities to Watch in 2017," *Social Media Week,* May 5, 2017, https://socialmediaweek.org/blog/2017/05/european-startup-cities-to-watch/.

41. Katie Perry, "10 European Startup Cities to Watch in 2017," *Social Media Week,* May 5, 2017, https://socialmediaweek.org/blog/2017/05/european-startup-cities-to-watch/.

42. Omar Mohout, "10 Things You Didn't Know About Europe's Tech Scene," *VentureBeat,* September 4, 2016, https://venturebeat.com/2016/09/04/10-things-you-didnt-know-about-europes-tech-scene/.

43. Aileen Lee, 'Welcome To The Unicorn Club: Learning From Billion-Dollar Startups," *TechCrunch,* November 2, 2013, https://techcrunch.com/2013/11/02/welcome-to-the-unicorn-club/

44. *Cowboy Ventures,* http://cowboy.vc/.

45. Sam Shead, "London Tech Startups Are Taking Almost All the VC Money in the UK," *Business Insider,* October 8, 2015, http://www.businessinsider.com/london-startups-bag-75-percent-of-uk-investment-2015-10?r=UK&IR=T.

46. Matthew Lynn, "Post-Brexit Britain Will Offer More for Start-ups," *The Telegraph,* July 11, 2016, http://www.telegraph.co.uk/business/2016/07/11/post-brexit-britain-will-offer-more-for-start-ups/.

47. *Direction Generale des Enterprises,* https://www.entreprises.gouv.fr/node/168501.

48. *Station F,* https://stationf.co/.

49. Romain Dillet, "With Station F, Paris Will Have the World's Biggest Startup Campus," *TechCrunch,* December 5, 2016, https://techcrunch.com/2016/12/05/with-station-f-paris-will-have-the-worlds-biggest-startup-campus/.

50. *Roxanne Varza,* https://twitter.com/roxannevarza.

51. "La French Tech," *Gouvernement.fr,* http://www.gouvernement.fr/en/la-french-tech/.

52. *French Tech Ticket,* http://www.frenchtechticket.com/.

53. Abby Young-Powell, "Six Lessons Berlin's Startup Scene Can Teach London's Tech Entrepreneurs," *The Telegraph,* August 25, 2016.

54. "Open Culture--A Definition," *Center International D'Art Contemporain Montreal,* http://www.ciac.ca/en/open-culture-definition-en.

55. Chris Hirst," 10 Ways to Create an Open Culture," *Fast Company*, September 5, 2012, https://www.fastcompany.com/1681531/10-ways-to-create-an-open-culture.

56. "Financing and Funding," *Make It in Germany*, http://www.make-it-in-germany.com/en/for-qualified-professionals/working/setting-up-a-business-in-germany/financing-and-funding.

57. *The German Startups Association*, https://deutschestartups.org/en/.

58. Omar Mohout, "10 Things You Didn't Know About Europe's Tech Scene," *VentureBeat*, September 4, 2016, https://venturebeat.com/2016/09/04/10-things-you-didnt-know-about-europes-tech-scene/.

59. Omar Mohout, "10 Things You Didn't Know About Europe's Tech Scene," *VentureBeat*, September 4, 2016, https://venturebeat.com/2016/09/04/10-things-you-didnt-know-about-europes-tech-scene/.

60. "The 2017 Global Startup Ecosystem Report," *Startup Genome*, https://startupgenome.com/report2017/.

61. "2017 Winter Asia Startup Ecosystem," *Asia Startup Ecosystem*, January 23, 2017, http://globalstartupecosystem.com/2017-winter-asia-startup-ecosystem/.

62. Alex Stern, "Revisiting The Unicorn Club," *Startup Grind*, https://medium.com/startup-grind/unicorn-club-revisited-e641f9c80e8d.

63. *DNI Fund*, https://digitalnewsinitiative.com/about/.

64. *DNI Fund Participants*, https://digitalnewsinitiative.com/participants/.

65. *DNI Fund Projects*, https://digitalnewsinitiative.com/dni-projects/.

66. *De-Escalation Bot*, https://digitalnewsinitiative.com/dni-projects/de-escalation-bot/.

67. *Wave*, https://digitalnewsinitiative.com/dni-projects/wave/.

68. *Connected Cars, Connected Audience, News Ecosystem (Round 3)*, Digital News Initiative, https://digitalnewsinitiative.com/dni-projects/connected-cars-connected-audience-news-ecosystem/.

69. *Companion App*, https://digitalnewsinitiative.com/dni-projects/nzz-companion-app/.

70. *Mural*, https://digitalnewsinitiative.com/dni-projects/mural/.

71. *PoliWatchBot*, https://digitalnewsinitiative.com/dni-projects/poliwatchbot/.

72. *Tagesspiegel Causa*, https://digitalnewsinitiative.com/dni-projects/tagesspiegel-causa/.

73. *Project Arete*, https://digitalnewsinitiative.com/dni-projects/project-arete/.

74. *Woodpecker Findings*, https://digitalnewsinitiative.com/dni-projects/woodpecker-findings/.

75. "DNI Funded Projects," Digital News Initiative, https://digitalnewsinitiative.com/dni-projects/.

76. James Breiner, "How J-schools Are Helping Students Develop Entrepreneurial Journalism Skills," *Poynter*, May 17, 2013, https://www.poynter.org/2013/how-j-schools-are-helping-students-develop-entrepreneurial-journalism-skills/213701/.

77. "Pioneers of Entrepreneurial Journalism in Europe," *Media Managers Club*, http://mediamanagersclub.org/pioneers-entrepreneurial-journalism-europe.

78. "Pioneers of Entrepreneurial Journalism in Europe," *Media Managers Club*, http://mediamanagersclub.org/pioneers-entrepreneurial-journalism-europe.

79. "Which Colleges or Universities Offer Entrepreneurial Journalism Programs?" *Quora*, https://www.quora.com/Which-colleges-or-universities-offer-entrepreneurial-journalism-programs.

80. "Spreadsheet: Entrepreneurial Journalism Programs in Universities," July 21, 2014, https://docs.google.com/spreadsheets/d/1AtmTF6sPZvo-EYm6F1CddSaYcxlOZZRulBPhUl1on_U/pub?output=html.

81. Anemona Hartocollis, "Building a Start-up Culture in a Broken-down Economy," *CNBC*, July 19, 2015, http://www.cnbc.com/2015/07/19/building-a-start-up-culture-in-greeces-broken-down-economy.html.

82. "Greek Start-ups Are Here," *Open Coffee*, July 18, 2007, http://opencoffee.gr/2007/07/18/declaration/.

83. *Open Coffee Club*, http://opencoffee.ning.com/.

84. "Open Coffee Athens Meeting VI," *Open Coffee*, http://opencoffee.gr/2007/11/29/open-coffee-athens-meeting-vi/.

85. Steve Case, "Get Ready, the Internet Is About to Change Again. Here's How," May 30, 2015, https://www.washingtonpost.com/business/capitalbusiness/steve-case-get-ready-the-Internet-is-about-to-change-again-heres-how/2015/05/29/d6c87f6c-0493-11e5-bc72-f3e16bf50bb6_story.html?utm_term=.44b24a0cce50.

86. *OpenFund*, http://theopenfund.com/.

87. *Marathon*, https://marathon.vc/.

88. Alfred Lua, "Social Proof," *Buffer Blog*, https://blog.bufferapp.com/social-proof.

89. Mike Butcher, "Witnessing The Rebirth Of The Greek Startup Ecosystem," *TechCrunch*, Jan 8, 2013, https://techcrunch.com/2013/01/08/witnessing-the-rebirth-of-the-greek-startup-ecosystem/.

90. "Ranking of Economies," *World Bank*, http://www.doingbusiness.org/rankings.

91. Itai Elizur, "The Emergence of an Ecosystem: 12 Startups Turning Greece Into a Startup Hub," *The Next Web*, April 2, 2017, https://thenextweb.com/contributors/2017/04/02/emergence-ecosystem-12-startups-turning-greece-startup-hub/#.tnw_05khlPl1.

92. "Greece's Jobless Rate Rises to 23.6 Percent in Fourth Quarter," *Reuters*, March 16, 2017, http://www.reuters.com/article/us-eurozone-greece-unemployment-idUSKBN16N16O.

93. Itai Elizur, "The Emergence of an Ecosystem: 12 Startups Turning Greece Into a Startup Hub," *The Next Web*, https://thenextweb.com/contributors/2017/04/02/emergence-ecosystem-12-startups-turning-greece-startup-hub/#.tnw_05khlPl1

94. Cate Lawrence, "Could the Greek Tech Sector Save the Greek Economy?" *Readwrite*, March 23, 2016, https://readwrite.com/2016/03/23/greek-tech-savior-ct4/.

95. *EBEA*, http://www.businessangelsgreece.gr/.

96. "Starttech Ventures Introduces Its 'Sidecar' Angel Group," *Starttech*, June 17, 2015, http://www.starttech.vc/blog/2015/starttech-ventures-introduces-its-side-car-angel-group/.

97. *Marathon VC*, https://marathon.vc/.

98. "Investments in Greek Startups, 2010-2016," *Marathon.vc*, July 27, 2017, https://marathon.vc/investments-in-greek-startups/.

99. *Entrepreneurial Journalism Medium Publication*, https://medium.com/entrepreneurial-journalism.

100. *Startup Weekend Entrepreneurial Journalism Athens Greece Publication,* https://medium.com/entrepreneurial-journalism.

101. Peter Diamandis, "Exponential Thinking Framework," *YouTube*, May 27, 2017, https://www.youtube.com/watch?v=65NgOzCk1aA.

102. Stephanie Marcus, "HOW TO: Organize A Successful Meetup," June 26, 2010, *Mashable*, http://mashable.com/2010/06/26/how-to-meetup/#CIbwNz1eAkqX.

103. "Create a Meetup," *Meetup*, https://www.meetup.com/help/article/865540/.

104. *Both Sides of the Table*, https://bothsidesofthetable.com/.

105. *BuzzMachine*, http://buzzmachine.com/.

106. *Fast Company Technology*, https://www.fastcompany.com/technology.

107. *Calacanis*, http://calacanis.com/.

108. *PressThink*, http://pressthink.org/.

109. Alex Stern, "Revisiting the Unicorn Club," *Startup Grind*, https://medium.com/startup-grind/unicorn-club-revisited-e641f9c80e8d.

110. *Startup Europe*, http://startupeuropeclub.eu/about-us/.

111. *Startup Europe Map*, http://startupeuropemap.eu/map/.

112. "The 2017 Global Startup Ecosystem Report," *Startup Genome*, https://startupgenome.com/report2017/.

113. *TechCrunch*, https://techcrunch.com/.

114. *@mediastartups*, https://twitter.com/mediastartups.

115. Connecting Cities, https://medium.com/connecting-cities.

116. Startup Weekend Entrepreneurial Journalism Athens Greece, https://medium.com/startup-weekend-entrepreneurial-journalism-athens.

# FROM THE FIELD: A SHORT HISTORY OF SILICON VALLEY

*Francine Hardaway*

What made Silicon Valley a Hub for entrepreneurs? And why has that become as much of a liability as an advantage?

Silicon Valley grew up in the area between San Jose, California, and San Francisco as a result of Frederick Terman, the legendary dean of Stanford engineering school during the 1940s and 1950s. He created the tradition of Stanford faculty starting their own companies. A number of companies we still reference came out of Stanford during those years, especially Hewlett Packard and Varian Associates.

The transistor was invented and manufactured in Silicon Valley, which gave the area a leg up in the radio and telegraph industries. And the Navy had a base in Sunnyvale. By 1957, Russia's success with Sputnik unleashed a big space competition, and the U.S. government founded NASA. At the time NASA opened at Moffett Field near San Jose, the only company able to build electronics for the space capsule was Fairchild Semiconductor.

The legend of Silicon Valley from the beginning of the transistor industry is well-known and has been written about and documented.[1] Most of the Valley's early success came from either components like Silicon chips (from which the Valley got its name) or the hardware into which the chips were placed.

It's actually fun to learn about the Valley's history, because the lesson is that the beginning of Silicon Valley was all about men and women, engineers, who had ideas out of science fiction about what technology could enable. Many of those ideas have now come true, like the personal computer and the iPhone, both envisioned by Steve Jobs. And we now wear what was once envisioned in a comic book as the "Dick Tracy wrist radio"–the Apple Watch.

Early engineers were not after money, they were about making things possible that had never been possible before, such as space travel. As a result, they received both government grants and venture capital. Before venture capital became a "thing," it originated from the financial centers like New York. Arthur Rock, for example, was an early investor in Intel, Apple, and Scientific Data Systems. The first Bay Area venture capital firms, who located on Sand Hill

Road adjacent to the Stanford campus, were Kleiner, Perkins Caulfield and Byers, and Sequoia Capital.

If you are interested in the history of Silicon Valley, you might want to watch the HBO show Silicon Valley, which tells you everything you need to know about where Silicon Valley is in the present, and also the fourth season of AMC's Halt and Catch Fire, which can take you from the 1980s to the rise of the World Wide Web.

We have now reached the point where Silicon Valley is a rich ecosystem where everyone with an idea eventually shows up because it's possible to sit in a coffee shop and form a team, raise some money, and get started. Numerous accelerators, such as Y Combinator make it easy to get a start, and the cost of starting a company has come down significantly due to Amazon Web Services (cloud-based infrastructure) and software development tools and frameworks.

However, we're also reached the point where Silicon Valley is a self-parody, with all the downsides of its own success: race, age, and gender discrimination, drug and alcohol abuse, suicide and depression.[2] Its "win at all costs mentality" has spawned excesses of every variety.

Not to mention the fact that it is now possible to start a company anywhere, especially near a university. Let's give Silicon Valley credit for establishing a culture of entrepreneurship, which is really a culture of resilience, and then understand that for digital media, it's not Paradise.

*As the founder of Stealthmode Partners,* **Francine Hardaway** *is a nineteen-year advocate and resource for entrepreneurs and intrapreneurs. She has consulted with more than 1,000 startups and blogs about technology, entrepreneurship, and health-care policy issues at* Huffington Post, Medium, *and* http://blog.stealthmode.com . *Reach her on Twitter at @hardaway.*

## Leave feedback on this sidebar.

## Notes

1. "Pirates of Silicon Valley," *Wikipedia*, https://en.wikipedia.org/wiki/Pirates_of_Silicon_Valley.

2. Why Silicon Valley is Going to Keep Having Sexual Harassment Lawsuits, *Mashable*, http://mashable.com/2017/06/08/silicon-valley-harassment/#sRm_EoiXdEqf.

# INSTRUCTOR RESOURCES

## Inside this section

We will be building out this section in spring of 2018 for an eventual instructor edition. Have a resource you'd like to contribute? Let us know by replying to this thread[1] in the Rebus Community Forum.

Note: All resources inside the book need to be licensed CC BY[2] (read why[3]) but we are glad to link from the book to resources you have hosted elsewhere.

# GLOSSARY

*Editors*

**angel investors.** Angels are "accredited" investors (who meet certain SEC criteria for net worth and income. Angels usually have little personal relationship with the founders. Usually they are investing in startups as part of their overall investment portfolio.

**audience.** The audience are the people who see your work. The audience is generally larger than your customer base and may include some of your customers.

**business owner vs. entrepreneur.** The key difference between an entrepreneur (of any type) and a small business owner (which are often confused) is one is searching to find a business model that works (entrepreneur) while the other is managing a business on a proven model (small business owner).

**content business.** A business whose core product is content, such as is the case in newspapers, television stations, films, video games, apps, or media companies.

**crowdfunding.** A method of funding innovative product ideas that are too early for investors. In this method, innovators reach out to like-minded supporters, early adopters and fans, who are enthusiastic about backing early stage ideas. The crowd not only contributes money to develop the product but offers something just as valuable: early market validation for the product, and a chance for the entrepreneur to build reputation and credibility.

**desirability-feasibility-viability.** The most valuable design sits at the intersection of three questions: can we do this; should we do this; do they want this?

**elevator pitch.** An elevator pitch is a business pitch or sales pitch told as a brief synopsis for the purpose of gaining the listener's interest in the hopes they will request more information or request to see the complete pitch.

**engagement.** 1. Any physical action that can be taken with digital content; e.g. a video view; a click or scroll; a like, share or retweet; reading a web page. 2. The practice of identifying, listening to, interacting with and activating digital audiences.

**engagement manager.** A person who manages connections to and conversations with audiences. Sometimes called a "community manager" or "social media manager."

**engagement rate.** The total number of engagements for a piece of digital content divided by the total number of the content's impressions. A measure of how "engaging" the content is.

**entrepreneur.** An entrepreneur is someone with a market-driven pursuit of a conceptual idea, who seeks a viable business model that succeeds in a target market.

**freelance consultant.** Someone who works independently to provide a service to a client. Typically consultants have control over how, when and where they perform the work. They are not considered employees. They are also subject to additional taxes that an employer normally pays.

**freemium.** A scenario in which people can use parts of a product for free, but must pay for upgraded functionality or features.

**goal.** A company's overall high-level business goals.

**sensor journalism.** A type of journalism in which sensor technology is used to collect data and journalists analyze and report on that data.

**impressions.** The number of times a digital platform served a piece of content to its users.

**initial public offerings.** When a company (and investors) first sell shares to the public (e.g. the stock market), the company can raise significant amounts of money to fund operations, growth, or new products. This also offers the investors (and founders) a chance to sell some of their stock for (sometimes significant) cash.

**intrapreneur.** An employee who innovates and thinks entrepreneurially to develop new lines of business, programs, or products within an existing organization or corporation.

**market risk.** The risk that a new product will not be needed enough that consumers will pay for it.

**measurable objective.** The specific, measurable metrics you will track to know if you have successfully executed your strategy. (You could say, our objective is to attain X percent user growth in a certain time period, for instance.)

**membership.** A subscription model under which the content can either be free or paid, but users who purchase a membership receive perks and bonus materials, exclusive access to supplemental materials and so forth.

**paywall.** A mechanism by which readers or viewers must pay in order to access content, such as on a news site.

**people risk.** The risk the founders or team members of a venture won't be successful managing the product or the business.

**private placement memorandum.** A private placement memorandum, or PPM, is also known as an offering document and includes disclosures for investors.

**product risk.** The unknowns surrounding whether a proposed product can be created or built at all.

**prospectus.** A prospectus is a detailed summary of a business plan put in writing. If a company wishes to sell public stock or to offer other financial instruments for sale, a complete prospectus includes many financial disclosures and the price of shares and number of shares to be offered.

**reach.** The number of accounts or users a brand or an individual piece of content was shown or served to.

**small business owner.** Someone who owns a for-profit, U.S. company that is independent and not dominant in its industry, according to government NAICS codes. "Small business" is a specific classification of business that may be eligible for some government contracts. Whether a business qualifies is based on "size standards,"[1] which take into account profits, number of employees and other factors.

**strategies.** The how of how a company plans to achieve its business goals–its approach.

**tactic.** The actions a company takes to meet its agreed-upon objectives.

**tweet.** A posting made on the social network Twitter.

**technology startup.** A scalable company providing a technology product, platform, or service.

**user personas.** A tool that entrepreneurs can use to drill down into the the ideal audience member and adds psychographic information such as behaviors and lifestyle information.

**venture capitalists.** A VC is a professional fund manager. They aggregate investment funding from large institutions then make investments in high-growth companies for potential high returns. VCs need their funds to make an extraordinary return on investment.

## *Notes*

1. "Small Business Size Standards," *SBA.gov*, https://www.sba.gov/contracting/getting-started-contractor/make-sure-you-meet-sba-size-standards.

# ACKNOWLEDGEMENTS

## A Collaboratively Created Open Textbook

This open textbook was built through a collaborative, grassroots effort of many educators in j-entrepreneurship, with project support from the Rebus Community for Open Textbook Creation.[1] There are numerous contributors to this, version 1.0, whom we would like to acknowledge and to thank.

**Dr. Michelle Ferrier**, president of Journalism That Matters and an associate professor in the E.W. Scripps School of Journalism at Ohio University; and **Elizabeth Mays**, operations and marketing manager for Rebus Foundation and adjunct faculty at Arizona State University, instigated and served as editors on the project.

The first edition features chapters by:

- **Jake Batsell**, associate professor at Southern Methodist University's Division of Journalism in Dallas and author of *Engaged Journalism*
- **CJ Cornell**, author of *The Age of Metapreneurship—A Journey into the Future of Entrepreneurship*
- **Geoffrey Graybeal**, assistant professor at Texas Tech University
- **Mike Green**, a New York Times Leadership Academy Fellow and co-founder of ScaleUp Partners
- **Mark Poepsel**, assistant professor, Southern Illinois University
- **Jessica Pucci**, professor of practice, Walter Cronkite School of Journalism and Mass Communication at ASU
- **Ingrid Sturgis**, associate professor, Howard University
- **Betty Tsakarestou**, assistant professor and head of advertising and public relations lab at Panteion University
- and a foreword by **Jan Schaffer**, executive director of *J-Lab.org*

In addition, multiple professionals contributed perspectives "from the field":

- **Lori Benjamin**, freelance content marketer
- **Dana Coester**, associate professor at West Virginia University Reed College of Media
- **Chris Dell**, founder of Go Baller Media
- **Dalton Dellsperger**, founder of *TownWave*

- **John Dille**, president of Federated Media
- **Amy Eisman**, director of media entrepreneurship, American University
- **Francine Hardaway**, founder of Stealthmode Partners
- **Coury Turczyn,** former editor of the *Knoxville Mercury*
- **Georgann Yara**, freelance journalist

Others, including **Ebony Reed**, and **Daniel Zayas**, provided interviews for the book. And **Cheryl Cuillier**, OER coordinator at the University of Arizona, helped to flesh out the (still-growing!) spreadsheet of foundations and contest funding for j-startups.

We would be remiss if we neglected to mention all those who volunteered to copy-edit chapters of the book, including **Leanne Page**, **Mary Brunskill**, and **Jay Hartwell**. (Peer reviewers will also be credited as a group here once we know all those who participated.) Finally, a thanks to the students and faculty who are beta testing the book in Fall 2017 and will help us improve it for the official release in January 2018.

**Apurva Ashok**, with help from **Zoe Wake Hyde**, formatted and designed the book using Pressbooks as well as product development for the software itself that will ultimately enhance the book's UX.

We would like to express our sincerest gratitude to all who contributed to this project to date.

This book is in public beta as of Fall 2017. The official release (ETA January 2018) will incorporate feedback received in beta testing. A future release will also include activities, ancillary materials, and faculty resources on media innovation for instructors. If you would like to help expand this book for the second edition and have a (CC BY) resource or additional chapter you would like to contribute, please volunteer by commenting here.[2]

## *Notes*

1. *Rebus Community for Open Textbook Creation*, http://rebus.community/.

2. "JMC Project Summary Media Innovation & Entrepreneurship," *Rebus Community Forum*, https://forum.rebus.community/topic/120/project-summary-media-innovation-entrepreneurship/21.

# COVER CREDITS

Cover image by Vancouver Film School, VFS Digital Design Agile Project Management. Image Licensed CC BY BY 2.0[1] Original found here[2] on Flickr.

The VFS Digital Design school (vfs.com/digitaldesign) educates students in agile project management practices.

## Notes

1. https://creativecommons.org/licenses/by/2.0/
2. http://bit.ly/mieOTcover

# LICENSE & REMIXING INFORMATION

This book is licensed CC BY[1] except where otherwise noted.

This license allows for reuse, adaptation, remixing, and redistribution of content, so long as you attribute it to the original author(s), indicate if changes are made, and link to the original, free content, found at https://press.rebus.community/media-innovation-and-entrepreneurship.

For attribution, please keep the entire copyright statement (found before the TOC in print, and below the CC BY license on the book's homepage, https://press.rebus.community/media-innovation-and-entrepreneurship/).

*Note if you are remixing this book: There are several images in this book that are not licensed CC BY but are used with permission here and clearly labeled with their copyright. You may want to seek additional permission before remixing if you plan to include these images.*

## Please credit us as follows:

*Redistributing the book verbatim:*
This material is created by Michelle Ferrier, Elizabeth Mays, Jake Batsell, CJ Cornell, Geoffrey Graybeal, Mike Green, Mark Poepsel, Jessica Pucci, Ingrid Sturgis, Betty Tsakarestou, Jan Schaffer, Lori Benjamin, Dana Coester, Chris Dell, Dalton Dellsperger, John Dille, Amy Eisman, Francine Hardaway, Coury Turczyn, and Georgann Yara, and produced with support from the Rebus Community. The original is freely available under the terms of the CC BY 4.0 license at https://press.rebus.community/media-innovation-and-entrepreneurship/.

*Revised or adapted versions:*
This material is based on original work by Michelle Ferrier, Elizabeth Mays, Jake Batsell, CJ Cornell, Geoffrey Graybeal, Mike Green, Mark Poepsel, Jessica Pucci, Ingrid Sturgis, Betty Tsakarestou, Jan Schaffer, Lori Benjamin, Dana Coester, Chris Dell, Dalton Dellsperger, John Dille, Amy Eisman, Francine Hardaway, Coury Turczyn, Georgann Yara, and produced with support from the Rebus Community. The original is freely available under the terms of the CC BY 4.0 license at https://press.rebus.community/media-innovation-and-entrepreneurship/.

*Individual chapters or pieces:*
This material is [created by or based on] original work by [chapter or piece author], and

produced with support from the Rebus Community. The original is freely available under the terms of the CC BY 4.0 license at https://press.rebus.community/media-innovation-and-entrepreneurship/.

## *Notes*

1. https://creativecommons.org/licenses/by/4.0/

# HELP TO EXPAND THIS BOOK!

This book is designed to be an ever-evolving and expanding resource of materials for faculty and students in media entrepreneurship courses. The beta version is an MVP, a minimum viable product, in itself. We hope that if you find it useful, you will also help to make it better.

Among the things we'd like to add:

- Instructor / ancillary materials: assignments and rubrics, lesson plans, presentations as well as pointers on how to teach a topic or grow capacity for teaching entrepreneurship in your institution
- Additional chapters or sidebars on relevant topics
- More glossary terms
- Links to resources elsewhere in the ecosystem

# FOR BETA TESTERS

Are you a beta tester? We've compiled a guide for beta testers that you can access here.[1]

It includes how to navigate the book, how to annotate your feedback directly on the book, and questions to guide your feedback.

You can also leave feedback in this project post[2] on the Rebus Community Forum.

## Notes

1. https://goo.gl/3nfhfJ

2. https://forum.rebus.community/topic/203/revision-requests-beta-version-of-media-innovation-entrepreneurship

# SUGGESTION BOX

We are actively and enthusiastically soliciting feedback from students, faculty and others using this book.

You can leave feedback directly on this textbook if you are logged into Hypothes.is. To do so, once logged in, from any chapter, click on the < symbol at the top right, sign up/log in to hypothes.is, click on the JMC Open Textbook group, highlight the text, click annotate, and post your comment.

You can also submit revision requests through the Rebus Community forum thread for this book here.[1]

Or, if you would like to send private and/or anonymous feedback to the editors of the Media Innovation & Entrepreneurship Open Textbook, you can do so using this form.[2]

*Notes*

1. https://forum.rebus.community/topic/203/revision-requests-media-innovation-entrepreneurship

2. https://goo.gl/T81NeX

# ERRATA

An earlier version of this text included a math miscalculation in the Engagement and Analytics chapter. The sentence has since been corrected to read:

"Did 1,000 people attend the festival (if so, you sold hats to 75% of them, and that's excellent!), or did 50,000 people attend (if so, you sold hats to only 1.5% of them, and that's not so excellent, assuming everyone at the festival had a head)?"

Printed in the USA
CPSIA information can be obtained
at www.ICGtesting.com
LVHW060308270823
756387LV00014B/1479